The Life and Writings of Ralph J. Gleason

The Life and Writings of Ralph J. Gleason

Dispatches from the Front

Don Armstrong

BLOOMSBURY ACADEMIC
NEW YORK • LONDON • OXFORD • NEW DELHI • SYDNEY

BLOOMSBURY ACADEMIC
Bloomsbury Publishing Inc, 1385 Broadway, New York, NY 10018, USA
Bloomsbury Publishing Plc, 50 Bedford Square, London, WC1B 3DP, UK
Bloomsbury Publishing Ireland, 29 Earlsfort Terrace, Dublin 2, D02 AY28, Ireland

BLOOMSBURY, BLOOMSBURY ACADEMIC and the Diana logo
are trademarks of Bloomsbury Publishing Plc

First published in the United States of America 2024
This paperback edition published 2025

Copyright © Don Armstrong, 2024

For legal purposes the Acknowledgments on pp. x–xi constitute
an extension of this copyright page.

Cover image: Photo by Barry Olivier. Courtesy of the Berkeley Folk Music
Festival Archive, Charles Deering McCormick Library of Special Collections,
Northwestern University Libraries.

All rights reserved. No part of this publication may be: i) reproduced or transmitted in any form, electronic or mechanical, including photocopying, recording or by means of any information storage or retrieval system without prior permission in writing from the publishers; or ii) used or reproduced in any way for the training, development or operation of artificial intelligence (AI) technologies, including generative AI technologies. The rights holders expressly reserve this publication from the text and data mining exception as per Article 4(3) of the Digital Single Market Directive (EU) 2019/790.

Bloomsbury Publishing Inc does not have any control over, or responsibility for, any third-party websites referred to or in this book. All internet addresses given in this book were correct at the time of going to press. The author and publisher regret any inconvenience caused if addresses have changed or sites have ceased to exist, but can accept no responsibility for any such changes.

Whilst every effort has been made to locate copyright holders the publishers would be grateful to hear from any person(s) not here acknowledged.

A catalog record for this book is available from the Library of Congress.

ISBN: HB: 978-1-5013-6698-7
PB: 978-1-5013-9352-5
ePDF: 978-1-5013-6700-7
eBook: 978-1-5013-6699-4

Typeset by Integra Software Services Pvt. Ltd.

For product safety related questions contact productsafety@bloomsbury.com.

To find out more about our authors and books visit www.bloomsbury.com
and sign up for our newsletters.

I dedicate this book to my wife, Jessica Armstrong, in memory of our son, Donald E. "Trey" Armstrong III.

Contents

List of Figures   viii
Acknowledgments   x

Introduction: The Number One Jazz Writer   1

1. The Horseplayer's Son (1917–34)   5
2. Hot Jazz Off the Record (1934–38)   17
3. The Politics of Jazz History-Telling (1938–46)   39
4. San Francisco (1946–56)   57
5. Winds of Change (1956–63)   81
6. An Entertainment of Dissent (1964)   107
7. The Jazz Liverpool of the West (1965)   129
8. A Sonic High (1965–67)   151
9. The *Rolling Stone* Generation (1967–69)   175
10. We've Had All That (1969–74)   191
11. Ralph, This is Your City (1974–75)   211

Conclusion: One Picket Left   233

Notes   235
Index   272

List of Figures

1.1 Ralph Gleason as a toddler in Chappaqua, New York, c. 1923. Courtesy of the Estate of Ralph J. Gleason — 8
1.2 Ralph Gleason with his parents Ralph and Mollie in Chappaqua, c. 1927. Courtesy of the Estate of Ralph J. Gleason — 9
1.3 Ralph Gleason at home in Chappaqua, c. 1932. Courtesy of the Estate of Ralph J. Gleason — 13
2.1 Gleason's picture in the 1938 Columbia University yearbook during his senior year. Courtesy of the Estate of Ralph J. Gleason — 34
3.1 The first issue of *Jazz Information*, September 1939, the hot jazz fanzine Ralph Gleason founded after college. Courtesy of the Estate of Ralph J. Gleason — 42
3.2 Ralph and Jean Gleason, c. 1941. Courtesy of the Estate of Ralph J. Gleason — 46
3.3 The last issue of *Jazz Information*, November 1941. On the cover: jazz pianist and composer James. P. Johnson. Courtesy of the Estate of Ralph J. Gleason — 47
3.4 Ralph Gleason working for the Office of War Information in the Hotel Lafayette, Greenwich Village, Manhattan, 1942. Courtesy of the Estate of Ralph J. Gleason — 50
4.1 Ralph Gleason (second from left) with Lionel Hampton (center) and music promotor Charles Sullivan (first from left), in San Francisco, c. 1955. Courtesy of Wesley F. Johnson III photo collection — 64
5.1 *Jazz: A Quarterly of American Music*, summer, 1959, founded by Gleason. On the cover: jazz saxophonist Julian "Cannonball" Adderley. Courtesy of the Estate of Ralph J. Gleason — 89
5.2 Ralph Gleason on the set of *Jazz Casual*, a jazz television show he produced and hosted that aired on KQED, a public television station serving the San Francisco Bay Area, 1960. Courtesy of the Estate of Ralph J. Gleason — 92
5.3 Ralph Gleason (center) with Miles Davis to his right and drummer Tony Williams to his left, at the Monterey Jazz Festival, 1963. Photo by Charles Robinson — 99

List of Figures

6.1 Ken Kesey with a trombone on the roof of Further, his 1939 school bus converted into a traveling home for his band of Merry Pranksters during their visit to the Gleason house in Berkeley, 1964. Courtesy of the Estate of Ralph J. Gleason 118
7.1 Ralph Gleason at his desk at the Monterey Jazz Festival, c. 1965. Courtesy of the Estate of Ralph J. Gleason 141
8.1 Bob Dylan and Ralph Gleason at the 1965 KQED press conference for Dylan, who was in the Bay Area for a series of concerts. Courtesy of the Estate of Ralph J. Gleason, photo by Eric Weill 153
8.2 Ralph Gleason with the Beatles backstage at their concert in Candlestick Park, San Francisco, 1966. © Jim Marshall Photography LLC 159
8.3 John Lennon and Ralph Gleason backstage at the Beatles concert in Candlestick Park, San Francisco, 1966. © Jim Marshall Photography LLC 159
9.1 Gleason in 1967. Courtesy of Northwestern University Libraries, photo by Barry Olivier 176
10.1 Ralph Gleason with Paul Simon (seated) and Art Garfunkel (standing) at Big Sur Folk Festival, 1969. © Jim Marshall Photography LLC 199
11.1 Ralph Gleason, c. 1975. Courtesy of the Estate of Ralph J. Gleason, photo by Phil Bray 229

Acknowledgments

The genesis of this book began with my article, "Dispatches from the Front: The Life and Writings of Ralph J. Gleason," co-written with my wife, Jessica Armstrong, and published in the inaugural issue of *Rock Music Studies*. Thank you to editors Gary Burns and Tom Kitts, for accepting my first foray into pop music studies. Simon Frith cited the article in the *Cambridge History of Music Criticism*, which boosted my confidence, and I thank Simon for his support. Also want to thank editor Ken Prouty for publishing my article "Hot Collecting Off the Record: Ralph J. Gleason's Start in Music Journalism," published in *Jazz Perspectives*.

Two books confirmed my belief early on that music journalism deserved scholarly study. John Gennari's outstanding *Blowin' Hot and Cool* set a bar for all of us in this field, so thank you, John, for writing this book and encouraging my research. Thank you to Steve Jones, whose introduction to his edited collection *Pop Music and the Press* confirmed my belief that Ralph J. Gleason was a founder of contemporary music journalism.

Interviews grounded my research and provided multiple perspectives. Thank you to music journalists Jon Landau, Greil Marcus, Alan Rinzler, Gene Sculatti, Davin Seay, Joel Selvin, and Jann Wenner. Also, the late Nat Hentoff, John Swenson, and Ed Ward. Thanks to musicians John Handy, Denise Kaufmann, Jorma Kaukonen, Sonny Rollins, and Grace Slick. Appreciations to Terri Hinte, Janet Minto Morrison, and Moana Wright. Special gratitude to the family and friends of Ralph Gleason whose interviews brought Ralph to life: Kehala Gleason, Kelly Gleason, Rebecca Adams, Steve and Richard Kaiser, Odette Pollar, John Sergeant, and Rose Van Thayer-Braan Imai.

This book was made possible by my long-distance friend, British author Simon Warner, who put me in contact with Bloomsbury Academic editor Leah Babb-Rosenfeld. Leah and editorial assistant Rachel Moore gave me the room I needed to write the best possible book I could, for which I am eternally grateful.

I want to thank a circle of individuals in Ralph's life who provided excellent background material for this book. Robert Zagone provided invaluable insights into the many television and film ventures he worked on with Ralph. Denise Kaufman, thank you for sharing your memories of Ralph, your papers on the San Francisco counterculture years, and your free-flowing positivity. Deep gratitude goes to Jann Wenner for sharing his recollections about Ralph and making available *Rolling Stone*'s Gleason files, which proved to be an invaluable trove of insights into one of the most significant working relationships in the history of music journalism.

Heartfelt thanks to Ralph's children, Bridget, Stacy, and Toby Gleason. The photographs, letters, and other materials you shared were essential to this book, and your memories added a richness to your father's story that only you could provide. You possess his integrity, passion, and humor.

Finally, thank you to my wife, Jessica, for her tireless editing, morale-boosting, and unconditional love.

Introduction

The Number One Jazz Writer

> *I'm sure, ladies and gentlemen, all of us are aware of the recent passing of truly the number one jazz writer Mr. Ralph Gleason [applause]. Without a doubt, this man had a sense of the music that is unprecedented in the annals of jazz. I'm going to compose a number now to Ralph and dedicate it to him ... we're going to play something, I have no idea what it is, but here it is.*[1]

With that, trumpeter Dizzy Gillespie's cheeks balloon as he improvises a blues motif on center stage at the 1975 Monterey Jazz Festival. The lament swells as the band joins in. Suddenly, the musicians break into an up-tempo groove. Reference to a New Orleans funeral procession is apparent: an introductory dirge, a joyous homage, a final goodbye. Sacred music rooted in spirituals and gospel hymns recast in jazz. As the notes ring out across the filled stands, one seat—stage right—remains empty. The seat occupied during the past twenty-eight festivals by Ralph J. Gleason.[2]

"Number one jazz writer." Gillespie's accolade reflects his belief that Ralph Gleason was the essential jazz critic of that time. Others called Gleason the most outstanding *rock* critic. While music scholars today avoid such rankings, they place Gleason among his time's most essential jazz and rock critics. Gleason earned this status across a forty-year career that began at Columbia University in 1936, where he fired off passionate opinions about swing jazz in the "Off the Record" column for the *Columbia Daily Spectator*. After college Gleason co-founded *Jazz Information*, a leading voice of the 1940s New Orleans jazz revival. He moved to San Francisco, the center of the revival, in the late 1940s. Gleason landed a job at the *San Francisco Chronicle*, where he championed revolutionary musicians who played in the Bay Area, such as Gillespie, Miles Davis, Hank Williams, Elvis Presley, and Chuck Berry. Gleason gained national recognition during the late 1950s when he edited a jazz anthology, *Jam Session*, launched a television show called *Jazz Casual*, and co-founded the Monterey Jazz Festival. His music columns hummed with social commentary inspired by the New Left, and Gleason advised activist groups such as the Berkeley Free Speech Movement. He played a crucial role in the San Francisco rock scene in the late 1960s and co-founded *Rolling Stone* magazine, where his name appears on the masthead today. By his death in 1975, Gleason had become a globally recognized cultural critic. Said his long-time friend and colleague, renowned jazz critic Nat Hentoff:

> Gleason's work is so important. He was one of the first, if not the first [jazz critic] to go beyond jazz. With Ralph, it was not only about the music. It was all about free expression. I miss him so much.[3]

Gleason cut a striking figure with his tweed jacket, deerstalker hat, drooping pipe, and khaki trench coat, Sherlock Holmes meets *Casablanca*'s Rick Blaine. Along with his black horn-rim glasses, Gleason's attire conveyed a sense of professorial playfulness. In conversation, he was relaxed but quick-witted; a humorous observation might follow a serious comment. Gleason's writings offered a similar play of light and gravity. Although he communicated through various media, his best-known texts were the columns he penned for the *Chronicle* from 1951 to 1975. Bay Area music critic Gene Sculatti calls these columns "dispatches from the front," messages from the cutting-edge of popular music.[4] Through his *Chronicle* columns and other texts, Gleason educated readers, infuriated editors, made reputations, sullied reputations, joined and repudiated political causes, and produced some of the most compelling prose of the mid-twentieth century.

Not to say that Gleason lacked human weaknesses. He could be irascible, thin-skinned, and shortsighted, although possessed of an uncommon ability to publicly recant ill-considered opinions. Gleason experienced a lifelong outsiderness that could make him defensive, yet lead him to empathize with artists marginalized because of their race, age, or rebelliousness.

Why should we care about a music journalist who wrote his last column almost a half-century ago? Gleason matters because he exemplifies the power of a single music journalist to catalyze influential music scenes. Gleason won the confidence of music producers and consumers because of his uncommon prescience, open-earedness, and intuition. But more than an influential critic, Gleason was an unapologetic polemicist fiercely dedicated to cultural democracy, especially needed today when multiculturalism and democracy are under fire.

Gleason's life and writings offer important lessons for contemporary music journalists. Today's music criticism has recently come under fire as journalists compete in a digital arena with 24–7 coverage, rampant celebrityism, and extensive lifestyle reporting. Some commentators see a decline in music criticism quality and blame it on factors such as the reduced need for music reviews when consumers can click on a link and assess the music themselves. One of the fiercest detractors of today's criticism is renowned music writer Ted Gioia, who wrote:

> One can read through a stack of music magazines and never find any in-depth discussion of music. Technical knowledge of the art form has disappeared from its discourse. In short, music criticism has turned into lifestyle reporting.[5]

According to Gioia:

> The biggest problem with lifestyle-driven music criticism is that it poisons our aural culture. Discerning consumers who care about music and have good ears should be the bedrock of the music business, but many of them have given up on new artists because they can't find reliable critics to guide them. Record labels, for their part, need frank, knowledgeable feedback from critics—both to keep them honest and hold them accountable—but such input is in short supply and veering towards extinction.[6]

Gleason's writings model the type of criticism Gioia yearns for. Gleason eschewed lifestyle reporting and celebrityism and raised his children to see great musicians as everyday people. Instead, Gleason concentrated on evaluating performances for readers, and as a drummer and pianist used his understanding of rhythm, melody, and harmony to do so.

Academic researchers have studied Gleason beginning in 1969 when R. Serge Denisoff wrote in the *Journal of Popular Culture* about Gleason's "participant observer status" within the San Francisco counterculture.[7] Since then, several academic books have provided essential insight into Gleason's role in the discourses of jazz and rock.[8] Additionally, several trade press publications have chronicled Gleason's role in co-founding *Rolling Stone* magazine with Jann Wenner, the most recent being Wenner's memoir.[9] The literature about Gleason divides between studies of his jazz writings and rock writings, depending on the genre affiliation of the author. But Gleason's important texts about folk music, country music, rhythm and blues, pop, and rock 'n' roll remain unexplored. Also uncharted are Gleason's writings about literature and stand-up comedy. Gleason's ideas about literature, humor, and the full spectrum of popular music genres underlay his views of jazz and rock. Another area of Gleason's life that has gone unexamined is his long history of activism from the 1930s through the 1960s and how activism meshed with his music writing.

This book explores how music critics like Gleason act as cultural mediators who bridge the gap between music producers and consumers. Through their mass platforms, critics shape the preferences of listeners by either legitimizing or discrediting musicians, recordings, performances, and music scenes. Their writings contribute to the overall conversation about popular music, which includes individual discourses about jazz, folk, and popular music genres such as country, R&B, and rock. While most music journalists specialize in covering a single genre, Gleason was a musical omnivore who contributed to all the discourses of American music, except for classical, from the 1930s to the 1970s.

During this time, American music underwent a series of disruptions caused by progressive forces such as racial and gender equality, antiwar sentiment, and free speech movements. Alongside advancing technology and the increasing empowerment of teens and young adults, forces that led to the emergence of new and disruptive forms of music, such as swing jazz, R&B, and rock. This book focuses on Gleason's contributions to these musical revolutions. It argues that Gleason, as a cultural mediator, used his constantly expanding platform to legitimize critical breakthroughs that innovated American music and kept it relevant to an increasingly diverse audience. He achieved this by shaping the discourse of American music and highlighting the progressive ideas that flowed between different genres. Supporting this claim are interviews with those who knew Gleason—musicians, colleagues, music journalists, family, and friends—along with unpublished correspondence and a deep dive into the thousands of writings Gleason left behind.

When Dizzy Gillespie stood on the stage at Monterey and said, "We're going to play something, I have no idea what it is, but here it is," he alluded to the improvisatory nature of his musical offering. Gillespie's words perfectly fit the ingenious spirit of Gleason's writing. Where lesser writers pondered, Gleason riffed. Where others wrote sweet, Gleason wrote hot. Where other columnists feared to tread, Gleason rushed in. A journey that begins when a handful of brilliant Black musicians cut loose with a propulsive new musical sound called swing.

1

The Horseplayer's Son (1917–34)

A room jumps with jazz on Chicago's South Side in 1932. On stage at the Grand Terrace Café, a trumpet fanfare blasts then dies away as piano chords fill the air. The orchestra plays a slow, swaying dirge while a lone trumpeter blows a down-and-out blues. As the notes fade, the piano returns, and the master of ceremonies calls out, "Fatha Hines! Fatha Hines!"

Suddenly, the orchestra wails. The drummer unleashes a lightning-fast volley on his high-hat cymbal. Pianist Earl "Fatha" Hines leads the band through chorus after chorus of propellant solos. The music sweeps through Hines, among history's most influential jazz pianists. Head back, eyes closed, and mouth wide open, caught in a hurricane of sound.

The music of Earl Hines travels far beyond the Grand Terrace Café that night. It's heard eight-hundred miles away in Chappaqua, New York, where fifteen-year-old Ralph Gleason recovers from measles in his darkened bedroom. Groping in the darkness, Gleason turns on the radio beside his bed, and its vacuum tubes glow. Crackling sounds fill the air. He twists the Bakelite dial and searches for a local station.[1] The radio speaker issues static-distorted Tin Pan Alley pop and vaudeville comedy routines. Gleason keeps turning the knob. More static, then one more twist and bang!

The powerful music of Earl Hines and His Grand Terrace Orchestra carries Gleason away as if he hopped on an express train speeding through underground Manhattan. This music evokes a big city's cacophony of sounds played with clockwork precision—chorus after chorus of exhilarating horn solos. Gleason has just discovered swing jazz played by Black bandleaders such as Hines, Duke Ellington, and Fletcher Henderson. These bandleaders inspired vibrant music scenes in Chicago, New York, and other destinations despite widespread racism. Although swing emerged in nightclubs it was not yet the national pastime it would become.

In addition to jazz, Gleason absorbed other influences during his childhood, such as his Irish American heritage and the entertainment columns of New York City newspapers he found lying on the bleachers of horserace tracks. These influences and others shaped Gleason's life as a music journalist, a life that began in a modest Bronx apartment.

A Fateful Birth

Gleason and a historic jazz record came into the world days apart. On March 1, 1917, thirty-one-year-old Mollie Gleason gave birth to Ralph Joseph Gleason in the Bronx walkup shared with her husband, Ralph Aloysius Gleason. Young Ralph entered the world with a bang when the delivery doctor slipped on a bedpan.[2] Across the city, another raucous birth is underway at Reisenweber's Cafe on Manhattan's Columbus Circle. A new type of dance band electrifies the cabaret crowd. Foxtrotting couples glide and swirl to the syncopated rhythms of the Original Dixieland Jass Band.

Six days after Gleason's birth, the band released a 78 rpm single, "Dixieland Jass Band One-Step," backed with "Livery Stable Blues." The disc became a hit and helped launch the "Jazz Age."[3] During this period in popular culture, jazz became the rage of America's first music-centered youth subculture. The music that got young couples foxtrotting was the earliest form of the genre; today referred to as "traditional jazz" or "New Orleans-style jazz." A band typically had five to seven musicians, and instrumentation included drums, piano, and a mix of wind and brass instruments.

As jazz bands spread the new music nationwide, journalists brought their readers into the action. For instance, in a Southside Chicago café called Schiller's, a local reporter said:

> Everybody was drinking, smoking, laughing, dancing. The dancing was as raggy as the music. Delightful Bohemianism prevailed. Lovely young ladies would come over to your table.[4]

Whether labeled "jass," "jazz," or "hot music," the rebellious new genre combined ragtime, dance band music, band marches, and other styles of the day. Jazz worked its magic through syncopation, a practice rooted in Africa which placed rhythmic accents *between* the beats instead of *on* the beat. In addition to emphasizing these "downbeats," jazz musicians played improvised solos that gave the music uncommon spontaneity. Jazz melodies often incorporated the African American folk form known as the blues, in which musicians bent, slurred, and roughened notes to express deep wellsprings of emotion. Syncopation, blue notes, and other devices disrupted the conventions of popular music and divided the listening public into fans and foes of jazz. Critics who rejected jazz included *New York Tribune* entertainment reviewer George S. Kaufman who wrote in 1917:

> The latest thing in the cabarets is the "jazz band," the name of which, presumably, is a contraction of the well-known jazzbo, which requires no introduction. The jazz band plays on mandolins, jugs, tin pans, and nerves.[5]

"Jazzbo," a derogatory term for Black people at the time, illustrates how the early criticism of jazz expressed thinly veiled racism. In some quarters, anti-jazz sentiment festered into a moral panic. For example, at a dance held by a women's dorm at the University of Chicago, the dean of women silenced the band's percussionist because "the drum arouses all that is base in young people and tends to provoke immorality."[6] Moral outrage took darker turns in other parts of the country, such as when a Milwaukee evangelist locked women parishioners in the church hall while he railed against dancing and gambling.[7]

Thus, as Gleason grew up a debate raged over jazz's moral and aesthetic validity. Mollie Gleason disliked the music, undoubtedly influenced by women's magazine writers and Roman Catholic clergy who declared jazz immoral. Gleason's father preferred Irish tenor John McCormack's operatic and popular songs. The Gleasons listened to music on their radio but did not own a phonograph player.

Gleason's father, Ralph A. Gleason, was born in the Bronx in 1883 to an Irish-born father—a shoemaker who struggled to support his nine children—and an Irish American mother.[8] Employed by the New York Telephone Company, Ralph A. rose from lineman to chief clerk of the company's Mount Vernon office. In 1911, Ralph A. wed Mary Quinlisk, known as Mollie. Born about 1886 in Ireland, Mollie came to America in 1900 as an indentured servant.[9] The couple lived in Fordham, Bronx, a Catholic Irish-American neighborhood. Ralph A. was a slender man with deep-set soulful eyes. Mollie had dark hair and a broad smile and wore a cross necklace as a devout Roman Catholic. Gleason's self-sufficient parents from humble backgrounds strove to give their son a better life.

For many Irish inhabitants of New York City, that meant leaving the boroughs for outlying communities with improved living conditions. The Gleasons joined this wave in 1919 when Ralph A. bought a parcel of land with two houses in Chappaqua, a rural hamlet in New Castle, Westchester County, New York. Quakers founded Chappaqua in the 1730s and established a culture based on pacifism and racial and gender equality, values Gleason upheld throughout his life. The hamlet grew from a settlement of neat, white clapboard houses to a grid of large farms. When Ralph A. and Mollie moved into their new home, farms had given way to subdivisions, and New Castle became a commuter suburb of New York City connected by the Harlem Line. The Gleasons moved into a white two-story clapboard house on Quaker Road with two fireplaces and a bay window overlooking shade trees.[10] The second house would be used for guests and as a rental property.

Within this rural setting, young Ralph started classes in 1922 at Roaring Brook grammar school, a traditional one-room schoolhouse with one teacher for seven grades.[11] In a photograph, young Ralph resembles Buster Brown, a popular comic strip character and Buster Brown Shoe Company symbol. Sporting a pageboy haircut, he stands beside a wooden scooter wearing a sailor smock, knickers, and knee stockings. In another photo, he sits on a wooden tricycle with a toothy grin and donning black patent leather shoes—a typical 1920s American kid.

Gleason's parents stayed in contact with their Irish relatives and likely taught him about his heritage and Ireland's troubled history. Part of the United Kingdom (UK), the island saw a rise in nationalism and anti-British sentiment following the Great Famine of the 1840s, which led to a call for Irish independence. In the Easter Rising of 1916, Irish nationalists turned to militant radicalism. This resistance led to the Irish War of Independence in 1919, a bitter conflict between the Irish Republican Army

Figure 1.1 Ralph Gleason as a toddler in Chappaqua, New York, c. 1923. Courtesy of the Estate of Ralph J. Gleason.

(IRA) and the British Army. As her homeland endured the war, Mollie agonized over her family's safety.

When the Gleasons embarked on an eight-day cruise to Ireland in the spring of 1928 to visit Mollie's sister, they landed in a new country.[12] After the war ended in 1921, the island was portioned into two countries, the Irish Free State, a predominantly Catholic nation, and Northern Ireland, primarily Protestant and part of the UK. But the IRA and other nationalists pressed to unify the island into a single independent Irish state. When the Gleasons arrived, the Irish Free State was just six years old, and young Ralph would have heard stories about the continuing conflict. Decades later in the 1960s, he would support global anti-colonialization and national wars of independence, including the IRA's fight.

After visiting Cobh, the family traveled to Ballygibbon, where Mollie's sister lived. Young Ralph disliked its primitive conditions but made a friend, the son of a prominent local family.[13] Ralph A. also made a friend, the local bookie, and waged bets on horse races during their entire stay. He told his son that the Irish weren't savvy

Figure 1.2 Ralph Gleason with his parents Ralph and Mollie in Chappaqua, c. 1927. Courtesy of the Estate of Ralph J. Gleason.

handicappers because they drank too much. After six months, the family departed Ireland on the S.S. *Cedric* ocean liner. A week later, they arrived at the Port of New York in time for Gleason to start high school in the fall of 1928.

Gleason identified with his Irish heritage throughout his life. He also experienced the outsiderness many Catholic Irish Americans bore in the 1920s Anglosphere. This alienation reinforced his later empathy for African Americans, another marginalized group.

The Horseplayer's Son

As Chappaqua's red maples and white oaks burst into showy color, Gleason started seventh grade at the newly built Horace Greeley High School. He later described himself as an "ordinary high school wise guy" who was "good in the 100-yard sprints, fair at basketball, and a terrible football player but a fast one with what we used to call 'the comeback.'"[14] He took his first job, lighting the wood stove each morning in the Chappaqua Friends Meeting House. In his spare time, he hunted and trapped muskrats; there is no account of what he did with them afterward.[15]

During Gleason's second year in high school, American capitalism collapsed. Wall Street crashed on October 29, 1929, triggering the Great Depression. Banks boarded up, leaving depositors penniless. Businesses folded, leaving millions of Americans jobless. Discarded newspapers called "Hoover blankets" warmed the homeless people forced to sleep on the city benches of Republican President Herbert Hoover's America. Yet, in Westchester County, life maintained a semblance of normality. *Blue Angel* starring Marlena Dietrich played at local movie theaters. The Port Chester basketball team advanced in their league tournament. Gleason's father kept his job at the phone company, a sign he was valued.

Ralph A. had an additional line of income: playing the horses. Although racetrack betting was a gentleman's sport popular with Irish American men, it carried a whiff of vice as a form of gambling.[16] A moralist in the *New York Times* wrote in 1924, "Wantonness, waste, jazz, gambling, drunkenness—all that is part of Satan's curriculum."[17] During the 1920s and 1930s, New York authorities cracked down on horse betting. Newspaper stories about arrests were familiar; some portrayed horse betting as being associated with violence and suspicious interactions between Whites and Blacks.[18] Others believed that gambling eroded America's work ethic. A horse bettor, explains sociologist Joan Allen, is "one whose risks symbolize an act of resistance to the expected patterns of expenditure and consumption."[19]

Successful racetrack betting requires skill and strong nerves. Serious bettors like Ralph A. assiduously study racing forms that provide statistics about horses' past performances. Bettors place wages with bookmakers, often called bookies, who accept and pay off bets at pre-determined odds. Ralph A. favored the racing forms of the *New York Morning Telegraph*, a leading source of racetrack news. He picked up a copy every morning at the Chappaqua train station and read the racing forms during the commute.[20] So intent was his focus that Ralph A. would ignore a cursory "good morning" from another passenger or answer with a terse grunt while rattling the paper to shoo them away.[21] He even handicapped horse races while at work. Instead of leaving for lunch with his co-workers, he volunteered to stay and collect overtime pay while he studied the racing forms. Gleason admired his father's subversiveness.[22]

Young Ralph soaked up horse racing during family vacations at New York racetrack towns like Belmont and Saratoga Springs during the summer. In a photograph, Gleason beams with pride in a pair of horse-riding breeches with long stockings and boots. He also loved the show-biz glamour of prestigious racetracks. In those days, movie stars such as tough guy George Raft attended races.[23] Gleason especially relished trips to Saratoga Springs because of the town's exciting milieu of casinos, clubs, and roadhouses.

Ralph A. was more than just a horseplayer; he was also a bookie. To bring in additional income during the Depression, he opened a business that young Ralph christened the "Greeley General Store." In addition to selling milk and eggs, Ralph A.

ran a bookmaking operation out of the store, and young Ralph helped by taking bets. Ralph A. arranged for the store to sell the *Morning Telegraph* so he could peruse the racing forms. Every night at 11:00 p.m., father and son went to the train station to pick up the next day's bundles of newspapers, giving Ralph A. an advanced look at the day's racing forms.[24]

These late-night jaunts to pick up the *Morning Telegraph* sparked Gleason's interest in journalism. The newspaper was in its tenth decade as a broadsheet devoted to theater shows and horse races. When racing rose in popularity after the First World War, notorious publisher Moe Annenberg bought the paper and turned it into an East Coast complement to his other publication, the *Daily Racing Form*. Annenberg's entanglements with organized crime eventually landed him in prison. Gleason found the *Morning Telegraph* fascinating. He fancied the newspaper's opinion pieces, such as those by Nelson Dunstan and Charles Hatton on horse racing.[25] But his favorite column was "Beau Broadway," written by Walter Winchell, the first gossip columnist in New York's theater district. Winchell wielded journalistic power and could make or break an upcoming entertainer. In "Beau Broadway," Winchell offered a hodgepodge of film and theater openings, cast changes, and insider news. Gleason relished Winchell's style, humor, and use of jazz slang.[26]

Gleason savored other New York dailies such as the *Times, Sun, World-Telegram,* and the *Times'* main rival, the *Herald Tribune*. Craving more information about the newspaper industry, Gleason learned all he could about journalism and saw reporters as "secular priests" who exposed corruption and upheld the First Amendment.[27] He never forgot the words carved in marble in the *Chicago Tribune* building: "And ye shall know the truth, and the truth shall make you free."[28]

Gleason carried this credo with him when he joined the staff of the *Greeley Tribune*, his high school newspaper. The *Greeley Tribune* reflected the rise in student newspapers between 1920 and 1940 as journalism professionalized and became an academic field of study. Aspiring journalists like Gleason benefited from these programs.[29] Gleason became editor of the *Greeley Tribune* and set out to expose unfairness and corruption. One day, an opportunity arose that tested how far he would go in upholding journalistic ethics.

Gleason discovered that the school principal changed the curriculum to accommodate the schedule of his secretary's daughter. The sudden change disrupted the graduation track of many students. Gleason had to decide whether to publish the story and face retribution from the principal or kill it and betray his ideals—an agonizing decision for a teenage editor. Gleason chose to publish. The principal punished his truth-telling by suspending him, but Gleason knew he did the right thing.[30] Later, as a music journalist, he became known for his steadfast integrity.

Gleason's interest in journalism coincided with the 1932 presidential election. Two years into the Great Depression, voters looked for an alternative to Hoover. Gleason's father supported Democratic candidate Franklin Delano Roosevelt, who vowed to address the economic crisis and its root causes. But Ralph A.'s boss at the phone company pressured employees to vote for Hoover. In defiance, Ralph A. proudly wore an "FDR for President" button to work and voted for Roosevelt.[31] His liberalness is unsurprising since Irish Americans belonged to a "core of minority group coalitions that made possible the New Deal."[32] Irish American scholar Lawrence McCaffrey wrote that the New Deal energized Catholic Democrats by appointing them to government positions where they played an essential role in creating the New Deal welfare state and an "expanding Irish social conscience."[33] Due to his father's influence, Gleason became a lifelong liberal Democrat.

As Gleason grew up, so did jazz. Ambitious bandleaders created a new streamlined version of jazz played by orchestras called big bands. Duke Ellington christened the new style swing, named for an expression coined by his trumpeter James "Bubber" Miley in their newly released record "It Don't Mean a Thing (If It Ain't Got That Swing)." This was the new music Gleason discovered by chance while recovering from a common childhood disease.

Strange Sounds in the Night

Childhood measles was nothing to trifle with in the 1930s, and it could cause vision loss and acute sensitivity to light. So, when Gleason contracted the ailment, Mollie kept his bedroom curtains drawn tight and the lights turned off while he recuperated. To help relieve the boredom, she put the family's Atwood-Kent radio in his bedroom. Through its tuner, Gleason explored the world of Depression-era radio broadcasting. Two networks dominated, the National Broadcasting Company (NBC) and the Columbia Broadcasting System (CBS). The airwaves teemed with serialized stories, highbrow lectures, classical music concerts, and dance band shows.

Networks scheduled these shows based on the performer's race. Programmers shunted the music by Black performers to late-night slots because companies based in the South wouldn't sponsor primetime shows by these artists. Therefore, Duke Ellington's orchestra and other Black bands had to accept time slots after 11 p.m. when most listeners were asleep. But Gleason did what any rebellious teen would do who didn't have to get up for school: stay up late and listen to the radio. That night, Gleason turned the radio's Bakelite dial, and Earl Hines' music flew out the speaker horn. From then on, he was hooked and returned nightly to the hurricane-force grooves, blues-based riffs, and riveting solos. "I could no more stop listening to music than I could stop breathing," he wrote.[34]

According to Neil Leonard, author of *Jazz: Myth and Religion*, jazz conversions are profoundly life-changing events similar to religious transformations.[35] These transfigurations lead to "redefinitions of the total image of the self and the world about it."[36] Gleason's dark bedroom provided a conducive setting for his epiphany. Dark space is "much more material, much more tangible, and even more penetrating than the limpid clarity" of well-lit space, notes French psychiatrist Eugene Minkowski.[37] The dark setting amplified the visceral intensity of big band jazz and made it a mysterious presence because "everything is obscure and mysterious within dark space. One feels as if in the presence of the unknown."[38] Gleason later referred to the "strange sounds" that emanated from the Atwood-Kent.

Figure 1.3 Ralph Gleason at home in Chappaqua, c. 1932. Courtesy of the Estate of Ralph J. Gleason.

Strange sounds to a White teenager living in a rural hamlet where only three African Americans resided.[39] Black swing bands introduced a new musical lexicon into the mainstream, such as the eerie voicings of Ellington's "East St. Louis Toodle-Oo" with trumpeter Bubber Miley's haunting wah-wah solos. Or Earl Hines' "Blue Drag" with its insistent tempo, pleading sax, and swirling horn sections. And Fletcher Henderson's "Sugar Foot Stomp," with one scintillating solo after another, each musician upping the intensity before coming together to bring it home.

"For those with open and curious minds," writes composer-historian Gunther Schuller, early jazz was met with a "mixture of captivation, allure, fear, mystery, incomprehension, and sheer fascination."[40] Swing scholar Lewis A. Erenberg explains why young White listeners flocked to Black jazz during the swing era:

> [It had] enormous vitality and spontaneity. On the segregated south side of Chicago and even more in New York's Harlem, black people created their cultural expressiveness in the area that was least policed – their music and dance. Jazz bore the spontaneous, improvisatory energy of this one realm of freedom and expressed the body as a natural and divine feature of human existence.[41]

Following his conversion, Gleason tuned in every night. "11, 12, one o'clock in the morning, bang! You'd catch Duke Ellington wailing, you know, and with all those mysterious sounds that didn't sound like anything else you'd ever heard."[42] In sharp contrast to daytime radio music, which Gleason compared to "somebody having a piano recital in the studio, you know, some corny mother whom you couldn't possibly listen to. And then, you'd hear Earl Hines singing through that piano at night."[43] He disliked the music of White bands who played "a distillation of Anglo-Saxon, Protestant, Puritanical dance music that, whatever it did, for God's sakes, don't let it swing."[44]

The Far-Outness of Duke Ellington in Chappaqua

Gleason adopted a new persona based on his love for Black jazz. Music scholar Simon Frith writes, "Music gives us a way of being in the world, a way of making sense of it; musical response is, by its nature, a process of musical identification."[45] That said, "Identity comes from the outside, not the inside; it is something we put or try on, not something we reveal or discover."[46] Most importantly, Frith points to the democratic nature of a fan constructing an identity around musicians whose ethnicity or gender differs from theirs.[47] Gleason became more egalitarian by building an identity around Black swing jazz. But with this new identity came alienation.

After he recovered and returned to school, Gleason excitedly told his friends about Ellington's music and the other "strange sounds." His classmates failed to grasp what he was so excited about:

> I went back to school, and I found I was a freak. Everybody else knows John Philip Sousa and "The Stars and Stripes Forever," and you know, whatever the hell a pop song was at that moment.[48]

As for Black jazz:

> The degree of far-outness of Duke Ellington in Chappaqua in 1932 was incredible. I heard all these weird exotic sounds in the middle of the night, you know, and I was the only one in the school that ever heard of him; nobody knew what I was talking about, and it freaked me out of my mind.[49]

Gleason discovered that praising unsung musicians could fall on deaf ears. So, he hatched a plan to bring jazz to Horace Greeley High. He and a friend brought a portable radio to the school auditorium and began to play jazz during lunchtime. Caught up in the rhythm, teen boys and girls paired off and danced. The girls taught the latest styles, like the jitterbug.[50] These radio dance parties caught on, and Gleason began his lifelong passion for introducing novices to jazz.

Gleason started to play jazz as well as listen to it. An amateur pianist, he formed a trio with a drummer and violinist. To learn songs, they listened to the "nighttime broadcasts of Paul Tremaine, Louis Armstrong, Earl Hines, Fletcher Henderson, and a host of others."[51] Gleason took lessons to sharpen his skills, learning "the Czerny exercises, 'Gollywog's Cakewalk,' things like that."[52] "Golliwog's Cakewalk" was written by French composer Claude Debussy as part of a suite about toys that come to life. The "golliwog," an anti-Black caricature and slur, came from a cartoon character and doll popular in the nineteenth century. That the song was used in 1930s piano instruction speaks to the pervasive presence of Black stereotypes at that time.

But it was three jazz tunes that Gleason's trio mastered and debuted at the Horace Greeley Friday Tea Dance. The event took an unfortunate turn, at least for Gleason.

As the dance gets underway, Gleason's trio starts swinging. Unexpectedly, in walks a group of out-of-town teens including professional pianist Graham Forbes. Wanting to check out his competition, Gleason let Forbes sit in. The pianist improvises solos that wow the crowd and leaves Gleason feeling so humiliated that he refuses to play for the remainder of the dance. From then on, Gleason mainly played piano for his amusement. He also learned to play drums, his musical skills broadening his understanding of jazz.

Gleason cultivated a group of friends who shared his taste for swing, and on weekends they drove to Long Island to listen to big bands. The teens piled into coupes and roadsters and made the cross-county drive, the sweeping fenders of their Fords and Chevies gleaming in the night. One evening it might be the casino at Roton Park; another evening, the dance hall on Glen Island, where they danced with local girls on the waterfront balcony.[53] Swing jazz would always conjure romance for Gleason, even late in life.

Gleason and his jazz-loving classmates belonged to the emergent swing youth culture.[54] These fans flocked to bandstands in ballrooms and parks, gathered around polished wood radios and phonographs, and spun discs on gleaming chrome jukeboxes. The youth of the swing era differed from their Jazz Age predecessors, according to scholar Lewis A. Erenberg. "Moving forward from the 1920s," he wrote, "we begin to discern subtle differences in the youth culture" of the 1930s. "Fired by economic collapse," he wrote, "youth behavior and popular music registered the cultural crisis of the day."[55] Gleason's generation witnessed the failure of capitalism and heard horror stories about the carnage of the First World War. They distrusted institutions and authority figures more than previous generations. This skepticism stayed with Gleason for the rest of his life.

In spring 1934, Gleason and his friends looked forward to graduating and moving on with their lives. Gleason planned to go to college and considered options with his parents. Mollie wanted him to attend an Irish Catholic university like Fordham or Notre Dame.[56] But Gleason refused because he had drifted away from the church. The family considered Trinity College in Dublin, a secular option, but it seemed too radical a change.⁵⁷ Having forsaken Jesus for jazz, another academic alternative appealed to the seventeen-year-old swing devotee: Columbia University. Although it was a private, Ivy League institution, Columbia offered student aid to Depression-era applicants from modest backgrounds like Gleason who met the academic standards.

At Columbia, Gleason would be within walking distance of clubs that roared with the sounds of Duke Ellington, Jimmie Lunceford, and other college favorites. An Ivy League degree would also give him a step up in life. And so, in the fall of 1934, Gleason left Chappaqua's curving roads for New York City's gridded streets. At Columbia, he would be just thirty miles from home but a short walk from where his real education would occur—the New York City jazz scene.

2

Hot Jazz Off the Record (1934–38)

Imagine Columbia University on September 27, 1934, the first day of fall classes. Students crowd the campus bookstore searching for textbooks and other items such as the latest Tommy Dorsey record or the latest issue of *Jester*, the student humor magazine. In classrooms campus-wide, faculty hand out mimeographed syllabi. Columbia was all-male back then, so students looked forward to the upcoming dance with neighboring Barnard, a women's college.

Topics more serious than social mixing dominated the newspapers that morning. In the *New York Times*, the Charles Lindbergh, Jr. kidnapping case and the indictment of Bruno Richard Hauptmann grab the headlines. On the front page of the *Columbia Spectator*, the student newspaper, a different charge: "Butler Charges Modern Youth Lack Manners."[1] In his opening address, president Nicholas Murray Butler had decried the younger generation's embrace of vulgar ways and lack of respect for authority figures, especially "those who are older in years."[2] For Gleason and other first-year students, the generation gap widened.

This fissure cut across political as well as social values. Gleason's generation grew up hearing about the horrors of the First World War, and many rejected militarism. In the *Columbia Spectator*, editors promised to use "every resource at our command to mobilize in significant proportions a university-wide movement against war."[3] Editors aimed the pledge at Butler, who barely tolerated the campus antiwar movement and its strident rhetoric.

On a lighter note, Duke Ellington led the list of artists slated to play at the 125th Street Apollo Theater. Jazz enthusiasts and jitterbugs alike welcome the news. Plus, an entertainment strip south of campus on 52nd Street shows signs of musical life thanks to the recent appeal of Prohibition. Club owners hire dance bands to draw drinking crowds. A new generation of jazz cognoscenti post themselves along the front edges of stages and take every note of every sax solo in silent benediction. These true believers congregate in the Commodore Record Shop, where owner Milt Gabler welcomes a new wave of Columbia jazz disciples. Gleason entered a new world of jazz, activism, and academics—a heady milieu for the Chappaqua escapee, one that would reset his life perspective.

Columbia University

At 17, Gleason cut a handsome figure, tall and slender with dark hair combed back and sporting a well-groomed yet offhand style. In a photo from that time, he wears a sweater vest over a shirt with the sleeves rolled up, ready to work. And high-waisted, wide-leg pleated trousers that were popular with Depression-era collegians and dapper movie gangsters. A sharp yet easy-going countenance. Self-aware but unformed.[4]

Located in Morningside Heights on the Upper West Side of Manhattan, the Columbia campus projected a nineteenth-century ideal of elite higher education. Symmetrical groupings of weathered stone buildings boasted bas-relief panels, garlands, and cartouches inscribed with the values of civic democracy. Such details hailed the nation's origins in European high culture. But just under five miles away, in Midtown, a new American order soared toward the sky. Skyscrapers like the Empire State Building signified a nation determined to redefine beauty and virtue and create its own culture apart from its European roots. A democratic order that found expression in the popular arts, including jazz.

This spirit of modernity animated Columbia despite its neoclassical image. The university boasted a progressive faculty, including Gleason's professor Lionel Trilling, an anti-communist Marxist on his way to becoming a leading twentieth-century literary critic. Trilling once said, "Between is the only honest place to be," a shades-of-gray principle that Gleason would also espouse.[5] In Trilling's classroom, Gleason learned how culture influenced politics, a central theme of his later writings.[6] In Trilling's "Great Books" course taught with venerated poet, novelist, and critic Mark Van Doren, Gleason read classic writers he would quote in future music writings. For social science, Gleason took courses by one of Columbia's most popular professors, William C. Casey.[7] Casey taught the new field of sociology, which introduced progressive thinking about economic justice, worker's rights, racial equality, and social services such as universal health care. Casey also engaged in activism, including the 1932 coal-mining protests held in Harlan, Kentucky that led to improved working conditions and some of the first protest songs.[8]

Such protests "marked the dawn of a new age in American student politics," according to historian Robert Cohen. "Shaken by the Depression, collegians began to discard their traditional political apathy."[9] Activism flourished in New York, which Cohen calls the "capital city of American radicalism during the Depression." Cohen said the "radical intelligentsia made New York its home and used the city as a base for publishing the nation's most important leftist magazines and journals," including *New Masses*, which Gleason read.[10] Columbia University became the city's center of student activism within this ferment.

But Columbia's president disdained student protest. Butler, a conservative Republican, established an anti-Jewish quota at the university and admired Benito Mussolini.[11] Such views put Butler at odds with his community. Cohen observes, "Within a 20-block radius of the Columbia campus lived the greatest assemblage of academic progressives and radicals in Depression America."[12]

Widen that radius several blocks, and you find the most vital jazz scene in Depression America. From Harlem to 52nd Street, musicians like Duke Ellington, Jimmy Lunceford, Tommy Dorsey, and Art Tatum spellbound audiences. Jazz permeated the Columbia campus, its dance halls, dorm rooms, and fraternity houses. During Gleason's first semester at Columbia, he immersed himself in a heady mix of academics and jazz beyond his wildest dreams.

From Harlem to Jazz Alley

You sit on the balcony of the Apollo and looked down at Earl Hines on that stage with that band, and he had on the fourth finger of his right hand a ring. And when he would play those trills, the right hand, [with] the treble way up on the top of the keyboard … cut through the brass and the saxophones, he'd stick his hand out there and just wail on those trills, and the spotlight would come down on that ring. And the whole stage would be dark, and all you'd see was Hines' hand and the top of the piano keyboard and that ring just glistening. It was insane. You know, blew me right out of my mind; I mean, you talk about mind-blowing experiences.[13]

Gleason dove into the New York jazz scene. He discovered the jazz greats he encountered on late-night radio performed just a few blocks off campus. The Apollo, Savoy Ballroom, the Renaissance, Strand, and Paramount theaters, Gleason spent every spare minute on his "jazz education," as he called it.[14]

Like other swing meccas in segregated America, the New York jazz scene straddled the color line. In Harlem, the showcase for popular music was the Apollo Theater. The music hall initially operated as a Whites-only venue, but by 1934 it catered to a predominantly Black audience. As historian Tuliza Fleming writes, "The theater was uniquely poised to take full advantage of Harlem's abundance of African American entertainers and burgeoning Black community."[15] Gleason discovered the Apollo soon after he started at Columbia. At that time, he commuted to Columbia every morning on the Chappaqua-to-Harlem train. One day Gleason gets off at the 125th Street station as he does every morning. Walking down the street, he stops dead in his tracks. Looking down at him is a ten-foot-tall image of Cab Calloway, part of an enormous sign announcing an upcoming performance by the riveting bandleader. Captivated, Gleason enters and catches his first Apollo show. From then on, he's hooked and frequents the Apollo regularly to watch musicians, comedians, and Westerns featuring pioneering Black cowboy star Herb Jeffries.

Gleason discovered that African American jazz musicians performed better at the Apollo than in front of all-White audiences. He wrote that it was a "strange experience to hear a band like Ellington or Lunceford at the Apollo one week and then downtown at the [white] Strand Theater," where they "never played badly, but at the Apollo, they were always on! Always."[16] Seeing "Chick Webb, hunched behind all those cymbals and gourds, Jimmie Lunceford waving that silly baton, Duke Ellington chewing gum and snapping his fingers—when they played the Apollo, they meant it."[17] For Gleason, the Apollo was "like a street corner. The audience was as fast as the comedian, and if he didn't cut it, they would cut him! Careers were made."[18] He said the Apollo "was the home of Black America laughin' just to keep from crying and the single greatest incubator of talent this country has ever seen."[19]

At the Apollo, Gleason acquired his interest in the social context of popular music. He saw music deeply interwoven with its community. There was "a dialogue between the performer and the audience at all times. I mean, Earl would say something or do something, and somebody would yell, and it wasn't a question of being heckled. It was a question of participation."[20] For the rest of his life, Gleason reported on the participatory nature of concerts by magnetic musicians, be it Earl Hines or the Beatles.

Gleason entered the complex world of 1930s race relations by venturing into Harlem. For many Harlem residents, the influx of Whites beginning in the 1920s created a "Caucasian storm," according to *American Mercury* writer Rudolf Fisher, a Black resident. "These places … are no longer mine but theirs … I am stared at; I frequently feel uncomfortable and out of place."[21] Black writer Langston Hughes also wrote about the White Storm:

> Ordinary Negroes [did not like] the growing influx of whites toward Harlem after sundown, flooding the little cabarets and bars where formerly only colored people laughed and sang and where now the strangers were given the best ringside tables to sit and stare at the Negro customers like amusing animals in a zoo.
>
> So, thousands of whites came to Harlem night after night, thinking the Negroes love to have them there and firmly believing that all Harlemites left their houses at sundown to sing and dance at cabarets because most whites saw nothing but the cabarets, not the houses.[22]

But as jazz historian John Gennari points out, not all White patrons of Harlem clubs were slumming or engaged in racial voyeurism. Jazz critics like Carl Van Vechten and others went to these clubs because of their near-religious devotion to Black jazz and used their positions to help artists and venues. Gleason followed this tradition.

Along with Harlem, New York's other jazz center was "The Street," a stretch of 52nd Street in Midtown Manhattan. Also called "Jazz Alley," this district nurtured one of the country's most vital music scenes.[23] Gleason wrote:

> You could wander all night long up and down that dingy thoroughfare lined with crumbling brownstone houses converted to theatrical rooming houses and small apartments. The basements and first floors of a really astonishing number of these buildings were converted into night clubs, the small, crowded, dark, and dingy club that was the prototype of the jazz joint.[24]

For Gleason, this was pure bliss,

> It was a natural ball. You could spend night after night wandering up and down, listening for a while in front of one club and then another before ducking around

the corner to the White Rose for a beer. They never seemed to mind the kids, who just stood around and listened. For that matter, you could get a pretty good basic course in jazz history just by walking The Street and listening to the conversations on the sidewalk among the musicians.[25]

Gleason avoided cover charges on a tight budget by standing instead of sitting at a table and nursing a bottle of Piels beer all night. "If you developed the capability for making yourself inconspicuous, you could hang around [even] on weekends without paying at all."[26]

It was on 52nd Street that Gleason first heard the sounds of traditional jazz by musicians such as Jelly Roll Morton, the Spirits of Rhythm, Red McKenzie, and Joe Marsala.[27] Big bands were yet to become regulars on The Street. However, swing musicians showed up for jam sessions. Gleason observes this at one of The Street's most popular nightspots, the Onyx Club. Performing is violinist Stuff Smith, an up-and-coming musician known for swinging improvisations devoid of ostentatious displays of technique. While Smith plays, pianists Fats Waller and Count Basie march into the club, two jazz giants. They join Smith's band in an impromptu jam session that thrills the audience. Gleason wrote, "I had an 8 o'clock class the next day. I don't think I made it. What could they tell me there to equal what I'd heard that night?"[28]

On another memorable night, the Count Basie band with saxophonist Lester Young squeezed onto the bandstand at the Famous Door, "a long thin box running back from the street," as Gleason described it. "The band was at the end of the room bunched together in echelons, stacked one over the other with the trumpet section blowing with their heads touching the ceiling," he wrote. But this didn't crimp their style. As Gleason said, "The power they had was breathtaking." When Gleason opened the door and walked into the club, the band "was like a blast of air in a wind tunnel. It almost knocked you down." Yet "they could come down to a whisper, so quiet you could hear glasses clink at the bar," and "never lose the pulse that swung you."[29]

Gleason experienced his first local music scene on 52nd Street. He communed with other enthusiasts and alleviated the sense of alienation that traveled with him to Columbia. But most importantly, Gleason learned that music scenes were more than the sum of their parts; they embody networks of information and camaraderie that can nurture unique musical creativity, even cultural revolutions.

A Beat-up Magnavox and a Box of Old Records

Gleason, who grew up without a phonograph, discovered the world of record collecting for the first time at Columbia. It happened one morning in spring 1935 as Gleason cleaned tables in the John Jay Hall dining room where he worked as a busboy. Alongside him is swing fan Kerry Merwin, a gangly premed student. Their conversation turns to jazz as they wipe up coffee rings and maple syrup drips. Merwin tells Gleason he has a phonograph and a box of jazz records, and would he like to hear some? Gleason answers, "Yes!" A few hours later, he sits in Merwin's dorm room as his new friend carefully places a shellac disc on the turntable. Merwin drops the cactus needle in place, and it rides the record's spiraling groove. Suddenly, the sound of the Jimmie Lunceford band ricochets off the dorm walls. A saxophone blows hot for a chorus, followed by a trumpet. Lunceford's smooth but swinging voice announces, "Rhythm is our business; rhythm is what we sell." For Gleason, Lunceford made the sale.[30]

In a foretelling move, Gleason cuts classes and spends the day in Merwin's room, where they listen to records by Lunceford, Henderson, and Ellington.[31] After the last disc ends, Merwin lends Gleason his phonograph and records. Gleason spends the weekend listening to deep cuts like Lunceford's first Decca records and pianist Teddy Wilson's "Rosetta," a lively performance with hints of modern jazz. After that weekend, Gleason said his "world was divided, with lovely bias, into those who dig jazz—and all those other people."[32] After discovering jazz on discs, "two things became apparent, I had to have a phonograph, and I had to have the records. I got them both as fast as I could."[33] Gleason purchases a "raunchy beat-up Magnavox" record player with a cactus needle that he sharpened with a "Red Top needle sharpener, the little sandpaper disc buzzing as you spun it."[34] Astute record collectors prized cactus needles because they produced a "softer tone without scratching the records."[35] He combed the Columbia Bookstore for jazz records:

> They used to appear on blue-label 35-cent discs every couple of weeks – two sides, 78 rpm, and you had to be there right on time, or the small allotment would be gone, and you would have missed the new Jimmie Lunceford record. If you were lucky, you got one, ran back to your room … and then sat back in ecstasy to listen to the sound.[36]

Gleason soon discovered a more comprehensive source of discs: the Commodore Record Shop. The tiny store faced the Chrysler Building on West 42nd Street and hosted the "most active cell of jazz enthusiasts New York has ever seen," according to Gleason.[37] The shop was run by Milt Gabler, a stout and balding jazz fanatic and "father confessor to a generation of musicians and buffs."[38] The Commodore was jazz central for Columbia University's "hot collectors."

As the name implies, hot collectors amassed collections of "hot jazz" records, discs containing intensely swinging performances with torrid improvisations. The term "hot jazz" had been used since the 1920s to reference the sizzling style of musicians like trumpeter Louis Armstrong. French critic Hugues Panassié, in his book, *Hot Jazz: The Guide to Swing Music*, codified the term with the precision of a classical music critic:

> In Jazz, we must distinguish between two ways of interpreting: "straight" and "hot." In general, you could say that straight playing is playing the piece just as it is written, without modifying it. To place straight is, then, to follow a direct line, to adhere to the tune …
>
> In a figurative sense, to play hot means to play with warmth, with heat. The expression was invented to describe the style of certain jazz musicians who played their solos with warm, eloquent intonations of a very special kind.[39]

Improvisation, Panassié wrote, was the key:

> One can hardly play hot while following the tune. Literally, for there is something about any tune, however beautiful, which is rigid, symmetrical, and unfriendly to that spontaneity necessary for hot interpretation.[40]

Panassié made clear that a musician could play swing jazz either hot or straight:

> Swing, that essential element of jazz, was the one element common to both kinds of interpretation. There can be as much of it in a good straight performance as in a hot performance. But there are degrees of swing, and almost always, hot interpretations have a greater swing than other performances. This is because phrases in that broken, syncopated, discreet style that hot musicians use lend themselves readily to extraordinary swing.[41]

Hot jazz was no more authentic than straight jazz, Panassié wrote, but it was aesthetically superior:

> It is straight jazz which has been diluted down into that spurious jazz which floods the whole world. It is a sort of straight execution without swing, which, popular opinion to the contrary, has the external form of jazz without its substance, the rime without the fruit ... Almost all the masterpieces produced by jazz are hot interpretations.[42]

Panassié's points became popularized in America through articles like "Collecting Hot," published by jazz historian Charles Edward Smith in *Esquire* in 1934.[43]

Hot collecting caught fire at Columbia, where four hot collectors wrote about jazz for campus publications. Robert Paul Smith penned "Off the Record," the record review column for the student-run *Columbia Daily Spectator*. Smith also published articles about jazz for *Jester*, Columbia's humor magazine.[44] Smith took his jazz crusade into the lecture hall and delivered a talk on swing music to the Philolexian Society, a campus literary group:

> An audience that jammed the Student Board Room was thrilled to a miscellany of Duke Ellington, Clyde McCoy, Louis Armstrong, and other exponents of the new jazz medium. Improvisation, said Smith, is the key to "swing," illustrating his statement with examples drawn from all varieties of recorded popular music.[45]

The Philolexian Society presented another program on swing by Barry Ulanov.[46] With his slight smirk and carefully coiffed hair, Ulanov exuded self-assurance. He published articles in the *Columbia Review*, including a piece on the "decline of the art of music," which he blamed on replacing melody with dissonance.[47] Ulanov also wrote on jazz for *Jester*.[48] There, he met another jazz fan, *Jester* editor Ralph de Toledano who wrote the magazine's record review column "Rocking in Rhythm." Toledano, a Julliard-trained violinist whose parents were journalists, grew up with music and writing. He and Ulanov belonged to the Boar's Head Society, a campus poetry-writing group that attracted guest speakers such as poet William Carlos Williams. Jazz and experimental poetry intermingled.[49]

Another *Jester* writer, Eugene Williams, a hot jazz fan, would play an essential role in Gleason's journalistic development.[50] Williams wore wireframe glasses, had a sensitive face, and liked to stir debate.[51] Gleason and Williams were part of the "Merton Circle" of hot collectors, named for their classmate and future theologian Thomas Merton. In his autobiography, Merton wrote how jazz lyrics fostered his empathy for struggling Black neighborhoods in the South. Merton said he learned "something true" about these communities through jazz records.[52]

The Merton Circle met at the Greenwich Village apartment of Eugene Williams to "hear jazz, meet musicians, and avoid going to class."[53] Fellow hot collector Ed Rice observed how "everything was influenced by [James] Joyce, down to our clothing—the necktie, the tweed jacket—and we imitated his way of writing."[54] Yet nothing was rarefied or pretentious about these young men for whom jazz and fun were interchangeable, said author Mary Cummings:

> If Joyce was their literary hero, jazz was their music. Everyone listened to Bessie Smith, Louis Armstrong, King Oliver, and Bix Beiderbecke's recordings. They frequented jazz joints and stole time from their studies to steep themselves in the jazzy atmosphere of Gene Williams's hip Village salon. If nothing special was on, Nick's on Sheridan Square usually rocked with jazz, or there was a party somewhere with enough booze, weed, and women to keep the wild anti-establishment ethos alive.[55]

Gleason began his lifelong habit of record collecting at Columbia, where he absorbed the hot jazz aesthetic framed by Panassié and other critics. One can imagine how this atmosphere of records, live shows, and passionate discussions set Gleason's mind afire with ideas about jazz. Back in Chappaqua, Gleason had dreamed of being a columnist, inspired by *Morning Telegraph* writers. His opportunity came in the spring of 1935 when word went out that Robert Paul Smith was leaving "Off the Record."

For Purposes Remotely Aesthetic

The *Spectator* was one of many student-run activities based in John Jay Hall, a stout neoclassical high-rise dubbed the "sky-scraper dorm." Merton described the importance of one section of the building in particular:

> The fourth floor of John Jay Hall was where all the offices of the student publications and the Glee Club, the Student Board, and all the rest were to be found. It was the noisiest and most agitated part of the campus. It was not gay, exactly. And I hardly ever saw, anywhere, antipathies and contentions and jealousies at once so petty, so open and so sharp ... It was all intellectual and verbal, as vicious as it could

be. Still, it never became concrete, never descended into a physical rage ... It was all more or less of a game that everybody played for purposes that were remotely aesthetic.[56]

Within this dynamic setting, the *Spectator* published daily editions from Monday to Saturday; its four pages were written and edited by students. The paper's editorial page contained several columns, including "Off the Record," which provided short reviews of popular music discs. Columnist Robert Paul Smith planned to graduate in a year, and Gleason wanted to fill the upcoming vacancy. The column came with a steady stream of free review records, and Gleason dreamed of hot jazz discs delivered to his door. And so, he applied to the *Spectator*. Applicants had to compete for staff positions:

> Classes under the direction of a member of the Managing Board will be held over several weeks to familiarize editorial aspirants with routine work. Reporting, feature writing, headline writing, editing, and other phases of journalism will be taught. After the course, those succeeding in the competition will be elected to the Associate News Board.[57]

Being editor of the *Horace Greeley Tribune* gave Gleason an edge, though he faced stiff competition among talented applicants.

The Managing Board appointed Gleason to the *Spectator* in April 1935, a life-turning event for the freshman.[58] Best of all, this put the budding hot collector on track to write "Off the Record" the following year. In the meantime, Gleason would learn the basics of journalistic writing. But before he wrote his first story, Gleason experienced the *Spectator*'s hardball politics. The managing editors announced the paper was on strike to protest interference from the Butler administration:

> [The strike came after] a long series of attempts, Administration-sponsored or encouraged, to throttle an independent student press ... It is one more phase of the concerted, ceaseless effort to "get the *Spectator*." ... Do we want to preserve the *Spectator* as an independent, critical organ? Or do we want it gradually transformed into a paper that says nothing and pleases everybody?"[59]

Gleason walked into a fight he would take up many times in his career, the battle for freedom of speech.

The *Spectator* and the administration resolved their differences, so Gleason the rookie journalist went to work on his first assignment. "Wolfe is Rated above Wilder" was based on an interview with an erudite soda fountain waiter about the relative merits of novelists Thomas Wolfe and Thornton Wilder:

> With one gesture of his lean hand, Jack the sandwich man and soda jerker dismissed Thornton Wilder's latest literary effort [*My Town*] as a "weakly naive work." He praised Thomas Wolfe as "the greatest poetic author writing in the

English language today ... Wolfe has put new life into literature; he has remade the novel into an instrument for his creative expression."

Another customer entered, and, as the soda had been finished, the session ended with Jack shouting: "Don't forget to read *Look Homeward, Angel.*"[60]

Gleason identified with Wolfe and *Look Homeward Angel*. The elegiac novel led future Columbia student Jack Kerouac to forsake his studies and read Wolfe, just like Lunceford's music led Gleason to skip classes and listen to jazz records.[61] Two decades later, Gleason would praise Kerouac's *On the Road*. From Wolfe to Kerouac and beyond, Gleason gravitated to novelists who used free-flowing prose to sanctify life's restless outsiders. "Wolfe is Rated above Wilder" was Gleason's first *Spectator* article and exemplified a strategy he used throughout his career: provide a platform for a colorful narrator—often marginalized—who has a worthwhile story that says something about creative expression.

That semester Gleason achieved another first, a slot on a campus dance committee. These groups organized social soirees that featured live music. Gleason helped plan the spring 1935 prom, which advertised with an art deco illustration of a curly-haired ingenue reclined in a club chair. "Meet this young lady at the John Jay Lounge at the Freshman Formal Dance," promised the ad.[62] Gleason helped book a band for the event, Wally Jaeger and his Islanders, a campus favorite that drew a big crowd.[63] Gleason continued to work on dance committees, where he learned how to audition bands and hire them, set up sound systems, and perform other tasks that went into organizing a show. This experience began his lifelong fascination with the mechanics of musical performances.

After the prom, the spring semester ended uneventfully. But that summer jazz history is made when clarinetist Benny Goodman and his orchestra start their show at the Palomar Ballroom in Los Angeles. The crowd appears listless, which frustrates the musicians. Exasperated by the crowd's lethargy, trumpeter Bunny Berigan yells at his bandmates, "Let's cut this shit!" With nothing to lose, Goodman pulls out all the stops and plays hotter. Jazz historian Lewis A. Erenberg describes the scene:

> As they reeled off one hot Fletcher Henderson arrangement after another, a roar rose from the crowd, which stopped its desultory dancing and surged around the stand to watch and listen. Goodman and his musicians were elated. The swing era, one of the defining moments in American popular music, was born.[64]

When Gleason returned to campus in the fall of 1935, swing and Goodman its King were in the air. "Benny Goodman now on the coast, and so good that words fail," wrote Smith in "Off the Record."[65] A new jazz craze swept the nation. Energized, Smith spent that fall reviewing a flood of swing discs.

Elsewhere in the *Spectator*, Gleason's byline appeared on "Sidelines," the paper's sports column. He gamely reported on campus athletics each week and developed a casual prose style. For example, he used his racetrack smarts to enliven one column with characters like Pete, "who rubs horses for twenty-five bucks a month, room and board, and makes bets on the ponies." And Flop, "who never gets into the track but hangs out at the poolroom across the street and books little bets from the stable boys."[66] These asides added a street hipness to his play-by-play summaries of campus sports.

That semester Gleason pledged Delta Upsilon fraternity. Columbia's fraternities played a central role in campus politics by running candidates for seats on the Student Board, an advisory council to the university's administration. A chief qualification for office was a portfolio of committee assignments, and Gleason acquired political capital when he became publicity chairman for the sophomore Easter dance in the spring of 1936.[67] Afterward, he moved into student politics and chaired the steering committee for the Independent Fraternity Party.[68] The party's platform included support for the American Student Union (ASU), one of the most influential left-wing student activist groups of the 1930s. Gleason's political evolution was underway.

Gleason stayed busy during the remainder of the semester. He compiled a solid record of accomplishments and had something to look forward to. Robert Paul Smith graduated, and "Off the Record" would be Gleason's when he returned in the fall.

We're Not Fred Astaire Fans

When classes resumed in September 1936, a dark wind blew through Europe, sending a chill across America. Adolf Hitler's army engaged in the most extensive military exercises since the First World War in Germany. In Italy, a parade of Hitler Youth marched in Rome's Piazza Venezia. A civil war broke out in Spain when right-wing Nationalists attacked the Republicans who held power. Despite fascism's spread across Europe, some American institutions maintained their ties with Germany. That summer, Columbia University sent a delegation to Germany for the University of Heidelberg's 550th anniversary. The decision generated controversy because the event began with a ceremony for the Nazi Party. Columbia activists staged a raucous protest in front of president Butler's residence that presaged a coming year of intense protests against fascism. Amidst political crisis and dissent, Gleason launched his career as a music critic.

But it was music, not protest, on his mind when Gleason received his first batch of review records. The novice writer expected hot jazz discs but instead received several recordings by dancer-singer Fred Astaire backed by bandleader-pianist Johnny Green. Six sides of lightly swinging tunes with no improvisatory heat. Gleason acknowledged his bias:

> Fred Astaire fans will go for these in a big way, but we're not Fred Astaire fans. Unfortunate but true.

> The first two [sides] are fair, except that recording devices cannot catch the subtlety of Astaire's dancing. The Bojangles side is the best of the poor lot. It may be a condemnation of Fred Astaire, but we thought he was at his best in the imitation of Bill Robinson in the current picture "Swing Time," from which these are the hit tunes.

> As for the last two, the "Waltz in Swing Time," whatever else it may do, certainly does not swing, and "A Fine Romance," we are afraid, is not one of Jerome Kern's better tunes. However, the waltz has one asset, Astaire does not dance. But Johnny Green makes a corny attempt to "swing in waltz time."[69]

Then the mood of the column lifted:

> Enough for the current releases. Jimmie Lunceford opened at the 125 Apollo Friday for a week giving the local cats a chance to peep at Willie Smith, Eddie Durham, Sy Oliver, et al before their expected opening at Larchmont again early in October. A slight tendency to go off-key is the only fault we've ever found with the Lunceford outfit. Oliver's arrangements alone are worth listening to.[70]

With this column, Gleason joined the discourse of American popular music. In it, he takes a stand for hot jazz and against straight jazz. Reviewing the Lunceford band required going into Harlem, where he had crossed the color line many times before, a signifier of credibility.

When Gleason took over "Off the Record" in October 1936, music critics around the country continued a vigorous jazz discourse that began in the 1920s. One of the first critics to take jazz seriously was Robert Donaldson Darrell, who in 1927 co-founded and became the leading critic for *Phonograph Monthly Review*, the "first American magazine about the appreciation and collecting of records by enthusiasts."[71] Another pioneering critic was Abbe Niles, who wrote the column "Ballads, Songs, and Snatches" for *The Bookman*, a literary magazine. For Niles, jazz records of the 1920s represented the birth of an authentically American culture. Some early critics argued that Black musicians invented jazz and that non-Black musicians diluted the music's essential features. One of these writers was Gilbert Seldes. The influential crusader for popular culture published *The Seven Lively Arts*, in which he made a case for the aesthetic value of lowbrow culture, including jazz. In a 1924 *Vanity Fair* article called "American Noises: How to Make Them, and Why," Seldes asked:

> What does jazz consist of? How is it created or produced?
>
> The most straightforward way to arrive at an answer, without becoming involved in technical details, is to compare the jazz band of ten years ago with that of today. The former was a jazz band and played jazz; the present one, if you follow either the learned Doctor Vincent Lopez or the eminent Professor Paul Whiteman, is "a small orchestra" playing "modern American music."
>
> The jazz of ten years ago is considered relatively low by the masters of modern effects. They are inclined to deny its good features, impudence, and vehemence. It was played on five instruments: the cornet, clarinet, trombone, piano, and

percussion; and the players improvised ad-lib, as do gypsy bands, Negro players, and others with an instinctive feeling of time and rhythm, which always brings them out right in the end.[72]

The first jazz press, led by three magazines, emerged in the early 1930s. *Esquire* launched in 1933 as a men's lifestyle magazine and by 1934 published important articles about jazz, such as Smith's "Collecting Hot." *DownBeat* started as a musicians' magazine that year and quickly became a platform for rising jazz writers including Paul Edward Miller, Marshall Stearns, and George Frazier. In the meantime, *Metronome*, a longstanding music magazine, increased its jazz coverage after George T. Simon joined the staff in the spring of 1935.

Although *DownBeat*, *Metronome*, and *Esquire* became the dominant outlets of the new jazz press, newspapers and left-leaning magazines also played an essential role. The *New York Times* largely ignored the city's vibrant jazz scenes. Still, other New York newspapers provided regular coverage, such as the *New York Age*, a Black newspaper, and the *Brooklyn Daily Eagle*, where writer John Hammond became an uncommonly passionate proponent of swing jazz. Hammond worked behind the scenes in the music industry and was an outspoken left-wing political activist.[73] In 1936, Hammond moved to *DownBeat* and also launched a music column in *The New Masses*, a Marxist magazine associated with the Communist Party, U.S.A. Concerned about government surveillance, Hammond wrote under the pseudonym "Henry Johnson." He wrote the column to get around his editors at *DownBeat*, who blocked him from writing about the racial discrimination faced by Black musicians.[74] Hammond titled his first *New Masses* column "The Development of Swing."[75] This piece was one of the first convincing attempts to analyze swing after it became a national pastime.

Gleason Off the Record

Hammond and other critics influenced Gleason, who readily absorbed the hot jazz aesthetic that valued warm intonations, powerfully swinging tempos, and expressive improvisation. Gleason applied this aesthetic in his "Off the Record" reviews.

His appreciation for hot jazz instrumentals is evident in this 1937 review of a groundbreaking artist:

> Coleman Hawkins, absolutely the best tenor sax that ever lived (come on now, boys, fight!), issues "What Harlem Means to Me" and "Meditation." The latter, his composition, is an exquisite number that demonstrates Hawkins' superiority beyond question. He is currently in Europe.[76]

Hawkins' solo on "Meditation" is sumptuous and deeply emotional. This review indicates Gleason's prescience and discriminating taste, which became hallmarks of his writing. He also enjoyed hot jazz performances with complex arrangements, such as "Caravan" by Ellington clarinetist Barney Bigard:

> The Bigard pressing of "Caravan" is one of the swellest tunes we've heard in ages and is presented with a background slightly reminiscent of "Alabama Home" that is nothing short of out-of-this-world. Lawrence Brown and Juan Tizol do marvelous work on trombones, and Barney proves his claim to the top listing in the clarinet field.[77]

The instrumental's growling trumpet interludes and lush trombone solos create a vivid soundscape. Gleason appreciated highly imaginative arrangements with diverse timbres and disparaged mono-color hit recordings. His criticism could cut deep, such as when he called the Tommy Tucker Orchestra "an insipid band" with "an insipid name" responsible for "a couple of insipid tunes."[78] Gleason called Bing Crosby a "wheezy tenor" and Guy Lombardo a "schmaltzy guy."[79] As for bandleader Shep Fields, "there seems to be no limit to the punishment the record audience will take."[80] Gleason judged each disc on its merits regardless of the artist. He sarcastically called a record by one of his favorite artists, Tommy Dorsey, "pure sugar from the sweet horn of Tommy."[81]

In "Off the Record," Gleason began his lifelong appreciation of one of the most respected jazz geniuses, Duke Ellington. "Ellington is God," Gleason proclaimed in his review of "New Black and Tan Fantasy" backed with "Steppin' into Swing Society."[82] "Fantasy" features a fascinating interplay between soaring solos and riveting ensemble work. Over the swinging rhythm, saxophonist Johnny Hodges plays with warm virtuosity.

In addition to recordings of contemporary jazz, Gleason reviewed reissues. He lavished praise on one in particular, the *Bix Beiderbecke Memorial Album*:

> As historical curiosities, these pressings are without peer, showing the development of "hot" playing as they do. For mere delight to the listener, almost every one of them is worth any two records you can get nowadays. Of course, this is exactly the type of thing we like, so we are voiceless with praise ... The space is much too small to list the wonders and delights of these six discs.[83]

Reissues like this energized hot collectors like Gleason, who held them up as exemplars of "true" jazz. Gleason and other hot collector critics sensed that some swing orchestras lacked the vitality and authenticity of these early records. Critics blamed this on the commercialization of swing jazz after it joined the mainstream of popular music.

Some musicians missed the fire of 1920s hot jazz combos and formed small groups that revived the sound of traditional New Orleans jazz. One of the more prominent of these bandleaders was clarinetist Joe Marsala who had recently moved from Chicago to New York. Gleason reviewed a jam session by Marsala and a special guest:

> Quite by accident, the other night, we got in on one of the nicest marmalade [jam] sessions we ever had the pleasure of hearing. We were at the Commodore listening to Tommy Dorsey [and then] afterward, we drifted to the Hickory House.

There we found Tommy and Bud Freeman and Carmen Mastren sitting with Joe Marsala and his boys. Bud took some almost unbelievable choruses on "You Took Advantage of Me" while Tommy squatted there with a grin of pleasure on his face adding his little bit now and again ... The whole evening couldn't have been better.[84]

One of the most influential hot jazz combos of the 1930s was the Quintette du Hot Club de France. French violinist Stéphane Grappelli and guitarist Django Reinhardt founded the group. Gleason gave them a mixed review:

Django Reinhardt and his brother, Joseph, French gypsies, are great admirers of the late Eddie Lang, whom Django occasionally surpasses in technique, if not feeling. Grappelli handles the violin work in the band and is adequate but a little too flashy for our taste. "Clouds" and "Avalon" are beautiful jobs.[85]

Reinhardt later influenced 1960s rock guitarists such as Jerry Garcia, whom Gleason later befriended and wrote about. Gleason's coverage of 1930s jazz artists provided him with historical context when he covered bands of the rock era, including the Grateful Dead.

Although Gleason mainly reviewed jazz records, he occasionally reviewed recordings from other genres. For example, he wrote positive reviews of Carlos Molina and his Orchestra, a Latin band; the Rhythm Wreckers, who played a blend of country, blues, and jazz; and washboard bands like the Washboard Serenaders and Clarence Williams and his Washboard Band.[86] Gleason also acquired a taste for records by obscure artists such as Boots and his Buddies, a Black band from Texas; Dolly Dawn and her Dawn Patrol, who influenced Ella Fitzgerald; and Sharkey and his Sharks of Rhythm, led by 1920s New Orleans trumpeter Sharkey Bananas.[87] Already, Gleason showed signs of the pluralist tastes that would distinguish him from critics who specialized in just one or two genres. Perhaps more importantly, Gleason was willing to review untested musicians unfamiliar to his readers, a critical role of cultural intermediaries who validate the "not-yet-legitimate arts" and the "marginal forms of legitimate art," according to French sociologist Pierre Bourdieu.[88]

From the fall of 1936, when Gleason wrote his first "Off the Record," to the spring of 1938 when he wrote his last, Gleason reviewed more than 400 records. He critiqued discs and concerts by some of the most significant jazz artists of the time, including Ella Fitzgerald, Benny Goodman, Andy Kirk with Mary Lou Williams, Red Norvo, and Chick Webb. Along the way, he developed a relaxed writing style, like a fan speaking to fellow fans. Gleason garnered authority as a music writer by demonstrating his knowledge about musicians, record labels, and what was happening around town. He didn't analyze *why* he liked or disliked a performance; that would come later in his career. His early reviews contain a subtext of aesthetic preferences that Gleason held throughout his career. He embraced music that was dissonant, discordant and distorted and rejected mainstream sounds. The music he loved demanded an openness to "strange sounds" that disrupted the norms of popular music.

Demonstrate Today!

Jazz wasn't the only rebellious presence in Gleason's college life; political activism thrived on campus and shaped his views as profoundly as a Johnny Hodges solo. Predisposed by his father's New Deal liberalism, Gleason's political values grew more radical at Columbia University. His protest activities at Columbia foreshadowed his deep involvement in student activism during the 1960s, particularly at the University of California, Berkeley.

The rise of fascism in Europe created the conditions for student activism in the 1930s. But the movement embodied two contradictory drives. The first was vehement opposition to fascism, and the second was equally fervent opposition to war, even if used to combat fascism. These two impulses spurred a debate about intervention versus isolationism regarding the possibility of another European conflict. Yet both sides agreed that a world devoid of fascism was the ultimate goal.

Activism began at Columbia in the early 1930s. The leading activist group was the Peace Council which sponsored an annual antiwar strike in which students and faculty skipped classes and demonstrated. The Peace Council interacted with campus chapters of national activist groups such as the Young Communists League, the American Student Union, and the American Youth Congress.[89] These groups sponsored swing music events, such as a dance rally starring Elmer Snowden, the Black banjo player who brought Duke Ellington to New York in the early 1920s.[90] The following year, Ellington performed a concert sponsored by the American Youth Congress.[91] This was the beginning of Gleason's association of music with protest; thirty years later he brought together 1960s UC Berkeley activists and San Francisco rock bands.

Like many at the *Spectator*, Gleason supported the antiwar movement. In March 1937, he joined the Peace Council and the staff of the Council's magazine, *University Against War*, along with fellow hot collector Ralph de Toledano.[92] Gleason wrote a *Spectator* article announcing the forthcoming strike and the Peace Council's call to demilitarize universities, defend "civil rights and academic freedom," and "keep America out of war."[93] Gleason also worked on the next issue of *University Against War*, to be published on the day of the strike. The magazine's dark satire presaged 1960s leftist magazines like *Ramparts*, which Gleason edited and wrote for. For example, one issue of *University Against War* included a macabre oil portrait of an American family sitting together, all wearing First World War gas masks. Even the family dog is masked.[94]

While he worked on the upcoming antiwar strike, Gleason continued to cover jazz in "Off the Record," including a historic Harlem show:

> Of interest to those local fans who have been swinging out for some time is the news that Count Basie is entertaining the boys and girls at the 125th Street Apollo. This place has pepped up its floor shows recently, and the whole tenor of the productions has changed. Watch the fiddler [Claude Williams] and drummer [Jo Jones] with the Count.[95]

The engagement marked Basie's Apollo debut. The bandleader had just moved to New York City, where he would influence the development of swing jazz.⁹⁶

The day of the antiwar strike arrives, but April showers disrupt the proceedings. Along a rain-glistened street in the middle of campus, a team of horses pulls a carriage displaying a pair of soggy placards. One calls for intervention, the other for isolationism, war versus peace. Rain forces organizers to move the event at the last minute to the gymnasium, which confuses participants. Despite the challenging conditions, about 1,500 student strikers show up. They fill the gym's seats as they had many times for pep rallies and basketball games. The cavernous space reverberates with students greeting friends and climbing bleachers. Once the protesters assemble, a series of speakers present their cases, some advocating for intervention, some for isolationism. *University Against War* sells out. Even though the protest failed to draw the 4,000 protesters who attended the previous year's strike, organizers proclaim the event a success.⁹⁷

But the next day, the *Spectator* blasted the strike organizers for the low turnout. On the front page, an uncredited writer said, "Campus politics were instrumental in harming the Anti-War Strike."⁹⁸ The editorial page contained a more detailed accusation:

> The prostitution of the peace movement to the needs of campus politics must bear the brunt of responsibility for the failure. Liberal activities do not survive when they are turned into war horses for ambitious Juniors.⁹⁹

These juniors included Gleason, president of his fraternity and now deeply involved in campus politics. The *Spectator* writer alleged that campus politicos landed appointments to the strike committees to bolster their political resumes. If Gleason felt stung by the controversy, he didn't let it show in his column that week:

> Tommy Dorsey's Clambake Seven just released their version of "Twilight in Turkey" and "Milkman's Matinee," which is far better than anything anyone has done to these two tunes previously. Even Ray Scott's Quintet can't touch the Dorsey interpretation of the classic, what with Jimmy Mince and Pee Wee Irwin riding all over the place, to say nothing of Bud Freeman and Tommy himself, backed up by the marvelous trap work of Dave Tough. This is a classic by all standards.¹⁰⁰

In another column, Gleason's sense of humor was in place as he ribbed two fellow music writers who dared to frown on Gleason's favorite musician:

> Princeton has some guy named Tab who writes a column called "Platters on Parade" who, like Barry Ulanov, writes with more cliches than Jim Ogle ever heard of. This Tab person is similar to the *Jester*'s Ralph Toledano (we left the De out because we knew him when). Both dislike Tommy Dorsey in a small way, which is the theme of this article.¹⁰¹

Gleason's column reminds us that other university newspapers carried swing-oriented music columns. Some of these papers nurtured future jazz critics.

Gleason rose in standing at the *Spectator* in April. A new Managing Board came into power led by editor-in-chief Irwin H. Kaiser, who would become a prominent physician and lifelong friend of Gleason's. The new Board appointed Gleason "News Editor." He had edited several issues and proved he was up for the job. These editing skills later came into play when Gleason edited magazines like *Ramparts* and *Rolling Stone*.

In his last "Off the Record" for the spring semester, Gleason offered readers some advice that combined music and activism: "Next fall, boys, we'll resume our rug-cutting and meanwhile don't miss anything by Lionel Hampton, Tommy Dorsey, Teddy Wilson, Duke, [and] the anti-Nazi demonstration on South Field."[102] But after the antiwar strike, Gleason left the Peace Council and stayed out of campus politics. The movement Gleason and his fellow activists belonged to continued to be the vanguard social justice crusade until the 1960s and the rise of the New Left. In the coming decades, Gleason advocated for leftist values, especially racial equality and workers' rights.

Figure 2.1 Gleason's picture in the 1938 Columbia University yearbook during his senior year. Courtesy of the Estate of Ralph J. Gleason.

Too Much Time on 52nd Street

Senior year is the final hurdle on a student's degree track when career plans begin in earnest. For Gleason, senior year was a turning point. When students returned to class in September 1937, president Butler warned on the front page of the *Spectator* that "within the decade, there have been more preparations for war, more talk of war, more fear of war than at any previous time in modern history."[103] Butler blamed fascism, and the newspaper's editors commended him for making the "liberal-anti-fascist argument that the major menace to democracy and peace today lies in the fascist powers."[104] Elsewhere in the paper were signs that everyday life went on. The Fifth Avenue Barnes & Noble offered deep discounts on textbooks. The rowing team began season practice. And "Off the Record" announced the return of saxophonist Sidney Bechet. But it wasn't Gleason's initials at the bottom of the column; the initials read "I.H.K." for editor Irwin H. Kaiser, who filled in for his friend.

Gleason wrote just one column during the fall of 1937, in which he wrote, "To anyone who may have been weak enough to wonder why this column hasn't appeared lately let it be said that Rush-week, etc., have interfered with any rug-cutting we might have liked to tell you about, so we've been silent."[105] For the remainder of the semester, the byline for "Off the Record" was "Archie," which may have been an alias for Gleason. According to his daughter Stacy, Gleason "was a big fan of the book *Archy and Mehitabel* by Don Marquis. I can imagine him using it as a nom de plume ... Archie is a cockroach who writes at night on a typewriter."[106] If "Archie" wasn't Gleason, his likes and dislikes and cutting style mirrored Gleason's. Gleason most likely wrote these columns, and the pseudonym was either a joke or a way to get around some sanction, such as curtailing extracurricular activities due to low grades.

In any event, Gleason resumed "Off the Record" full-time in the spring of 1938. His first column humorously began, "R.I.P. Archie—1936–38."[107] Gleason followed with a tribute to one of his favorite musicians, multi-instrumentalist Adrian Rollini:

> Records that the Westchester ace made with Bix Beiderbecke and other immortals years ago are now collectors' items. Rollini is, without doubt, the most incredible bass sax player who ever lived and is considered by many critics, ourselves included, as the best on the vibraharp. We like his work, especially on the Adrian Rollini Trio and Quartet numbers.[108]

In his next column, Gleason moved from praise to disdain in his review of bandleader Larry Clinton:

> Being a good seller doesn't detract from the fact that he is perhaps the least noteworthy of all the current bands. Completely taking advantage of the popularity of swing, he has issued tune after tune stolen from previous numbers and arranged in his own queer little monotonous fashion. Such tripe as "Military Madcaps," "Abba Dabba," etc., are direct steals. The public eats it up. Victor makes money. God, what horrible stuff.[109]

Unlike Clinton, one of Gleason's favorite musicians forged an original sound by reinterpreting the spirit of early jazz. Bob Crosby, Bing's brother, led a combo popular with collegians. Gleason ordained the group the "only white band worth its salt" in a review of Crosby's "Gin Mill Blues," a piano-driven instrumental with a soulful clarinet solo atop a stop-time rhythm.[110] In the same column, Gleason reviewed a show by the Crosby band at the Hotel Pennsylvania:

> For the sheer joy of playing and versatility, no one can touch [the Crosby band] ... Eddie Miller shyly plays powerful tenor, Matty Matlock roams all around a clarinet, and the rhythm section can't be beat ... Bob Zurke plays a fistful of piano with imagination and technique that is little short of miraculous ... Great credit should go to [arranger] Dean Kincaid for whipping this outfit into shape and giving us the real Dixie, the old New Orleans stuff—a band that honestly likes to play.[111]

"The real Dixie, the old New Orleans stuff," came back on college campuses and nightclub districts like 52nd Street in the late 1930s. Hot collector critics like Gleason helped popularize this revival, letting their joy for the music spill off the page.

As the semester rolled on, Gleason continued to post his columns. In his March 30, 1938 "Off the Record," Gleason wrote:

> Spring certainly has gotten into the musicians' blood and given them collectively a fine case of wanderlust. Men have been switching around most of the major bands to beat all blazes ... The next few weeks should prove interesting.[112]

But Gleason wouldn't cover these changes in the *Spectator*. This column was his final "Off the Record." After reviewing hundreds of singles and numerous live shows, Gleason left the column for good. There is no information explaining why he stopped so abruptly.

Gleason's "Off the Record" columns illustrate the critical role of college record columns during the swing era. Back then, as well as today, college music columns provided training for upcoming critics, a safe space for students to learn from their mistakes and find their writing voice. Gleason's "Off the Record" columns represent his earliest body of work as a music journalist and provide an intimate look into the mind of an early hot collector embedded in the country's most fertile jazz scene. A New York swing-era narrative, these columns hum with the excitement of a scene in the making.

Having written his last "Off the Record," Gleason joined his fellow seniors in preparing for graduation. But when the registrar published the list of graduates, Gleason's name wasn't on it. There are three accounts as to why he didn't graduate. Gleason said his grades suffered because he "spent too much time on 52nd St." and neglected his studies.[113] In another statement, he recalled being ill at the end of the semester and unable to finish his coursework. According to his daughter Stacy Gleason, he completed his course requirements but didn't graduate because he incurred fines on overdue library books and stubbornly refused to pay.[114] Perhaps it was a combination of all three reasons. But one factor is apparent, by the end of his senior year, Gleason loved music writing. He was in good company forging ahead without a college degree. John Hammond dropped out of Yale University a few years earlier and became the country's most respected jazz critic. Gleason realized he didn't need a degree to pursue a career in music journalism.

Gleason's fellow hot collectors, including Thomas Merton, Ralph de Toledano, and Eugene Williams, graduated on schedule. Another classmate, Walter Schaap, graduated earlier and was translating the works of Charles Delaunay and Hughes Panassié into English. Barry Ulanov graduated the following year and became editor of *Metronome*. Gleason had to make a hard decision. Return to Columbia, hit the books, and earn a degree? Or forget the diploma and pursue a career in music journalism? The stakes were enormous. A degree from Columbia University could fix him for life in a well-paying job. He could continue his family's upward mobility. But Gleason was a horseplayer's son, unafraid to play a long shot. He chose jazz over college.

And so, amid the post-graduation hoopla, Gleason left Columbia and returned to Chappaqua with an uncertain fate. But Cab Calloway was on the airwaves along with Ellington, Armstrong, Hines, and Henderson. A great summer lay ahead.

3

The Politics of Jazz History-Telling (1938–46)

After he left Columbia, Gleason embarked on an eight-year journey of self-discovery as he established himself as a music journalist. He dove into the New Orleans jazz revival just as an internecine war of words broke out between traditionalists like him and modernists who saw swing as an evolution of jazz from its roots. This was a profoundly formative period for Gleason in which he discovered the politics of jazz history-telling.

The Era of Good Feeling

By 1938, many of the pioneers of New Orleans jazz had retired from playing music. After the start of the swing era, their music fell into disfavor with the public. But musicologists like Alan Lomax and writers like Frederic Ramsey understood these musicians' historical significance and continuing relevance as performers of a fading musical tradition.

One of these New Orleans innovators was pianist Ferdinand Joseph LaMothe, known as Jelly Roll Morton. After a highly productive and influential career, Morton found it challenging to interest clubs or record companies in his style of ragtime-infused jazz. Jobs for traditional jazz musicians had grown scarce, even on 52nd Street, where the music once flourished. In the summer of 1938, Morton found work at the Onyx Club, but management limited his playing to intermissions between the central performances. As a result, his engagement drew little interest from jazz fans, except Gleason. He goes to the Onyx one night, and although the audience ignores Morton's keyboard inventions, Gleason listens with rapt attention. He notices an unoccupied drum kit on the stage and plays along with Morton, making it harder for the audience to ignore the pioneering musician. A night Gleason never forgot.[1]

Gleason experienced another memorable night on Sheridan Square in Greenwich Village in December 1938. It was the opening of Café Society, one of America's first racially integrated nightclubs. A doorman wearing a tattered tuxedo directs the crowd downstairs, where they are greeted by an effigy of Adolf Hitler with a monkey's body and a hangman's noose dangling from his neck, actually a clay statue on display in the stairway.[2] The shocking countenance reminds patrons that Café Society boasts an anti-elitist, anti-fascist spirit. Pianists Pete Johnson, Albert Ammons, and Meade Lux Lewis jam in the basement club. And Billie Holiday sings. Gleason later wrote:

> She was simply shocking in her impact. Standing there with a spotlight on her great, sad, beautiful face, a white gardenia in her hair, she sang her songs, and singers were never the same after that.[3]

Although he lacked a journalistic platform, Gleason continued to frequent jazz performances with the keenness of a music critic. But he had to make a living now that he was out of school. The college dropout found a job that placed him in the middle of the Long Island Sound casino circuit, where the swinging sounds of saxophone sections reverberated across the moonlit waterway. The position was publicist for the waterfront Playland Amusement Park in Rye, New York. The Park attracted thousands of yearly visitors who rode its thrilling roller coaster and sunbathed beachside under colorfully striped umbrellas.

Five miles south of Playland was the Larchmont Casino. Bandleader Jimmie Lunceford and his manager Harold Oxley bought the restaurant in 1936 to give the Lunceford band a reliable venue during a time racial barriers limited the opportunities of Black artists.[4] Gleason became a regular:

> Every night after I closed up [Playland] at 11 or midnight, I ran over to the club and heard the [Lunceford] band till the club closed.
>
> The ballroom usually wouldn't let you stand in front of the band. You had to keep dancing (no chore to *that* band), but sometimes you could cluster at the edge of the bandstand ...
>
> The best place, though, was in front of the band, where you could see and hear it all as you danced along very slowly and watch the trumpets twirl and the trombones wave and see those eyes of saxophonist Earl Carruthers look to his section mates as he rocked backward in the chair, anchoring the sax section. And where you could see the wisp of a mustache on Willie Smith and the sly look in his eyes as he leaned forward to sing.[5]

Perhaps one of Gleason's dance partners was Jean Rayburn, a young blonde in her early twenties. Gleason met Rayburn at Columbia through her brother. At a card game one night, Bill Rayburn told Gleason he had a sister who loved jazz. Interested, Gleason asked Rayburn out. One date led to another, and the couple fell in love. Gleason introduced Rayburn to the New York jazz scene, and it was no come-on when he told her, "Stick with me, kid, and you'll hear some great music."[6]

Rayburn, Gleason, and his former Columbia classmates, Eugene Williams and Ralph de Toledano, began toying with the idea of founding a hot jazz magazine. It would follow the lead of *Jazz Hot*, the magazine of Hot Club de France founded by Hugues Panassié. Hot jazz magazines increased in the 1930s as an alternative to mainstream jazz magazines like *DownBeat*. New York City had one, the *HRS Society Rag,* founded in 1938 by magazine illustrator Stephen W. Smith, owner of the Hot Record Society Shop, which had a friendly rivalry with Milt Gabler's Commodore Record Shop, both located in Midtown Manhattan.

The founders and writers of these magazines believed that New Orleans style jazz was "a wellspring from which all other 'hot' variants derived," writes jazz historian Bruce Boyd Raeburn:[7]

> "Traditional" New Orleans style was thus defined by its protagonists as an original, "pure" jazz archetype that represented the unmediated creative potential of an underclass whose cultural products "trickled up" from the bottom of society, reversing the flow of cultural dynamics as it was then conceived ... "Hot" collectors found themselves inevitably drawn to the political left in their pursuit of the "righteous cause" of jazz advocacy.[8]

Gleason, Rayburn, Williams, and de Toledano took up this "righteous cause." They presented their magazine idea to Milt Gabler, who enthusiastically supported it. Williams took the lead, becoming editor and financing the project. Gabler provided workspace and a mimeograph machine at his Commodore Record Shop. He also offered a subscriber mailing list and came up with the magazine's name, *Jazz Information*, based on the belief of hot collectors that dominant jazz magazines like *DownBeat* provided inaccurate information. They decided to begin with a weekly newsletter to test public response.

Jazz Information, Please

Early fall in Manhattan can be hot and humid, and September 8, 1939, was an exceptionally muggy day. Inside the stifling storeroom of the Commodore Record Shop, jazz history is about to be made, just days after global history was made when Nazi Germany sparked the Second World War by invading Poland. But in the US, life proceeds as usual. Within the front room of Gabler's record shop, customers leisurely peruse 78s by artists like Red McKenzie and Art Tatum. In the backroom, a band of hot jazz crusaders scrambles to meet a deadline. Rayburn types their mission statement on a defective typewriter that misaligns the 'J' in "jazz":

> *Jazz information* is not designed to compete with any existing trade papers or jitterbug sheets. We feel that *Jazz Information* fulfills a unique and important function in American jazz music. Being a non-commercial venture, the continuance of *Jazz Information* depends entirely on what support it receives from those whose interests in jazz go beyond Tin Pan Alley and the sensationalism of the swing fad. We believe that there are many such people to keep us alive.[9]

Once the mimeograph stencil sheet is complete, Rayburn types the remaining three pages. Williams and his crew have created the first issue of *Jazz Information*, a four-page weekly fanzine with hand-ruled borders at ten cents an issue. A small publication with a strong message. All the latest news about the world of hot jazz, along with ads selling records. Milt Gabler watches in awe as the intense foursome assembles the inaugural issue.

The team works into the night, printing pages as ammonia fumes fill the oppressive air. They crank out 4,000 8.5" × 11" sheets, staple them into issues and bundle them for distribution. Before the night ends, the crew slaps an address label on each copy, using Gabler's nationwide mailing list of hot collectors. At daybreak, they stack one thousand copies in Gleason's Dodge station wagon and deliver them to the Radio City Post Office. Along the way, they leave a few copies at record stores and then go home to bed.

Within days, subscriptions come in from all over the world. Williams financed the magazine through his trust fund and placed ads in *DownBeat* and *Tempo*, a popular swing magazine. The staff holds meetings at Williams' Greenwich Village apartment and local bars. Gleason, de Toledano, and Williams make up the editorial board. Rayburn is the circulation manager, and Gleason runs the news department. Each type

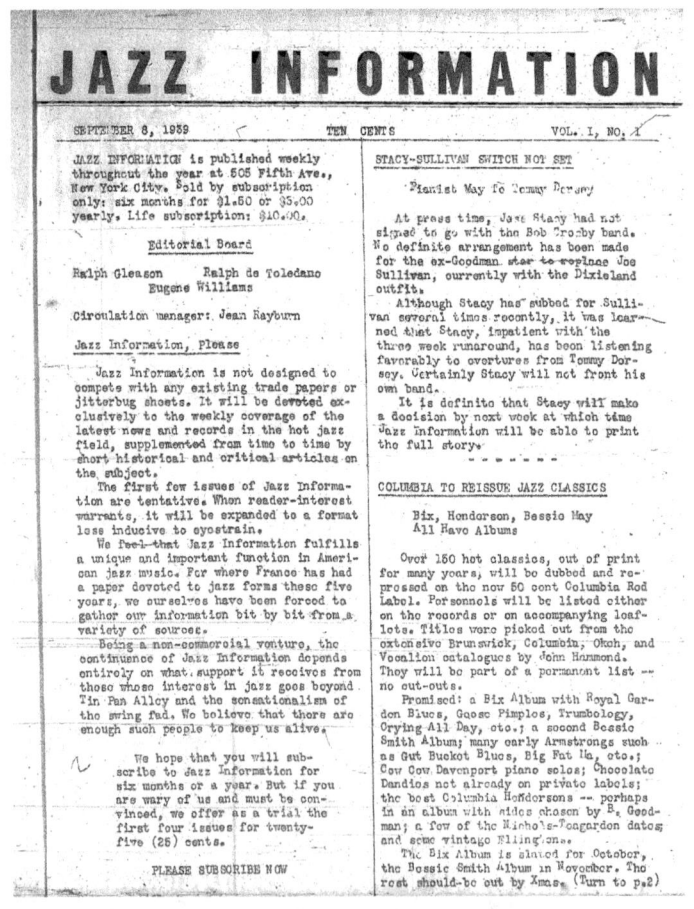

Figure 3.1 The first issue of *Jazz Information*, September 1939, the hot jazz fanzine Ralph Gleason founded after college. Courtesy of the Estate of Ralph J. Gleason.

mimeograph stencils, crank the copier, and distribute the issues. All-nighters were common when an issue went to press.¹⁰

Jazz Information's three editors applied the skills they acquired at Columbia University working for campus publications. Gleason had edited the *Spectator*, and Williams and Toledano edited the *Jester* and other campus magazines. They understood the process of putting a periodical together on a deadline. A do-it-yourself endeavor, *Jazz Information* preceded the mimeographed rock fanzines of the 1960s, such as the early issues of *Crawdaddy*, *Creem*, and *Mojo-Navigator*. Like its descendants, *Jazz Information* provided solid writing on a shoestring budget. Its homemade look belied the intent of its founders: to use the power of information to upset the hegemony of magazines like *Metronome*, *DownBeat*, and *Esquire*.

Jazz Information was inclusive, covering hot swing as well as traditional jazz. For example, the magazine followed the development of pioneering swing saxophonist Coleman Hawkins, whom Gleason lauded in "Off the Record." The "Hawk" had just returned from a lengthy tour of Europe and settled in New York City, where he formed a band with Lionel Hampton and guitarist Charlie Christian.¹¹ *Jazz Information* announced Hawkins' opening at Café Society and his historic stint at Kelly's Stables, where Hawkins took jazz a step closer to bebop with his rule-breaking improvisations on the pop standard "Body and Soul."¹²

Gleason saw Hawkins perform thanks to his friend Oran "Hot Lips" Page, a Black trumpeter "addicted to wearing green suits and greener ties" who could "sing and play the blues fit to make you think it was Armstrong."¹³ Accompanied by Page, Gleason goes to an all-night jam session at a Harlem nightclub owned by saxophonist "Happy" Cauldwell. As they enter, Page tells the burly bouncer, "This is a friend of mine; treat him right." They find a table, and Gleason becomes so absorbed in the all-night session that he is still there at 10 a.m. the next day, "stuffing myself on hot rolls and honey while Coleman Hawkins played."¹⁴ Gleason had launched *Jazz Information* from the center of the country's most innovative jazz scene, where change was in the air. He developed relationships with musicians, club owners, and others who shared news tips he included in *Jazz Information*. He learned how to create a network of contacts, an essential skill in journalism.

Three months after *Jazz Information* launched, a book called *Jazzmen* boosted the interest in New Orleans-style jazz and energized the hot collecting movement. Collectors Fredric Ramsey, Jr. and Charles Edward Smith produced the reader to "relate the story of jazz as it has unfolded about the men who created it, the musicians themselves."¹⁵ To that end, Ramsey and Smith conducted extensive interviews with musicians nationwide. They discovered many early jazz pioneers, including retired New Orleans trumpeter Willie Gary "Bunk" Johnson, who wrote the introduction for the book. Although *Jazzmen* referenced swing jazz by Ellington and others, the book focused on music before the 1930s. Ramsey and Smith's portrayal of Bunk Johnson as an exemplar of jazz in its pre-commercial state sparked a new movement in jazz: the New Orleans revival.¹⁶ *Jazzmen* and *Jazz Information* promoted the idea that New Orleans-style jazz was the only "true" jazz.¹⁷ This view provoked intense debates between traditionalists and swing modernists in jazz magazines. At *Jazz Information*, the stakes grew higher. The definition of jazz was up for grabs.

Rebirth and Revival

The magazine faced challenges as it committed itself to the revival. Like most music fanzines, *Jazz Information* struggled because it operated on a tight budget, had a small staff, and catered to a niche fanbase. After its sixth issue in October 1939, the magazine experienced another set of problems. First, Toledano left and became editor of the *New Leader*, the magazine of the Socialist Party of America. Two months later, in December, Gleason temporarily quit for undisclosed reasons, which meant Rayburn had to leave because she depended on Gleason for a ride into the city. Williams soldiered on alone, but the strain took its toll. To make matters worse, *Jazz Information* and its competitor, the *HRS Society Rag*, came to blows. The once-friendly rivalry between the Commodore and the Hot Record Society devolved into hostility.[18] The two shops cultivated opposing attitudes towards hot jazz, with the Commodore group taking a more serious approach. Jazz historian Bruce Raeburn said, "What separated these 'hot' factions was a mixture of different personalities and preferences."[19]

The mounting problems affected Williams' health. He suffered a mental breakdown and suspended the publication of *Jazz Information*. In need of respite, Williams put the contents of his Greenwich Village apartment in storage and moved into a cottage in Chappaqua near where Gleason lived with his parents.[20] The old friends often met to discuss *Jazz Information*'s future and listen to jazz records. One particular disc stood out: an interview with Bunk Johnson. The recording left a deep impression on Gleason and Williams, intensifying their commitment to the revival.

Inspired, Gleason, Williams, and Rayburn upgraded *Jazz Information* in 1940. They turned it into a twenty-four-page monthly digest with photos and illustrations. Williams told readers he intended "to fill a long-neglected gap by publishing an independent, non-commercial, intelligent magazine devoted entirely to hot jazz." He went on:

> Never a fan magazine, [*Jazz Information*] has always tried to penetrate to the essential values beneath the fanfare of publicity which afflicts both swing and, often, "non-commercial" hot jazz. Never dilettante, it has avoided pseudo-literary jazz criticism and pretentious intellectualizing.
>
> Our aims remain the same.[21]

In his credo, Williams expressed values dear to Gleason, a professional approach to music discourse that communicated the deeper meanings of the music in a natural way.

A few weeks later, in August 1940, Gleason wrote his first credited article for the magazine, "On the Air: An Interview with Ralph Berton."[22] Berton hosted *Metropolitan Review*, a radio show on New York's WNYC. Gleason called Berton a "missionary" who wanted to "run a program of real jazz records, something the radio had been neglecting."[23] Gleason applauded Berton for attacking "Jim Crowism" when Berton chastised a listener who complained that he played too many records by Black musicians. This article marked the first time Gleason wrote about racism in the music industry. Racial inequality became a recurring theme in his writings.

With Ralph and Jean back in the fold, the magazine flourished. Williams brought in new writers from New York City and Chicago. The magazine continued to document significant events in the New York jazz scene, such as Lester Young replacing Coleman Hawkins at Kelley's Stable, a turning point in the development of modern jazz. Rising jazz critic George Avakian wrote the magazine's record review section, and Hugues Panassié contributed an article. As Gabler and other hot jazz cognoscenti had done, Williams created a record label. Named for the magazine, Jazz Information reissued 1920s records such as King Oliver's "Mandy Lee Blues" and later recorded early New Orleans artists.

October 12, 1940, saw a significant milestone in Gleason's life; he and Jean wed in the Church of St. John's and St. Mary's in Chappaqua.[24] Jean became a guiding force in Gleason's life and played an essential role in every step of his career. Born in Pittsburgh in 1918, Jean grew up in Briarcliff Manor, a Westchester County, New York, village where her parents raised their children to be highly self-reliant. Rayburn's mother was a weaver, and her father was a furniture maker. After Ralph and Jean married, Gleason's father soon introduced Jean to a family tradition—horse racing. Ralph A. took them to the Empire City racetrack in Yonkers and asked Jean to pick a nag for him. Although the 100-to-1 shot didn't place, Rayburn fell in love with horse racing. The following summer, she and Gleason went to the races at Saratoga, planning to stay for the weekend. Rayburn bet on a maiden, a horse that had never won a race. The long shot paid off, and Rayburn won so much money that she and Gleason extended their weekend stay to three weeks.[25]

Ralph and Jean forged one of music journalism's most remarkable husband–wife partnerships. Ralph found an alter ego in Jean, who shared his dedication to jazz. He also found a collaborator, the only person he would trust to edit his work and tell him the truth even when he didn't want to hear it. Jean became an indispensable catalyst for Gleason's development as a journalist. Together, they would experience tremendous highs and lows. Jazz historian Bruce Raeburn notes that Rayburn became one of the unsung "women of hot collecting" along with Marili Morden, who ran the Jazz Man Record Shop in Los Angeles. These women navigated the male-dominated power structure of jazz, and their contributions deserve greater recognition.[26]

Gleason lost an important woman in his life at that time. Mary A. Gleason died in her early fifties after living the hard life of an Irish immigrant. Mollie ensured Ralph appreciated his Irish heritage, a legacy he never forgot. Gleason left *Jazz Information* again, not to return, probably to be present for his father, now a widower. Williams now piloted the magazine alone, an overwhelming job.[27]

About six months after his wedding, Gleason wrote his first freelance article, "A Short Analysis of Hot Jazz Record Collecting," published in the spring 1941 *Hobbies* magazine. The piece followed the tradition of earlier articles on hot collecting by Charles Edward Smith and Stephen W. Smith.[28] But Gleason focused less on the music and more on its socio-historical context. He explained to his general readership that jazz existed before the Original Dixieland Jass Band released the first jazz record:

Figure 3.2 Ralph and Jean Gleason, c. 1941. Courtesy of the Estate of Ralph J. Gleason.

> The music … had existed long before that time in the bordellos and dance halls of New Orleans, on the Mississippi and Ohio riverboats, and in the night spots of Chicago, Kansas City, and New York.

> As this music started out in the beginning as musicians' music, played only for the love of playing and for the enjoyment of the musician, commercial companies did little recording along this line … However, a demand was finally created for this type of music by both the musicians and the negro population. The negro people, as a matter of fact, didn't have to take to jazz—it was theirs in the first place.[29]

With this article, Gleason began his lifelong practice of narrating jazz history using rich contextual details. In the *Hobbies* piece, Gleason also asserted that African American musicians invented jazz, a position he held until the end of his life. Another custom that Gleason began with this article was to examine the sociology of popular music fandom. In this case, the habits and attitudes of hot collectors.

A few months later, in November 1941, Williams published the final issue of *Jazz Information* after a two-year run. It had been a challenging year for the young editor. He dealt with missed deadlines, a lowered page count, and a "tricky lung condition that sometimes goes with a physical breakdown," probably the type of breathing problems accompanying mental collapses.[30] Williams said a lack of staff, not finances, forced him to stop publication.[31]

Although he was no longer an editor, Gleason published two articles in the final *Jazz Information*. The first, "Something Keeps A-Worryin' Me," was a half-page spoof of George Frazier, who covered the Boston jazz scene for *DownBeat* at the time and

Figure 3.3 The last issue of *Jazz Information*, November 1941. On the cover: jazz pianist and composer James. P. Johnson. Courtesy of the Estate of Ralph J. Gleason.

wrote for *Mademoiselle*, a women's magazine that featured excellent writers. Jazz scholar John Gennari wrote:

> Though his politics were unclear and his musical taste unpredictable, Frazier's writing style could affect a young fan's hormones in much the same way as the heartthrob-of-the-month girlie pictures. The purpose of jazz criticism, in Frazer's view, was to "send you." And Frazier was sending more swing fans than any other critic, save, perhaps, the ubiquitous Hammond. In singularly cavalier language, Frazier told his readers what he liked and what he disliked. He didn't like Martha Tilton when he heard her sing with Benny Goodman in 1938, and so the headline of his next *DownBeat* column read, "Martha Tilton Stinks."[32]

Frazier's writings struck a chord with Gleason. He grew "madder and madder at Frazier" yet confessed he had liked the provocative critic during the "stink-is-a-lovely-word day and age of *Mademoiselle*."[33] Gleason absorbed Frazier's forthrightly provocative style and willingness to go after revered musicians such as Benny Goodman. Gleason even picked up Frazier's use of sartorial status details, such as the make of a performer's suit.

Gleason wrote a second article in the final *Jazz Information*, a review of the novel *Send Me Down* by Henry Steig.[34] He said Steig wrote "authentically of the background of musicians" and said, "The best thing about the book is its real 'feel' for hot music."[35] Gleason wrote that *Send Me Down* addressed "commercial music and art-for-art's-sake music, and the solution is a compromise."[36] A belief Gleason held for the rest of his life.

Williams wrote a candid eight-page editorial for the final issue that seethed with frustration. He called swing music the "watered-down, emasculated, often hysterical remnants of the jazz tradition" and declared "real jazz" the "stuff which came out of New Orleans."[37] Williams railed against the "pseudo-critics" who wrote for "the popular magazines" like *DownBeat* that derided hot collectors.[38]

Swing proponents like Barry Ulanov and Leonard Feather bristled at such criticism and grew tired of being targeted by hot collector writers. Tensions developed between traditionalists and modernists, bad enough that some called it a war. But Gleason and other draft-age men across America suddenly had a real war to contend with.

London Blues

On December 1941, Japanese fighter jets bombed the US naval base at Pearl Harbor, and the country entered the Second World War. Following the attack, the number of Americans drafted rose dramatically. Jazz musicians Glenn Miller, Dave Brubeck, and a young Charlie Parker fan named John Coltrane went to war, as did jazz writers such as John Hammond. At home, jazz provided respite for soldiers on leave and their families. Overseas, the military used jazz in propaganda campaigns.

Gleason received a draft card in 1940 and, though he didn't get called, he indeed felt the inevitability of wartime service. In the meantime, life went on for the Gleasons. A photograph at the time shows Gleason playing music on an upright piano at home. He sits erect and smiles for the camera, clearly enjoying himself. Horseracing remained another pastime. Gleason bought a Saratoga racehorse for $25 and kept the yearling in his father's garage where he groomed it for racing. The horse underperformed during its first season, and Gleason sold it for a profit after it became ill.[39]

During that time, Gleason worked several jobs and continued to write freelance articles. Though freelancing gave him an outlet, he undoubtedly yearned for full-time work writing about jazz. The twenty-three-year-old moved restlessly from employer to employer: Playland, an ad agency, and an advertising journal called *Printer's Ink*. He also worked as a general assignment reporter for several Westchester County newspapers. Then came a significant career jump when Gleason landed a position at Columbia Broadcasting System's headquarters in New York City, where he became the CBS trades news editor in 1942.[40] Although the post brought perks such as being mentioned in magazines like *Billboard* and *Variety*, working for a corporation clashed with Gleason's values. At CBS, he "saw big business as it really was," the corporate equivalent of a sharecropper's company store.[41]

The president of CBS was famed broadcaster William S. Paley, who made the radio network a global success. After the start of the Second World War, Paley went to London to serve in the United States Office of War Information (OWI). President Roosevelt started the organization in 1942 to produce propaganda about the war effort in various media, including phonograph records. To that end, the OWI recruited jazz revivalists like Frederic Ramsey and Charles Edward Smith to make recordings of New Orleans jazz musicians to broadcast overseas to soldiers.[42] Gleason, a pacifist, joined the organization in January 1943 in lieu of serving in the military. "R. J. Gleason Joins OWI" read the front-page headline of his local *New Castle Tribune* as it touted a hometown boy going to war.[43]

Gleason went to work in the OWI's New York office but, after several months, was assigned to open an OWI office in Lisbon, Portugal. Gleason said goodbye to Jean, his father, and friends and traveled to Lisbon. The ancient peninsular city teemed with spies from both sides and was named the Capital of Espionage. Lisbon also abounded with jazz in clubs like the *Hot Clube de Portugal*. For pleasure, Gleason put together a jazz combo with himself on piano backed by "a Vichy French clarinetist, an English bass man, and a West African drummer."[44] Once Gleason established the Lisbon office, the OWI assigned him to London, which continued to experience German bombings. Gleason spent Christmas Eve 1943 listening to the "crack of the ack-ack and sometimes the boom of the Big Guns in the Park or the whoosh of the rockets on the other side of Park Lane. And then the slow, steady, deep grunt of the bombs as they marched along in their giant steps of three or four or five."[45]

More welcoming sounds also pierced the London night—hot jazz rhythms. In clubs, on records, and in radio broadcasts, the insistent tempos of Louis Armstrong and King Oliver filled the air. England even had a hot jazz magazine, *Jazz Music*, edited by A. J. McCarthy and Max Jones. McCarthy wrote "Collectors' Corner" in *Melody*

Figure 3.4 Ralph Gleason working for the Office of War Information in the Hotel Lafayette, Greenwich Village, Manhattan, 1942. Courtesy of the Estate of Ralph J. Gleason.

Maker, and Jones wrote for a radio program. After Gleason discovered *Jazz Music*, he introduced himself to McCarthy and Jones. The three formed a lifelong friendship that would impact the founding of *Rolling Stone* magazine 20 years later.[46] While in London, Gleason made another lifelong friend, Bill Ballentine. After the war, Ballentine became a Barnum & Bailey Circus clown and founded the Ringling Bros. and Barnum & Bailey Clown College.[47]

Although he made lasting friends in London, Gleason admitted in a letter to Jean that he disliked his overseas post and couldn't wait to come home.[48] The day finally arrived, and Gleason returned to the states in June 1944. Photos show him joyfully running to Jean when she met him at New York Harbor. They joined young couples nationwide, relieved to have the war behind them and ready to pursue their dreams. Gleason became the trades news editor at a new radio group, the Blue Network, launched by the National Broadcasting Company.[49] But jazz soon pulled him in another direction.

From One War to Another

While American soldiers wound down a military war, American jazz fans launched a cultural war. In a blistering article in *Metronome*, Barry Ulanov blasted traditionalists as "moldy figs" who prevented jazz from modernizing.⁵⁰ Similar articles in *Metronome* and elsewhere vilified the revival as a retrograde movement that kept jazz from updating. Revivalists like Gleason fired back in a new crop of hot collector magazines such as *Record Changer*.

Founded in 1942 by Gordon Gullickson, *Record Changer* became the leading source for hot collectors after the demise of *Jazz Information* and the *HRS Rag*. Gullickson recruited knowledgeable writers such as Nesuhi Ertegun (brother of Atlantic Records co-founder Ahmet Ertegun), Frederick Ramsey, Charles Edward Smith, and Eugene Williams. Gleason wrote three articles for *Record Changer,* beginning with "London Blues," published a month after he returned home from England in the summer of 1944. The article's title alludes to the demise of the UK hot collector magazine *Jazz Music*, founded by the writers Gleason befriended during the war. The loss of *Jazz Music* left British jazz coverage to *Melody Maker*, a publication loathed by Gleason and other hot collectors because of its pro-swing stance. "Dribbling, commercial, inaccurate and tasteless" was how Gleason characterized the magazine's record reviews. He fumed that the magazine catered to "record companies and commercial dance bands" and called *Melody Maker*'s reviews the "London equivalent of Leonard Feather's nonsense."⁵¹ With that, Gleason had attacked one of the most potent jazz critics of the time.

Feather made a name in British radio broadcasting before coming to America in 1939. In addition to writing, he represented Ellington, Lionel Hampton, and other leading jazz musicians. Feather wrote for the swing-centric *Metronome*, but it was at *Esquire* where he drew the wrath of hot collectors. One night, Feather, historian Robert Goffin, and *Esquire* editor Arnold Gingrich listen to the Ellington Orchestra in a club called the Hurricane. Feather and Goffin pitch a novel idea to Gingrich: run a jazz poll in which critics, not readers, pick the winners.⁵² Gingrich liked the idea, and in 1943 *Esquire* conducted a critics' poll that included Feather, Goffin, George Avakian, John Hammond, Barry Ulanov, and Charles Edward Smith.⁵³ The list of winners was published in the 1944 *Esquire Jazz Book*, a special annual edition. The magazine arranged for the top-winning musicians to form the "*Esquire* All-American Band" and record an album for Commodore Records with jazz classics like Billie Holiday's "Strange Fruit." Traditionalists immediately attacked the poll results as having a pro-swing bias. They went after Feather and Ulanov in particular because they represented the "ultramodern vanguard" to traditionalists.⁵⁴

Gleason dove into the melee with a 1944 *Record Changer* article called "Featherbed Ball." He said London jazz fans disparaged Feather and his "line of jive" during the war.⁵⁵ Gleason railed against Feather's coverage of jazz in *Esquire*, calling it inaccurate, and said it "stinks, is offensive and ruinous to good jazz."⁵⁶ He wrote that the jazz revival needed "feature articles done by guys who will get the facts straight in a fashion that will sell to [mass circulation] magazines and reach the kids in high school and the general public."⁵⁷ Gleason said hot jazz enthusiasts should write for mainstream magazines like *Esquire* instead of dismissing them. Sounding more like a social organizer than a critic, Gleason called for a media campaign by revivalists to disrupt swing music's status. He called for a more definitive definition of jazz:

Before we can make any progress via the written word, educationally, we will have to have a semantic house cleaning. Until you can establish a static meaning for "jazz" or substitute another word or words for its various meanings, we will make slow progress.[58]

For Gleason and other revivalists, "jazz" was the New Orleans-style music of King Oliver and Louis Armstrong and the hot music that followed. For them, 1940s swing departed from that music. Jazz historian Bernard Gendron wrote that revivalists believed "no music could be called jazz that wasn't collectively improvised and whose melodies, rhythms, phrasings, and timbres were not primarily derived from African American sources."[59] The problem for traditionalists was convincing the public to accept this restricted definition. Gleason made an audacious proposal:

> I don't know the answer to this semantic merry-go-round; maybe there is no answer except for us to usurp the fountainheads of information ourselves."[60]

In other words, beat the pro-swing critics at their own game. Spread the traditionalist message by writing for jazz magazines like *DownBeat* and mass-circulation magazines like *Life*. In his call to action, Gleason struggled with a perennial problem faced by music journalists who support marginalized movements—how to get the mass support needed to sustain these movements.

After Gleason identified the problem and posed a solution, he might have ended his article there. Instead, he criticized one more critic. "Okay, so Rudi Blesh is writing a book. What jazz *doesn't* need right now is a book, even if [early New Orleans cornetist Buddy] Bolden wrote it."[61] Blesh, jazz critic for the *San Francisco Chronicle*, would strike back in six months. But before Blesh's retaliation, Gleason took his own advice and began writing for a leading "fountainhead of information."

Crawl Out of Your Featherbed

One night Gleason sits in the Ross Tavern on New York's Sixth Avenue and waits for his friend Art Hodes to play. The lights dim, and the pianist starts one of the many blues songs in his repertoire. His light touch and insistent rhythms draw the crowd in. Playing along is clarinetist Rod Cless with his searching solos. In a musical conversation with Hode, Cless's clarinet whispers in response and then cries out in cascading passages. The crowd listens quietly, not wanting to break the spell. Traditional jazz at its most sublime.

After Gleason saw Cless play, the clarinetist fell on hard times. Following a late-night drinking bout, Cless accidentally went over the balcony of his apartment building and plummeted to his death. Gleason wrote a remembrance of the clarinetist for *DownBeat*, a bittersweet article called "Cless Played Heart Out to Deaf Town." A breakthrough piece for Gleason, his first article in a major jazz magazine, and the only press coverage Cless ever received besides his obituary. Gleason wrote, "What really killed Rod Cless was New York and people who didn't know how a clarinet should sound in a band." What also killed him, Gleason surmised, was a lack of appreciation for the subtleties of traditional jazz. He believed swing fans and critics placed too much emphasis on technical ability and overlooked musicians like Cless. "Rod played his heart out in New York. And nobody listened."[62] The remembrance marked the beginning of Gleason's long association with *DownBeat*.

Two months later, Gleason was on the receiving end of criticism. Rudi Blesh finally responded to Gleason's attack on him in *Record Changer*. A leading figure in the San Francisco jazz revival, Blesh reviewed music for the *San Francisco Chronicle*, lectured on jazz at the San Francisco Museum of Modern Art, and worked as an interior designer. He produced a concert by Bunk Johnson, an icon of the jazz revival after the publication of *Jazzmen*. *Time* magazine covered the concert and published a highly appreciative article called "Bunk Johnson Rides Again."[63] The Office of War Information broadcast the show to service members worldwide. Blesh helped make San Francisco the West Coast center of the jazz revival.

Blesh was working on on a book, *Shining Trumpets: A History of Jazz*, which had prompted Gleason to write in "Featherbed Ball," "Okay, so Rudi Blesh is writing a book. What jazz *doesn't* need right now is a book."[64] Gleason argued that books had been ineffective at explaining jazz to the American people in a "non-technical language they can understand without a course in music theory."[65] But Blesh disagreed and responded in a *Record Changer* article addressed to Gleason, "Crawl Out of Bed—Winter is Over." He wrote that "Featherbed Ball" exuded a "personal defeatism" and said Gleason should show a more "generous spirit" toward fellow hot collectors.[66] Blesh stated, "More books are needed to furnish the wide range of viewpoints which the understanding of a great art requires and which are indispensable to a well-founded school of criticism and appreciation."[67] He implied that Gleason lacked gravitas as a critic because he wasn't a full-time writer. He wrote that a "featherbed is neither inspiring nor compelling. Perhaps he should crawl out of his private one. Pack his briefcase with the right contents and, with better motives than Feather's, hit the trail that Leonard has blazed."[68]

Unsurprisingly, Blesh's article incensed Gleason. He countered two months later in another *Record Changer* article and sneered that his article riled the "inferiority complex of a young but bearded prophet, Mr. Rudi Blesh."[69] Blesh was "so aroused that he devoted some 1,500 words to replying."[70] Gleason noted that when he and Williams launched *Jazz Information*, Blesh was merely "decorating interiors."[71] Gleason said that jazz discourse had grown pretentious and cited a passage by Blesh about an "improvised instrumental polyphony on either a harmonic or melodic theme."[72] The two writers represented opposite positions within the emergent hot jazz intelligentsia. Whereas Blesh was a traditional intellectual with ties to institutions such as the San Francisco Museum of Art, Gleason was an organic intellectual educated in nightclubs and outside the culture industries.

Although this was Gleason's final article for *Record Changer*, his role in the jazz revival had just begun. He, Jean, and Eugene Williams took on an ambitious project within the rapidly changing New York traditional jazz scene.

When Louis Does Up, I Does Down!

The musical lineup on 52nd Street had changed since Gleason watched Count Basie bring down the house in the 1930s. Balloon-cheeked trumpeter Dizzy Gillespie brought his combo to the Onyx in 1944, followed by saxophonist Charlie Parker at the Three Deuces. They introduced the new bebop style, expanding jazz's melodic, rhythmic, and harmonic possibilities. Gleason discovered the unique sound on the radio in 1945:

> The new music of Gillespie and [Charlie] Parker was brought instantly, if only occasionally, to the vast Metropolitan New York [radio] audience. It took a little while to spread around the country, but it caught on in New York with the young jazzmen, like a flu virus in midwinter.

Gleason admitted that he initially disliked bebop, as did Jean.[73]

Despite the infusion of modern jazz, a few New York clubs kept the jazz revival going. One was Jimmy Ryan's, a brownstone basement where Milt Gabler ran public jam sessions that featured jazz veterans such as stride piano pioneer James P. Johnson.[74] One spring night in 1945, Bunk Johnson played Ryan's, and Gleason covered the show for *DownBeat* while Jean wrote about it for *Record Changer*. Jean had come into her own as a respected writer within the New York revival.

The night Johnson plays Ryan's, Jean and Ralph find a table in the crowded club, get out their reporter's notebooks and wait for the show to start. Johnson takes the stage, a lean and wizened figure who began his career on the streets of New Orleans. He announces, "Don't expect me to sound like my boy Louis [Armstrong]. When Louis does up, I does down!"[75] With that, the trumpeter launches into "Careless Love," a swaying Dixieland tune. Johnson interweaves a languidly deliberate trumpet solo with Sidney Bechet's saxophone filigrees and Sandy Williams' growling trombone response. Ralph and Jean surrender to the music, enthralled.

Ralph wrote that Johnson "stood up on the bandstand [a humble wood-frame platform], grey-haired, hands gnarled and calloused from rice field labor, and 'drove down the blues.'"[76] Jean showed her allegiance to traditional jazz and said Johnson "plays the melody with variations which bear no resemblance to the meaningless riffs and flashy solos characteristic of the present 'swing' style." She described Johnson's tone as "indescribably lovely, and the simplicity and delicacy of his phrasing superb!"[77] Jean had evolved into an astute and sensitive music writer.

Johnson's performance electrified the city's revivalists. Gleason said, "Four days later, they were still talking about him in the Commodore."[78] Inspired, Eugene Williams arranged to mount an ambitious comeback tour for the trumpet player. With the Gleasons helping, Williams scheduled a series of shows for Johnson in Boston, backed by the Sydney Bechet band. A pioneering saxophonist and clarinetist, Bechet came up in the 1910s New Orleans jazz scene along with Johnson. Mercurial and abrasive, Bechet could be difficult to work with. Gleason and Williams booked an engagement for Johnson and the Bechet band at Boston's Savoy Café. Although the shows went as scheduled, tensions erupted between Johnson and Bechet. Johnson drank heavily, acted erratically, and gave spotty performances, which infuriated Bechet.[79] After a month, Johnson fired Bechet and returned to Louisiana, leaving Williams in the lurch.

Yet Williams and Gleason remained faithful to the trumpeter. Gleason became Johnson's informal publicist and wrote his promotional materials. In late 1945, Gleason, Williams, and jazz historian William Russell made plans to bring Johnson back to New York for a long-term engagement at the Stuyvesant Casino, a top revivalist venue. Williams invested his remaining inheritance in the venture. Gleason announced the Stuyvesant engagement in an "exclusive *DownBeat* interview" with Williams on the front page of the September 15, 1945, issue.[80] Announcements ran in the *New York Daily News* and *New York Age*.

Despite their strong promotion, Williams, Gleason, and Russell lost money on the engagement. Gleason later wrote that Williams and Russell were "accused of exploiting an old, tired man for their financial reward, though the truth was that everyone made money out of Bunk's various appearances except those who promoted him."[81] Johnson biographer Christopher Hillman said that on opening night, the casino teemed "with 400 enthusiasts, among them many musicians, and most were very excited by what they heard."[82] Gleason said the Stuyvesant engagement brought Johnson publicity in *Vogue*, the *New Yorker*, and *Collier's*. "Almost every magazine did interviews, reviews, and ran pictures."[83] The promotion brought Johnson more engagements, and he played at a concert hosted by Orson Welles at the New York Town Hall in 1946.

With his comeback underway, Johnson received a contract from RCA Records and recorded *Bunk Johnson and His New Orleans Band—Hot Jazz*. The bound set of four 10" shellac singles hit record stores in April 1946. Gleason penned the liner notes, the first he had ever written. In the notes, he constructed a detailed narrative of Johnson's career that began in a "Creole legitimate band of reading musicians."[84] Gleason recounted how Johnson toured with circuses, played steamboats, and worked the "dance halls and honky tonks of the fabulous Storyville," New Orleans' red-light district.[85] His liner notes describe how Johnson retired from music, became a laborer in the "rice fields of New Iberia," and "hauled sugar cane to the mills."[86] Gleason described how authorities stopped a Johnson concert in San Francisco because segregation laws prohibited the trumpeter from having White musicians in his band. These liner notes established the template Gleason used throughout his career. He would outline the musician's story and sprinkle it with colorful details. When writing about Black musicians, Gleason often cited instances of racial injustice. Gleason became one of the most prolific liner note writers of his time.

In the summer of 1946, Gleason traveled to San Francisco. He likely went to help Eugene Williams with his new project, an extended engagement of veteran New Orleans trombonist Edward "Kid" Ory at a San Francisco venue.[87] While there, Gleason soaked up San Francisco's Dixieland jazz scene, still going strong in the mid-1940s. Gleason had developed into a professional music writer who crossed the continent to soak up the music he loved, wrote for *DownBeat*, and wrote liner notes for a major record label. Yet, as Blesh spitefully told the readers of *Record Changer*, Gleason still relied on a day job to support his jazz writing. Competition for full-time music writing jobs was intense in New York City. Maybe that was why Blesh advised Gleason to "crawl out his featherbed," pack a suitcase, and "hit the trail that Leonard has blazed."[88] That's precisely what Gleason did.

4

San Francisco (1946–56)

And in that vale of light
  the city drifts
    anchorless upon the ocean
              "The Changing Light," Lawrence Ferlinghetti[1]

Music had long swayed to the pulse of this drifting city, even before Jelly Roll Morton founded San Francisco's Jupiter Club in the 1910s. Swinging tempos set feet to dancing, ears to listening, and minds to opening. These rhythms were a siren call that lured Gleason to San Francisco. A city free of puritanical repression, wrote poet Kenneth Rexroth:

> San Francisco was not just a wide-open town. It is the only city in the United States which was not settled over land by the westward spreading Puritan tradition, or by the Walter Scott, fake-cavalier tradition of the South. It had been settled mostly, in spite of all the romances of the overland migration, by gamblers, prostitutes, rascals, and fortune seekers who came across the isthmus and around the horn. They had their faults, but they were not influenced by Cotton Mather.[2]

Ralph and Jean Gleason joined this western migration of adventurers in the fall of 1946. Their summer trip to San Francisco likely paved the way for the move. Although New York gave Gleason his start in music journalism, it had become a cold town for hot jazz. Why remain in New York when the true center of the jazz revival was San Francisco?

Fillmore Street Jumps

With his suitcase barely unpacked from the summer trip, Gleason loaded the Stutz Bearcat, and he and Jean headed for the West Coast.[3] On the week-long journey, they stopped in New Orleans, then onward across farmland, deserts, and mountain ranges. An endless stream of sights punctuated by bizarre roadside attractions—gigantic dinosaurs, spacemen, whales, and colossal fruits. And natural wonders—purple mountains, painted deserts, and red river valleys. The Gleasons saw the American landscape before the homogenizing forces of retail chains and corporate architecture robbed the country of its singular sense of place. They saw Jack Kerouac's America, with "nothing behind me, everything ahead of me, as is ever so on the road." A shimmering asphalt ribbon that ended where the Pacific Ocean flowed into the San Francisco Bay. After days of traveling, the Gleasons arrived with only one mishap. During an overnight stay, thieves broke into their car and stole several items, including family photographs, as if fate erased all connections to their past.

The Gleasons settled into their new home, a second-floor apartment in Berkeley.[4] The college town sat across the bay from San Francisco and extended from the water's edge to the Berkeley Hills. Gleason found a job at the *California Aggie*, a newspaper published by students in the agriculture department of the University of California. The job provided income but no intellectual stimulus.[5] For that, there was the San Francisco jazz scene. Although the city remained a bastion of traditional jazz, more modern sounds emerged, like bebop.

On a foggy night in 1946, Gleason decides to give bebop jazz a second chance. He squeezes into a "cramped ballroom on Fillmore Street ... that doubled as a roller rink," probably the Primalon Ballroom, a dance hall in the predominantly Black Fillmore district of San Francisco.[6] Called the "Harlem of the West," the neighborhood nurtured up-and-coming musicians who played jazz, blues, and a rebellious new sound—rhythm and blues (R&B).

Gleason went to the nightspot to hear trumpet virtuoso John Birks "Dizzy" Gillespie, twenty-nine years old at the time, Gleason's age. Gillespie had honed his skills in two bands that modernized jazz in the 1940s, Earl Hines' orchestra and Billy Eckstine's band. The trumpeter joined a handful of young musicians who developed a new jazz language called bebop. Based on a chromatic twelve-tone scale, bebop opened up new possibilities for melodies and harmonies. A fresh sound reflective of modern urban life. A sound Gillespie brought to the West Coast.

Packed into the club, Gleason listens to Gillespie play in front of a predominantly Black audience. The trumpeter's setlist at that time included bebop classics like "Salt Peanuts," "Groovin' High," "Anthropology," and others. This music broke most of the rules of Dixieland yet delivered everything Gleason loved about jazz: blazing improvisation, a hot swinging beat, irreverent patter, and thought-provoking complexity. All these elements are in Gillespie's closing number, a revved-up version of Earl Hines' "Second Balcony Jump." Beginning with a deceptively old-school swing chorus, Gillespie launches an extended bop solo followed by soaring sax solos. The punchy riffs by the horn section make the tune a great set closer. As Gleason and the crowd watch, Gillespie suddenly leaps on the piano and yells, "All the men go home, and all the women stay right here!" The room erupts in laughter.[7] After that show, Gleason went to see Gillespie's band whenever it was in town. "The sound of Dizzy's big band was one of joyous exultation," Gleason later wrote. "They were as exciting as anything I have ever heard, before or since."[8] The two developed a lifelong friendship.

The Gillespie show redefined Gleason's tastes. He let go of the revivalism that closed his ears to bebop. Gleason wasn't alone. Jazz historian Bruce Raeburn said that during the postwar years, "most of the hot collectors learned to move on. Jazz purism had given way to a relativistic universe in which aesthetics and historiography reflected stylistic pluralism."[9] In Gleason's case, this burgeoning pluralism would go far outside the boundaries of jazz to encompass the whole of popular music.

Swingin' the Golden Gate

Gleason continued to freelance after he moved to the Bay Area. One of his first articles was an *Esquire* profile of Nat King Cole, "Just Can't See for Lookin'." Cole led a trio with guitarist Oscar Moore and bassist Johnny Miller, playing a swinging style of bop-influenced pop. The group hosted a nationally sponsored radio program, *King Cole Trio*, the first radio show in America presented by a Black musician. Gleason noted this:

> The Trio is allowed to pick its own tunes (as they generally do on Capitol), and the sane, adult, and fair treatment of the Trio on the show, as contrasted with radio's usual Uncle Tom approach to the Negro artist, has brought compliments.[10]

Gleason continued writing for *DownBeat* and became their West Coast correspondent. A 1947 article illuminated Gleason's radio-listening habits:

> The programs from the various Negro churches provide the best music on the air. There are several, and they make Sunday night jump like mad with sister Loretta Peavey singing loud and clear.[11]

Gleason appreciated Black gospel music and wrote that it was an "unknown area to most whites," including jazz fans.[12] One exception was Loretta Peavey, whose music gained widespread popularity in the Bay Area. Gleason discovered gospel in New York when he heard Mahalia Jackson perform in a Harlem ballroom.[13] He took Atlantic Records' Ahmet Ertegun to hear Jackson, but she had already signed with another company.

In October 1947, *DownBeat* editor Ned Williams gave Gleason his own column, "Swingin' the Golden Gate" covering the San Francisco jazz scene. "San Francisco Jumps with Visitors, Natives," proclaimed the first column.[14] Gleason introduced readers to visiting blues musicians T-Bone Walker and Lowell Folson and jazz vocalist Bulee "Slim" Gaillard. The new *DownBeat* columnist extolled local musicians such as R&B guitarist Saunders King who played at Harold Blackshear's Café Society, an upscale nightclub in the Fillmore district. Gleason credited Blackshear with energizing the San Francisco jazz scene by presenting musicians from the bands of Walker, Gaillard, and other West Coast bandleaders. Gleason showcased another Black-owned nightspot, the Swing Club in West Oakland, a historically Black district with a rich musical history. Clubs in West Oakland and the Fillmore district hosted some of the leading blues, jazz, and R&B artists of the time, such as vibraphonist Lionel Hampton.

Gleason had praised Hampton's playing since his *Columbia Spectator* days. In a 1937 "Off the Record," he wrote, "Benny Goodman has brought Lionel Hampton on from California for his Quartet, and the negro rhythm artist's work on the vibraphone is excellent."[15] After Hampton's stint with Goodman, he returned to California, formed the Lionel Hampton Orchestra, and released best-selling singles such as "Flying Home," a precursor to R&B. He lived in Los Angeles and frequently played San Francisco. "Hamp" pioneered jump blues, a new genre that evolved into R&B. The Oakland-Fillmore circuit of Black clubs was a key incubator.

Gleason published a lengthy review of Hampton's band in a 1947 *DownBeat* article in which he took note of a rising young bassist:

> Hamp's rhythm section has all the old kick in it now. The addition of Charlie Mingus may be the reason; I don't know. But I know that … Mingus, the great drummer Earl Walker, and William Kackel jump like mad, rock like mad, swing like mad, and do anything rhythmically that needs to be done.[16]

Gleason had expanded his aesthetic over the past decade. He now thrilled to music that swung hard, "jumped," and "rocked," characteristics that defined an emerging new postwar sound in popular music. Artists like Hampton predisposed Gleason to this new direction and revolutionary genres like rhythm and blues.

As the Bay Area R&B scene blossomed, Gleason covered it for *DownBeat*, including a show by Johnny Moore's Three Blazers, whose "Driftin' Blues" featured vocals by Charles Brown. Two decades later, Gleason re-introduced the vocal group to a new generation of readers and lamented their omission in music histories of the time.[17]

Gleason saw how White and Black audiences in the Bay Area reacted differently to Black artists, differences similar to those he had observed in New York. For instance, he wrote that a Slim Gaillard show at a White venue wasn't well-attended because the vocalist "was too hip for San Franciscans, raised on a diet of cowboy music and hotel bands."[18] On the other hand, when Gleason saw T-Bone Walker play at Blackshear's, the audience went wild. The blues guitarist recently released "Call It Stormy Monday (But Tuesday is Just as Bad)," and it climbed the *Billboard* "race records" charts. Gleason makes the half-hour drive from Berkeley to hear Walker on a cold Monday night. The acrobatic guitarist electrifies the crowd:

> He jumps. He swings. He rocks. He does tricks. He makes the audience cry when he's sad and laughs when he's happy.
>
> Possessed of a remarkable stage presence, he paces his show superbly, building up to a terrific climax, at all times doing exactly what he wants to.
>
> T-Bone is one of the great entertainers of our day.[19]

"Swingin' the Golden Gate" redefined the San Francisco music scene as a setting that nurtured modern jazz and popular music trends such as R&B. Gleason introduced the evolving Bay Area milieu to a national audience. Once solely identified with Dixieland jazz, San Francisco became recognized for its modern jazz, blues, and R&B, thanks to Gleason. The freshly minted columnist found a new purpose as the city's musical ambassador. But Gleason's professional progress was soon overshadowed by grievous losses.

My Father was a Great Man

After the California move, Gleason remained in touch with his old friend Eugene Williams, who traveled to San Francisco frequently to promote traditional jazz. Williams booked New Orleans trombonist Kid Ory at the Green Room, a San Francisco union hall. A scandal occurred when Williams recorded the performances without telling Ory because he wanted to capture an unselfconscious replication of original New Orleans jazz. The stint lost money and damaged Williams' reputation when word got out about the secret recordings. Williams wrote about the incident in a contrite but meandering *DownBeat* article published in 1947. He surprisingly said he lacked jazz expertise and admitted that "you can do a lot of harm, without intending any, when you don't know what you're doing."[20] Only in his early thirties, Williams made the shocking announcement that he planned to quit writing. Ten months later, on May 5, 1948, Williams committed suicide by jumping off the roof of a building in Manhattan.[21]

The tragedy shook Gleason, but he never wrote about his close friend's death. Other critics publicly praised Williams' significance. Nesuhi Ertegun proclaimed Williams "one of the very best among jazz writers."[22] Williams greatly influenced Gleason and started him on his path of working behind the scenes to help musicians he believed in. An under-recognized voice in 1940s jazz discourse, Williams' life and writings warrant future research.

Three months after Williams took his life, Gleason suffered an even greater loss when his father, Ralph A. Gleason, died on August 7, 1948.[23] Gleason didn't attend his father's funeral because he couldn't afford the cross-country trip. This speaks to the Gleasons' hardscrabble life at the time, making ends meet on Ralph's income from low-tier jobs augmented by freelance checks. Gleason was at peace with his decision because he believed his father wouldn't have wanted him to borrow money to make the trip.[24] Ralph A. left an indelible imprint on his son's values. Gleason later wrote to a friend:

> My father was a great man because he was for me in whatever it was I really wanted to do, because he believed in people, in humanity, and hated bullshit and phoniness … We sat up night after night after night after night drinking beer and talking politics and talking life … Even when I screamed at him, I thought he was the

absolute living end … He loved young people, and he was tolerant … When people said I was nuts to be hung up on jazz, he didn't.[25]

Fate had an even worse loss in store for the Gleasons, preceded by a joyous moment. Jean gave birth to the couple's first child, Timothy R. Gleason, just after midnight on New Year's Day, 1949. But joy turned to tragedy a few weeks later when Jean found Timothy lifeless in his carriage, likely a victim of sudden infant death syndrome (SIDS). Gleason's daughter Stacy said, "I'm sure they were devastated, and they never told us about Timmy until we were teenagers."[26] As was the case with Williams, Gleason never wrote about losing his infant son.

Life went on for Ralph and Jean despite their unspeakable loss. Gleason plunged into a variety of jazz-related activities. He appeared on the new "Discs and Data" radio program hosted by disc jockey Jimmy Lyons, an avid proponent of modern jazz who would play a critical role in Gleason's career.[27] The DJ used his radio show to mediate modern jazz by playing records and interviewing young Bay Area musicians such as pianist Dave Brubeck.[28] Gleason wrote a cover story about Lyons' radio program in *DownBeat*. It detailed Lyons' on-air symposium in defense of bebop with a stellar set of musicians that included Woody Herman, Nat King Cole, Mel Torme, and June Christy. Gleason published most of the exchange, and quoted Herman that, "Bop is the music of the youth, and anywhere youth is, it must be served." Herman added, "We'd better listen to youth because when we stop, we become doddering old men,"[29] a belief Gleason embraced.

A somber *DownBeat* assignment had Gleason covering Billie Holiday's second arrest for narcotics which occurred in San Francisco's Hotel Mark Twain.[30] The luminous singer's addiction had taken a toll since Gleason saw her at Café Society in the 1930s. In more sad news, Bunk Johnson passed away on July 7, 1949. After Gleason heard, he stayed up all night and wrote "Bunk's an Amazing Story," a two-page *DownBeat* tribute. Drawing on the liner notes he wrote for Johnson's RCA album, Gleason framed Johnson as a "peculiarly eloquent raconteur" who bridged the eras of New Orleans jazz and its revival.[31] Gleason highlighted how dedicated supporters like Eugene Williams brought the struggling artist back into the limelight. He refuted the view that Williams exploited Johnson and opposed claims that Johnson was a minor jazz figure. "His importance in the history of the development of American jazz," Gleason wrote, "is undisputed."[32] Today, Johnson remains a controversial figure. Evidence surfaced that the trumpeter was younger than he claimed. This undermines Johnson's claims that he played with New Orleans jazz originator Buddy Bolden and performed in nineteenth-century traveling shows. But for Gleason and other young revivalists, Johnson was a vessel into which they poured their fantasies of early jazz as an unfettered folk form, a people's music.

Johnson's departure came as the jazz revival wound down. But the revival established traditional jazz as a living art that continues today. Gleason mediated New Orleans-style jazz until his career's end, bringing the music to future generations of listeners. Now established as a respected jazz critic, Gleason undoubtedly longed for a full-time position as a music journalist. A few weeks after he memorialized Bunk Johnson, he took a critical step in that direction.

The *Chronicle*

In late-1940s San Francisco, the only option for pursuing a full-time music journalism career was to write for one of the two daily newspapers, the *Examiner* or the *Chronicle*. Gleason would have found the Hearst-owned, conservative *Examiner* to be unappealing. Conversely, the *Chronicle* had a record of serious jazz coverage dating back to the 1920s. No better way to get his foot in the door than to contribute freelance articles.

Gleason wrote his first *Chronicle* freelance piece in the summer of 1949. The article showcased Nellie Rose Lutcher, a pioneering Black R&B singer who recently crossed over to the pop charts. Gleason reviewed her performance at Ciro's, a San Francisco nightclub, and captured Lutcher's compelling style:

> She takes the melody of a song, plays with it, and improvises on it and on the chords which the melody and her improvisation suggest. The result is a lacy, titillating, insinuating style of singing that intrigues and excites the listener. And, of course, it is all founded on a solid beat.[33]

The article ran in *This World*, the *Chronicle*'s Sunday magazine, where the highbrow and the middlebrow coexisted once a week. Each issue carried reviews of art, literature, theater, films, television, and radio. The editor was Denise McCluggage, a friend of pianist Dave Brubeck. McCluggage frequented the San Francisco jazz scene, where she would sip a Coke and listen to the likes of Ella Fitzgerald or pianist George Shearing.

McCluggage must have liked Gleason's article because others followed. In "Jazz at the Philharmonic Fights Discrimination with Music," Gleason applauded the pro-integration efforts of Los Angeles promoter Norman Granz. The impresario created a touring music series, Jazz at the Philharmonic (JATP), featuring integrated bandstands and audiences. JATP tours made regular stops in San Francisco and influenced its burgeoning modern jazz scene. Gleason's title for the article conveyed his belief that music can change society, a conviction held his entire life.

In 1950, Gleason wrote an inspired *Chronicle* article about Lionel Hampton, a JATP musician. Hampton's music had a kinetic and visceral kick that Gleason loved and praised with a fan's enthusiasm and a music critic's ear for sonic drama:

> Hampton throws himself into each show with a burst of energy that is positively awesome. He plays the vibraphones slowly and sweetly, gradually working up to a frenzy. He flails the piano with his special two-fingered technique, playing boogie-woogie at incredible speeds; he pounds tom-toms and drums leading up to his stock finale, where he leaps high in the air and lands on the big tom-tom as the band hits the final chord.[34]

In addition to Hampton and Lutcher, Gleason penned *Chronicle* articles about Nat King Cole, Billie Eckstine, Ella Fitzgerald, and boogie-woogie pianist Julia Lee. As Gleason's writing schedule picked up, he and Jean became parents again. Just days after Gleason's thirty-third birthday, Jean gave birth to Joyce Bridget Gleason on March 22, 1950,

Figure 4.1 Ralph Gleason (second from left) with Lionel Hampton (center) and music promotor Charles Sullivan (first from left), in San Francisco, c. 1955. Courtesy of the Wesley F. Johnson III photo collection.

part of the baby boom generation that reshaped American society and popular music. Bridget grew up in an unconventional household where great musicians regularly stopped by, and music was always in the air. Having a child undoubtedly filled Gleason with a greater sense of responsibility and a more pressing desire for a full-time job as a music critic. The opportunity soon came when McCluggage decided to add a new music column to *This World*.

This decision came during an exciting period in American jazz and popular music. A key factor was the rising generation of teens and young adults able to buy more records and concert tickets than their predecessors because of postwar prosperity. Another factor:

> Musical genres regarded as marginalized by the industry came to influence even more strongly the musical taste of middle-class white Americans ... country and western music had expanded its audience during the war, and this trend continued through the early 1950s. The market for Black popular music, rechristened rhythm & blues, also expanded ... The market was supported by a new generation of record labels.[35]

The upswing of independent labels also benefited jazz, which "moved beyond the big band era and was beginning to experience both an economic resurgence and signs of growing cultural legitimation," according to music historian Matt Brennan.[36] In San Francisco, a new generation of innovative musicians such as Dave Brubeck, Cal Tjader, and Vince Guaraldi created a modern jazz scene that attracted touring artists from Los Angeles, New York City, and elsewhere.

McCluggage wanted *This World* to reflect these changes in jazz and popular music. The Sunday magazine's one music column was in a classical rut. Columnist R. H. Hagan recently tried to get readers excited about "Harpo Marx conducting Beethoven's Fifth Symphony without the support of an orchestra" and "Charles Laughton reading selections from the Bible with the support of the Vienna Choir Boys."[37] The most extensive and stimulating *Chronicle* coverage of jazz and popular music occurred not in *This World* but in a weekday teen column called "Juke Box" in the women's section. Columnist Marjorie McCabe had reviewed records at the *Chronicle* since 1946 and possessed a pro-jazz sensibility. A thorough researcher, in 1947 McCabe expertly reviewed a set of Jelly Roll Morton recordings previously unreleased.[38] McCabe's prose, redolent with hipster jargon and deep knowledge of jazz, presaged an emergent generation of women reviewers in newspapers, magazines like *DownBeat*, and other publications. Her "Juke Box" column foreshadowed the first newspaper rock music columns, many written by women writers. But "Juke Box," buried in the women's section, ended in late 1950. The *Chronicle*'s coverage of jazz and popular music was at a low ebb except for Gleason's occasional articles.

The *Chronicle* had been covering jazz and popular music since the 1920s with articles about musicians such as bandleader Paul Whiteman, who started his career in the San Francisco Symphony. The newspaper also covered local shows by jazz musicians like Cab Calloway, Earl Hines, and Louis Armstrong. During the swing era, the paper had a columnist named "Jive," likely Rudi Blesh, who had engaged in a war of words with Gleason in *Record Changer*. "Jive" had an extensive knowledge of jazz history and wrote insightful criticism, despite sometimes using flowery language. Their column, "On the Records," was the *Chronicle*'s first critical discourse about jazz.

In 1945 the *Chronicle* hired a new jazz critic, Robert Liles, who wrote a column with the intriguing title of "Tongs and Bones." The column lasted only six months, followed by "New Popular Records in Review," which appeared in *This World*.[39] A string of different reviewers wrote the column, which covered a range of genres from jazz to folk to pop. It ended after sixteen months. Thus, after three decades of vigorous music coverage, the *Chronicle* lacked a focused column about jazz and popular music.

In 1951, the newspaper pop music column was already thirty years old, dating back to the Jazz Age. These columns mainly consisted of record reviews and covered all genres of discs, including classical music. During the postwar era, top newspapers across the country had columns that emphasized jazz, like John W. Riley's "Popular Records" in the *Boston Globe* and Fred Reynolds' "Platter Chatter" in the *Chicago Tribune*. The *New York Times* launched a column called "Records" by Gama Gilbert, who reviewed both classical and pop music records. After Gilbert's passing, the column was taken over by Howard Taubman, a music editor and hot jazz enthusiast at the *Times*.

The American music column after the Second World War lacked substance and direction. It was mostly published on weekdays, and not in the prominent weekend arts and entertainment sections. Most columns were brief and focused mainly on reviewing records. However, with the exciting changes happening in jazz and popular music, it was time for a fresh perspective on what a newspaper music column could offer. Denise McCluggage had this vision and chose her young freelancer, Ralph J. Gleason, to write the new column. They called it "Rhythm Section."

Rhythm Section

The *Chronicle* began advertising Gleason's column in February 1951, spotlighting the column's multi-genre scope. Its eye-catching announcement titled "Sweet 'n' Hot" featured a cartoon sketch of a trombone player pumping a slide:

> Whether it's hot jazz or sweet melody, cowboy or Calypso—if you like popular recorded music, you'll enjoy *This World*'s new "Rhythm Section." Here are profiles of top artists and reviews of their latest recordings.[40]

"Rhythm Section" debuted in the February 11, 1951 *This World*. The Sunday magazine's cover featured Rudolph Valentino's intense gaze from the 1921 silent film *The Sheik*, while inside, readers found a review of the newly released biopic *Valentino*. As its name suggests, *This World* also provided a weekly summary of global events. One article discussed how Democratic President Harry S. Truman was handling the Cold War, while others covered the Korean conflict, atomic bomb testing, and the House Un-American Activities Committee's vehement opposition to Communism. Five years after the end of the Second World War, America faced challenges both domestically and internationally.

Although *This World* reflected growing sociopolitical tensions, it also showed the emergence of postwar consumerism. There were numerous advertisements showcasing contemporary furniture and the latest fashion trends. Home entertainment systems took center stage, featuring a combination of television, radio, and a three-speed record player in an elegant oak-veneered cabinet. *This World*'s ads and columns provided the reader with recommendations on what to watch, listen to, and read.

"Rhythm Section" met the demands of this new wave of middlebrow consumption by mediating high-quality music. Fans of contemporary jazz who were anticipating an expanded version of Gleason's *DownBeat* column may have been surprised at the eclectic mix of torch singers, crooners, big band leaders, and jazz instrumentalists such as Red Norvo and Lionel Hampton. The column lived up to its advance publicity pledge by catering to readers with wide-ranging tastes.

This can be seen in Gleason's first "Rhythm Section." A headline announced the lead article, "A Handsome Kid with an Accordion," about Italian American pop musician

Dick Contino, popular with bobbysoxers. A fine musician, Contino garnered respect in the jazz community and appeared in *DownBeat*. Gleason warmly described a Contino performance he attended in which the accordionist brought his father onstage to sing "The Butcher Boy," a Sicilian tarantella and popular wedding song. The lyrical music enraptured the audience, including Gleason, who revealed his appreciation for pop music for the first time.[41]

Following the Contino profile were three other features written by Gleason. "On and Off the Record" brimmed with tidbits about the music industry and the San Francisco music scene, including an upcoming stint by the Red Norvo Trio with Charles Mingus on bass. On the next page was a profile of bandleader Billie Eckstine and "Some New Discs in Brief Review." In it, Gleason reviewed records by Patti Page, Erroll Garner, Doris Day, and several other artists, a mix of jazz and pop musicians. The recordings were all singles, which in early 1951 meant the same type of 78 rpm discs he reviewed since his *Columbia Spectator* days.[42]

In his first "Rhythm Section," Gleason stretched into pop territory with the Contino profile and reviews of records by artists such as Doris Day. No mention of country or R&B yet, but that would come. This first column established the template for future columns: a three-part format consisting of an article, a set of news briefs, and a collection of record reviews. Although all three of these types of music features were common in newspapers of the time, to collect them within a single column under one byline was novel. This format gave "Rhythm Section" a personal touch; to read it was like sitting in Gleason's living room as he warmly and wittily raised your appreciation for high-quality music. For Gleason, securing "Rhythm Section" and a full-time position as a music writer was the most crucial turning point in his career. No longer would he divide his energy between music writing and dull day jobs.

"Rhythm Section" was a milestone in music journalism history. Its three-part format across two pages provided an unprecedented depth of pop music coverage for a newspaper music column of that time. This came with unparalleled discursive power for a single music columnist within a regional music scene. In this case, the San Francisco modern jazz scene on its way to national renown thanks to Gleason's *DownBeat* column. Gleason brought the world of jazz and popular music together in "Rhythm Section." It would be another year before *DownBeat* expanded its scope into pop, rhythm and blues, and eventually, Country & Western.[43] Gleason brought new legitimacy to the humble newspaper music column. But most importantly, he became the first nationally known jazz critic to embrace popular music.

Extended Lines of Improvisation

With "Rhythm Section" up and running, Gleason confirmed his status as the San Francisco music scene's resident pop music critic. He celebrated noteworthy artists, previewed upcoming shows, and reviewed the latest batch of discs to hit the local record stores. Equally important, Gleason began to play a pivotal role in a rising genre—West Coast jazz.

"Dave Brubeck opens with his new four-piece unit Tuesday at the Blackhawk," announced Gleason in a July 1951 column.[44] A mini-milestone in jazz history, the Brubeck engagement was another step in the visionary pianist's development. After serving in the Second World War, Brubeck studied music at Oakland's Mills College under Darius Milhaud, the influential French composer who pioneered Third Stream, a genre that fuses jazz and classical music. Brubeck caught the ear of San Francisco disc jockey Jimmy Lyons, whom Gleason had written about in *DownBeat*. Brubeck and Lyons developed a friendship, and in 1949, the pair organized San Francisco's first outdoor jazz event, the Festival of Jazz.[45] In 1950, Brubeck recorded for a new Bay Area record label, Fantasy Records, owned by brothers Max and Sol Weiss. Fantasy would later play an enormous role in Gleason's life.

The following year, the Brubeck quartet debuted at a nondescript club called the Blackhawk in San Francisco's gritty Tenderloin district. Over the next several years, the club became the "most illustrious jazz corner in all of San Francisco," according to Ted Gioia.[46] Fantasy Records musicians found a "home base" at the club "from which they could launch their distinctive assault on the world of contemporary jazz."[47] Gioia notes, "If San Francisco could ever lay claim to a truly indigenous jazz style, it sprang from the *sui generis* modernism sponsored by the Blackhawk and Fantasy Records."[48]

Gleason frequently covered the Brubeck band in "Rhythm Section." But while he praised the other members of the group, such as vibraphonist Cal Tjader and saxophonist Paul Desmond, Gleason admitted that Brubeck didn't swing enough for his tastes. Gleason did admire Brubeck as a serious artist who succeeded without compromising his musical values and wrote, "It's impossible not to admire his courage and musical integrity."[49] When *DownBeat* proclaimed the quartet "Best Small Combo of 1953," Gleason presented the award.[50] And when Brubeck recorded his second album for Fantasy, *Distinctive Rhythm Instrumentals*, Gleason wrote the liner notes. "In the short space of two years," Gleason wrote, Brubeck had "risen from the obscurity of an unknown jazz pianist to a point where he is accepted in this country and abroad as one of the leaders of the modern school of musicians."[51]

Gleason and other music writers in the early 1950s used liner notes as a new form of jazz discourse. The oversized covers of long-playing (LP) albums had enough room on the back to print lengthy commentary. Author Tom Piazza, who wrote a book about liner notes said they "play a special role in a jazz fan's development. They have often been where a new fan first begins to learn about the musicians and the repertoire of jazz."[52] During the 1950s and 1960s, "jazz liner notes entered a golden age" in which most notes were penned by "working jazz writers."[53] Gleason wrote liner notes for other Bay Area musicians. When Tjader left Brubeck's group, Gleason covered the vibraphonist in his *Chronicle* column and wrote the notes for his Fantasy albums. Gleason proclaimed Tjader a "modernist, yet a swinging modernist."[54]

Gleason's *Chronicle* writings and Fantasy liner notes connected the dots between the key elements of the burgeoning San Francisco modern jazz scene: the Blackhawk, Fantasy Records, and the radio program of Jimmy Lyons, whom a *Chronicle* reporter described as a "slight, dapper young man who speaks of bop as the new American culture and will put nothing on the air, without some reluctance, unless it's composed of flatted fifths."[55] Lyons' midnight show "Discapades" was required listening for Gleason, and influenced his growing taste for modern jazz.[56] Lyons recalled a fateful discussion he had with Gleason in the late 1940s:

> Ralph and I had some kind of instant rapport ... we discussed, wouldn't it be nice to have a sylvan setting with lots of trees and grass and all that and the best jazz people in the world playing on the same stage and having a whole weekend of just getting drowned in jazz?[57]

Their idea materialized eight years later when Lyons and Gleason co-founded the Monterey Jazz Festival.

Gleason brought attention to yet another rising star in the San Francisco ferment, pianist Vince Guaraldi, who would go on to score the soundtrack for *A Charlie Brown Christmas*. As with Brubeck and Tjader, Gleason covered Guaraldi in his column and wrote liner notes for his albums on Fantasy. In his notes for *The Vince Guaraldi Trio*, Gleason praised the pianist's angst-free personality as "not ridden by an unconscionable demon to prove something; he just loves music and loves playing and swinging."[58] Gleason said Guaraldi's "uncomplicated approach ... enables him to like, appreciate and want to play all sorts of numbers [from chamber jazz to pop]. It enables him to play simple, emotionally pure piano and to [also] get funky and hard-swinging."[59] He wrote that drummer Eddie Duran solos "with authority, taste and a classic sense of construction."[60] After Gleason wrote the liner notes for another Guaraldi album, he called the pianist and told him, "It's a damn good album, Duran is a bitch on it."[61]

In addition to local musicians like Guaraldi, Tjader, and Brubeck, the 1950s San Francisco music scene depended on a steady flow of musicians from outside the Bay Area. Vital music scenes rely on these infusions of new ideas that diversify the local soundscape and connect it to the global stage. Although the San Francisco scene produced innovative musicians, it also attracted progressive musicians from other cities, such as self-taught prodigy Charles Mingus. Gleason recognized the bassist's potential early on and conducted a lengthy *DownBeat* interview with Mingus in 1951. But after the exchange, Mingus felt dissatisfied and wrote Gleason a long letter that described his jazz views. Mingus wrote, "This way, I didn't know what you would ask, so I am only quoting my beliefs."[62] Gleason chucked the original interview and based his article on the letter, an extended argument that improvisation was a form of composition. Mingus noted that when Charlie Parker improvised, he created "clearly thought-out compositions of the melodic line" that were just as legitimate as any music "written down by Brahms or Chopin or Tchaikovsky."[63] Mingus lamented that racial segregation blocked gifted Black musicians from getting classical training and playing in symphonies. He deplored the systemic racism that shunted these musicians to demeaning jobs like burlesque shows. Two years after the interview, in 1953, Fantasy Records released *The Charles Mingus Duo and Trio*. Gleason gave the album a positive review and called him a visionary musician.

Another jazz innovator Gleason wrote about was trumpeter Miles Davis. When Gleason wrote his first review of Davis in the spring of 1951, the musician struggled with addiction but pioneered a new idiom called cool jazz. Influenced by farsighted arranger Gil Evans, Davis sought a counter to bebop's high-speed virtuosic soloing. Cool jazz musicians introduced a more relaxed sound akin to the human voice. Through saxophonist Gerry Mulligan and others, cool significantly influenced postwar California jazz, later labeled "West Coast jazz," centered in Los Angeles and San Francisco.

Gleason adored the *Miles Davis All-Stars Volume 1* and devoted an entire column to it in 1955. The reader always knew Gleason had wholly entered into a piece of music when he wrote a focused passage like this:

> On the opening side, "Bag's Groove," after an introductory cymbal crash, Davis takes a long chorus in which he toys with several figures and then quotes from Victor Herbert before introducing [Milt] Jackson, who plays a delightful solo with [Thelonious] Monk feeding him chords in the background. A simple solo from Monk follows, and then Davis plays a short, sweet bit before the final unison ending."[64]

Gleason always covered Davis when he was in town. During a 1956 visit Gleason wrote, "One of the most important musicians in the history of modern jazz is currently playing at the Blackhawk."[65] He called Davis an "improviser in the freest jazz tradition," who brought "simplicity and authority back to the blues." Gleason noted that an upcoming young musician had joined Davis's band, groundbreaking saxophonist John Coltrane. Gleason wrote:

> In the work of such young men as Sonny Rollins and John Coltrane, the makings of a new style are simmering ... It will include the use of longer lines of solo structure (à la Parker), a more intimate relationship to other instruments, particularly the drums, and a return to the central driving core of the Hawkins style—the straight-ahead, non-inferential swinging. It will also, once the tone softens, be particularly adapted to melodic clarity in ballads.[66]

Gleason wrote that Davis, Rollins, Coltrane, and other modernists were "demanding form, restraint, control and above all, extended lines of improvisation and the utilization of the full range of harmony and rhythms possible to jazz."[67] Their music was "at once complex and orderly; whose excitement is controlled; where the soloist utilizes structure as well as dynamics to create a climax and where inspiration finds logical channels for expression."[68] Gleason's ability to listen intently and to describe what he heard had grown immensely since he penned his first "Rhythm Section" in 1951.

2835 Ashby Avenue

As Gleason's professional life evolved in the early 1950s, so did his domestic life. He and Jean had their second child, Stacy Rayburn Gleason, on November 25, 1951. Two months later, Gleason shared a glimpse of a family night in the Gleason household:

> We played a nifty little game at our house last weekend. It is based on the new RCA-Victor album, *Your Horoscope is Your Music* … A gentleman by the name of Dewey Bergman has written and conducted a series of 12 short compositions based on the signs of the Zodiac.
>
> You play the selection for Aries the Ram, and [it says]: "You are a pioneer—bold and adventurous. You're the first to try something new. You lead, and others follow." This happens to fit to a T, Joyce Bridget Gleason, age 23 months.
>
> Sagittarius the Archer means "Laughter—that's you. Going through life with a smile." Stacy, age 2 ½ months, fits this. Laughter, that's her. In between colic spells, that is.[69]

In the summer of 1953, Jean gave birth to a son, Toby Ralph Gleason, who one day would make his father's writings and films available to the world. Bridget, Stacy, and Toby became recurring characters in Gleason's *Chronicle* columns, along with Jean.

The family outgrew their apartment and moved to a cozy bungalow-style house on a busy street fewer than two miles from the campus of UC Berkeley.[70] 2835 Ashby Avenue became the center of Gleason's professional and domestic life. He and Jean turned the living room into an inviting place lined with floor-to-ceiling shelves for their growing collection of books, records, and music ephemera. Gleason created an office in an attic dormer that overlooked Jean's rose garden and an apricot tree. He worked from an old rolltop desk surrounded by books and an extensive library of newspaper and magazine clippings.

But just as Gleason settled into an idyllic home life, he was diagnosed with type 1 diabetes, usually found in children and adolescents. This incurable condition causes tiredness, irritability, and weight loss and can shorten life expectancy. Gleason began to inject insulin daily and follow a strict diet. Family life centered on Gleason's care, and Jean based family meals on what he was allowed to eat. According to Gleason's daughter Bridget, her father had "brittle diabetes," a rare variation with severe blood sugar fluctuations that can lead to anxiety and depression. Bridget recalled:

> Diabetes was a pervasive presence in the household. Everything revolved around [Ralph's] schedule and needs, exacerbated by the fact that he worked from home. He routinely suffered from low blood sugar because of the fragility of his diabetes. That ruled our household because high-stress levels and unpredictable behavior accompanied it.[71]

Despite his diabetes, Gleason remained uncommonly creative and productive. Each morning he ate breakfast in bed. After breakfast, he sat in his favorite leather chair in the living room and thought through his current assignment. Once visualized, Gleason typed the article in his attic office. Jean proofread the piece and made editing notes on a carbon copy which she put on the morning bus to the East Bay terminal in San Francisco, where a copyboy from the *Chronicle* received it from the driver.

For the remainder of the day, Gleason worked at home. He worked on in-progress articles, reviewed records, interviewed musicians, and wrote correspondence, one of his passions. He might leave the house to meet musicians in their hotel rooms or attend a daytime musical performance. Work began again after dinner, making rounds of Bay Area music venues. Once inside a nightspot, Gleason leaned against a wall and wrote in his reporter's notebook. Returning home, often late at night, he might work on the piece before bed.

A grueling workload for anyone, let alone someone with diabetes. A workload that grew in the spring of 1953 when the *Chronicle* assigned Gleason a second column called "Lively Arts." In addition, he continued to write his *DownBeat* column and freelance for *Variety* and other publications.[72] On top of that, Gleason turned out liner notes for Fantasy, Atlantic, and other record companies, over twenty-five sets of liner notes from 1950 to 1956. He maintained this workload for the next two decades while adding ambitious side projects to his busy schedule.

Gleason kept up this schedule because he enjoyed his work, which put him in touch with people throughout the Bay Area who became lasting friends. One was Scott Newhall, the new managing editor of the *Chronicle*. A lanky adventurer who loved sailing, Newhall started at the paper in the 1930s as a photographer and later became a writer and editor. Newhall closed the newspaper's circulation gap with the *Examiner* by hiring writers who reflected the Bay Area spirit of literariness, irreverence, hedonism, and tolerance.[73] Author Kevin Starr wrote that Newhall changed the *Chronicle* into a "daily magazine of feature columnists and cultural critics." Starr said the *Chronicle* was "sustained by an assumption that San Francisco and its environs were the most privileged place in America."[74] Writer David Talbot noted that under Newhall, "The *Chronicle* did not just give voice to San Francisco; it invented the city" and turned it into a place of "fizz and fun."[75] Newhall loved jazz and said Gleason was "always a courtly companion when it came time to stroll the boulevards of San Francisco after the sun had set" and take in the city's music scene.[76]

Anything from Hymns to Hillbilly

From 1951 to 1956, Gleason increasingly covered jazz in "Rhythm Section." But as earlier noted, he wrote about other genres as well. These included pop music and Country & Western.

Gleason's favorite pop vocalist was Frank Sinatra. After a career lull, Sinatra recorded an astonishing series of albums for Capitol Records that Gleason praised. He called Sinatra "one of the great ballad singers of our time" and a "master of phrasing, one of the necessities of a good singer."[77] Gleason's favorite Sinatra album was *Songs for Swingin' Lovers!* which he called "one of the best vocal albums I have ever heard."[78] After playing the album repeatedly for three days, he was "unable to find anything wrong with it."[79] Sinatra "had an uncanny instinct for the right tempo. And this enables him to set a mood, phrase easily and give the proper emphasis to the lyrics."[80]

Gleason also appreciated jazz singer Jeri Southern's voice, which he described as "soft as velvet yet retaining the slight romantic huskiness of too many cigarettes or too many late hours."[81] He wrote about Southern's early career in "gin mills and jazz joints in Chicago, Los Angeles, and other cities" where "jazz musicians were crazy about her from the first. Miles Davis, Nat Cole, and many other well-known jazz stars raved about her singing, but the public passed her by."[82] That changed when Southern launched a successful series of albums for Decca that brought her to Gleason's attention. Gleason listened to the new pop singers as closely as he did to Cal Tjader or Miles Davis. For pop stylists like Southern, Gleason learned their stories and teased out the emotional threads that ran through their music. Another vocalist Gleason enjoyed was Patti Page. The Oklahoma-born singer sold three million records, including the countryish "Tennessee Waltz." Gleason wrote that Page's voice had a "warm, friendly quality" and her "versatility is truly remarkable. She can sing anything from hymns to hillbilly. In the opinion of many, she is an almost perfect singer, with great natural phrasing, warmth, and swing. And always on pitch."[83]

In addition to country-influenced pop, Gleason came to appreciate pure country music. In the decades after the first "hillbilly" records hit the market, a new style emerged in the rural bars of the American southwest called "honky tonk":

> To entertain roadhouse patrons, honky-tonk bands offered a mix of fast instrumental numbers, slower dance numbers, and songs describing the life experiences of patrons. In these increasingly personal and candid songs, instrumentalists moved to a supporting role, providing the context for the lyrics offered by the guitar-playing bandleader vocalist.[84]

No vocalist could pack more longing into a honky-tonk lyric than Hiram "Hank" Williams. Gleason wrote a profile of Williams in 1952 when the lanky Alabamian was high in the pop charts with "Cold, Cold Heart." But Williams struggled with an addiction to alcohol and pills that weakened his constitution and caused the Grand Ole Opry to sack him. When meeting Williams at Oakland's Leamington Hotel, Gleason recoils. Stooped, skeletal, and pallid with hollowed cheeks and haunted eyes, Williams had sunk low since the glory days of "Move It On Over" and "Lost Highway." As he shakes Gleason's hand, Williams grabs a handful of pills off the dresser and slugs them down. Fortified, he takes Gleason downstairs to the coffee shop for the interview. Williams eats breakfast and recounts early memories of singing gospel tunes at the Mt. Olive, Alabama, church where his mother played the organ. He reminisces about Rufus "Tee-Tot" Payne, the elderly Black blues guitarist who taught Williams how to play. Williams makes it clear that he performs folk music, not country music. Straight-from-the-heart music with no pretense. Williams says, "A song ain't nothin', but a story just wrote with music to it."[85] When the interview ends, Gleason notices that the color has returned to Williams' face.

That night Gleason drives to a small club surrounded by cotton fields twenty miles outside of Oakland. He parks in a muddy lot and enters the club, an extended dance hall with a crude stage at the end. Williams' band, the Driftin' Cowboys, warms up the crowd. Williams strides on stage, resplendent in a rhinestone-encrusted Nudie suit. As he hunches over the microphone and starts to sing, people flock to the dance floor, driven by the fiddle and pedal-steel guitar sounds. And the lonesome voice of Hank Williams, which could tear your heart out and leave you wanting more.

Artists like Williams brought Country & Western music into the mainstream during the first half of the 1950s. Magazine publishers responded. At least fifteen country music magazines hit the stands in the 1940s and 1950s, including the standard bearer *Country Song Roundup*. *DownBeat* initially besmirched country music and took the position that it was responsible for swing music's commercial decline. "Hillbilly Boom Can Spread Like Plague," trumpeted one cover story, sounding like the anti-jazz rhetoric of the 1920s.[86] But when *DownBeat*'s editors began to diversify the magazine's coverage in the early 1950s, they included country music.

Gleason helped to legitimize country music as it distanced itself from its "hillbilly" appellation. He wrote profiles of musicians such as T. Texas Tyler, who gave his explanation of the music's new wave of popularity:

> It was all due to the war. The war put so many people together—from every hamlet and hollow. It showed exactly how trustworthy and how big a heart a man can have. When a man gets lonesome, there's nothing that can replace a lonesome song, and there were plenty of lonesome nights in the war.[87]

In his profile of Eddy Arnold, the "Tennessee Plowboy," Gleason described country music as a "strange mixture of simple singers, pseudo-cowboys who never rode a horse, and Arkansas fiddlers from Arizona." He appreciated Arnold's genuineness because he started "working on a farm and playing rural radio stations." Arnold sounded "authentically folksy as a sunbonnet and a corncob pipe."[88]

The American protest song entered country music through singer-songwriter Merle Travis. Gleason reviewed his song "Sixteen Tons" as recorded by Tennessee Ernie Ford. The song told the story of a sharecropper perpetually indebted to the "company store":

> It's no moon-June song; it's no teenager nonsense number, and if it has any hidden meanings, they certainly won't run counter to our moral code – although Senator McCarthy might not appreciate the general tenor of the song."[89]

Gleason referenced red-baiting Republican Senator Joseph McCarthy. Travis's songs about the hardships of coal miners and sharecroppers got him into trouble with the FBI, who pressured a Chicago radio station not to play Travis's music because of its possible associations with labor unions and Communists.[90]

Curiously, Gleason covered very little folk music in the *Chronicle* during the first half of the 1950s, when the national folk revival centered in New York City was well underway. He commented positively on the Weavers, the Greenwich Village folk music quartet. Gleason noted when member Pete Seeger was called to testify before House Un-American Activities Committee. The *Chronicle*'s coverage of folk music went to other writers such as R. H. Hagan, Marjorie Trumbull, and Alfred Frankenstein, the paper's classical music critic. But Gleason did cover another recently renamed genre: rhythm and blues.

Up-to-Date Blues with a Beat

> Rhythm and Blues? That's the folk music of the American Negro of the Fifties. It's generally a vocal blues emphasizing rhythm and a tenor saxophone played as emotionally as possible.[91]

When Gleason wrote this in 1955, he added that R&B had been there "all the time, but no one noticed it."[92] Gleason heard it in the jump blues of musicians like Louis Jordan, whom he saw perform in the Fillmore district in the late 1940s.[93] And in the wailing saxophone solo by Illinois Jacquet on Lionel Hampton's "Flying Home." And the first sounds of R&B in the gospel-tinged vocals of Ruth Brown, who sang in the Basie band, and the rocking guitar of Sister Rosetta Sharpe.

When Gleason discovered these R&B precursors, their recordings were labeled "race records," a catch-all term for discs marketed to Black consumers. By the late-1940s, some music critics considered the term disparaging, including *Billboard*'s Jerry Wexler, who convinced the magazine to replace "race records" with "rhythm and blues." The name stuck. Wexler preached R&B like Gleason had preached New Orleans jazz. He published an article in *Saturday Review*, "Rhythm and Blues in 1950," that compared R&B with hot jazz. Wexler lamented the commercialization of R&B but said discerning listeners could separate "the hot from the hoke."[94] Wexler practiced what he preached and went to work for Ahmet Ertegun's Atlantic Records, one of the first independent labels to record R&B. In 1954, he and Ertegun wrote an article for *Cashbox* that explained how a genre created by African American musicians became popular with White listeners:

> The southern bobbysoxers began to call the R&B records that moved them "cat" music. And what kind of music moves them? Well, it's the up-to-date blues with a beat, infectious catchphrases, and highly danceable rhythms. It has to have a kick; it has to move, and it has to have a message for the sharp youngsters who dig it.[95]

The article describes how New York music publisher Howie Richmond discovered R&B on a trip to the South, where he saw how "white high school and college kids were picking up on the rhythm and blues records—primarily to dance to."[96] Gleason read the article and realized that a new generation of White listeners had fallen in love with Black music just as his age group did in the 1930s. He increased his coverage of R&B in "Rhythm Section."

Gleason reviewed dozens of R&B records in the early 1950s. Annisteen Allen, Fats Domino, the Metrotones, Nappy Brown, Buddy Johnson, and Chris Powell all had discs reviewed in "Rhythm Section." Gleason wrote two major articles about R&B, beginning with "Sharp Youngsters Dig Rhythm, Blues Records," written in 1954. He recounted Wexler and Ertegun's story about White Southern teens dancing to "cat music." Gleason said teens who liked R&B were aware, open-minded listeners, not dumbed-down consumers as portrayed by anti-R&B critics.[97]

In 1956, Gleason wrote a second analysis of R&B titled "Rock 'N' Roll Took Because the Kids Had to Dance." At that time, "rhythm and blues" and "rock 'n' roll" were often used interchangeably. The article was about an R&B revue at the Oakland Paramount Theater that Gleason covered for the *Chronicle*. His narrative foreshadowed his later coverage of San Francisco ballroom shows in the 1960s in its observations of the dress and comportment of fans:

> It was apparent that this was no ordinary stage presentation. Bobby Soxers, teenagers, leather-jacketed motorcycle riders, and platoons of high school students stormed the box office to attend ... They recognized every tune, knew the words, and sometimes chanted them. At other times they swayed back and forth, clapping their hands in time to the music, and occasionally, in a burst of uncontrollable energy, leaped to their feet and danced in the aisles.[98]

Gleason felt the intense synergy between the performers and the integrated audience, similar to what he had experienced at the Harlem Apollo and Black clubs in the Bay Area. The "youngsters searched for something to dance to, and they found it in R&B."[99] He wrote that the genre existed "since the beginning of the phonograph record and possibly before" in the form of hot jazz and blues dance music.[100] Gleason knew R&B made his generation nervous, and he tried to counter it: "Every parent remembers the hysteria attendant on the swing era and the Benny Goodman band whose fans danced in the aisles of the New York Paramount much as today's fans dance to R&B." He said the "prophets of doom regarded [the swing youth culture] with as much dismay as today's critics of R&B." Pop songwriters since Cole Porter also used euphemisms for sex in their lyrics, he added. R&B songwriters were more direct.[101]

A Critic's Explanation of Rock 'n' Roll

On Christmas day, 1955, Gleason announced his new "Record of the Week":

> A railroad blues done somewhat in the manner of Leadbelly, and it's an effective number. He comes on like a hurricane.[102]

The "railroad blues" was "Mystery Train" by Elvis Presley, not yet a household name. This review started Gleason's sometimes knotty writings about the King of Rock 'n'

Roll. Initially, Gleason appreciated Presley and called him a "guitar-twanging, blues-shouting youngster who is a minor sensation currently. He is derivative but has strength, swing, and a certain raw courage."[103] He referred to Presley's debut album as "all blues and western folk songs."[104] When Presley's "Heartbreak Hotel" topped the *Billboard* charts for pop, country, and R&B, Gleason knew Presley was an artist to contend with. He devoted most of a *Chronicle* column to the rockabilly rebel:

> He plays the guitar with the strong, twanging, terrifically rhythmic approach of an old-fashioned blues artist. He sings in a more virile version of the Johnnie Ray style or in a sort of amplified rhythm and blues voice, similar to Leadbelly or Arthur Crudup.
>
> What this does to teenagers is rather frightening. They mob him.[105]

Gleason witnessed Elvis's effect on an audience at the Oakland Auditorium in June 1956. Before the show, Gleason goes backstage and interviews Presley, the picture of cool with slicked-back hair, striped jacket with a black velvet collar and black loafers. This is the Elvis of "Hound Dog" and "Jailhouse Rock," a charismatic mix of sincere hill-country shyness and 1950s teen rebellion. Presley paces the room full of pre-show energy, sticks his head through the stage curtain, and calls out to fans. When it's near time to go on stage, Presley calls a police guard to escort him to the men's room; Gleason finds this need for security shocking. Ready to go onstage, Presley replaces the striped jacket with a bright red one and steps into the deafening roar of adoring fans. Gleason watches the show, transfixed.

Crouched with the mike stand tipped at an angle, Presley launches into his first song. When Presley wiggles, girls scream, prompting him to wiggle more suggestively. The performance represents more than a revolution in singing style; it marks a new high in audience nirvana, a heightened experience in which artist and audience work themselves into a fever pitch akin to a Pentecostal tent revival. Presley aroused drives long suppressed in popular music, most notably sexual desire.

After the show ends, Gleason returns to Presley's dressing room and watches the police escort the singer to his car. A mob of fans breaks through the protection to grab their idol, and he kisses a few fans on the cheek. As Presley is driven away, fans scream in adulation.

Adulation isn't what Gleason felt. Now aged thirty-nine with two young daughters, Gleason was repelled by Presley's raw sex appeal to teen girls. Gleason expressed his disapproval in "Presley Leaves You in a Blue Suede Funk."[106] He wrote that Presley's performance, "grotesque as it may be, was deftly aimed at his fans whom he deliberately raised to an emotional pitch." Presley's "emotional power is frightening," Gleason said, and his "musical performance is as elemental as the gyrations of an 'exotic' dancer in the Tenderloin district."[107]

Gleason continued his tirade in *DownBeat*, where he referred to Presley as the "newest phenomenon in the strange, perverted taste of the American public."[108] Presley's erotic appeal aimed at teen girls was "sickening," and the rock star sold "sheer sex."[109] Gleason said, "I'm no prude, and I don't think rock and roll is a national menace," but

Presley "should not perform such provocative actions in public."[110] Gleason called out what he saw as Presley's unhealthy obsession with teen girls. This fixation has come to light in recent books such as Joel Williamson's *Elvis Presley: A Southern Life*. Elizabeth King wrote in *Vice* that "in addition to nabbing the title of 'the King of Rock and Roll,'" Presley was "just as much the king of exploiting teenagers for sex and treating women like shit."[111] The issues Gleason raised continue to roil rock discourse.

"Presley has a rival," Gleason wrote a few months later with a tone of hopefulness. The rival was then-rockabilly singer Johnny Cash. Gleason attended a Cash show and wrote, "unlike Presley, there are no bumps and grinds in his routine." And unlike Presley, Cash "composed the words and music to the first four tunes he recorded."[112] Cash carried Gleason's review in his pocket for years.

Gleason didn't let his dim view of Presley dampen his enthusiasm for rock 'n' roll. He wrote an animated 1955 profile of singer Bill Haley whose song "Rock Around the Clock" topped the charts after it appeared in the film *Blackboard Jungle*. Gleason sketched the rocker's colorful roots just as he had for early jazz musicians like Bunk Johnson. Haley began his career "on the carnival circuit, yodeling with a band, trouping with a medicine show playing all the open-air parks and fairs of the Middle West."[113] Gleason called Haley a "longtime student of the blues":

> What is Haley's Style? Well, it is strictly blues and strictly rhythm. A drummer bats the off-beat as hard as a pile driver, and an electric guitar twangs away while Haley and his Comets shout the lyrics. It may not be artistic, but it certainly produces hits.[114]

Few music writers of that time gave rock 'n' roll a fair hearing like this.[115] Gleason took the genre seriously and enlightened his readers in articles like "A Critic's Explanation of Rock 'n' Roll Music":

> "Rock 'n' roll" is a name for a particular kind of blueish dance music. It is a style of playing, not a dance, not a composition, and it is the direct descendant of the blues singers and artists of the '20s and '30s ... The vocalist, in general, seems to shout and weep a little more than ordinary, and the groups have a stylized out-of-tune sound to them ... But the real tipoff, aside from the out-of-tune singers, the piano hammering away in the top, and the heavy beat, is the tenor sax chorus ... When you hear a snorting, howling, honking, squalling tenor roaring away in the middle of a tune, the chances are that's rock 'n' roll, Virginia.[116]

Gleason extended his discourse about rock 'n' roll into broadcast media. In August 1956, he provided research on the roots of rock 'n' roll for a local television show broadcast on the newly launched KQED, one of the country's first public television stations. This was the start of Gleason's lifetime relationship with the station. His research for the show went into an article he wrote about the similarities between the moral panics over jazz in the 1930s and rock 'n' roll in the 1950s.[117]

Even as Gleason advocated rock 'n' roll—and produced some of the first rational discourse about its history and aesthetics—he remained overwhelmingly focused on jazz. For example, of Gleason's favorite albums released in 1956, 75 percent were by jazz artists. Yet he cared enough about rock 'n' roll artists to study their records and attend their shows. He resisted the temptation of other middle-aged journalists to ridicule the music or call it a social menace. Gleason gave a music critic's ultimate homage to a genre: educate readers about its history and analyze its aesthetic. In this sense, Gleason's rock 'n' roll writings foreshadowed his later rock criticism.

Gleason's first "Rhythm Section" columns show him smoothly transitioning from jazz to other genres. Among his greatest gifts to music journalism is how Gleason applied the passion and intellectual rigor of jazz criticism to other genres. Ten years had passed since Gleason moved to the West Coast. Ten eventful years in which he brought readers into the fast-changing landscapes of jazz and popular music. A decade of living in a city that drifted "anchorless upon the ocean," free of earthbound conventions. A city about to re-discover its bohemian past.

5

Winds of Change (1956–63)

One June night in 1956, Gleason sits in the smokey confines of the Cellar, a new jazz club in San Francisco's North Beach neighborhood. He and the audience of jazz lovers and poetry devotees groove to the improvisations of Milton "Brew" Moore. The saxophonist captivates Gleason with his simple, profoundly expressive playing, a contrast to the intellectualized virtuosity of bebop. "Freedom and movement. They're important," Moore tells Gleason.[1] This is an apt pair of words for the winds of change sweeping America and the world—and howling through new forms of music, literature, and even comedy.

A Coterie of Clever Bohemians

Another vital writer found inspiration in Brew Moore during his North Beach stint:

> First thing I'm gonna do is hit that ofay sweet saxophone Cellar. Where I'll immediately go for the Sunday Afternoon jam session. O they'll all be there, the girls with the dark glasses and blond hair, the brunettes in pretty coats … raising beers to their lips, sucking in cigarette smoke, beating to the beat of the beat of Brue Moore the perfect tenor saxophone—Old Brue he'll be high on Brew, and me too.[2]

In this passage from *Desolation Angels*, novelist Jack Kerouac expresses his rapture at a North Beach jam session led by Moore. Several years earlier, in 1954, the saxophonist drove his Buick from New York to San Francisco and decided to stay. By the following year, Kerouac frequented the city and contributed to the rising San Francisco Renaissance, a flowering of experimental poetry, art, and music. Moore and Kerouac joined the many cutting-edge novelists, poets, musicians, and comedians attracted to North Beach as it became the western counterpart to New York's Greenwich Village. These two neighborhoods became the poles of a new subculture, writes author Stephen Duncan:

> Despite the affluence that defined much of the post-war era, the specters of atomic apocalypse, the Cold War, racial oppression, the triumph of corporate liberalism,

and concomitant conformity led some Americans to wonder whether the promise of plenty was worth less than the sum of its parts. This discontent spawned a national community of bohemians and cultural dissidents in the two decades following World War Two.

> [They gathered in] night spots as social and cultural institutions, nocturnal nodal points that connected social networks into a national circuit … What the radical poet Ken Saunders has called, collectively, the Rebel Café.[3]

Jazz musicians like Moore played a key role in this emerging circuit. Gleason continued to follow Moore's music and wrote the liner notes for his 1956 Fantasy album, *The Brew Moore Quartet and Quintet*. "Brew has two absolutely golden gifts," he wrote. "He swings like mad, and he has soul. These are things you cannot learn by woodshedding, or in any conservatory. You have to be born with them or learn them by living."[4] Listening to Moore at the Cellar, Gleason experienced the emerging "Rebel Café" culture.

This culture infused the history of San Francisco. In 1865 a *Chronicle* writer wrote:

> There is a coterie of clever Bohemians around town writing for the weekly literary papers who are bent on smashing up all the old creeds and bringing in the "religion of the future." These young men of gigantic intellect think that Christianity is played out … They consider Milton, Newton, Bacon, and the other old fogies who swallowed such nonsense as imbeciles.[5]

Mark Twain was among these "clever Bohemians." Twain worked as a journalist when he moved to San Francisco in 1864 and fell in with writer Bret Harte and other self-identified literary bohemians. The group produced a distinctly American style of writing that was more conversational than its European antecedents. San Francisco poet George Sterling described the lifestyle of these writers:

> There are two elements, at least, that are essential to Bohemianism. The first is devotion or addiction to one or more of the Seven Arts; the other is poverty. Other factors suggest themselves: for instance, I like to think of my Bohemians as young, as radical in their outlook on art and life, as unconventional, and, though this is debatable, as dwellers in a city large enough to have the somewhat cruel atmosphere of all great cities.[6]

Gold Rush-era short story author Bret Harte wrote that San Francisco embodied the rebel lifestyle:

> Bohemia has never been located geographically, but any clear day when the sun is going down, if you mount Telegraph Hill, you shall see its pleasant valleys and cloud-capped hills glittering in the West …[7]

Seventy years after Harte wrote these words, the Telegraph Hill neighborhood and adjacent North Beach had become home to a community of poets who joined other "radical moderns" around the country who rewrote the rules of poetic expression and performed poetic experiments in which "nouns are made to serve as verbs, colors are used to describe sounds, words run together."[8] These North Beach poets came together through the Federal Works Progress Administration (WPA) and the Federal Writers' Project (FWP), which gave work to Bay Area writers during the Depression.

One of these writers shaped the direction of American poetry in the postwar era. Thirty-year-old Kenneth Rexroth moved to San Francisco from Chicago, where he had read poetry in clubs while jazz musicians performed. Rexroth continued to do so in San Francisco and became "the focal point for practically every poet who came to the Bay Area," according to historian Michael Davidson. Starting in the early 1950s, Rexroth hosted Friday night open-house poetry readings at his home that included not only poets but "political activists of various sorts … anarchists, longshoremen, and radical journalists."[9] One of the regulars was Lawrence Ferlinghetti, a provocative but unassuming young poet whose suit, tie, and receding hairline belied an unfettered imagination.

In early 1957, Ferlinghetti joined Rexroth in a daring experiment. "There was a jazz and poetry night last week at the Cellar," wrote Gleason, who took an interest in the sessions.[10] To the accompaniment of the Cellar Quartet, Rexroth and Ferlinghetti read imagistic poems that laid bare the realities of postwar America. The poets continued their experiments into the spring, and Gleason covered the performances. "To adopt poetry to jazz (or vice versa) is no easy task," he wrote, but the Cellar artists "have been working at it with some success."[11] Gleason's friends at Fantasy Records were also impressed and decided to record a Cellar performance. Gleason attended the session.

Gathered around café tables that night is a mix of regulars and newcomers unsure what to expect. Rexroth walks onstage, his suspenders and slight potbelly remind Gleason of a country doctor. Then a single note from a trumpet cuts through the din, followed by a muted military drum cadence. The crowd grows quiet as Rexroth intones, "They are murdering all the young men. For half a century now, every day, they have hunted them down and killed them."[12] Rexroth recites his indictment of war with the dispassion of a television news announcer. An ominous bass riff wells up amidst handfuls of discordant piano notes as he speaks. Rexroth's voice and the instruments convey a darkly beautiful sense of dread.

Ferlinghetti's turn to recite. Tall and bearded, the first-generation Italian American from Yonkers reads his poem "Autobiography." He spins vivid images of nightmarish places like the "Dante Billiard Parlor," and memorable characters such as the "Laughing Woman at Loona Park." Ferlinghetti tells a fantastical tale of an "American boy" who had seen "Egyptian pilots in purple clouds" and ate "potato salad and dandelions at anarchist picnics."[13] His surrealism continues, "I have heard Kid Ory cry. I have heard a trombone preach. I have heard Debussy strained thru a sheet." Words and saxophone alternate in call and response. Engineers from Fantasy Records capture it all on audiotape as Gleason takes notes.

The poems continue, and then Ferlinghetti concludes:

> I must arise and go now
> to the Isle of Manisfree
> way up behind the broken words
> and woods of Arcady.[14]

The performance concludes with a single trumpet note hanging in the air.

Fantasy released *Poetry Readings in the Cellar* in August 1957 with liner notes by Gleason:

> The experiment was an attempt to meld the twin forms of modern expression—jazz and poetry.
>
> The Cellar jazz-and-poetry sessions are a natural result of the continued cultural turbulence in San Francisco since the end of World War II and exemplified by the poetry of Allen Ginsberg ... the novels of Jack Kerouac ... the rise of numerous modern jazz groups, and the migration to San Francisco of creatively active people from all over the United States.[15]

Gleason jumped into this "cultural turbulence" and became its narrator, promotor, documentarian, and critic. But as he championed jazz poetry's values, Gleason criticized its flaws, such as the contradictory aims of poets and the jazz musicians with whom Gleason naturally sided with. In the avant-garde magazine *Evergreen Review*, Gleason said the jazz poetry experiments were "far from aesthetically satisfactory to the [jazz] performers involved."[16] In *DownBeat*, he wrote how jazz poetry had become a "sort of freak attraction in San Francisco." "Not until a poet comes along who learns what jazz is all about and then writes poetry will there be any merger. What we have now is a freak, like a two-headed calf. That's all."[17]

Although skeptical of jazz poetry, Gleason praised Jack Kerouac's novel *On the Road*, a crucial work of the Beat Generation. The semi-autobiographical book recounts road trips and searches for kicks by protagonist Sal Paradise and his friend Dean Moriarty. The novel divided America's literary critics. Many were dismissive. Thomas Sherman of the *St. Louis Post-Dispatch* wrote that Kerouac's writing "is full of provocative sound and fury but with as much philosophical meaning as a Sears Roebuck catalog."[18] The *Atlantic*'s reviewer called *On the Road* "most readable," but "it disappoints because it constantly promises a revelation or a conclusion of real importance and general applicability and cannot deliver any such conclusion because Dean is more convincing as an eccentric than as a representative of any segment of humanity."[19] The most lacerating assessment came from Robert R. Kirsch in the *Los Angeles Times*, who concluded, "Mr. Kerouac calls this 'The Beat Generation,' but a much more accurate description would be 'The Deadbeat Generation.' I don't know whether such people really exist, but if they do, he has thoroughly failed to make them believable."[20]

Yet, in the Beat Generation's twin cities of New York and San Francisco, critics applauded *On the Road* as a groundbreaking novel illuminating a rising youth subculture. In the *New York Times*, Gilbert Millstein lauded the book as an "authentic work of art." Millstein proclaimed it as the "most beautifully executed, the clearest and the most important utterance yet made" by the Beat Generation.[21]

Gleason was equally captivated by *On the Road*. A few days before the *Times* review, Gleason and Kenneth Rexroth published side-by-side reviews of the book in the *Chronicle*'s book section. The reviews offered contrasting interpretations of Kerouac's characters, members of the Silent Generation who came after Gleason's Greatest Generation. Rexroth saw them as "hypertrophied" versions of "the most conformist members of the middle class they despise."[22] Gleason, though, identified with the emergent Silent Generation:

> They swing. And this means to affirm. Kerouac leaves you with no feeling of despair but rather of exaltation. This is really the quality we get from jazz, even from the lowest of lowdown blues. Ellington's lyric, "The saddest tale on land or sea is the tale they told when they told the truth on me," has exaltation in it. And *On the Road* certainly does.[23]

Gleason called *On the Road* a jazz novel "in that it reflects, immediately and vividly, to those who have been stricken with the jazz virus, a knowledge of their own struggle to get straight," to build an authentic identity despite living in a world of conformity.[24]

> Faced with a society which he considers has rejected him (and the fact that he believes this makes it real if not a fact), the young intellectual has come to identify himself in a great degree with jazz music because this is also the position of the jazz artist ... Put him down anywhere and the jazz fan finds himself at home as soon as he has discovered the nearest brother-jazz fan.
>
> Kerouac writes from this point of view. His book assumes a knowledge of the language and litany of jazz.[25]

This piece had a limited readership because Gleason had yet to become a nationally known figure. But the editors of *Saturday Review* liked the article and reprinted it with the title "Kerouac's 'Beat Generation'" in their January 1958 issue.[26] The *Chronicle* column marked Gleason's turn from reviewing only music to covering other popular arts. These arts included stand-up comedy, and Gleason began to champion a satirist unafraid to poke fun at popes, presidents, and pompous hypocrites of all types.

Lenny

In addition to jazz musicians and Beat poets, North Beach nightclubs nurtured the early careers of Mort Sahl and other stand-up comics who skewered social hypocrisy.

Gleason took an interest, and picked Sahl's *The Future Lies Ahead* as "Album of the Week" in a spring 1958 *Chronicle* column.[27] In the same column, Gleason introduced another stand-up comic: "Musicians who have heard Lenny Bruce have been talking about him for the past year as another wild wit somewhat akin to Mort Sahl."[28] Bruce had just opened at Ann's 440, a North Beach lesbian bar whose new owner upped the focus on entertainers. Gleason learned about Bruce in 1957 from saxophonist Paul Desmond and discovered that the comic was popular with jazz musicians. Intrigued, Gleason took Sol Weiss and Saul Zaentz of Fantasy Records to see Bruce perform in Los Angeles. Unfortunately, Bruce didn't appear because he'd been fired for removing his clothes on stage during the previous show.

That might have ended Gleason's interest in Bruce if not for recording engineer Wally Heide, who gave him a tape of a Bruce performance. The tape included Bruce's monologue "Religions, Inc." where religious leaders gather at a business convention to view merchandise like a "gen-u-ine Jewish star and a lucky cross-cigarette lighter combined." The bit included an enactment of a collect phone call to Pope "Johnnie" by a Pentecostal preacher who opposed school integration and assured the Pope: "We had to give them the bus, but there are two toilets," a reference to forced busing and segregated restrooms.

Gleason loved the bit and sent the tape to New York jazz writer Ira Gitler who played it for journalists such as Dorothy Kilgallen, who failed to show an interest in writing about Bruce.[29] Gleason resolved to bring Bruce to a broader audience, and so, when the satirist performed at Ann's 440 in the spring of 1958, Gleason covered the show for the *Chronicle*. After Bruce performed, Gleason introduced himself and discovered that the young comedian loved jazz and deeply knew the music. The two became fast friends.

Gleason wrote a review of the show and noted how jazz musicians and the new satirists went after sacred cows:

> Fundamentally, this is an attitude of irreverence ... It is evidenced today by the jazz musicians' admiration of the nightclub social commentary of Mort Saul and Lenny Bruce.
>
> The jazz musician is a rebel. But he is a rebel with humor, something that is too often forgotten. There is no more wildly effective putdown of the political speeches, the incongruity of everyday life, and the fatuous posing of the tent show religious carnivals than that which goes on in the conversation of the jazz musician.
>
> For the jazz fan, there is the same urgency in Bruce's monologue as exists in a Charlie Parker chorus.[30]

With this, Gleason began his lifelong practice of drawing comparisons between musicians and artists in other fields. This allowed him to frame individual creative works as part of broader social, cultural, and political movements.

The New York-based Bruce became a de facto member of the North Beach scene because he performed there regularly. The comic joined a cast of characters, rebellious musicians and writers, who became regulars in Gleason's *Chronicle* columns. One of these characters was a figment of Gleason's comic imagination, "Boris the Beatnik." Gleason derived the personality from another fictitious figure, "Shorty Petterstein," created by San Francisco humorist and avant-garde musician Henry Jacobs. In one tale, Gleason satirized the actual outlawing of the book *Howl* by Allen Ginsberg on charges of obscenity. In Gleason's telling, Shorty shows up on Gleason's doorstep with a bundle of hot contraband, a brown-paper-wrapped copy of *Howl*. Starting in 1960, Gleason used the same hipster personage under a new name, Boris, who was "once a tenor saxophone player, but his beard grew so long (and letting it grow is de rigueur) it hampered his embouchure."[31]

Gleason voiced his own opinions through Boris. For example, when the clean-cut John F. Kennedy ran for president in 1960, Boris said, "It's the Kingston Trio we're nominating. This is the high point of the Organization Man. Interchangeable parts. And they don't swing."[32] Boris said the election was bought and paid for, and "if there was a chance for a third party, I'd be for it."[33] As for the Democratic convention, the "ghost of Roosevelt hung over that place like Bird's music hangs over modern jazz."[34]

In the Boris columns, Gleason used humor to deliver social messages. But Gleason began to be more direct in his social commentary. For instance, he wrote a passionate *DownBeat* column about the link between "the music of Charlie Parker and Miles Davis, the poetry of Dylan Thomas and Allen Ginsberg, and the comedy of Lenny Bruce. All part of a growing body of dissent from the status quo that is gradually effecting a fundamental change in many attitudes."[35] He continued, "Once struck by jazz music, you are never the same. Once hit by the impact of the poets or touched to wild laughter by Bruce, things are never the same either."[36]

A Jazz Fan's Paradise

Though he took side trips into literature and comedy, Gleason remained focused on his first love, jazz. From 1957 to 1959, he undertook several ambitious projects to create a broader public awareness of jazz and its musicians.

The first was *Jam Session*, a jazz anthology published in 1958 by G. P. Putnam's Sons. Gleason stated his intent in the introduction:

> Gathering the material for this book has been, in the musicians' terminology, a ball! Back through the years, I've tried to read or look at everything that appeared in print about jazz ... This is not a collection of pieces about *every* jazz artist and jazz style. It cannot be. If I help make jazz more interesting to the uninitiated and if I offer something new to the initiated, I will have succeeded.[37]

Jazz anthologies were relatively new. Others included *Frontiers of Jazz* (1947), by Gleason's Columbia classmate Ralph de Toledano, and *Treasury of Jazz* (1956) by Eddie Condon and Richard Gehman. Such collections reflect the anthologist's tastes, agenda, and awareness of their field's literature. What an editor excludes is as telling as what they include. Gleason's exclusions were critics he'd crossed swords with over the years such as Leonard Feather, George Avakian, and Barry Ulanov. Among those included were Otis Ferguson of the *New Republic*, Irving Kolodin of the *Saturday Review*, and music writer Gilbert S. McKean, co-founder of the US branch of Decca Records and father of actor Michael McKean. In addition to their contributions, eight articles were by Gleason: five reprints, and three new essays including "Toward a New Form: Jazz and Poetry." He wrote that the hybrid art could bring American literature "closer to its audience and farther from the formalized atmosphere of the classroom and the lecture hall."[38]

Gleason also wrote introductions to the articles that illuminate his viewpoints at the time. For instance, in his preamble to an essay by blues singer Lead Belly, Gleason said jazz "never really got away from the blues" and "if it lacks the blues feeling, it ... fails to be authentic jazz."[39] The link between jazz and Beat literature showed up in several articles. For example, Gleason included Anatole Broyard's "Portrait of a Hipster" in the anthology to explain the relationship between Kerouac and jazz. Gleason said Broyard's article provided insight into the psychological and social drives of the Black musicians who pioneered modern jazz. He quoted Broyard that these musicians were "always of the minority—opposed in race or feeling to those who owned the machinery of recognition," a trait shared with Beat writers.[40]

Released in early 1958, *Jam Session* received generally positive reviews. "Some of the finest writing on jazz that has appeared in the past two decades," stated a reviewer for the *Raleigh News and Observer*.[41] In the *New York Times Book Review*, Arnold Shaw said he liked *Jam Session*'s pieces on early jazz musicians but noted the absence of articles about Duke Ellington, Louis Armstrong, and Charlie Parker. The reviewer for the *London Observer* called *Jam Session* the "most entertaining book about jazz" since *Hear Me Talkin' to Ya: The Story of Jazz by the Men Who Made It* edited by Nat Shapiro and Nat Hentoff.[42]

As reviews for *Jam Session* came in, Gleason celebrated another career milestone. In the summer of 1958, the *Chronicle* syndicated "Rhythm Section" in six newspapers, including the *Boston Globe*. By the end of the year, syndication grew to over fifteen papers, including the *Los Angeles Mirror News*, the *Philadelphia Inquirer*, and the *Des Moines Register*. American jazz fans from the Eastern Seaboard to the Great Plains and beyond read Gleason with their morning coffee.

With his reputation growing, Gleason embarked on his next project, a journal called *Jazz: A Quarterly of American Music*. In his first editorial, Gleason wrote:

> Our aim is to provide as broad as possible coverage of jazz music. We will examine all types and styles of jazz and hope to extend this discussion to areas other than musicological ... We deem it our duty to seek out and print new, provocative, and refreshing viewpoints.[43]

The magazine was digest-sized, 6" × 8" like its predecessor, the second iteration of *Jazz Information*. But in form and content, the journal was a significant step up with glossy pages and a bright red cover with professional typography. Devoted to "American music," the journal reminded readers that jazz was a homegrown cultural

Figure 5.1 *Jazz: A Quarterly of American Music*, summer, 1959, founded by Gleason. On the cover: jazz saxophonist Julian "Cannonball" Adderley. Courtesy of the Estate of Ralph J. Gleason.

form. Contributors to the inaugural issue include notable writers George Frazier, Studs Terkel, and Philip Elwood, who later became a music critic for the *San Francisco Examiner*. Another contributor was Louis Gottlieb, comedian and bassist for the Bay Area folk trio The Limeliters. Gleason published *Jazz: A Quarterly of American Music* from the fall of 1958 to the winter of 1960. Although it only lasted for five issues, it contributed to a new wave of critical discourse about jazz that rose in the late-1950s. The journal preceded *The Jazz Review*, launched a month later in New York by Nat Hentoff, Martin Williams, and Hsio Wen Shih. Hentoff, Gleason's junior by eight years, was part of a generation of young critics such as Ira Gitler who shaped jazz journalism in the 1950s. A pioneering jazz radio broadcaster, Hentoff was the New York editor of *DownBeat* from 1953 to 1956, a columnist at the *Village Voice* from 1958 to 2009, and like Gleason, on the way to international renown in 1958. Hentoff became close friends with Gleason, and said readers could rely on Gleason to give them a full and pure account of what they were hearing or seeing. "Recalled Hentoff, "He enjoyed what he was doing. He found his true life's work. He energized you just by reading his work. He was curious, and a good judge of what he was listening to or watching. I first heard about Lenny Bruce by reading Ralph, who became a close friend of mine … Lenny changed the scope of comedy, and Ralph had the ear to understand Lenny's voice."[44] Asked if he ever felt he competed with Gleason, Hentoff said, "We were never in competition. I learned from him and hope he learned a little from me."[45]

One thing Hentoff and Gleason had in common was their belief in jazz festivals as sites of racial rapprochement. Yet the leading American event, the Newport Jazz Festival, experienced friction between its multi-racial audiences and local residents. Hentoff, a civil rights activist, accused Newport of racism. And so, when Gleason joined a team planning a California jazz festival, his dream was to create an event that fostered harmony between the festival and its surrounding community.

The West Coast lacked a jazz festival. For a decade, Gleason and Jimmy Lyons fantasized about starting a California jazz fest. Their fantasy materialized in the fall of 1958. After bringing in Dave Brubeck to sell the Monterey City Council on the idea, Lyons and Gleason formed a non-profit corporation with Lyons serving as the festival's general manager and Gleason on its board of directors and advisory committee.[46] Gleason began a blitz of *Chronicle* columns promoting the event with titles such as "Monterey Will Be a Jazz Fan's Paradise"[47] and "Jazz Fans Flocking to Monterey Festival."[48] Although he wholeheartedly supported the festival, Gleason never accepted payment for his involvement so he could write about the performances independently.

When the festival premiered on October 3, 1958, Gleason and his family watched from their special box in the bleachers. The City Council authorized a crowd of 5,000, and that many showed up, from hipsters to socialites to everyday jazz fans. Master of ceremonies Dizzy Gillespie opened with "The Star-Spangled Banner." Well-known musicians such as Louis Armstrong and lesser known such as Pete Daily and the Abalone Stompers captivated the audience. In between shows were forums, including one by Gleason, "Jazz: An International Language," a roundtable with Dizzy Gillespie, Louis Armstrong, Dave Brubeck, and Gleason's wartime London friend, Albert McCarthy.[49]

On the final day, drummer Max Roach and the Symphony Percussion Section performed "Monterey Concerto for Percussion," a piece composed for the festival that left Gleason spellbound.[50] Billie Holiday managed to sing on the final night, despite suffering from undiagnosed cirrhosis that weakened her powers and eventually killed her. Although still a successful recording artist, Holiday spiraled downward, reflected in her diminished singing capacity.

Gleason witnesses Holiday's failing health the next day at Monterey's San Carlos Hotel. The legendary singer sits stiffly on the periphery of the lobby. A group of jazz musicians walk past, paying her no mind. In their eyes, Holiday is washed up. In a ravaged whisper, she calls out, "Where you boys goin'?" As they stared blankly at Holiday's ghostly countenance, she added, "They got me openin' in Vegas tonight."[51] Holiday died less than a year later, but her music uplifted Gleason for the rest of his days.

Notwithstanding this sad afternote, the festival was a success. Gleason took his family each year, and it became an important outing. Bridget Gleason recalled a memorable performance by Jon Hendricks, an originator of vocalese, a jazz style in which the voice imitates the instrumental components of the song. Hendricks performed "The

Evolution of the Blues," a song cycle that traced the development of blues music from African songs to spirituals to jump jazz. Surrounded on stage by children, including Gleason's two daughters, Hendricks sang, "Once upon a time, music was born in the heavens on high ..." As Hendricks incanted his song-stories, fellow musicians and the audience fell under his spell. Bridget became a lifelong fan of Hendricks and his vocal trio Lambert, Hendricks, and Ross.[52]

A year after he co-founded the Monterey Jazz Festival, Gleason launched *Jazz Casual*, a television series he produced for KQED, San Francisco's public television station. There had been short-lived jazz series, such as *The Stars of Jazz* (1956–8), and documentaries, such as *The Sound of Jazz* (1957) by Hentoff and Whitney Balliett. But *Jazz Casual* ran for thirty-one episodes from 1960 to 1968, into the rock era. The first episode to carry the name *Jazz Casual* aired in September 1959 and featured Black vocalist Ernestine Anderson and the band Mastersounds.[53] This program and Gleason's columns about Anderson brought her to the attention of *Time* magazine's San Francisco bureau chief and resulted in an article that boosted Anderson's career.[54]

Gleason produced a second episode of *Jazz Casual* in July 1960, which he considered the actual pilot of the series. The filming gets off to a rocky start. With ten minutes until cameras roll, guests Duke Ellington and Billy Strayhorn haven't arrived, leaving Gleason in a sweat. With five minutes to go, Ellington walks in without Strayhorn, who was scheduled to discuss jazz with Ellington on air. Gleason stutters, "Duke, the, er, format." Ellington raises his eyebrows in mock dismay and replies, "Format? Anybody can do it with a format, sweetie. The trick is to do it without one.'" From that point on, Gleason produced the show with "no format, no script, ad-lib all the way ... the musical director for each show is the leader of the jazz group involved. He plays what he wants and sets up his musicians so they are comfortable playing."[55]

The next *Jazz Casual* aired in January 1961 and featured Gleason's friend Dizzy Gillespie. The show opens with the trumpeter's quintet performing "Norm's Norm." Bassist Bob Cunningham sets a fast-swinging tempo. Saxophonist Leo Wright plays the first solo, followed by Gillespie, pianist Lalo Schifrin and back to Cunningham, whose calm demeanor belies an inner intensity. The camera cuts to Gleason, leaning back in a canvas director's chair, his hair in a crew cut, and dressed in his trademark tweed jacket and black-frame glasses favored by jazz musicians. After introducing the band, Gillespie joins Gleason, who flashes an engaging smile then laughs, clearly delighted to settle into a warm conversation with his old friend Dizzy. They discuss the blues roots of jazz, and Gillespie reminds viewers that blues is more than a twelve-bar song structure; it is a feeling rooted in experience. Gleason asks Gillespie how soloing had changed from swing to modern jazz and Gillespie explains that most modern soloists play piano, increasing their awareness of their solos' harmonic aspects. As the two men converse, a long shot shows Gleason semi-slouched in his chair, legs crossed at the knee with his socks showing. Casual.

One after another, Gleason turned out episodes that featured many of the top jazz artists of the day, such as the Dave Brubeck Quartet, Carmen McRae, and the Cannonball Adderley Quintet. In the spring of 1962, National Educational Television syndicated *Jazz Casual*, beginning with an episode featuring hard bop sax player Sonny Rollins.

The episode helped Rollins' career, along with a review by Gleason syndicated in the *New York Post*. Rollins recalls, "It was a very good article for me because jazz musicians had a tough time getting recognition, promotion, and recordings. *Jazz Casual* was a groundbreaking show that treated musicians with great dignity."[56] The series ran until 1968 on sixty stations nationwide, including New York City, Boston, and Chicago.[57]

Jazz Casual reveals why Gleason was among the best interviewers in jazz history. His open demeanor and genuine enthusiasm put guests at ease. They felt like they were chatting in his Ashby Avenue living room rather than in a television studio. Gleason's spontaneous verbal prompts, facial expressions, and emotional responses kept the conversation flowing. Leaning on a piano or reclining in his director's chair, Gleason focused keenly on the musician's reactions to his questions. The camera caught poignant moments, such as the tender reaction from Sonny Rollins when Gleason told him how much young players looked up to him.

As immersed as Gleason was in jazz during this time, one might think he wouldn't have much to say about teen music. But having been an adolescent jazz enthusiast led Gleason to empathize with the rock 'n' roll generation. And he knew how to calm moral panics over rebellious music.

Figure 5.2 Ralph Gleason on the set of *Jazz Casual*, a jazz television show he produced and hosted that aired on KQED, a public television station serving the San Francisco Bay Area, 1960. Courtesy of the Estate of Ralph J. Gleason.

A Natural Thing that Feeds the Audience's Desires

"Rock 'n' Roll Show Turned Into Bedlam."[58] The *Chronicle* article by an uncredited writer described a rock 'n' roll concert at New York's Paramount Theater where teens "smashed glass, danced barefoot in the aisles, and their screams drowned out the heavy beat of the music ... Groups of boys roamed the theater like wolf packs, picking up girls. Necking was open and unrestrained."[59]

Such Sodom and Gomorrah imagery echoed the anti-jazz rhetoric Gleason heard in the 1930s. The year before the Paramount riot, a disturbance erupted at a Fats Domino concert in North Carolina that resulted in police tear-gassing the audience. Domino blamed the melee on tensions over racial intermixing at the show. Gleason wrote:

> The Domino band was officially exonerated of all blame, but the syndrome had been set in motion, and for the rest of that year, whenever he went across the country, everybody wanted to riot because they thought they were supposed to, and all the square reporters were looking for exactly this to happen.[60]

Gleason understood the underlying racism of these expectations:

> There is a concentrated effort on the part of municipal officials ... to freeze out rock and roll shows, especially those featuring Negro artists ... The official reason behind this has been, of course, the widely publicized images of riots at rock 'n' roll and rhythm and blues affairs in recent years. Underlying this, too, is the corollary image of the riot potential of a Negro crowd as opposed to a white one.[61]

But for Gleason, rock 'n' roll was the vernacular music of the new generation. He said there were "two underground cultures in our society today that are particularly interesting, the Negro and the teenager."[62] He called Chubby Checker's "Pony Time" "one of the natural folk songs of high school America."[63]

> In a way—and this is something the folklore fanatics seem determined to avoid at all costs—the hit disc lyrics that are entering into the common speech of the new generation are contemporary folk songs, and the creators of these songs are characters in the folk mythology of our times ... What do Elvis Presley, Chubby Checker, Bobby Darin, Connie Frances, the Shirelles, and the rest of the hit makers offer their teenage audience? Believe me, their success is not manufactured ... Whatever it is that starts their success is a natural thing that feeds the audience's desires and cannot be predicted."[64]

Gleason remained steadfast in his support for rock 'n' roll even as it generated controversy in the late 1950s and lost many of its leading lights. Presley enlisted in the U.S. Army, Little Richard became a minister, Chuck Berry spent time in prison, and Jerry Lee Lewis's career cooled off after he married his thirteen-year-old cousin. The violent deaths of Buddy Holly, Ritchie Valens, and Eddie Cochran seemed to mark the death of rock 'n' roll. On top of this came a scandal over payola, the illegal music industry practice of paying commercial radio stations to play records without disclosing the payment. In 1958, the US House Oversight Committee publicly investigated hundreds of cases where disc jockeys accepted payola. These revelations fed the public view that rock 'n' roll's success had been bought and paid for. Thus, by 1959 rock 'n' roll signified death, racial anxiety, and corruption.

In response, the music industry manufactured a new generation of squeaky-clean artists. While the fan press plastered photos of heartthrobs like Bobby Rydell across the insides and outsides of teen magazines, Gleason saw the makeover as an attempt to erase the influence of Black music on rock 'n' roll. Case in point, Pat Boone:

The reason I do not like young Mr. Boone is that I find him pretentious and even a bit of a phony ...

He has a consistent record of picking up the songs of other artists, such as Ivory Joe Hunter, and redoing them in a paler and more popular version ... His voice, as his personality, never gets very definite. It's always a 'safe' sound. I think of Pat Boone as an Organization Man type of singer. Nice, clean-cut, even antiseptic, and also spiritless and pallid ...

You have to have a bit of life in you to sing songs of the blues types.[65]

Gleason continued this critique into the 1960s. For example, he savaged the 1963 Grammy television show, charging racial bias. "It was a bland panel and utterly false picture of the record business," he said and added that the judges should be ashamed of themselves. Gleason asked, "Where were Bobby Blue Bland, Freddie Scott, Johnny Mathis, Jackie Wilson?"[66]

But one of Gleason's favorite musicians did win a Grammy that night. Ray Charles won the Best Rhythm & Blues Recording award for "I Can't Stop Loving You." The song was a track from Charles' genre-bending album *Modern Sounds in Country and Western Music*. Gleason applauded the album's covers of country songs, transformed by Ray's "great emotional authenticity."[67] Gleason especially fancied how Charles performed "You Are My Sunshine" like it was "sung (and swung) on a Sunday night radio broadcast from a gospel choir."[68]

Gleason had covered Charles since 1957 when he praised the pianist's album of jazz instrumentals, *The Great Ray Charles*:

It is a thrilling album. Charles has the blues feeling so naturally that everything he does contains it ... The point about this album is that there is a thin line between the true folk blues and the raucous commercial product we usually hear. The folk blues are right there in Ray Charles and in Fats Domino, too ... With Charles, the blues again become uncluttered lyric emotion with dignity and relevancy.[69]

Gleason reviewed a concert by Charles at the Fillmore Auditorium, a Black venue, in 1959. He described the pianist's struggles:

> Ray Charles is a musician and a player of considerable talents. The value of none of these things is weakened by the fact that he is also blind, a Negro, and an admitted narcotics addict, any more than the qualities of writers from Edgar Allan Poe and Baudelaire through Aldous Huxley and W. Somerset Maugham have been debilitated by experiments with drugs.[70]

Charles helped usher in a new genre which came to be called "soul music." Gleason was a fan and especially liked singer Sam Cooke, who crossed from gospel to soul music in the late 1950s. Gleason named Cooke's debut LP "Album of the Week" in 1958. "This is a superior rock 'n' roll singer," Gleason wrote.[71] In his review of *Nightbeat*, Gleason said Cooke had a "fine sense of phrasing and a deep feeling for the blues."[72]

Cooke, Charles, Checker, and other Black musicians kept youth-oriented music vital when the music industry tried to homogenize it. Gleason supported these musicians and called out the underlying racism behind attacks on their music. When the teen-music industry entered a cycle of safe alternatives to the earlier rock 'n' roll hell-raisers, Gleason saw through this too, especially the watered-down appropriation of Black rock by White singers such as Pat Boone. And why should he listen to schlock 'n' roll when he could be deep in conversation with a revolutionary saxophonist?

See What I Can Hear

It's May 1961, and John Coltrane settles into the plush leather chair in Gleason's living room. As a tape recorder runs, the two talk about music—King Kolax's big band, flamenco, and the different capabilities of tenor and soprano saxophones. Gleason asks, "How do you work out a tune when you're composing?" Coltrane answers, "Well, I've been going to the piano and working these things out. Now I think I'm going to move away from that … I think I'm just going to write for the horn from now on, just play around on the horn and see what I can hear."[73] A few weeks later, Coltrane recorded a new composition called "Ole" that manifested the ideas he discussed with Gleason. Breaking with jazz tradition, "Ole" is an instrumental that utilizes a repeating modal motif rather than a set of chord changes. "Ole" led off Coltrane's final disc for Atlantic, *Ole Coltrane*. Gleason wrote the liner notes, which included parts of his interview with Coltrane.

These home-taping sessions became an essential part of Gleason's research during a critical point in the development of jazz.[74] Although some content from the interviews went into various texts by Gleason, the recorded exchanges were unrelated to specific writing assignments. The conversations were an oral-history project Gleason conducted to preserve the legacy of jazz. Toby Gleason explained his father's intent:

> From 1959 to 1969, my father decided to tape-record interviews with musicians he knew who made their way to San Francisco on tour. He intended the talks to

provide invaluable background information for his work as a journalist, and tape recording the conversations would make this background easily available.[75]

Hentoff admired Gleason's interviewing skills:

> Ralph did some extraordinary interviews. He never put himself in the role of the interrogator. He didn't have a "gotcha!" interview style. He made a point of learning all he could about the people he interviewed. He got to the foundation of what he was interested in. A critic has to be a good listener, a deep listener, and Ralph certainly was. His questions would get [his subjects] to start thinking about themselves in ways they might not ever have done. He enlarged the person he was interviewing.[76]

Gleason's gift for bringing his subjects to a new level of self-awareness is seen in his November 1960 conversation with Les McCann. The pianist played soul jazz, a hard bop variant that reflected Black musicians' desire to draw on the traditions of African American blues, gospel, work songs, and rhythm and blues. An early example of soul jazz was "The Preacher," a gospel-infused piece composed and recorded by pianist Horace Silver in 1955. By 1960, jazz record labels used the term "soul jazz" as a marketing tool, which caused some critics to be skeptical of the genre. This distrust erupted into an uproar in the mid-1960s when McCann released his first album, *Les McCann Ltd. Plays the Truth*. Leading the charge with a one-star review in *DownBeat* was critic Ira Gitler who said, "McCann is working out of a cocktail bag," with his "phony funk."[77] McCann responded by adding a new piece to his repertoire, "Ira Gitler's Homogenized Funk."

The following week in his *Chronicle* column, Gleason joined the fray and mocked soul jazz as a marketing ploy by record companies. Not that Gleason wasn't a fan of Black gospel music, he listened to it regularly on the radio. And he praised soul jazz pianist Bobby Timmons of the Cannonball Adderley Quintet. Gleason wrote that Timmons "has roots in both the blues and gospel music, and the spirit that pervades both comes through in all he does."[78]

But Gleason initially failed to hear this spirit in McCann's piano playing, which he called "monotonous" in a 1960 column.[79] *Downbeat* published another critique of McCann that contained an ominous undercurrent of racial paranoia. Critic John Tynan identified a relationship between soul jazz and the Nation of Islam. He said Black Nationalism gave rise to a "'soul brother' mentality ... a basically undemocratic and backward attitude."[80] Tynan painted a hellish picture of soul jazz as a wave "about to engulf us, and jazz listeners are plunging into its boiling core."[81] Tynan interviewed McCann for the article and asked aggressive questions like "Are you helping to prostitute church music?" McCann's answer: "I've been around gospel music all my life, and I'm very proud of it."[82]

When Gleason interviewed McCann, the pianist was in San Francisco for an engagement at the Jazz Workshop. He just released his second album *Les McCann Ltd.*

Plays the Shout. Like many Gleason interviews, the conversation begins with a lengthy, free-flowing discussion of the artist's background. But then, Gleason disrupts the flow:

> Gleason: You got the whole jazz world split right down the middle.
> McCann: Got the whole jazz, what do you mean by that?
> Gleason: Well, I mean, the reaction is either pro or con.

Both interviewer and the interviewee seem uneasy at this point.

> Gleason: Well now, why do you think that the music that you've, that the records that you've, well, this is an awkward question ... why do you think that what is on the records upsets people so much?

This frank question might have derailed the interview. Instead, the conversation evolves into a lengthy discourse about gospel music as a legitimate source for jazz, just like blues. The two agree that African American musicians' facility for jazz stems from environmental factors like the church, not genetic factors, as some still believed. They discuss the spiritual nature of jazz brought out by gospel influences. McCann concludes the interview by disclosing that he identifies with Ray Charles, who was accused of jumping on the soul jazz bandwagon and degrading gospel music.

In the month since Gleason panned McCann in his column, he came to appreciate the pianist's music. The same day of the interview, the *Chronicle* published a profile of McCann by Gleason:

> The McCann style is a hybrid of the spatial devices and apparent simplicity of Ahmad Jamal and the earthly spiritual jazz of Bobby Timmons ... on some numbers, he brings the house down to a hush with delicate and lacy improvisations, and when he begins his own revival meeting, he shakes the walls.
>
> Jazz can use more players in their ranks who are not afraid to have a good time when playing.[83]

In contrast to the negative *DownBeat* articles by Gitler and Tynan, Gleason set aside the soul jazz controversy and gave his readers an alternative view of McCann based on his live performances. In listening with an open mind to McCann's music and his ideas, Gleason saw how the rising Black Nationalist spirit inspired the young pianist to proudly display his roots in African American music.

Beauty, Emotion, Abruptness, and Discontinuity

As soul jazz gathered steam, Miles Davis explored a new direction in his music. Gleason witnessed the trumpeter's latest innovations at the Jazz Workshop in September 1963.

In his review, Gleason looked at the complex dynamics between Davis and his new bandmates:

> I sometimes think it would be next to impossible for Miles to play anything that was not pretty. His driving intense solos, with their dramatic use of bursts and overtones from the microphone, which characterized the up-tempo numbers, have a naked, fierce beauty all their own.
>
> And when he plays the ballads, like "Stella by Starlight," "My Funny Valentine," "All of You," a sheer exuberant joy of living; a mad, intense delight in beauty for its own sake, positively shine through …
>
> Miles has a group which inspires him … Keystone of the group is the young drummer, Tony Williams. Drummers are always the keystone, and this youngster has the fire of a great drummer and the uncanny ability to predict the logic of a solo that characterizes the handful of master drummers.
>
> Williams plays duets with Davis, long exchanges of ideas and rhythmic patterns during Miles' solos, which send Davis up another notch in his own playing. He does the same thing in a slightly different way with pianist Herbie Hancock, whose solos have a curiously intriguing, impressionistic sound to them at times. With Hancock, the drummer seems to talk back and forth and then anticipate the rhythmic construction.[84]

It had been fourteen years since Davis birthed the cool sounds that underpinned West Coast jazz. After that, a series of other idioms surfaced, from Third Stream to hard bop. But the most radical departure from cool was "free jazz," which liberated musicians from the norms established by early modernists such as Davis.

Gleason discovered free jazz through the albums of iconoclastic saxophonist Ornette Coleman. The former elevator operator started out playing R&B and bebop in clubs before joining a circle of avant-jazz musicians in Los Angeles and forming a quartet that included trumpeter Don Cherry. In a 1959 column, Gleason described Coleman as an "exciting young alto saxophonist who is just beginning to make a name for himself in jazz."[85] Later that year, Gleason wrote a profile of Coleman after he released the groundbreaking *Shape of Jazz to Come*:

> Ornette is working toward a freer form of jazz improvisation in which the actual bar number may be whatever the improviser desires; in which the harmonies develop as the soloist improvises and are not the structuring factor; and in which the broadest possible range of sounds is utilized. There is a great similarity to the human voice in the way in which Ornette plays with highly charged emotion, abruptness, and discontinuity.[86]

Gleason acknowledged that he did not "derive any pleasure from Coleman's music nor from that of [free jazz pianist] Cecil Taylor, to be frank." But he planned to "suspend

Figure 5.3 Ralph Gleason (center) with Miles Davis to his right and drummer Tony Williams to his left, at the Monterey Jazz Festival, 1963. Photo by Charles Robinson.

judgment on what he is doing to see where it goes ... his work is only a beginning ... the saxophone and possibly jazz may never be the same."[87] True to his word, Gleason continued to follow Coleman's music. After the release of Coleman's *Change of the Century* in the spring of 1960, Gleason linked the visionary musician with other cultural revolutionaries:

> Just as the publication of *On the Road*, whether or not Jack Kerouac is a great writer, is coming to be recognized as a turning point in American literature, and just as the emergence of Mort Sahl and Lenny Bruce indicates a turning point in American humor, so does the emergence of Ornette Coleman mark the end of something in jazz music and the beginning of something else.[88]

Gleason saw Coleman's music as a disruption of the history of jazz up to that time, noting how it "breaks through the old boundaries of the bar structures and the chord changes into a new individual cry. It has less debt to Parker than it has to the seminal roots of jazz itself."[89]

For some, free jazz symbolized the wave of decolonization occurring around the world. Independence movements raged as the United States and Soviet Union engaged in proxy wars in developing countries. One of these nations was Cuba. In 1959, a guerilla army led by Marxist revolutionary Fidel Castro overthrew Cuba's US-backed military dictator Fulgencio Batista. After John F. Kennedy became president in January 1961, he launched a failed attack to oust Castro in the Bay of Pigs Invasion. Kennedy was staunchly anti-communist and in a speech to the American Newspaper Publishers Association, urged publishers to keep any content that had a whiff of communist sentiment out of their publications. His message reached conservative editors of newspapers and magazines that employed leftist journalists like Gleason.

The Cuban revolution thus came at a time of global decolonization and wars of independence. Some rulers began to accept the inevitable end of colonialism. British Prime Minister Harold Macmillan addressed South Africa's parliament in February 1960 and said, "The wind of change is blowing through this continent. Whether we like it or not, this growth of national consciousness is a political fact."[90]

Gleason used the same metaphor in his April 27, 1961, *DownBeat* column. He compared musical rebels like Charlie Parker, Miles Davis, and John Coltrane to political revolutionaries:

> Today the winds of change are blowing the world over, from the Tokyo students to Fidel Castro and the veterans of Sierra Maestra to those who are beginning the good fight against the Dark Ages view of social illness as evinced in the Harrison Act as well as the House Un-American Activities Committee.[91]

Gleason was referring to insurgents around the world: Japanese students who protested the presence of US military bases; Fidel Castro; Americans who opposed the Harrison Narcotics Tax Act that treated addiction as a crime; and those who refused to cooperate with the House Un-American Activities Committee as it blacklisted Americans suspected of having communist ties. Gleason was heartened by the "increasing involvement of the jazz musician, after decades of isolation, in the problems and worries and work of the rest of the world."[92]

Soon after the column was published, Gleason and *DownBeat* permanently parted ways. According to Gleason's colleague at the magazine, critic Frank Kofsky, the break-up came over the "winds of change" column. "The publisher and advertisers were aghast. The word quickly came down to Gleason from on high: *Cut out that Commie crap!*"[93] Longtime *DownBeat* editor Gene Lees told a different story:

> If I had stayed at the magazine a few more weeks, I'd have done it myself [fire Gleason] for being a prima donna about any editing done to his prose, which was usually slapdash, sometimes incoherent, and sometimes even ungrammatical; for writing over length; and above all for missing deadlines. Castro had nothing to do with it, although I am sure Ralph circulated that story to explain away his dismissal.[94]

Gleason was already on thin ice at *DownBeat*. In a 1959 *Chronicle* column, he brusquely wrote that the magazine had no "literary style" and that it "varied from crusading to irresponsibility and periodically has gone through upheavals that rivaled the Mount Pelee eruption."[95] A likely reference to the firing of Nat Hentoff in 1956 when he insisted the magazine hire Black staff.[96] Columnist Dorothy Kilgallen wrote that Gleason and other writers quit because editors were "cutting their reviews and altering the meaning of them," something Gleason had publicly complained about.[97] But Gleason's son Toby said his father's split with *DownBeat* was amicable. Gleason likely parted with *DownBeat* for a combination of reasons, including his disappointment with its direction and his vehement dislike of editorial changes to his copy. His public criticisms of *DownBeat* and political commentary likely factored in as well.

The Appalling Condescension of the Well-Meaning Caucasian

The "winds of change" column illustrates how Gleason's liberal views intensified in the early 1960s. A lifelong Democrat like his father, Gleason had been influenced by the 1930s student activist movement and its pro-labor, anti-fascist, and antiwar views. During the 1950s, he used his column to speak out against racism. But like many liberals, he grew impatient with the pace of the civil rights movement. Inspired by writers like C. Wright Mills and James Baldwin, Gleason embraced the New Left and its critique of Cold War liberalism.[98]

As his views moved leftward, Gleason began to feel out of touch with colleagues who still looked to traditional liberalism to change the country. These associates included a circle of Bay Area activists, professors, and writers who met for dinner parties to discuss the day's issues. After one of these dinners, Gleason wrote a friend to complain how the "square, myopic, UNHIP left antagonizes me like the banderillas in the bull."[99] African American activists were "making a social revolution while [liberals] think and talk in political terms ... You make your social revolution first and then politicize it."[100] For Gleason, this social revolution would be inspired by subversive artists like John Coltrane, Fats Domino, Lenny Bruce, and a new wave of dissident novelists.

At these social gatherings, he met several of these writers, including Ken Kesey, whose novel *One Flew Over the Cuckoo's Nest* had just been published, and James Baldwin, who laid bare the realities of the Black experience in books such as *Notes of a Native Son*. Gleason reviewed Baldwin's *Nobody Knows My Name* and declared him "the most important American essayist." He said Baldwin's book "firmly establishes him as the painful voice of desperate sanity in a world still hiding as best it can from the problems surrounding it."[101] Around this time, Gleason worked on a television documentary with Baldwin called "Take This Hammer" that focused on racial discrimination in San Francisco.[102]

Gleason also befriended Nelson Algren, author of *The Man with the Golden Arm* and *A Walk on the Wild Side*, novels that showed empathy for life's down-and-outers. Gleason wrote, "Like the artists in jazz whom he so greatly resembles," Algren "hurls himself against the superstructure of the Establishment, going for broke every time he writes."[103] The two began corresponding and mailed each other books, newspaper clippings, and records. Algren sent the Gleasons a two-page set of unpublished song lyrics called "Epilogue: The Moon of the Arfy Darfy." The title refers to a short story Algren published in the *Saturday Evening Post* about a dive-bar pianist who sang about losing at the racetrack and losing at life.[104] Gleason identified with Algren, Baldwin, Kesey, and other writers whose marginalized protagonists exposed the duplicities in American society.

And no figure in America attacked hypocrisy with the ferocity of Lenny Bruce. Gleason wrote, "No one has expressed the sadly inadequate understanding and the appalling condescension of the well-meaning Caucasian better than Bruce."[105] But the comic paid a heavy price for his daring monologues. On October 4, 1961, San Francisco police arrested Bruce for saying the word "cocksucker" on stage at the Jazz Workshop. Police had been monitoring Bruce's shows because of his reputation for using strong language, and his recent arrest in Philadelphia for possessing narcotics.[106] Gleason was in the audience when police seized Bruce and looked on in horror as his friend was taken away. The tenacious Bruce returned to the club for a late-night show after being booked. Gleason covered the arrest in his column and said: "The word he was arrested for using, and which describes in street argot certain aspects of homosexuality, is familiar to every schoolboy."[107] Bruce was a "semanticist" who refused to attribute evil "to words themselves."[108]

Bruce's obscenity trial began in November and ended the following March. His defense team called Gleason as an expert witness, and he provided lengthy testimony over two days. On the first day of the trial, Bruce's attorney Al Bendich asked Gleason about the nature of his work at the *Chronicle*, to which Gleason replied, "A column of comment on contemporary culture."[109] Gleason fielded a series of questions and remained composed despite constant objections by the prosecuting attorney. Asked by Bendich about his experience observing nightclub audiences, Gleason said, "In writing about a show, it is often very useful to study the crowd and speak of the crowd's reaction. You are trained to do this over the years."[110]

Gleason told the court that Bruce's performances had social relevance. Bruce revealed "the hypocrisy inherent in the fact that you can discuss these things [even though] you aren't supposed to."[111] Bruce differed from other satirists because he attacked the "fundamental structures of society, and other comedians deal with it superficially."[112] Under cross-examination, Gleason resisted leading questions aimed at weakening Bruce's case. The prosecutor showed Gleason a simmering article that condemned Bruce's strong language. It was written by *Variety* editor Abel Green, who had stirred up moral panic in the 1950s with articles about R&B "leer-ics." Using Green's article as an example, the prosecutor asked Gleason, "So all experts don't agree with you in your testimony?" Gleason replied, "No, they don't. They seldom agree totally on any subject."[113] Asked if the word "cocksucker" made the bit funnier, Gleason said, "I think it was more authentic, not necessarily more funny."[114] Touché.

"Lenny Bruce Cleared," declared the *Chronicle* the next day. After 25 minutes, the jury acquitted Bruce. He told the press: "I'm never going to say any four-letter words again. I'm off for a bigger mission. I'm going to thwart pseudo-Christians and make them live their religion or back down."[115] Nine months later, in December 1962, Chicago police arrested Bruce for obscenity at the Gate of Horn folk club. The following year, Bruce was barred from entering London.[116]

Gleason kept track of his friend's travails and invited Bruce to his house when the comic was in town. He and Jean allowed Bruce to babysit their children, the ultimate mark of trust. Toby Gleason recalled a night when Bruce told him bedtime stories in a Dracula à la Bela Lugosi accent that haunted Toby's dreams for years. But Toby loved Bruce's routines and memorized many, which delighted Bruce. The comic's presence in the Gleason household even expanded Bridget's vocabulary, albeit in an unplanned way. One day, she repeated a curse word she heard Bruce say. A father–daughter talk followed, and Ralph gently counseled, "People don't like little girls who say motherfucker." Bridget tested her dad's statement at school the next day, prompting a call from a very rattled teacher.[117]

Man-Sized Rumbles

According to scholar Paul Lyons, although Bruce's monologues weren't explicitly political, they taught audiences "how to cope within an existential alienation, how to beat oppressors and the fates to the punch with self-deprecating humor, how to find meaning in tragedy, nobility in vulgarity; how to be survivors."[118] Beneath the street humor of Bruce's monologues, the existential terror of James Baldwin's essays, and the ordered tumult of Ornette Coleman's free jazz, Gleason saw a vision of a better society in which tolerance and personal expression reigned. He wrote that John Coltrane was "linked inextricably with those creative artists such as Joseph Heller, Ken Kesey, Lenny Bruce, and others who are searching for what Kesey refers to as a 'new way to look at the world, an attempt to locate a better reality.'"[119] These words foreshadowed those of music scholar Barry Shank, who wrote that "the experience of beauty is the recognition of the way things could be, the way things should be. The ability to produce beauty, therefore, is an index of the ability to imagine a better future." For Shank, this ability to envision a better tomorrow was the "political force of musical beauty."[120]

Gleason understood the political power of popular culture and went to great lengths to amplify it through his writings. For instance, in a 1963 column about Dick Gregory, Gleason explained how the activist gave up a lucrative engagement at the hungry i nightclub to go to Jackson, Mississippi, at the behest of civil rights leader Medgar Evers to speak at a voter registration rally. Evers, an African American, was a leading civil rights activist who helped end segregation at the University of Mississippi. Gleason used his review of Gregory to comment on the state of American racial injustice:

> Dick Gregory left the hungry i and went to Jackson [as a] personal gesture, and wars have been won, and dynasties tumbled by such. It may seem odd for a nightclub comic to dramatize a moral issue, but somebody has to. The President rides in a helicopter with the governor of Alabama, and the Attorney General laughs when

James Baldwin and others suggest that the President make a personal gesture, even lead a [black] student into Alabama State.

It doesn't seem to me that the leaders of this country have awakened to the fact that [racial equality] is now past politics. A power vacuum is developing in the human rights movement. It can be directed for humanity, as Baldwin, Gregory, and King stand for, or for bloodshed and riots with some extremist yet to arise.[121]

A week later, a White supremacist murdered Evers in the driveway of his Jackson ranch house. Gleason felt the tremors of American society on the brink of a race war. He continued to highlight the story of two countries, one Black, and one White. He devoted a column to Black journalist Dan Burley, who wrote for the *New York Amsterdam News* and other African American newspapers. Gleason used the column to shine a light on the ignorance of Whites about the African American community. And even worse, the invisibility of African American journalists in their own communities:

Like a shadow that can't be photographed, this Negro subculture has risen in the past few decades in the midst of the established American Society. Dan Burley wrote about how it was to live in this other world, the invisible man whose name nobody knows on the flat pavements of Harlem, the windy street corners of Chicago, and the ramshackle tenements of Kansas City and the other Negro ghettos.[122]

Columns like this show how Gleason's social commentary became more impassioned in the early 1960s as the civil rights movement escalated and the Cold War heated up. But Gleason's *Chronicle* editors disapproved of his ramped-up commentary. Even executive editor and fellow jazz fan Scott Newhall told him to stop. A cat-and-mouse situation developed as Gleason tried to blend social commentary into his music columns, only to be called out by editors. This added to the stress caused by the *Chronicle* increasing his workload to include five weekday columns called "On the Town."

By summer 1963, Gleason was forty-six and worried that his schedule at the *Chronicle* prevented him from reaching his potential as a writer. He expressed these frustrations in letters to activist lawyer Alexander P. Hoffman in 1963. "I have a great panic about time going by these days and my not accomplishing anything I consider worthwhile, and I'm not at all convinced that the goddam [sic] column is worthwhile."[123]

Over time, the exhaustion and editorial conflicts taxed Gleason's health, already weakened by diabetes and its side effects: depression and anxiety. Under doctor's orders, Gleason took a two-week sabbatical with Jean at a beachfront house in Carmel-by-the-Sea, California, in the summer of 1963.[124] An idyllic vacation that allowed Gleason to reflect on his goals. But when Gleason returned to work, his problems awaited him. "I'm having a lot of man-sized rumbles with the *Chronicle*," Gleason wrote to Hoffman and told him he considered resigning.[125] As the tensions escalated through the end of 1963, Gleason expressed his distress in a letter to another friend, British Marxist historian Eric Hobsbawm:

> I have got to get off this treadmill before I collapse. I don't have time to think, and there is neither money enough nor joy enough in writing a daily column so heavily concerned with show biz and in which I get continual static and tsuris [Yiddish for aggravating trouble] whenever I move into politics or anything OUTSIDE show biz."[126]

A national tragedy eclipsed Gleason's problems. On November 22, 1963, a former Marine sharpshooter opened fire on President Kennedy while he traveled in a motorcade in Dallas. Gleason is at home when his friend, concert promoter Mary Ann Pollar, calls with the grim news. Like most Americans, he rushes to the television and tunes in to the famous Huntley-Brinkley Report on NBC, where events quickly unfold in one news bulletin after another. Soon newscaster Chet Huntley confirms the worst, Kennedy is dead. Gleason sits in near shock as he watches a mélange of black and white newsreel clips, eight-millimeter amateur film strips, and fuzzy shots of John and Jackie Kennedy in the backseat of their limousine. Police take into custody a dead-eyed Cuba sympathizer named Lee Harvey Oswald. Footage shows Jackie Kennedy in her pink Chanel suit and matching pillbox hat splattered with her husband's blood.

After he recovered from the shocking events, Gleason's journalistic sensibilities kicked in. That day, he drove to the UC Berkeley campus to gauge student reaction to the assassination. News had spread within the activist community that Oswald supported the leftist organization Fair Play for Cuba, which had a student chapter at Berkeley. Members were more upset about possible repercussions for them than the assassination itself. A young woman told Gleason, "I am sorry any man is killed, but to put it in the proper perspective, I am sorry for all the people in Venezuela who are killed every day," referring to leftist guerillas in that country's civil war.[127] Gleason softly replied, "No, that didn't put it into perspective." When his words went unheard, he despaired.

As day turned to night, Gleason continued to seek reactions to the assassination. He ventured to North Beach, where the lights were on in some clubs and off in others. Strippers continued to strip, and musicians pondered whether to go on stage. Ella Fitzgerald canceled her show, but at another club, Trini Lopez sang "If I Had a Hammer." Dazed people passed Gleason on the street. He later wrote Hobsbawm that the reactions around town deeply disturbed him. "Right when I needed to talk to some political soul brothers, if such exist, the most I had was none. I'm too young or too old, too left or too right. I don't fit!"[128]

This had been the central conflict of Gleason's life since he converted to jazz back in 1930s Chappaqua. From then on, he ceased fitting into society's neat categories. Even within the groups he identified with, from the hot collector movement to the American Left, Gleason occupied positions between the extremes. And now, just as he began connecting with a rising youth culture committed to activism, Gleason again took the middle way.

"A Violent Act Defines Us," proclaimed the title of Gleason's column about the assassination. "What I find now disturbs me more fundamentally than the act itself ... A terrible schizophrenia in us today, a gap between the generations and their attitudes which came as a shock to me."[129] In words that presaged the coming counterculture, Gleason declared the "children of the Atomic Age, raised under a mushroom cloud and sentenced to soldiering," could not process Kennedy's death.[130] Some of the students, he wrote, shared an "alienated feeling the event had no meaning for them, just an episode in a world they never made."[131] Gleason noted that he often disagreed with Kennedy's views, but "I respected him."

Yet Gleason didn't believe the students should be condemned for their misguided reactions. He wrote that it would be a "perversion of everything we stood for if we allowed the sublimation of our sense of shame and guilt to result in blind lashing out at others."[132] Gleason ended the column with an excerpt from the song "Please Send Me Someone to Love" by Percy Mayfield: "Hate will put the world in flames, what a shame, what a shame." Gleason concluded, "What a shame indeed if we let that fatal turn be taken ... We bred [Kennedy's] murderer, our society produced him, and he is, in one sense, a part of all of us."[133]

Five years later, a revolution-touting Mick Jagger barked out a similar indictment in "Sympathy for the Devil":

I shouted out
Who killed the Kennedys?
When after all
It was you and me.[134]

6

An Entertainment of Dissent (1964)

In 1964, the Beatles revolutionized pop music and birthed a new genre called "rock." This updated version of rock 'n' roll gave voice to the rising baby boom generation, who aimed to challenge the traditions of their elders. From the shrill harmonies of "I Want to Hold Your Hand" to the soul sway of "Time is on My Side," the songs of the British bands synthesized American rock 'n' roll, blues, and R&B into a thrilling new sound. The Cold War generation now felt a warming glow of hope.

Boomers also turned to a new wave of folk singers. Bob Dylan, Joan Baez, and others expressed in their song lyrics what the British Invasion bands expressed in their sound—a fierce protest against the "establishment," the dominant culture of conformity, racial injustice, and war. Gleason understood the messages of the new rock bands and folk singers. Still, more importantly, he grasped how these messages needed successful messengers to influence a mass audience and change society. In his writings, he advocated for musician-envoys such as the Beatles and Dylan, who transformed American culture through an entertainment of dissent.

A Wild, Roaring Sound

Gleason entered the emergent cultural revolution thanks to his ability to change his mind. He never shied away from reversing his positions in public and could let go of his outdated opinions as quickly as a pair of worn-out socks. In early 1964, the forty-seven-year-old music critic changed his mind about two of the decade's most impactful artists, the Beatles and Bob Dylan.

Gleason produced his first writings about the Beatles in January and February 1964, during which their success in America was still being determined. Gleason published his first reaction to the band in January, before the Beatles visited the country and before they had any American hit records. He dismissed the Beatles as a commercial gimmick, writing:

> The Beatles, apparently a British version of Elvis Presley manipulated by an apparatus of managers and companies, including the one which makes "Beatles wigs," are trying to be a hit in the U.S. pop market and will probably make it. If they succeed, they will be the worst thing the British have sent over since Burgoyne.[1]

Gleason referred to eighteenth-century British General John Burgoyne, who lost the American Revolutionary War for England.

Gleason's initial reaction to the Beatles was unsurprising. His interest in White rock 'n' roll subsided in the early 1960s, and in January 1964, he focused on artists like jazz pianist Hampton Hawes and singer-guitarist Sister Rosetta Tharpe. Unlike in England, there was no rock press in America at that time except for fan magazines, which were generally uninterested in the Beatles in January 1964. Many US newspapers reacted negatively to the first reports of British Beatlemania. "Beatles 'Infest' England" and similar headlines likened the band's growing popularity to an invasion of creepy-crawlies.[2] A *New York Daily News* entertainment writer said the Beatles' taped appearance on the "Tonight Starring Jack Paar" confirmed that British rock 'n' rollers are "worse than their American counterparts."[3]

It wasn't until "I Want to Hold Your Hand" and *Meet the Beatles!* skyrocketed up the American record charts that a pro-Beatles chorus began in the press. Then across the twenty-nine days of February 1964, the Beatles wrought a cultural revolution that reverberates today.

During that time, only a small group of American writers, including Gleason, John S. Wilson, and Tom Wolfe, recognized the significance of the Beatles' music. Gleason was among the first American music critics to take the Beatles seriously. In a reversal of his initial position, Gleason depicted the Beatles as a constructively subversive force out to return vitality to popular music.

This can be seen in his February 5 column, "The Beatles' Mersey Sound."

> A spectre is haunting Europe. Four young men called the Beatles, who wear medieval haircuts and leather jackets and sing with a wild, roaring sound, are threatening to dominate the popular music lists in the Common Market.[4]

Gleason borrowed his beginning line from the *Communist Manifesto*, a call to overthrow bourgeois hegemony that begins, "A spectre is haunting Europe—the spectre of communism." Gleason uses the quote to needle conservative readers and depict the Beatles as musical subversives. For the remainder of this column and the next two, he legitimized the Beatles by taking them seriously enough to narrate their story without snarky asides. He presents them as young rebels out to capsize the music industry as delegates for a new generation. The Beatles "represent something almost sacred in British culture, akin to the feeling for Elvis Presley and [James] Dean here."[5] In his next column, Gleason wrote:

> Their records sound like a thesaurus of all the influences in American popular music's wide spectrum. There are elements of gospel, country and western, traditional jazz, rock 'n' roll, and contemporary rhythm and blues. In all the Beatles' records, these things are present, and although none of them are new, the Beatles are the first to put them all together all the time.[6]

Because of the Beatles' longstanding global influence on popular culture, we must remind ourselves that the world once existed without them. Gleason was evaluating the Beatles with fresh ears and could appreciate their multi-genre sound because of his deep-rooted coverage of these genres. Once Gleason understood the Beatles' singular synthesis of American musical forms, he abandoned his initial shortsighted view of the band. He realized that John, Paul, George, and Ringo fought against the insipidness of 1960s teen music with their "wild, roaring sound." He likened the Liverpool band to the teens in Colin MacInnes's book *Absolute Beginners,* who mounted a "revolt against today's adult world."[7] An adult world Gleason belonged to but failed to identify with.

Gleason initially underestimated Bob Dylan as well. "One more banjo twang and my ears will start bleeding," he wrote after a weekend of vernacular music at the 1963 Monterey Folk Festival.[8] Stoking Gleason's fears of an olfactory bleed-out, Bob Dylan, a young folkie with a "mop of fuzzy hair, beat-up looking work pants, thin as a rail," who sang with a "gen-yew-wine twang."[9] Gleason yawned:

> His songs have social significance, I am told by the remnants of the Cultural (and square) Left …
>
> I am in sympathy with his protests against The Bomb and for Humanity, but I find he tends to bore me and sound oppressively mournful.[10]

For Gleason, Dylan in 1963 represented the outmoded principles of the Old Left. He lumped the singer-songwriter in with the "skyscraper hillbillies and those fleeing from the reality of America by vicariously living the American myth through song."[11] Gleason continued, "There is more vitality, humor, and reality in the best of rhythm and blues than we got out of anything at Monterey. And it swings. The folk music at Monterey may come from the soul, but it does so by way of the nasal passages too much of the time."[12] Two months later, Gleason told a friend that he considered the Monterey Folk Festival "a disaster" and said, "the whole folknic movement ought to be abolished."[13]

Yet one song Dylan played at the festival stuck in Gleason's memory. "A Hard Rain's a-Gonna Fall," written by Dylan, departed from his practice of covering traditional folk songs. In referencing nuclear fallout, Dylan expressed his generation's dread of atomic war. The song resonated with Gleason. The younger generation's music reflected grave social realities caused by the political establishment. Gleason began to rethink his view of Dylan:

> The post-bomb babies simply aren't having any of what we, their parents and their elders, have been putting down. The way they express it may not be as gracious as we may wish, but the strength of their denial is in the truth of their position, and the truth of Dylan's position is in the words of his songs."[14]

"The truth shall make ye free," the declaration that called Gleason to journalism now called him to the music of a new generation. He felt this verity in the songs of another emergent folk singer:

> Joan Baez is slim, bird-quick, and starkly simple in manner, dress, and presentation … Her hair is extra-long and hangs down the side of her pale, thin face. She brushes it aside continually in quick, nervous gestures. Her voice is flat, almost metallic, as she makes brief Salingeresque announcements.[15]

From then on, Gleason enthusiastically supported Baez and Dylan in his columns. He called their generation "an American version of *Absolute Beginners*" who were "beyond politics in a curious way, beyond it and in favor of humanity."[16]

Dylan surprised his followers in February 1964 when he released *The Times They Are a-Changin'*, an album of all-original songs. In the LP, Dylan took on racism, poverty, and the growing generation gap. Gleason sees Dylan perform at that time at the Berkeley Community Theater. Imagine the scene as Gleason takes his seat, surrounded by the first blush of Mod fashion as young people fill the hall. The house lights dim, and Dylan stands still as a statue center stage, his pale face crowned by curls, his eyes both wary and trusting. Dressed in a suede jacket, green shirt, stovepipe trousers, and work boots, he channels his hero Woody Guthrie while tapping into the style of the times. Dylan addresses Gleason's generation:

> Come mothers and fathers throughout the land
> And don't criticize what you can't understand
> Your sons and your daughters are beyond your command
> Your old road is rapidly aging
> Please get out of the new one if you can't lend your hand
> For the times, they are a-changin'[17]

Baez joins Dylan to sing "Blowin' in the Wind." Gleason grasps the song's meaning for the first time and realizes Dylan's prowess as a songwriter. In his review of the concert, Gleason wrote:

> Dylan's special gift lies in the creation of poetic images that clearly pose the moral dilemmas of our society. He is a magnificent songwriter (his repertoire is all his own, like Ellington and Monk). In his small boy's anti-formal manner, he is advocating a moral and social revolution that is long past due.[18]

Gleason depicted Dylan as part of a broader cultural upheaval:

> All our values and all our concepts are being challenged by the Miles Davises, the Bob Dylans, and the rest of the poets and prophesiers of the new generation. A hard core of reality connects the music of Dylan, the best of jazz, contemporary poetry, painting, and all the arts, in fact, with the social revolution that has resulted in CORE and SNCC, Dick Gregory, James Baldwin, and the rest.[19]

A skeptic no longer, Gleason became one of Dylan's staunchest interpreters. A longtime follower of organic folk musicians such as Lightnin' Hopkins and Leadbelly, who grew up in vernacular settings, Gleason was slow to respect what he saw as the "skyscraper hillbillies" of the Greenwich Village folk scene. And folk music hadn't been part of Gleason's beat, as it was covered primarily by the *Chronicle*'s classical music critics (a common occurrence in newspapers then). As with the Beatles, once Gleason understood Dylan as a harbinger of a coming youth culture, he saw him in a new light. As mentioned earlier, one of Gleason's gifts was his ability to publicly change his mind about revolutionary artists.

A Thousand Shimmering Pieces

As Gleason opened up to a new generation of pop musicians, the descendants of Ellington, Hines, and Armstrong lit up the skies of modern jazz:

> Miles played the whole line of a ballad through once, slowly, and breathily with infinite tenderness and beauty before blasting it joyously into a thousand shimmering pieces in a wildly swinging second chorus.[20]

In passages like this, Gleason brought the reader into his heightened experiences, such as listening to a groundbreaking album for the first time or sitting in a club immersed in a powerful performance. Through empathic listening and metaphor-rich prose, Gleason captured exciting moments in the history of San Francisco jazz, including this performance at the Jazz Workshop on an April night in 1964:

> Miles Davis was playing a long series of soaring passages filled with little bursts of notes ranging up and down the scale. It sounded like a musical impression of a surf rider swooping and sliding as he maneuvered the crest of the wave.
>
> Tony Williams, Miles' youthful drummer, was snapping along behind Miles and began a series of explosions that were perfectly contrived to the end, in one crashing meteor-landing burst, just as Miles ended his solo.
>
> "Wipeout!" somebody said at the bar.[21]

The addition of Williams and keyboardist Herbie Hancock created a "wildly swinging, swift-paced rhythm section that excites Miles."[22] Being a drummer, Gleason closely observed Williams's technique and how he took the "rhythmic accents in phrases by the soloists as take-off points for counter-rhythms."[23] Davis, Gleason wrote, played "with sheer brilliance. He blows duets with the drums, the bass, and the section as a whole."[24] Gleason championed Davis's band because it took post-bop jazz to new heights. At the time, Williams was just seventeen and Hancock twenty-three, and within a few years, they would join Davis in pioneering a new genre—jazz rock, also called fusion.

Gleason supported another promising artist, Oakland saxophonist John Richard Handy III. Gleason heard Handy's band play at a Bay Area benefit for the Congress for

Racial Equality, an influential civil rights group, and wrote, "The band is excellent; it has exciting arrangements and plays them with spirit and fire and a fine swinging beat. Handy is a major league player."[25] A few weeks later, Gleason saw the Handy Quintet at the Jazz Workshop and wrote that new member Mike White is an "astonishing violinist ... a gas."[26] White foreshadowed jazz rock with his electrified violin sound.

When deeply inspired by a live performance, Gleason lit up the page with lively prose informed by the details of a performer's technique. For instance, after he heard a show by Art Blakey and the Jazz Messengers, Gleason effused:

> Art Blakey has stamped his personality on every group he has had to a greater degree than any other drummer. This is true because of the Blakey concept of drumming, which is orchestral. He doesn't play the sort of drums that are simply an accompaniment for the soloist or a background for the ensemble passages. He plays a style that spreads out as a foundation for everything that is being done by the other members of the group, which fills in, supports, surrounds, lifts up, and swings.
>
> Like John Coltrane, Blakey deals in sheets of sound. His [signature] is a rushing, roaring whirlwind of sound in which crescendos and acute attention to dynamics, fascinating cross-rhythms, and accents give a highly individual flavor.
>
> Yet, if you take any single aspect of his drumming, say the cross-rhythms he plays on the tom toms and the snare (with rimshots), a rhythmic line which is integrated into the solo line and the phrasing of the tune is always present.
>
> Doubling of time, cutting it in half, and mixing up both is another way in which he makes tension appear and disappear while maintaining the surging swing that marks everything he does.[27]

That "surging swing" had drawn Gleason to jazz shows since he discovered the Apollo Theater in the 1930s. Gleason frequently recalled early jazz experiences in his column, such as his teenage discovery of a long-forgotten swing band who played a roadhouse "set on a bluff up off the Saw River Road halfway from Pleasantville to Tarrytown," seven miles outside Chappaqua:

> The White Tower was a Negro nightclub, a rare and exotic flower in suburbia of the 30s, and it was off bounds for high school kids like me from adjacent communities, but who was to know? Which is how I got to hear, one brief night, a group later to become famous in jazz as the Savoy Sultans.
>
> In the words of Dizzy Gillespie ... "They was the swinging-est band EVER!" and it was only a nine-piece group.[28]

Such accounts were more than mere nostalgia. Recollections like these bolstered Gleason's credentials as a jazz authority; in this case, a White kid's willingness to cross the color line. These remembrances often focused on long-forgotten artists whom Gleason brought to the attention of contemporary readers.

The delicate play between a musician's artistry and their widespread success had always fascinated Gleason. In March 1964, Gleason explored this balance in a television series presented on National Educational Television called *Anatomy of a Hit*. He co-produced the three-part series, which documented the making of "Cast Your Fate to the Wind," a piano instrumental composed and recorded by Vince Guaraldi. The disc became the first hit single for Fantasy Records and won the 1963 Grammy Award for Best Original Jazz Composition.

Gleason followed the song's genesis beginning when Guaraldi recorded it for his album *Jazz Impressions of Black Orpheus*, released in the spring of 1962 with liner notes by Gleason. As he admitted, Gleason initially found "Cast Your Fate to the Wind" pleasant but unimpressive.[29] But he was deeply taken by *Jazz Impressions of Black Orpheus*. Guaraldi based the first side of the album on music from the soundtrack of the 1959 French movie *Black Orpheus*, an interpretation of the Greek legend of Orpheus and Eurydice set in the slums of Rio de Janeiro during Carnival. The soundtrack by Antônio Carlos Jobim and Luiz Bonfá popularized Bossa Nova and won over Fantasy's Max Weiss, who worked with Guaraldi to record *Jazz Impressions of Black Orpheus*, including "Cast Your Fate to the Wind." In his liner notes, Gleason said that Guaraldi and his trio created a "vivid impression of the gloriously blazing sound that marked the film music."[30]

After "Cast Your Fate to the Wind" became the breakout track from the album, Gleason convinced KQED to make a television documentary about how the song was created and marketed. He co-produced and narrated the mini-series, which went into production in the fall of 1963. Gleason filmed interviews with Guaraldi and others, including Fantasy's Max Weiss. Guaraldi visited Gleason at his house weekly while they worked on the series.[31] They had a tight budget, and the project was another labor of love for Gleason in his quest to bring jazz to a general audience.

In the film, Gleason narrates between clips of Guaraldi and his trio playing songs. Laying back in an overstuffed club chair and smoking his pipe, Gleason also interviews Guaraldi about his music. In one exchange, he asks the pianist how he composes, to which Guaraldi replies, "I prefer a strong melody. It's something that stays with you. I can't think of an instance where anybody's walking down the street whistling the chord changes."[32]

Anatomy of a Hit offers hope to struggling musicians. It demythologizes the star-making process by showing everything from cluttered, makeshift recording studio setups to the unplanned and unexpected breakout of "Cast Your Fate to the Wind." In one talk-over, Gleason begins, "Dreams are fascinating things," and then describes the archetypical American dream to become a star and how every musician, no matter how dedicated to their art, "wants to hear himself come back at himself out of all the transistor radios that his friends have, and from all the juke boxes and all the soda fountains and coffee shops, and from the hit parade on all the Top 40 radio stations that he listens to all over the country."[33]

As *Anatomy of a Hit* showed, Gleason saw fame as a vehicle for innovative artists to spread their messages across society. For Gleason, the key was for a musician to maintain authenticity while achieving success. And he was troubled by the lack of genuineness in the American folk music scene.

The Voices of a New Generation

After the Kingston Trio caused a commercial boom for clean-cut White guys in striped shirts singing catchy folk songs like "Tom Dooley," Gleason had largely ignored the 1950s folk revival. One exception was Odetta, an Alabama-born Black singer who made her name in the San Francisco folk circuit. Odetta influenced Dylan and Baez, and Martin Luther King praised her political activism. Gleason wrote that Odetta "has that cry in her throat, that piercing electricity, that instant drama of word and line that marks a great folk singer, to the tradition born or not."[34]

For Gleason, genuine folk music expressed the joys and miseries of the working class. His views of folk music somewhat paralleled his 1940s ideas of New Orleans-style jazz as a form of vernacular music descended from work songs, fortified with a roughhewn vitality born in brothels and bars, and passed down from musician to musician. Back then, he despaired whenever record labels and musicians commercialized jazz in a way that sapped its earthy origins. Gleason saw the same thing happening in folk music:

> It has long been obvious that in an affluent society within a free, competitive economy, the authentic art form does not necessarily become the most successful. If that seems an understatement, it is just as true that the authentic need not be commercially unsuccessful (witness jazz in which Miles Davis, the Modern Jazz Quartet, Erroll Garner, Count Basie, and numerous other authentic artists have been and are commercial successes). Conversely, the unauthentic, deliberately contrived, does not always become successful either.[35]

Gleason wrote, "Folk music is commercial," not bad in itself, but it gave in to a mass culture market "of superficiality" because of the "swiftly shifting currents of trend and taste."[36] Yet he held out hope:

> There is a market for the real, the authentic. It's a market created by the value of the thing itself on the one hand and by a curious law that seems to operate at the base of the mass culture: Every superficial trend creates a great market, even for the basic and the real.[37]

Race is a factor, he wrote in a later column:

> Folk music, like Dixieland and traditional jazz, is by definition preteristic [focused on the past]. And although one of the most vital strains of American folk music is that of the Negro, [the current folk scene] is remarkable for the absence of any important degree of Negro participation either as performer or audience.[38]

Gleason contrasted "genuine" folk singers like Huddie Ledbetter (Lead Belly) with "those folk singers two years out of college" who "structure their performance to the audience taste, not to their own. You have to be as big and strong and deeply angry as Lead Belly" to not bend to popular tastes.[39] Gleason believed there was "more genuine contemporary folk art" in popular songs like "Kansas City" or "Alley Oop" than in contemporary folk songs.

Gleason's standards for folk authenticity underpinned his coverage of the 1964 Berkeley Folk Festival held on the UC Berkeley campus. Founded in 1958 by Bay Area guitar teacher Barry Olivier, the festival joined the "emerging international circuit of folk music festivals in the 1960s" and created a "crucial gathering site for the West Coast folk revival."[40] The Berkeley event occurred in the "very same spaces on the University of California campus that were centers of the tumultuous politics of the 1960s."[41]

Gleason took in many of the 1964 festival's performances, including Doc Watson, a blind guitarist from North Carolina who dazzled listeners with his flat-picking style. Although Gleason believed the "hillbilly tradition is the voice of the reactionary Southern bigot," he saw Watson as a modern traditionalist who broke this custom by absorbing ideas from contemporary records.[42] After Watson's show ended, Gleason listened to the remainder of the day's performances and joined the crowd for the festival closer. Joan Baez enchanted the audience with a concert in the Greek Theater, a landmark amphitheater on the Berkeley campus. As the last notes died out, strands of twilight fog cooled the air, and the festival ended.[43]

Gleason had much to say about the festival and devoted several columns to it. He praised Baez and other young artists who "sprung out of the prison of strict tradition" and broke "the iron bars of antiquarianism."[44] The younger generation, he wrote, reached out to the marginalized while the old guard just talked among themselves. Gleason asked why the folk movement attracted so few Blacks, even though African American musicians significantly contributed to the nation's vernacular music. He wondered if that was because folk music carried the "taint of hillbilly twang which equates to Southern Jim Crow."[45] Gleason hailed Baez and Dylan for addressing their songs to a diverse audience, which is "what a true folk singer really does."[46]

Gleason befriended Baez during that time. His daughter Stacy recalled a day when Baez pulled her robin's-egg blue Jaguar XKE into the Gleason's driveway for a visit. When it was time to go, the Jag wouldn't start, so Baez stayed overnight:

> I gave her my room, and I remember sitting with her on the floor in front of the living room fireplace as she twisted her gorgeous long black hair and looked incredibly beautiful, but talked about how she was so nervous performing that she got sick to her stomach every time. I was smitten but, of course, had to be cool.
>
> I didn't change the sheets on my bed for weeks after.[47]

Stacy said this story exemplifies how her parents "opened up their house" to famous musicians and treated them like ordinary people.[48] But she admits someone of Baez's stature could sweep up her and her siblings.

Bridget's high school friend Rebecca Adams recalls washing dishes with Baez one evening after a social gathering at the Gleason's. "There had been some speculation that Dylan might show up, but he didn't. It was just a normal activity to find myself washing dishes with Joan Baez. Nothing dramatic here at all!"⁴⁹ Another visitor to the Gleason house was the emerging folk rock duo, Simon & Garfunkel. Toby recalled a day they came over with their manager and gave Ralph and Jean the shock of their life. The couple wasn't home, so, to kill time, the musicians and their manager took Toby to a nearby pizza parlor for lunch. As a joke, they left a fake ransom note signed, "The Green Phantom." Unbeknownst to the phony kidnappers, Ralph had received many threatening letters in his career because of his controversial views and took the note seriously and called the police. Toby says his parents "almost fainted with relief when we came home, fed, happy, and covered with pizza sauce."⁵⁰

Gleason began to support Baez after he changed his mind about Dylan. Navigate the byways of Gleason's 1964 writings on folk music, and you find Dylan around every corner. One aspect of Dylan that Gleason identified with was the songwriter's romance with Beat poetry. Dylan emulated the Beat life and, in early 1964, took a cross-country car ride like the protagonist Sal Paradise of Kerouac's *On the Road*. During the journey, Dylan read Arthur Rimbaud and other French symbolist poets who inspired the Beats. Dylan applied their free-associative, beatific style to his next album, *Another Side of Bob Dylan*. Music writer Tim Riley called the LP a "rock album without electric guitars," which puts Gleason's review in with the emergent rock criticism of that time:⁵¹

> It is a collection of poetic comments on the journey of the continuing innocent in the corrupt world, a reaction in song to the past few years of Dylan's turbulent life.
>
> If you listen to what Dylan says (and the sound of his singing is enough to carry you along most of the time), he makes you face yourself just as Lenny Bruce makes you face yourself. It is the humanity in his view and the acceptance of the imperfection of man that moves you like that.
>
> Bob Dylan is a great deal more than a young kid with a guitar, a harmonica, and unruly hair. He's the voice of the new generation, challenging all betrayers of ideals and the compromisers with truth and destroyers of beauty.⁵²

A month later, Gleason defended Dylan from his critics:

> The one unforgivable sin in the American money culture is to break through to the top rungs of success while, at the same time, spurning the power apparatus.
>
> Do that, and the demons that lurk beneath the surface come up and attack you, whether they are the mass media magazines or the Inside Dopesters and their barroom gossip.
>
> This has been the fate of Bob Dylan.⁵³

These demons included members of the folk establishment, distressed because Dylan no longer wrote protest songs:

His protest songs have earned him the admiration of a great body of people interested in social change and who see the world in terms of moral issues.

Yet Dylan eschews politics.

Dylan dropped the writing of protest songs to turn to his own direct experience.[54]

Gleason, too, repudiated politics as the answer to society's problems. Even though he identified with the New Left, Gleason lost faith in political institutions, believing it would take revolutionary musicians and writers to change America, not political ideologues.

Kesey

These revolutionaries included novelist Ken Kesey. In 1962, the author of *One Flew Over the Cuckoo's Nest* moved to the rural community of La Honda, about an hour south of San Francisco. There he worked on his next book, *Sometimes a Great Notion*. Gleason admired Kesey's writing and wrote that he sought to "break the confines of the novel" just like modern jazz players such as Davis and Coltrane sought to "find new forms, new methods, and new ways of expressing themselves."[55] When Gleason first met Kesey at a literary party in 1963, he reminded Gleason of *Catch-22* author Joe Heller, another novelist he admired. Kesey and Heller, he wrote, were writers who appealed to "young people who have a conviction that the world is perhaps even more absurd than Beckett."[56]

Gleason and Kesey became friends and frequently corresponded. In a 1964 letter to Gleason, Kesey foresaw the coming counterculture:

> There's a scene a-building. All the labels are being repealed. For nearly a year now, I have worked on whatever it is that I have been working on. Not a book or nuthin' like that but (I steadfastly refrain from calling it music) SOUND! And soon will have some tapes and maybe some films to subject you to.[57]

Kesey drew inspiration from hallucinogenic drugs such as lysergic acid diethylamide, called LSD, or "acid." He had taken part in government studies of psychedelics and came to value their creative and recreational potential. At his La Honda ranch, Kesey hosted LSD-inspired happenings with a circle of friends known collectively as the Merry Pranksters. Kesey recorded the La Honda parties, multimedia events with music, taped sounds, and light shows.

Six days after Kesey wrote to Gleason, the Pranksters took off on a cross-country road trip to New York City to promote the upcoming publication of *Sometimes a Great Notion* and see the 1964 World's Fair.[58] They journeyed in a 1939 International Harvester school bus christened Furthur that Kesey and the Pranksters painted in swirling psychedelic patterns and outfitted with cameras, microphones, and speakers. It was like a rolling set for a crazed reality TV show, a happening on wheels. As novelist Tom Wolfe said, "It was sloppy, but one thing you had to say for it, it was freaking lurid."[59]

As Kesey and his crew made their way to New York, advance copies of *Sometimes a Great Notion* went out to book reviewers, including William Hogan, literary editor of the *San Francisco Chronicle*. The novel tells the story of an Oregon logging family fighting against nature and their self-defeating impulses. Hogan passed the book on to Gleason, who wrote a two-page review praising Kesey's ability to use the family's struggles as a means for literary experimentation:

> Getting into [*Sometimes a Great Notion*] is getting into a fascinating, crazy world of a fascinating, crazy family that has a throbbing reality and a desperate dedication to living. These are strange people but not frightening people, and you move among them with a highly intense sense of participation.[60]

After the review ran, Gleason briefly glimpsed into Kesey's world. One day, he picked up the phone to hear Kesey say, "Come meet us, and we'll do a thing we do." Soon after, Further pulled into Gleason's Berkeley neighborhood:

> Like a huge, mottled, turret-topped beetle, the bus turned the corner onto Telegraph Avenue and pulled up by the Shell station. The wild shades of yellow, orange, pale blue, and ochre shimmering in waves along the sides looked like World War II camouflage for autumn in New York.[61]

Figure 6.1 Ken Kesey with a trombone on the roof of Furthur, his 1939 school bus converted into a traveling home for his band of Merry Pranksters during their visit to the Gleason house in Berkeley, 1964. Courtesy of the Estate of Ralph J. Gleason.

"Get on! Get on!" yells a Prankster dressed as a pirate. Gleason climbs aboard, where he's greeted by driver Neal Cassady, the inspiration for Dean Moriarty in Kerouac's *On the Road*. Cassady fires off a "fuel-injected stream of monologue, bucking and swaying like a rodeo rider in action."[62] Cassady tells Gleason about the beginning of the Prankster's California-to-New York City trip with jazz flutist "Roland Kirk blasting away on those tapes and me jumping up and down with the music, driving the bus."[63] Gleason meets other Pranksters, including "Intrepid Traveler," Kesey's best friend and sound engineer Ken Babbs. All have inspired nicknames such as Stark Naked, Zonker, Speed Limit, and Slime Queen. As Cassady drives, Pranksters play musical instruments, film the action, and tape the sounds. After his brief ride, Gleason says goodbye, hops off and watches as "the bus coughed, the flutes blew, the guitars hummed, and the Intrepid Traveler waved his wooden sword and shouted to straggling Pranksters to get on board." Cassady heaved the steering wheel rightward, and Further rolled off to its next adventure.

Girls Continued to Scream

What do Ken Kesey and British rocker Gerry Marsden have in common? Gleason wrote about both in 1964, which shows his eclectic coverage. Three months after he rode on Furthur, Gleason took in a show by Gerry and the Pacemakers at the Oakland Auditorium, with opening act Billy J. Kramer and the Dakotas. Newspaper writers covering the Pacemakers' tour across the United States limited their reportage to announcing the shows and providing basic information, such as contests to win tickets. Gleason wrote a review which expressed his mixed feelings:

> The affair was singularly unsuccessful, but it had some interesting aspects. The kids stood in their seats and screamed and waved at the performers, provoking the police to use flashlights and occasional strength to restrain them. In fact, the cops patrolled the small audience like it was a prison camp. One girl, obviously incensed because she was prevented from standing up, expressed a desire that a police officer perform an act even contortionists have historically found impossible and was hauled away for her brashness.[64]

Gleason didn't have the same enthusiasm for the Pacemakers he showed for their fellow Liverpool band, the Beatles:

> The concert, if you can call it that, was sloppily produced and replete with awkward pauses and confusion. The sound of the Merseybeat, if this was a fair sample, is pure overwhelming noise. It was impossible to distinguish many of the lyrics or to tell what kinds of voices the British singers had because of the souped-up loudspeakers and the shrill screams of the audience.[65]

Gleason gave a hilariously scathing description of the opening act, a Los Angeles duo he referred to as "Sonny and Sherri," likely Sonny and Cher, who sang in a "slow, screaming drawl while grinding around on stage." Sonny, he joked, "wore his hair Ringo-style and shook it unmercifully at strategic moments." The climax of the set, he wrote, was Sherri "writhing on the floor to the beat of the music, her hair flying, while Sonny, kneeling, huddled over the microphone, his hair flopping, shrieked the magic words—'John, Paul, George, Ringo!'"[66]

Gleason was still trying to get that image out of his mind when he saw the Dave Clark Five (DC5) at the Cow Place a few weeks later. He sat through tedious opening acts, including a "desultory big band, led by a bouncing man wearing glasses."[67] Finally, the house lights dimmed as security guards tried to quell young fans bent on touching their idols:

> The Dave Clark Five filed out on stage, their cuffs and collars shining in the darkness, the red bulb in the bass drum flashing off and on, and the photographers' light bulbs popping. It looked like a combination of Dante's Inferno and the re-creation of the Battle of the Marne [a bloody First World War battle].
>
> The audience screamed. Throughout the first tune, all you could hear was the thumping of the drums and the screams of the kids. At the end of the first tune, the band filed off stage, and a disc jockey came on and said, "I told you naughty children this would happen. STAY IN YOUR SEATS!"[68]

After the audience sat down, the DC5 returned and "continued to pound out music" while "the girls continued to scream."[69] The show concluded, and the DC5 bolted to a waiting car that carried them through screaming crowds of fans. Once again, Gleason felt thwarted in his desire to review a Merseybeat show because of crowd chaos. As a jazz critic, he liked respectful audiences quietly listening to music. Even at the 1950s rock 'n' roll and R&B shows he covered, noise and distractions were less intense.

Most music writers outside of fan magazines ignored the 1964 British Invasion. But a few open-minded critics paid attention, such as Jane Scott, who wrote a teen column for the *Plain Dealer* and began covering Cleveland rock shows in 1964. Another was Jim Delehant, a contributing editor to *Hit Parader*, one of several song lyric magazines with solid writing published by the Charlton Publishing Corporation. These writers and others occasionally produced good articles but with little critical analysis. Baby boom critics had yet to express their generation's identification with the music.

Another reason for the lack of critical discourse about rock music in 1964 was that the new sounds demanded a set of aesthetic standards that didn't exist. Outside of avant-garde music, no case had been made for the artistic value of loud, dissonant, distorted sounds and highly amplified electrified instruments. There were no principles for assessing a musical performance that triggered audience participation so extreme as to risk bodily harm to musicians and fans.

Consider how far Gleason had come since his initial dismissal of the Beatles. Unlike most—if not all—of his middle-aged colleagues, Gleason now gives the music a fair listen and ponders its meanings. He also sees how rock fans use music to cope with alienation and compares them to the antihero of MacInnes's *Absolute Beginners*.

As Gleason slowly warmed to the new British bands, he also embraced Black artists who influenced the direction of rock music. For example, when young British fans flocked to ska music, Gleason paid attention. Originating in Jamaica as a precursor to reggae, ska had a lightly swinging rhythm that dancers loved. By the 1960s, youth subcultures in the United Kingdom and the United States made ska a commercial success. Gleason's old friend, Nesuhi Ertegun of Atlantic Records, flew to Jamaica and recorded the Maytals and Prince Buster, the Ska Busters, and other groups. This inspired Gleason to write a column about the genre, known in London club culture as "Blue Beat." Gleason noted that Jamaican sax player Bertie King called ska "very relaxed rock and roll" and quoted producer Ziggy Jackson saying that ska was a "fusion of beat music and the blues."[70]

Gleason also wrote about two Black artists who influenced rock guitar. Sister Rosetta Tharpe brought gospel music to a pop audience in the 1930s and stirred controversy with secular songs like "I Want a Tall Skinny Papa" that mixed swing jazz and blues. In 1964 Gleason saw Tharpe perform at the hungry i nightclub in San Francisco and wrote:

> Rosetta Tharpe is a great artist, a genuine artist, and one of the most moving, gifted, and authentic singers you're likely to encounter these days. ... Tharpe has a voice that can belt and can whisper but is always throbbing with vitality, plays the kind of guitar one usually associates with, say, T-Bone Walker, thus stating again the implicit bond between gospel music and the blues.[71]

Tharpe's performance triggered pleasant memories for Gleason, such as hearing blues singer Bertha "Chippie" Hill at Jimmy Ryan's in the 1940s. Gleason also recalled hearing Tharpe herself at that time, at Café Society, where the rocking gospel singer played to a mixed-race audience similar to the hungry i's. Sharing such memories enriched Gleason's writings during the rock era. He provided readers with historical context based on personal experience.

Gleason greatly admired the music of Chuck Berry, another African American electric guitar pioneer. After Berry was released from prison in 1963, he began a comeback aided by British musicians covering his songs. Gleason reviewed Berry's 1964 performance at the Cow Palace for a teen rock show:

> Berry came on in the middle of the evening, sang a short set, and completely dominated the proceedings ... [He] plays the guitar, dances, and sings and is the most impressive performer to arise from the rhythm and blues and rock 'n' roll ranks since Ray Charles.
>
> He has already joined Charles as a major influence [on] rock 'n' roll music. His guitar playing and his singing and his compositions are one of the main sources of the Beatles' music ... Berry has the kind of stage presence that is charismatic. He just walks onstage, and the atmosphere changes. He is an exceptional guitarist with a wildly swinging style and a singer who can move any audience.[72]

Gleason worked to re-legitimize Berry, a fallen Black performer he believed in, just like he worked to revitalize the career of Bunk Johnson in the 1940s. In this review and others of 1964 rock shows, we see how Gleason changed his focus depending on the nature of the concert. At chaotic shows, he focused on the mayhem; at relatively orderly shows, he focused on the artist. As he had his entire career, Gleason stood up for Black musicians knowing the barriers they faced. Despite the passage of the Civil Rights Act of 1964, these musicians continued to face widespread discrimination. Racial injustice sparked student activists at UC Berkeley to step up their fight for equality and other causes, such as the antiwar movement. Gleason joined the fight.

The Berkeley Rebellion

October 1, 1964. Sproul Plaza. Located in the center of the Berkeley campus, this hub of student activity fronts its namesake Sproul Hall. On this day, the imposing neoclassical building, with its orderly arrangement of Ionic columns, overlooks a distinctly disorderly scene in the plaza below. Hundreds of chanting protesters surround a campus police car and prevent it from moving. In the back seat, activist Jack Weinberg watches the crowd grow.

Hours before, Weinberg defied university rules against political speech when he set up a table and distributed literature for the Congress of Racial Equality (CORE). This leading civil rights group fought segregation and organized voter registration drives for African Americans. For his offense, campus police arrested Weinberg and placed him in their car. Protesters formed a human wall around the vehicle within minutes.

"We can all see better if we sit down," shouts a student, so hundreds of students sit on the plaza ground. Then one at a time, demonstrators remove their shoes and climb onto the roof of the police car and give speeches that boost the protesters' morale. Day turns to night and back to day, and the vehicle remains surrounded with police and Weinberg trapped inside. The crowd has grown to 3,000. Several hundred Alameda County sheriff's office deputies arrive and stand by. Though the potential for violence hangs in the air, the demonstration is peaceful.

Meanwhile, protest leaders negotiate with administrators to end the stalemate. A bushy-haired activist in a rumpled sports jacket named Mario Savio hops on the roof of the police car. An agreement has been reached, Savio says, and asks the protesters to "rise quietly and with dignity and go home." The crowd complies, and the police drive Weinberg to the station, book him, and release him.

Over the following days, campus activists meet and consider their next step. A new organization emerged called the Free Speech Movement (FSM). All this occurred just a few miles from Gleason's home, where he undoubtedly followed the breaking events. Recall that Gleason had earlier interacted with Berkeley activists, such as when he interviewed them about the Kennedy assassination. So, it's no surprise when FSM leaders contact Gleason for help with their public relations strategy. One of these leaders was twenty-four-year-old Michael Rossman:[73]

Someone said, "Hey, this guy Gleason might be crazy enough to care," and a few of us went to see him. He said, "Well, I write a music column, but you might talk to [*Chronicle* reporters] Pimsleur and Hochschild." We kept coming back to Ralph, and not just for reports on his behind-the-scenes struggle against the *Chronicle*'s top-desk censoring of the free speech movement coverage. Something more was going on that made us take time out from the constant operational demands of crisis to brief him and consult with him. Our perceptions of social real reality had been wrenched violently. We were lonely for some fuller understanding.[74]

Rossman noted that the *Chronicle* failed to provide this "fuller understanding." Instead, the newspaper published headlines like "Kerr Links Demonstrator, Reds." In the article, *Chronicle* reporter Malcolm Smith wrote:

Among the "hard-core" demonstrators at the University of California last week were some "who are sympathetic with the Communist approach and skilled in tactics used by the Communist movement," UC president Clark Kerr said yesterday."[75]

To counter this misrepresentation, the Gleasons invited Savio, Rossman, and other FSM leaders to their house and provided much-needed advice and moral support. Rossman wrote:

We came, late at night, to the warm house on Ashby Avenue; the crates of records and the wilderness of memorabilia lining the living room were in shadow, the only light, four lux-o-lamps cantilevering their low pools over the slumping chairs ... Jeanie rose to bring us coffee and cake and left us feeling not simply at home but in family, as we talked about strategy and tactics, conspiracy indictment threats, the unquenchable antic impulse that moved in us also, survivors rocking the crazy lifeboat of our time.[76]

Rossman said Gleason "got" the FSM:

Ralph recognized beneath its political façade the lonely perception of Lenny, the sardonic truth of the Beats, phasing into mass uplift commitment. His sense for watersheds minor and major was extraordinary; when the FSM exploded in his hometown and living room, he grasped at once that it was an action one step nearer to challenging the justice of the deeper processes of our social reality and was enrolled.[77]

In Ralph, we found someone who spoke our language more fully than any other observer. He shared our commitment to the goals of justice and had a keen avocational appreciation of the military strategies of their achievement. He had a nose for the authoritarian style of bureaucrats under pressure. And he had a sense of theater, rooted in the drama of movement actions and events to the deeper play of complex human values acting on the social stage.[78]

As the Free Speech Movement energized Bay Area activists, Gleason continued to share his expertise and advice with other leftist groups. For example, in November 1964, he gave a lengthy presentation on public relations to the West Coast Friends of the SNCC Conference. SNCC stands for the Student Nonviolent Coordinating Committee, a leading civil rights group. Gleason participated in a panel discussion called "Press and Public Relations" and advised the audience of activists on how to garner press attention for protests:[79]

> It is necessary to understand certain things about newspapers and newspapermen in order to discuss how to deal with them. A daily newspaper is a profit-making organization. They like to see themselves as "public servants." In fact, they are public servants only as much as they can afford to be.

> Newspapers, in general, are owned by Republican conservatives. They are staffed by clerks, i.e., reporters and editors. This staff averages out as "Kennedy Democrats." There is a silent struggle—the staff tries to get into print what the management wouldn't want to be there.[80]

This advice came firsthand from Gleason's continual wrangling with *Chronicle* editors over social commentary in his columns. He told the group to "establish a personal relationship with a member of the newspaper staff. You must impress the reporter with your trustworthiness and sense of responsibility." In particular, "personal contact is important."[81]

> If you want to get your material into a column, find out what the columnist is interested in and how he works. Send him the kind of material that will fit into his column. If he works at home, don't send the material to the office and expect it to get to him in time. Getting things in on time is extremely important.[82]

Gleason explained that a typical columnist writes about social issues with "some intrinsic news value in relation to the kind of material he handles."[83] In Gleason's case, that was music, and he began to work the Berkeley protests into his columns. One example is "An Aural Record of The U.C. Struggle," in which he described the role of songs in the FSM. "Free speech on phonograph records and free speech in song," he exalted, "the winds of change are blowing again."[84]

But these winds faced resistance. On November 20, the UC Berkeley Board of Regents met at University Hall to consider disciplinary actions against students involved in the fall protests. They also consider removing the prohibition against political activities, yet Mario Savio and other FSM representatives are barred from speaking at the meeting. Outside, several thousand demonstrators rally in Sproul Plaza and then march to University Hall. Joan Baez joins the protesters and leads them in song. The ebullience dies when Savio reports that the university will continue prohibiting political speech.

The weekend after the University Hall march, activists raised their spirits by holding post-protest dances. In one living room, students play Beatles records and sing a new batch of songs created by the FSM and sung at their protests. Students cavort to "Twist and Shout" by the Beatles and "Mockingbird" by pop-soul duo Inez and Charlie Foxx. In the kitchen, activists plan the next demonstration.[85]

Two days later, Gleason wrote about this marriage of music and politics in "Songs Born of The UC Rebellion":

> Answering Sartre's question, "What is literature?" Nelson Algren defined it as "being made upon any occasion that a challenge is put to the legal apparatus by a conscience in touch with humanity."
>
> The Cal students who marched 7000 strong Friday in a quiet, orderly, responsible demonstration to University Hall are not only making literature, they are making folk music.
>
> What I mean is that folk music, in the true and not the academic sense, is made upon any occasion that the pressures of a restrictive society become comparable to consciences in touch with truth.[86]

Unknown to Gleason, his column caught the eye of a staffer for the California House Un-American Activities Committee (HUAC) investigating the Berkeley demonstrations. The column earned a place of honor in the Senate Committee's files. Gleason had first come to the Committee's attention after he made a speech at a local DuBois Club meeting in the early 1960s, and now HUAC monitored his columns on the Free Speech Movement.[87]

Although HUAC saved Gleason's column as evidence of communist sympathies, the piece was about the connection between protest and music. Recall that at Columbia University, members of the peace movement Gleason belonged to held post-protest dances with swing jazz. After college, Gleason learned about the propagandistic power of popular music during his stint in the US Office of War Information. Twenty years later, he applauded Dylan and Baez because their songs expressed the will of a new generation to ban the bomb, establish racial justice, and end the Vietnam War. Gleason saw rebellious music and radical politics come together again in the Free Speech Movement.

That conflict peaked a week after Gleason's column ran. On December 2, 1964, a crowd of singing activists led by Baez entered Sproul Hall and staged a sit-in. Savio delivered his now-immortalized "Bodies Upon the Gears" speech:

> There's a time when the operation of the machine becomes so odious, makes you so sick at heart that you can't take part! You can't even passively take part! And you've got to put your bodies upon the gears and upon the wheels, upon the levers, upon all the apparatus—and you've got to make it stop! And you've got to indicate to the people who run it, to the people who own it—that unless you're free, the machine will be prevented from working at all![88]

Buoyed by Baez's ballads and Savio's salvos, protesters held their ground into the night. But as the demonstration dragged into its second day, government officials put their machine into operation. Hundreds of police officers swarmed the building and began arresting students.

Tragedy at the Greek Theater

For twelve hours, police arrested protesters, jailing nearly 800. Joel Pimsleur, the *Chronicle* reporter Gleason introduced to the Free Speech Movement, observed the mayhem. Pimsleur wrote for *This World* as an associate editor, but it's unclear why he attended the Sproul Hall sit-in and the arrests. What is certain: nothing could have prepared him for the excessive force he witnessed.

The day after the arrests, Pimsleur sent Gleason a lengthy letter dated December 3, 1964. He wrote:

Ralph,

This is as much personal catharsis for me—purging Thursday's nightmare by putting it on paper—as it may be an assist to you. But there are certain things that should not go unspoken …

Make no mistake, Ralph, the police weren't simply doing their duty. If they'd merely been the machines, the automatons, the privates in the army of the politicians, they'd have been much better.

There was much hilarity in the ranks, as the students were dragged the gauntlet down the long corridors to the stairwell. Very few of them struggled or resisted in any way save going limp, but they were deliberately hauled down the stairs on their backs and tailbones, their arms and wrists twisted—all to the immense amusement of the Oakland police. And lest anyone think I exaggerate, listen to the cops themselves …

While a pair of cops dragged a student down two flights of stairs, a third, surveying the scene from a landing, remarked:

"Hey, don't drag 'em down so fast—they ride on their heels. Take 'em down a little slower—they bounce more that way."

Since when does the press meekly submit to its own suppression? Where were the outraged editorials? Where were the complaints about press censorship, amid all the howls for law and order?[89]

Berkeley activists copied and disseminated Pimsleur's letter, likely with Gleason's help. The truth got out, but it required an underground network.

Four days after the demonstration on December 7, the Berkeley administration announced its response. President Clark Kerr stands before a crowd at the Greek Theater, where the previous summer Joan Baez brought her message of peace to the Berkeley Folk Festival. But now it was winter, and Kerr delivered a more chilling message. "The acts of civil disobedience on December 2 and 3 were unwarranted," he proclaims, making it clear the university stood firm against campus political speech.[90] As Kerr finishes his speech, Savio steps onto the other end of the stage and stands quietly until Kerr adjourns the event. Savio then bolts to the podium. Campus security approach, but allow him to speak. Addressing the crowd, Savio implores, "Please leave here, clear this disastrous scene."[91]

On December 9, 1964, Gleason published "The Tragedy at the Greek Theater," one of the most potent columns of his career. He began by quoting Savio's powerful "Bodies Upon the Gears" speech, followed by his outrage over the police brutality:

> In the face of a university that abandoned its nerve center to armed police, on the first university campus outside Mississippi to be taken over by the cops, dragged to jail by cops who removed their badges so as not to be identified, in the face of a torrent of apoplectic outrage from the elders of the tribe who felt their positions threatened, this generation has stood up and continued to speak plainly of truth.[92]

In the same edition of the *Chronicle* is a political advertisement, a proclamation:

> We support the free speech movement.
>
> We believe that traditionally a university is a sanctuary for ideas, any ideas, their exploration, and expression.
>
> We believe this tradition was violated by the administration of the University of California when it ruled—and they have not backed down from this rule—that students might be expelled for on-campus advocacy and/or off-campus participation in possibly unlawful political activities, such as some civil rights demonstrations ...
>
> We call on the governor and the administration to recognize their error, to guarantee the political rights not be denied students by the university, to help ensure that charges are dropped against those demonstrators recently arrested, and to recognize that the traditions of the university and democratic society cannot so easily be destroyed.[93]

It was signed by notable Bay Area cultural rebels: Lawrence Ferlinghetti, Jon Hendricks, Malvina Reynolds, Ken Kesey, John Handy, Morton Subotnick, Alan Watts, and others. And, of course, Ralph J. Gleason.

Nine days later and almost 3,000 miles away, another newspaper carried the story of the Sproul Hall protest. "Conflict at Berkeley: An Inside Story" appeared on the front page of the *Columbia Spectator* on December 18, 1964. Pimsleur, a Columbia alumnus and former *Spectator* writer, penned it. Articles like this supported the rise of a new era of student activism at Columbia, where, twenty-seven years earlier, Gleason wrote in the *Spectator* that plans were in the works for the 1937 Antiwar Strike. As 1964 ended, Gleason saw history repeat, a recurrence he helped spark.

7

The Jazz Liverpool of the West (1965)

> *Yes, I know this is a jazz column, and yes, I know, the Beatles are not usually considered a jazz group. But it has come upon me with increasing strength recently that the Beatles are a lot more than they may seem to be, and I offer as evidence this album.*[1]
>
> Ralph J. Gleason, review of *Beatles '65*

Gleason addressed readers who thought a "jazz column" should exclude rock music. Though Gleason continued to write influential jazz criticism, he increasingly devoted column space to rock music as the genre evolved. Gleason became especially fascinated with rock's social messages to the new generation. He wrote, "The Beatles strike a responsive chord with youth by their flat-out rejection of the values of the established society ... the Beatles are rebels and rebels of the most virulent kind. Successful rebels."[2]

The revolutionary sound of the British Invasion and the songs of young folk singers like Dylan echoed across the Bay Area in 1965. They influenced local musicians such as Marty Balin, George Hunter, Country Joe McDonald, Grace Slick, and Jerry Garcia who developed the "San Francisco Sound," which blended the electronic experimentation of rock with the poetic sensibility and protest messages of folk music. One young promoter said San Francisco could become the "Liverpool of the West." Enveloping this new scene was the city's jazz milieu, which infused the rock community with its traditions of improvised dance music and avant-garde experimentation.

Gleason Beat

And it was jazz on Gleason's mind in January 1965 when he lectured students at Sonoma State College, about fifty miles north of San Francisco. Hands in pockets, Gleason gently rocks side-to-side as he introduces his new course, "Jazz in American Society," at the start of the spring semester. Gleason pulls out a letter and says, "I received my first piece of fan mail." He reads it to the class while interjecting his comments:

Letter writer: The course is a grave mistake.
Gleason: And he may be right [nervous laughter from students].
Letter writer: Ralph Gleason does not have a California state teacher's credential.
Gleason: Which is absolutely true, I do not.
Letter writer: Mr. Gleason is a graduate of no college.
Gleason: Well, I've heard about Noh plays and Noh poetry [a reference to classical Japanese drama and poetry], but not about Noh college, that's a new one [round of laughter].
Letter writer: Mr. Gleason is, however, an advocate for narcotics and sex deviation and had called for integration with Negroes.
Gleason: So now you know what the course is really about [great laughter]. And we'll get into all of those things, and we'll practice integration and turn on and sex deviation and all the rest of it.

Won over, the students relax back into their seats, and Gleason begins his lecture. On the chalkboard is a quote from Bunk Johnson: "Jazz is playin' from the heart. You don't lie."[3]

All this was filmed by a British Broadcasting Corporation (BBC) crew for an episode of a documentary series called *Inside America*. The program profiled thirteen Americans, focusing on their professions and home life. Director Robert Kitts said Gleason had been chosen because he wasn't an "obvious spokesman" for jazz and would avoid clichés.[4] Kitts liked Gleason's embedment in the Bay Area jazz scene and knowledge of the city's Beat poetry movement. The episode was called "The Gleason Beat." Over ten days, the crew captured Gleason in various settings: a local nightclub, his home, the studios of KQED, a restaurant (with Jimmy Lyons), the *Chronicle* newsroom, and his classroom at Sonoma State College. Formatted like today's reality TV, each scene was set up beforehand, including dialogue, but allowed for impromptu moments. We see an unprecedented look at a leading music journalist at work.

True to its title, the documentary begins with a typical work night for Gleason as he takes in a show by Vince Guaraldi and Bola Sete at a local club. Afterward, Gleason and Guaraldi stroll North Beach, Gleason dressed in his signature tweed coat, tie, and sweater vest. He reveals that he started wearing a tie after covering shows in North Beach so he wouldn't be mistaken for a beatnik.

The documentary takes us into Gleason's Ashby Avenue house the following morning. Gleason walks into the living room and slips an LP onto a turntable. He greets his family as they finish breakfast and the children leave for school. Gleason tells Jean about the Guaraldi show when the phone rings. The caller is saxophonist Stan Getz, known for his collaborations with Bossa Nova virtuosos Antônio Carlos Jobim, João Gilberto, and his wife, Astrud Gilberto. Chatting on the phone with Getz, Gleason recounted the Guaraldi show and complained that the audience talked over the music, a pet peeve of Gleason's. After the call ends, Gleason climbs the stairs to his attic office while lighting his pipe. Seated at his cluttered desk, he faces the camera and says: "Well, this is where it all starts. I go to a nightclub or a concert, and I go home, and I think about it, and I get up the next morning, and I have breakfast, and I come up here, and

I try to write a column about it."[5] Gleason speaks the same way he writes, in a flow of uninterrupted clauses.

The camera pans across his desk covered with a music writer's detritus—promotional circulars, photographs of musicians, newspaper clippings, and a copy of *Variety*. On the adjacent wall, bookcases overflow with additional ephemera. A sign reads "Think," an appeal to reason within the cluttered office. Gleason clicks on his electric typewriter, faces the keyboard, and says, "It all starts with my sitting down here, looking at the typewriter, and then trying to write a sentence that makes sense."[6]

Downstairs, Jean, slender with her hair in a ponytail, pulls an album from the wall of records in the living room. In a voiceover, Gleason says, "I married a jazz fan twenty-five years ago." When they met, Jean had a "Chu Berry record that I dug and had a better phonograph than I did." Finished with his review of the Guaraldi show, Gleason walks downstairs and sits with Jean, who is sewing. After reading his mail, Gleason leaves to drive into the city as Jean calls out, "Don't forget your milk!" and hands him a thermos. As Gleason pilots his Volvo across the Bay Bridge into San Francisco, the city comes into view. "There are elements of progress that I find absolutely abominable, and I'd like to stop right now," he says. Gleason criticized the city's tendency to demolish old buildings and replace them with "prisons of plate glass and concrete" that are "cold and don't have the warm feeling" San Francisco once had.[7]

Gleason pulls into the KQED-TV studios, where he watches a videotape of a recent *Jazz Casual* show. He tells a producer that the episode is about the "sociology of a jam session." The producer asks, "You're really an academic at heart?" Gleason smiles and replies, "Yes." With that, Gleason is back in his Volvo as the camera takes in the city and zooms in on Alcatraz prison in the distance. Gleason, in voiceover, reflects on jazz and race:

> The role of the white jazz musicians today, who feel uncomfortable, or slighted or even put upon because of the accepted superiority or validity of the negro musician, is rather similar to that of the white liberal, faced with the fact that his former role as a pioneer and discoverer is obsolete because we are in a transitional period and jazz reflects this. In this country, the color of the skin of the jazz artist interferes with our hearing.[8]

Gleason's poignant words resonate today.

Gleason pulls up to the *Chronicle* building and enters the newsroom, where his colleagues try to ignore the film crew. He hands his editor the Guaraldi review. As Gleason walks to the mailroom, he flashes his winning smile as he passes row after row of desks. After leaving the *Chronicle* building, he makes the forty-mile trek to Sonoma State College, delivering a lecture that challenges preconceptions about jazz.

In the documentary's final scene, Gleason drives home as he sums up the meaning of jazz:

> So, this is the jazz message, the dignity of man. It is expressed and repeated from the beginning right down to the latest free-blowing session in a smoky nightclub. And

in reality, it's the message of art itself. And in the attitude of American society to these arts. And to this art is the implicit self-judgment of the values of this society. Even in his own craft union, the AFM [American Federation of Musicians], the musician is classified as a performer, not as an artist, and his concerts are not concerts but variety shows.[9]

Arriving home, Gleason walks to the front door as the camera zooms in on a hand-painted campaign poster: "Dizzy for President." As the film ends, Gleason says, "It is a tragic thing that we have never known the names of the greatest artists we have produced in this society. The rest of the world knows their names very well indeed."[10] That's what drove Gleason to shine a light on musicians in the shadows of American culture.

The Black Priest of Disorganized Religion

Gleason saw in Bob Dylan the imagination, irreverence, and spontaneity of jazz musicians such as John Coltrane and Archie Shepp. He recognized that Dylan, like those artists, spoke for an alienated segment of society.

Dylan performed at the Berkeley Community Theater in April 1965. The buzz of anticipation electrifies the room as Gleason takes his seat in an audience of old-school folkies and new-generation rock fans. He sees a different Dylan than the scruffy folk singer from the Monterey Folk Festival. His hair is longer, and he wears a mod-style, houndstooth-pattern jacket. Dylan sings songs of true love, lost love, and brotherly love. The transcendent performance inspires Gleason to pen an inspired review:

> This identification with the lonely, the lost, and the misunderstood makes Dylan, the Black priest of disorganized religion that he is, speak for his generation … His chains of flashing images were like a gospel preacher's parables. Dylan, like Lenny Bruce, is delineating a highly moral position … He is sui generis, alone and unique, and a seething wellspring of creativity.[11]

Dylan just released his fifth album, *Bringing it All Back Home*. The first half of the LP was recorded with an electric band, a radical departure for a folk artist. Gleason adulated the album, especially one song in particular:

> Dylan achieved the goal of every major poet in history: to speak with conviction and authority to a mass audience of his generation … "Subterranean Homesick Blues" is a pure rock 'n' roll blues-oriented piece with lyrics that are a poem to the teenager's hopeless position in a world he never made … more and more of the lost, the lonely and the disillusioned youth are harking to his words.[12]

The album also caught the attention of the new generation Bay Area musicians, such as guitarist Jerry Garcia:

> I never used to like Bob Dylan until he came out with electric music ... Boy, when *Bringing It All Back Home* came out. Yeah, lovely ... Beautiful, mad stuff.[13]

Garcia, like Dylan, began as a folk musician and moved to rock music, in his band the Warlocks, later called the Grateful Dead. Other Bay Area folk musicians began switching to rock and experimenting with electronic sounds. They also began to experiment with their look. Musicians took on the frontier-era style of the San Francisco Barbary Coast decked out in fringed suede jackets, cowboy vests, wide-brimmed hats, and for women, high-necked Victorian dresses in floral calicos. Counterculture scholar Nadya Zimmerman observed how the early San Francisco rock bands such as the Charlatans cultivated a "Wild-West-outlaw-meets-young-White-rebel look" even before they nurtured their sound.[14] Gleason dubbed these musicians and their followers the "buckskin brigade."[15]

Although change was in the air, it hadn't coalesced into an actual music scene. According to author Gary Kamiya, many factors worked against a city-wide cultural revolution:

> In 1965 San Francisco was rolling comfortably along on post-Eisenhower cruise control, a prosperous, increasingly corporate city busy tearing down its poor neighborhoods and historic buildings and throwing up high-rises and freeways. For all its vaunted bohemianism, its power structure was deeply conservative.
>
> The old Beat haunt, North Beach, had been taken over by topless clubs. In Berkeley, the free speech movement had galvanized students a year before, but there was no evidence that anything weird was brewing.[16]

Despite lacking an established music scene, San Francisco rock fans enjoyed a steady fare of high-quality music by significant recording artists. These included the new folk rock musicians such as the Byrds, whom Gleason heard in May 1965 at the Peppermint Tree, a well-liked San Francisco go-go club. Gleason focused on the audience's appearance and dance style:

> Everybody goes out there and wails away in his or her own individual fashion, and the dancers generally ignore one another, preferring the fullest flower of individual free enterprise. One male in jeans and a striped shirt had a head of hair that looked like Medusa's snakes, and he shook it with abandon.[17]

Not a single word about the Byrds' music other than "they do a lot of Dylan songs."[18] Except for the Beatles and Dylan, Gleason was less interested in rock's aesthetics than rock's sociology, audience behavior in particular. Unlike most pop music writers, Gleason saw something bigger at stake than the sales of records and concert tickets. Something was happening in American society, and the signs were everywhere: the lyrics of Bob Dylan, the sounds of the Beatles and John Coltrane, the happenings of Ken Kesey, and a new rise of activism on the UC Berkeley campus.

Three Moments in a Revolution

By the spring of 1965, the Free Speech Movement had run its course. But as America became more deeply involved in the Vietnam War, a new wave of protests rose. The United States had just entered the ground war in Vietnam and launched an aerial bombing campaign called Operation Rolling Thunder. In response, student antiwar activists around the country utilized a new form of protest—the teach-in, derived from the civil rights movement's sit-ins. Teach-ins originated in the spring of 1965 as political forums leading to action, typically protests against the Vietnam War. During teach-ins, participants held seminars, debates, marches, and other events designed to spark dialogue.

No one could spark a dialogue like Jerry Clyde Rubin. The former Berkeley student had moved away from the Bay Area before the Sproul Hall protests but recently returned, teeming with unspent political ambition. One day in 1965, Rubin and his girlfriend Barbara Gullahorn hit on the idea of holding a teach-in at Berkeley. Knowing Gleason was a sounding board for campus activists, the couple walked to Gleason's house and pitched the idea. Gleason loved the proposal and suggested possible speakers for the event, christened "Vietnam Day."[19] In planning the teach-in, Rubin and other activists founded the Vietnam Day Committee (VDC) and contacted antiwar groups and protesters worldwide. The idea snowballed into a global demonstration with Berkeley as one of the two sites in the United States.

Vietnam Day came on what was a busy May weekend for Gleason. On Friday night, May 21, 1965, he attended a special concert by Vince Guaraldi at San Francisco's Grace Cathedral. Prominently located on the top of Nob Hill, the towering English Gothic church was consecrated in 1964 after a 44-year construction process. The Episcopal parish celebrated the cathedral's completion with a year-long "Festival of Grace" featuring performances by notable jazz musicians. This came during a period in which several Black jazz musicians around the country composed "sacred jazz" pieces such as Max Roach's "We Insist! The Freedom Now Suite" and Mary Lou Williams' hymn "Black Christ of the Andes." Guaraldi's composition for the "Festival of Grace" was a "jazz mass," the first of several performed by various artists in the 1960s. Fantasy Records recorded the performance as Gleason watched, spellbound.

The following night, Gleason experienced a different type of spiritual epiphany at the Vietnam Day teach-in where he heard speakers such as writer and antiwar activist Norman Mailer. Gleason saw a transcendent connection between the teach-in and the Guaraldi performance:

> Guaraldi's religious music, which was lyric and outgoing and swung lightly in the setting of Grace Cathedral, is but another move in the religious revolution that is sweeping society. It is a natural outgrowth of the whole thrust to involve the worshippers, to feed back the service directly to them and not to a wall ...
>
> Vince Guaraldi's music, flowing, melodic, and pulsing with the life thrust of jazz, was successful ... It was a religious demonstration of the revolution

of creativity, of the philosophy of improvisation rising up against the deadening influence of formality, of the calcified establishment and breaking through to the people themselves ...

The revolution of creativity marked the two-day affair at the University of California, too. It throbbed day and night with the vitality of improvisation ... [It was] as peaceful as a religious revival ...[20]

The Vietnam Day Committee continued to hold successful antiwar protests in San Francisco and became the new face of Berkeley protest. Emboldened, Jerry Rubin and other organizers began planning a second teach-in for the fall of 1965.

Gleason called the Guaraldi concert and the VDC forum "two moments in a revolution." That May, he experienced a different revolution when the Rolling Stones came to town. The bad boys of British rock hit big with *Rolling Stones, Now!* and its single, "The Last Time." Gleason experienced the excitement at their Civic Auditorium show with opening act, the Byrds. Before the concert, he hung out backstage with the band:

Mick Jagger and Keith Richards kidded Charlie Watts and Ian Stewart (who manages the equipment and used to play piano with the group when it was more traditional-jazz oriented). "Groovin' with Ornette Coleman," Mick Jagger taunted the jazz lovers and was promptly wrestled against the wall while the road manager howled, "Don't break the guitars." ...

Charlie Watts and Stewart cross-examined the visiting jazz critic [Gleason] about who was playing where in San Francisco and complained bitterly that in New York, Roy Eldridge and Coleman Hawkins had been playing somewhere, but no one knew exactly where.

When the Byrds were playing, the door to the dressing room was open so the Stones could hear them. Charlie Watts stood listening and clapping a set of claves, the Latin rhythm blocks. The road manager wouldn't let any of the group go outside to listen. "They'll tear you apart," he said, wise with the experience of two US tours with the Stones.[21]

Stewart was right, and after the Rolling Stones walked onstage, Gleason experienced the bedlam:

The shrill feminine cries were so loud one could hardly hear the group at all. Periodically, the press became so acute that the cops would lean over the lip of the stage and extract some wiggling body from the blob of flesh, throw her backward, like a sack of wheat, across the stage, and march her down the exit steps to the side ...

A blonde girl waved a red and white rugby shirt. A heavy girl, minus a shoe and limping on an injured leg, was hauled up by the cops on stage. Slim, younger girls followed and slouched on the music cases, sobbing. Suddenly one of them leaped on drummer Charlie Watts from the back.

Watts patiently extricated himself and kept on drumming while the cops pulled her off him. Pieces of paper, candy boxes, and handkerchiefs were thrown down on the stage. Mick Jagger, who backstage had been full of humor, twisted and wiggled in his dance, clutching the microphone like James Brown …

A thin boy, mildly hysterical, was thrown back into the crowd from the stage by the police as his friend shouted, "He'll go quietly." … The lights went up, and the Stones raced for the stage door and into a waiting limousine.[22]

Gleason captured the chaos and drama from the storm's center. His review contained a theme that began to underpin many of his rock concert reviews, the excessive force by police officers put into an impossible situation as they tried to control ecstatic young fans.

The Stones show, the Guaraldi concert, and the Vietnam Day forum were only three events in Gleason's May 1965 schedule. Still, they brought him deeper into a swirling cultural transformation spun off turntables rotating 33 1/3 revolutions per minute.

Four-Minute Suspensions of Disbelief

Gleason believed in the power of phonograph records. He saw the Stones, Beatles, and Dylan as pop propagandists, secular evangelists who used records to spread their vision of a better way of life. Gleason witnessed shellac discs' power to fight fascism during his stint in the Office of War Information when jazz records carried the clarion call of democracy into European and American households.

Songwriters like Dylan, Gleason observed, "consciously or unconsciously transformed the phonograph record from pure entertainment to that of the communication of ideas, and made the concert hall a political platform."[23]

There is a deep thing at work in all of this. The Reality behind the American dream and the truth behind its mythology is being attacked relentlessly by a generation that takes nothing for granted from its elders. They have added the weight of words to the anti-establishment humanitarian position the jazz musicians have wordlessly occupied for years.[24]

In the summer of 1965, electric guitars and drums amplified Dylan's messages to the audience of the Newport Folk Festival. Wearing a black leather jacket and sunburst Stratocaster, Dylan takes the stage with a rock band and launches into "Maggie's Farm." Rock fans cheer, but folk fans boo. Gleason read about the show and called it a merger of "poetry and popular music" unlike anything in recent cultural history.[25] Dylan's

Newport set animates a discussion Gleason leads a few weeks later at the Big Sur Folk Festival. He asks the panel, "Why the sudden surge of interest in popular music" by folk musicians? Panelist Malvina Reynolds, a notable Bay Area folk singer, responds:

> Even if an audience doesn't get every word of a lyric, even if all that comes through from Bobby Dylan's song "Subterranean Homesick Blues" is the one line "Don't follow Leaders," then it's worthwhile."[26]

Gleason participated in the festival during a two-week vacation in July 1965. When he returned to work, he wrote a *Chronicle* column about the meaning of rock music:

> Rock 'n' roll constitutes the contemporary folk music of the world's teenagers.
>
> The twin themes it strikes me are exemplified by the Beatles and Bob Dylan. The Beatles are when all is said and done, a roaring, raging, riotous protest in favor of life and love and laughter and thrill of living and against pretense and pomposity and falsehood. Dylan wears more than one hat, but the two which have had the biggest effect on popular music are his teenage protest songs such as "Subterranean Homesick Blues," which says that society will blame the kids no matter what really happened, and his lyric songs of alienation with their great poetic imagery.
>
> Then there's the dancing, which poet Allen Ginsberg refers to as a revolution of the psyche and a discovery of the body antithetical to the Protestant prudery that dogs this culture. Then there is the sound itself, with the reverberating electric guitars and the yelling and screaming of the audience.
>
> In a way, this strikes me as reflecting the sound of modern society, freeways, and jets, and the songs themselves, little three and four-minute suspensions of disbelief.
>
> What these songs are doing, it seems to me, is speaking of the realities behind the American Dream, attacking the stereotype of the American Dream World of Success.[27]

In this column, Gleason brought together thoughts from his past writings to analyze the themes of rock music. This was likely the first attempt by a music journalist to do so.

Gleason vigorously supported Dylan's music in a full-page review of *Highway 61 Revisited*. Dylan's lyrics, he wrote, "represent for the first time in our society a merger of poetry with popular music which can have a deep and lasting effect on our entire society."[28] He said Dylan met the aim of the jazz-poetry movement to "get poetry out of the hands of the professors and out of the hands of the squares."[29] Gleason also compared Dylan to Ken Kesey, Joseph Heller, and James Baldwin with their "growing realization of the surrealism of the world."[30]

In his lyrics, Dylan ranges over the whole scene surrealistically, linking together his mosaics of images like a ceiling by El Greco. He sings of alienation, of the futility of politics, of the emptiness of the values of the adult society, but he is not negativistic. He sings in favor of life, just as the Beatles do in a different way, and is no coincidence that Dylan and the Beatles share a huge audience.[31]

Highway 61 Revisited, *Beatles '65*, and *Bringing It All Back Home* transformed Gleason. He began to write about music with a newfound sense of purpose. Recall that two years earlier, Gleason verged on leaving the *Chronicle* in a fit of existential despair. Alienated from his Old Left cronies, he now found a place within a new generation. This generation's music enthralled Gleason, and he wanted to use his column to cultivate an appreciation for the new sounds, as he had for rock 'n' roll in the 1950s. Case in point, Gleason's August 1965 column called "On Listening to Rock 'n' Roll,"

> You listen to Top 40 music in several ways. On your LPs for dancing, for the beat, to hear and feel the rush of sound or the words. The same applies to radio except that you have the addition of disc jockeys who are themselves entertainers, bright, witty, hip, and irreverent.
>
> You go to see the shows at the Cow Palace or the Civic Auditorium, however, to experience the thing, not to hear it. These are not concerts; these are shows. The ritual of participation takes over, it's a happening ... The sound of the music is the sound of the electronic age, a dissent from earlier forms. The [performers'] costumes are a dissent from the Ed Sullivan slick. And a relief, I might add. These performers never have a nose bob or cap their teeth.[32]

Gleason had come to understand the ritualistic, participatory nature of rock concerts and how the audience noise and excitement that drowned out the music were part of the show. He reflected this understanding in his coverage of the Beatles Cow Palace concert on August 31, 1965.

In a column that ran before the concert, Gleason helped his readers understand the social and aesthetic revolution the Beatles wrought. He contrasted their music with Tin Pan Alley pop and noted the Beatles' popularity in folk music circles and within the Free Speech Movement. He championed the Beatles' irreverence and lack of hypocrisy. And praised "the ingenuity of teenagers in crashing the gate." Prophetic words.

On concert day, Gleason arrived before the afternoon show and attended a press conference with the Beatles. He found them to be "human, quiet, reasonable citizens, living in the midst of a fantastic uproar with the calm of fatalists."[33] Gleason witnessed that uproar at the concert. Now accustomed to fan mayhem, he enjoyed the snatches of music he heard between waves of screams. But he didn't appreciate how security manhandled fans. And Gleason didn't like how the *Chronicle* framed the chaos. "Beatles Play S.F. as a Riot Rages," shouted the headline. At the show, "Wave after wave of little girls trampled and clawed through the ranks of outnumbered Cow Palace police."[34] The article, and others like it during the tour, gave the impression that the

Beatles' music provoked riots. Gleason had defended rock 'n' roll musicians like Fats Domino against this charge, and in his review of the Beatles concert, he blamed the chaos on lax security. "The problem is not the Beatles," he wrote, "unlike some other groups," the band discourages fans from charging the stage.[35] Gleason said the Beatles "sing well, write excellent tunes and sounded ... when I could hear them, as though they were much more musically sophisticated than one might imagine."[36] Even though the screams drowned out the lyrics, "the kids never missed one tune, and they sang and chanted along with it all."[37]

As the summer of 1965 ended, Gleason had covered concerts by the era's most influential rock artists: Bob Dylan, the Rolling Stones, and the Beatles. These concerts transformed Gleason and the world, triggering a cultural revolution. More and more, rock music fascinated Gleason because it provided a new sonic ecosystem to explore, teeming with diverse lifeforms and new realms of aural experience.

A Raging Torrent of Sound

Gleason's interest in rock music didn't impede his jazz writing. Although he was fascinated by the rising San Francisco rock scene, Gleason's coverage of jazz remained more extensive than his coverage of rock.

John Coltrane's new music captivated Gleason like no other. "What we are confronting is an artist searching for new ways of perceiving reality," he wrote of the sax player's masterwork *A Love Supreme*.[38] Gleason told readers the album had a "different sound ... the newness and the strangeness of those experiments will repel some and discourage others."[39] No stranger to the revelatory power of "strange sounds," Gleason urged readers to open their minds and said *A Love Supreme* conveyed Coltrane's "profound religiosity" and intent to "express love through music." Coltrane's quartet transformed the "conflicting and clashing series of emotions and kaleidoscopic scenes" of the mid-1960s into an "ordered universe of intense emotional feeling."

> [The musicians] attempt to strain or even break the bounds of expression previously laid down for each instrument. The music they produce is the kind that simply cannot be audited with half an ear. It must be listened to with intensity, blocking out all distractions.
>
> Done this way and by someone who has surrendered himself to the music by abandoning his preconceptions of what it should be, it becomes all-encompassing music that brings the listener a high degree of emotional charge.[40]

In September 1965, Coltrane came to town, and Gleason heard him at the Jazz Workshop:

> On the opening night of a beautiful ballad, Coltrane began slowly and, with infinite pain, carefully lined out the lyrical melody. Then he broke it up, rephrased it, and

used the fragments as platforms for further explorations, building the whole thing in a series of pyramidal structures into a raging torrent of sound."[41]

September was also the month of the annual Monterey Jazz Festival. Gleason had an understanding with his co-founder Jimmy Lyons that he would receive no compensation for his work with the festival so he could objectively cover the event. Gleason exercised that right in his scathing critique of the 1965 festival. Backstage he witnessed problem after problem, such as unrehearsed bands and poor staging. Frustrated that the festival he co-founded put on a poorly organized event, Gleason wrote that an "agonizing re-appraisal is needed if Monterey is to maintain its stature as America's best jazz festival."[42] He also criticized the heavy police presence at the festival, a reaction to the recent Watts race riots in Los Angeles. Gleason blamed racism for excessive security at the peaceful festival:

> It is pitiful … what this episode implies about white America. About you and me, brother. The Monterey Jazz Festival is a thing of beauty and joy to all just because it is a three-day hiatus of racial tension and a three-day vision of how the world should, can, and must be someday. But Negroes in groups scare white people. Especially the security-conscious white people.[43]

Despite his misgivings about the festival's organization and security, Gleason enjoyed sets by Duke Ellington, the Denny Zeitlin Trio, and others.[44] But the standout performance for Gleason was the John Handy Quintet, a "personal triumph for the San Francisco State College saxophonist" and "one of the most musically satisfying performances" in the festival's recent history.[45] Incredibly satisfying for Gleason because he helped make it happen.

The story began when Gleason heard the Handy Quintet at the Both/And Club in San Francisco the previous summer. The thirty-two-year-old saxophonist eschewed the experimentalism of free jazz for a straightforward melodicism that nonetheless expressed an intensely creative imagination. When the group launched into their showcase "Spanish Lady," Gleason said it was like "a wind tunnel had been turned on. At first, I didn't believe it. Really. I thought it was an illusion. The drummer was completely impossible to believe, he swung so much."[46] Handy said that when he spotted Gleason in the audience, he signaled his bandmates, and they played "as if in front of 10,000 people."[47] The inspired performance brought record crowds to the Both/And. Knocked out, Gleason took his friend Jimmy Lyons, manager of the Monterey Jazz Festival, to hear Handy play and consider him for the upcoming festival. Lyons listened to "Spanish Lady" from start to finish and told Handy, "You're at the festival."[48] So, as Gleason watches Handy's performance from his festival box, he's glad to see the saxophone prodigy and bandmates get the accolades they deserve.

In September 1965, Gleason experienced another gratifying concert in which he played an important role. "A Concert of Sacred Music" was staged by Duke Ellington and combined old and new compositions specially arranged for a religious setting. The concert was part of Grace Cathedral's year-long "Festival of Grace," in which Gleason

Figure 7.1 Ralph Gleason at his desk at the Monterey Jazz Festival, c. 1965. Courtesy of the Estate of Ralph J. Gleason.

saw Vince Guaraldi perform his jazz mass. But Gleason played a critical behind-the-scenes role in the Ellington concert—he filmed the performance for KQED public television, where he produced and hosted *Jazz Casual*.

On the concert day, Gleason arrives early to greet the film crew led by his friend, cinemaphotographer Robert Zagone. This sets a positive tone for the project. The team sets up their equipment with Zagone perched high on a platform above the orchestra. The doors opened, and the audience fills the pews. Ellington and his musicians take the stage, resplendent in white tuxedos, looking like they stepped out of the Cotton Club c. 1929. Ellington cues the orchestra and leads them through their first piece, "In the Beginning God," named for the first words of the Old Testament. The majesty of Ellington's music fills the space. The concert's highlight is when twenty-four-year-old Black gospel singer Esther Marrow takes the stage, demurely dressed in a white shift dress. Marrow performs a quietly killing interpretation of "Come Sunday" from Ellington's 1942 suite "Black, Brown, and Beige." The song's wide melodic span perfectly represents Marrow's extraordinary range. The recitation stuns the audience.

Zagone, perched overhead, is mesmerized. Rifling through his gadget bag for equipment, he abruptly stops, overcome by the beauty of Marrow's soaring voice. Below, Gleason stands transfixed. After Marrow's performance, Ellington plays the final numbers. What Ellington, Gleason, and Zagone accomplished was not only satisfying but transgressive; to perform secular music in a sacred space at that time was controversial.[49] The experience inspired John Handy to such a degree that he became a college teacher and taught at San Francisco State University, Stanford University, UC Berkeley, and the San Francisco Conservatory of Music.[50]

During this period, Gleason produced another Ellington documentary with his KQED crew, *Love You Madly*. He filmed the bandleader onstage, backstage, and in hotel rooms—capturing all the "sophistication and humor, popularity, and charm of his childhood hero."[51] In his autobiography, Ellington called Gleason's two documentaries the best films to have been made about him. Gleason established his credentials as a documentary filmmaker in his three television documentaries: *Love You Madly*, *A Concert of Sacred Music*, and *Anatomy of a Hit*. In addition to *Jazz Casual*, these TV films were broadcast on National Educational Television and introduced Gleason to a national audience. Unfortunately, the programs didn't garner much attention from critics. However, Percy Shain in the *Boston Globe* wrote that *Anatomy of a Hit* "caught the easy formality of pop musicians going to work on a studio date, but it rambled and wandered too much in a formless way to keep one's attention riveted" and offered "little insight into what makes a hit."[52] Today, *Anatomy* and the Ellington films are considered essential documents of jazz history, precisely what Gleason intended.

As he made films, wrote his column, and took in San Francisco's kaleidoscopic music scene, Gleason remained active in the city's literary world. He developed an association with *Ramparts*, a glossy New Left magazine that recently moved to San Francisco under new editor Warren Hinckle. That April, Gleason had written an article about Dylan and protest music for the magazine, "The Times They Are A-Changin'." From there, Gleason became a *Ramparts* editor and created an arts-review feature called "Ephemera." He kicked off the segment with a short piece called "Manifesto":

> Very possibly, it seems to me, literature has never had a more important role to play in American life than it does today, and the most useful thing a critic or editor can do is to be aware of that fact …
>
> That major literary talents such as Allen Ginsberg should have had to resort to underground publication is a terrible commentary on the literary world. We can, if we believe in life and have some poetry in our souls, do no less than try to see that it does not happen again. "My rock and roll is the motion of an Angel flying in a modern city," Ginsburg said. And Bob Dylan adds, "those not busy being born, are busy dyin.'"
>
> We aim to live.[53]

Gleason assigned reviews for "Ephemera" to an eclectic group of his friends, including Nat Hentoff, Bishop James Pike of Grace Cathedral, up-and-coming music writer Jonathan Cott, and Nelson Algren, who reviewed a recent book by his lover, philosopher Simone de Beauvoir. Adding to the chumminess, Gleason reviewed his friend Algren's novel *Notes from a Sea Diary: Hemingway All the Way*.

In *Notes*, Algren described a tanker voyage to India during which he reflected on Ernest Hemingway. Gleason wrote that Algren, like John Coltrane, let go of traditional forms of expression to say something "relevant to today's turbulent scene."[54] Algren's language, "sings and moans and keens and wails."[55] When Algren read Gleason's review, he sent Gleason a letter and joked that he enjoyed it "even though I didn't know what you were reviewing."[56] Algren recommended Tom Wolfe's *Kandy-Kolored Tangerine-Flake Streamline Baby*, one of the first works of New Journalism. Algren told Gleason that Wolfe was "new and good, and everybody hates him because he'd found a new way to say things."[57] But Algren criticized the *Ramparts* review of the Beatles' *Hard Day's Night* by Jonathan Cott, who watched the movie two times to review it. Algren said Cott was "dealing with half a deck" because "nobody in his right mind" would want to see the film twice.[58] Yet Cott's fascinating but overlooked article foretold the free-wheeling and irreverent style of rock writing soon to come.[59] Cott would work with Gleason at *Rolling Stone* magazine in a few years.

Gleason remained deeply involved in jazz and literature as he covered the San Francisco rock scene, which underwent a history-changing metamorphosis in the summer and fall of 1965, with Gleason playing an essential role.

Sound and Style

Gleason received phone calls from enthusiastic music fans urging him to review a musician or band. But never so intently as the caller who implored him to rush out to see a band that had just debuted at a local club. Gleason casually replied, "Yeah, sure. People keep telling me about these groups. I try to check 'em out; you know how it is."[60] Just another tip that won't pan out.

The caller was Bay Area journalist Hunter S. Thompson whose article "The Motorcycle Gangs: Losers and Outsiders" had just been published by the *Nation*. Soon book offers would come in, but for now, Thompson wrote for a Berkeley underground newspaper called the *Spider*. He called Gleason about a new San Francisco band with an intriguing name—the Jefferson Airplane. Despite Thompson's frantic pleadings, Gleason initially declined to cover the Airplane, so the *Chronicle* gave the assignment to their young theater critic John Wasserman.[61]

Gleason finally gets curious and decides to give the Airplane a listen. And so, one night, he drives his Volvo to the Marina district to hear the band, passing antique shops, bars, and Italianate townhouses with bay windows and bracketed cornices. Gleason parks at the Matrix nightclub, a nondescript building except for its distinctive ziggurat-shaped façade. Entering, he finds a spot where he can observe the stage and take notes on his reporter's spiral pad. He blends in, though old enough to be the parent of many in the young crowd. At forty-eight, he maintains his slender, square-shouldered build. Well-liked by musicians and fans, he's a familiar sight in the local music scene, dressed in his signature trench coat or tweed jacket.

Gleason sees the earliest incarnation of the Jefferson Airplane that night. Lead singers Marty Balin and Signe Toly Anderson tear through electrified versions of folk standards such as "High Flying Bird." At the same time, lead guitarist Jorma Kaukonen fills the air with shimmering blasts of vibrato-laden sounds. The rhythm section of Paul Kantner, acoustic bassist Bob Harvey, and drummer Jerry Peloquin propel songs forward or in some cases, provide a delicate wash of rhythmic color.

The Jefferson Airplane win over Gleason. It was the first time he listened to a live rock band undistracted by screaming fans or flamboyantly dressed dancers. Instinctively comparing the band to a jazz combo, he likes their fusion of rock, blues, and R&B. Gleason appreciates how Anderson smoothly transitions between solos and background parts like a seasoned jazz vocalist and how Kaukonen improvises his guitar parts. Although he spots weak areas in their performance, Gleason likes the Airplane's raw sound, especially its visceral force. The band didn't strive for the polished harmonies of folk rock bands like the Byrds, whose voices and instruments blended into a seamless whole. Instead, the Airplane constructed an assemblage of vocals and instrumental passages that expressed each member's identity—music of angular melodies and rough timbres.[62]

The next day in his office, Gleason types his title, "Jefferson Airplane—Sound and Style," followed by "Er, ah, it seems kind of lonely out here, doesn't it?"[63] Is Gleason lamenting a lack of musical communalism around the Bay? If that was the case, he found hope in the Jefferson Airplane:

> They have style, which is the first thing and is indicated by their name. Secondly, they have a good sound with both voices and guitars and bass … It's really not a rock 'n' roll group. Few are any longer. It's a contemporary-popular-music-folk-rock unit and we have no less cumbersome phrase to use so far. They will obviously record for someone …[64]

Gleason was right. The column caught the attention of music scouts for major recording labels. Balin recalled that soon after Gleason's review appeared, "every record company was sitting in the audience, offering us a deal."[65] Jefferson Airplane biographer Jeff Tamarkin said Gleason gave the band "a legitimacy it couldn't have bought with a million buttons and stickers."[66] Bassist Bob Harvey noted that after Gleason's article, "there was pandemonium. I never believed a newspaper column could have that effect until I saw it happen."[67] Balin summarizes the Gleason effect: "There wouldn't have been a Jefferson Airplane without Ralph Gleason."[68]

The American Liverpool

Gleason's Jefferson Airplane column caught the eye of a young concert promoter. With her waist-length hair and flowing gowns, Luria Castell could have walked out of a Pre-Raphaelite painting. A well-known figure among the Bay Area Left, Castell defied the State Department ban on Cuba travel in 1963 and visited the country with local activists. They met with Fidel Castro, who showed them the results of the revolution.[69] After the trip, Castell engaged in demonstrations throughout 1964 and spent fourteen days in jail for trespassing during a teach-in—the twenty-year-old embodied resolve.

And a rock 'n' roll spirit. Castell belonged to the local chapter of the W.E.B. DuBois Club, a leftist group sponsored by the Communist Party USA. Gleason had recently lectured on jazz for the group and likely met Castell.[70] The DuBois Club was known for holding wild celebrations after demonstrations that brought together Bay Area radicals, musicians, and rock fans.[71] Recall when Gleason was an activist at Columbia University, Popular Front organizations held post-demonstration dances with swing bands. He understood the power of music to rally political causes.

Castell and her roommates convened these post-protest bashes at their home called the "Dog House" in honor of a beloved canine pet. In the summer of 1965, Castell and her roommates helped establish the Red Dog Saloon, a bar in Virginia City, Nevada, 230 miles northeast of San Francisco. The Old West-styled club recruited the Charlatans as the house band. Emboldened by the success of the Red Dog Saloon, Castell and her roommates returned to San Francisco and formed a production company called the Family Dog. They planned a dance at Longshoremen's Hall, a union hall well-known to Bay Area activists. The Family Dog named the event "A Tribute to Dr. Strange" after the wizard in the Marvel comic book *Strange Tales*, popular with Castell and her roommates. Castell arranged for a slate of Bay Area bands to play at the event, including the Charlatans, Great Society, and Jefferson Airplane.

Castell read Gleason's review of the Jefferson Airplane's show at the Matrix, and one line grabbed her attention, "It's a shame there isn't dancing."[72] Castell couldn't agree more. She calls Gleason, arranges for a meeting, and on the scheduled October afternoon, the Family Dog members sit in Gleason's living room surrounded by his floor-to-ceiling record library. Castell makes her case: "San Francisco can be the American Liverpool."[73] Why San Francisco?" Gleason asks. Castell responds:

> San Francisco is a pleasure city, the only city in the United States which can support a scene. New York is too large and confused, and Los Angeles is super-up-tight plastic America ... Rock and roll is the new form of communication for our generation. We want to bring in the artistic underground, using light machines – boxes projecting a light pulse from the tonal qualities of the music.

> We want to have a good time and meet people and not be dishonest and have a good, profitable thing going on. I think that rock 'n' roll people are just starting to know how to use their instruments. They're doing new things in electronics; the generation brought up in the insanity [of the nuclear era]. Young people today are torn between the insanity and the advances of the electronic age.[74]

Castell became more animated as she talked, her face flushed with excitement:

Music is the most beautiful way to communicate; it's the way we're going to change things. Dancing is the thing. When I heard the Lovin' Spoonful in Hollywood, I couldn't stop. It was such an enveloping sound."

They've got to give people a place to dance. That's what's wrong with those Cow Palace shows. The kids can't dance there. There will be no trouble when they can dance.[75]

Castell's speech echoed many of Gleason's points about rock music. That rock is a form of communication that provides a catharsis to Cold War anxieties. That rock fans need places where they can dance to live music—all part of Castell's vision of a San Francisco rock scene. A few weeks later, Gleason's column spread the news across the Bay Area rock community: "The Jefferson Airplane, the Great Society, and other rock groups will be at the Longshoremen's Hall Saturday in a concert and dance."[76]

Home on the Range

There was another layer to the planning of "Dr. Strange." The dance concert was coordinated with a massive demonstration planned for the UC Berkeley campus the same weekend. "On October 15 and 16, the Vietnam Day Committee is planning a teach-in to protest the war in Vietnam and a mass march from the campus to the Oakland Army Terminal where acts of civil disobedience are threatened," announced the *Chronicle*.[77] Since that day earlier in the year when Gleason encouraged Jerry Rubin to hold the first teach-in, the VDC had grown into a national force in the antiwar movement.

Rubin and the teach-in organizers created a simple agenda for the two-day event. On Friday, there would be forums all day, followed by an antiwar march from Berkeley to the army induction center in Oakland. On Saturday, more seminars. But the mayor of Oakland had his agenda and refused to issue a permit for the march. When the VDC predictably announced it would march anyway, the Oakland police chief said his officers would be waiting at the city limits.

Against this looming showdown, 14,000 antiwar activists from around the world gathered at the Berkeley campus on the morning of October 15. Enthusiasm built into the afternoon as one speaker after another spoke out against the war. Ken Kesey, one of the final speakers, made a splash by driving onto campus in Furthur, freshly repainted by the Pranksters. The infamous bus was tricked out in swirling multi-dayglo patterns, a red background, and military symbols from hammers and sickles to Iron Crosses—a mockery of militarism in all its forms. Bob Dylan and the Beatles blasted from the tape system. Kesey walks to the podium and starts his speech. It isn't what the VDC expects:

You know, you're not gonna stop this war with this rally, by marching ... That's what they do ... they hold rallies and march ... and that's the game you're playing—their game.[78]

Then Kesey pulls out a harmonica and starts to play "Home on the Range," occasionally making asides such as comparing the previous VDC speaker to Mussolini. Having said his piece, Kesey leaves the podium, and the final speaker tries to undo the damage with a rousing call to march. It works, and demonstrators start their seven-mile trek to the Oakland Army train terminal, where soldiers departed for Viet Nam. But at the Oakland city limits, police block the march as promised, and the demonstrators return to Berkeley.

The next day the determined marchers return. Kesey and the Pranksters led the way, and even though Kesey had given his anti-VDC speech the day before, the organizers welcomed his participation. The Pranksters led the marchers in singing the Beatles' "Help," and Allen Ginsberg conducted peace chants. Once again, at the Oakland line, marchers run into a police blockade. Assisting the officers is the Hells Angels motorcycle gang. The bikers, some who are military veterans, supported the Vietnam War and helped law enforcement aggressively stop the march. Ironically, Kesey had just started to use the Angels for security at his LSD-fueled parties at La Honda.

When Gleason heard the news about the failed march, he was outraged that the Angels obstructed the marchers. He confronted Kesey and vented his disgust. To Gleason's dismay, Kesey found poetic justice in an antiwar march coming to a warlike end.[79] Gleason was stunned; the Angels' pro-war stance appalled him despite their recent acceptance in hip circles.

Although the marches failed, the VDC teach-in succeeded because it brought together many of the world's leading antiwar protesters. And now organizers looked forward to their traditional post-demonstration dance with live rock music. They cleaned up, dressed in their freaky finery, and headed across the Bay Bridge to Longshoremen's Hall, where Gleason had just pulled up.

Dr. Strange

The residue of the day's ugly events had dissipated, and "A Tribute to Dr. Strange" takes place as planned. Gleason arrives early and surveys the surrealistic scene as he strolls across the parking lot. The hall's saucer-shaped form sits before him, looking like a spaceship at the bay's edge. In the background, the restored nineteenth-century sailing ship *Balclutha* bobs on the water. Costumed rock fans give the event a celebratory air that reminds Gleason of early Christian feast days. Even the concert's title, "A Tribute to Dr. Strange," reminds him of the saint's days he once observed as a young Catholic boy. Gleason thought, "A new religion is in the process of evolving."[80]

Stepping into the hall, Gleason enters an alternative reality. Lines of dancers in army surplus and thrift shop regalia hold hands and sweep through the crowd. Musicians and the audience move together to pulsing rhythm sections and fuzztone guitar riffs. The hall's great dome of raw concrete ribs belies the tender bodies gyrating below, a cradling grid that shelters the dancers.

The music of the Jefferson Airplane, Charlatans, and Great Society reverberates throughout the hall. The Great Society's vocalist, Grace Slick, resplendent in a purple miniskirt and stockings, represented an advance guard of liberated women vocalists who shaped the new music coming out of San Francisco. Artist Bill Ham projects light through a multicolored mixture of oil, water, and glycerin between panes of glass, which beams ameboid patterns across the musicians and dancers. Cannabis and incense infuse the air. Reveling in sensory overload were Allen Ginsberg and rising rock musicians such as guitarist John Cipollina, who formed the Quicksilver Messenger Service following the concert. Great Society co-founder Darby Slick recalled the night:

> The overwhelming part of the experience for me, and I think for virtually everyone who attended, was the certainty of the birth of a scene. We had arrived, and there were so many of us, and we were weird and interesting, and lovable. The excitement was intense and vibrant. The atmosphere was completely different from the commercial concerts put on at the Cow Palace.[81]

Gleason watched with awe from the balcony surrounding the dance floor. The forty-eight-year-old journalist had witnessed the birth of the swing era the same way, from the balcony of the Apollo Theater, where he watched acrobatic couples dance the Lindy Hop. And now, a new music scene swept him up and radically reshaped his worldview. He began as an outsider in both settings, the Harlem jazz scene and the San Francisco counterculture. But became an insider by earning trust and proving his value.

Descending the balcony stairs, Gleason spots Luria Castell and a few of her friends dancing and joins in, unusual for Gleason, who rarely danced in public since his New York days.[82] He sees Jon Sagen, a Capitol Records promoter dressed in a fur jacket like Admiral Robert E. Peary at the North Pole. As Gleason chats with Sagen, a young woman with luxuriant dark hair wearing an American flag dress greets Gleason. It's his friend Denise Kaufman.

Gleason mentored Kaufman, a UC Berkeley freshman and aspiring musician. That past summer, Gleason heard Kaufman perform at the Berkeley Folk Festival and mentioned her in his column:

> Two young guitarists and a wild girl harmonica player did Beatles songs, rhythm & blues, Rolling Stones numbers, and other examples of contemporary folk music on the Plaza. It was a delightful change.[83]

The untamed harmonica player was Kaufman. The article caught the eye of a representative of the Hohner Harmonica Company, who contacted Gleason and said Hohner would like to sponsor Kaufman. He shared the news and began to mentor Kaufman, who says Gleason became "my dear friend; I called him my godfather."[84] He gave her stacks of records to listen to and took her to hear various musicians. "He'd say, 'You need to go hear Ray Charles or some other musician.'" Kaufman would check them out, part of her musical education.[85] In turn, Kaufman helped Gleason by informing him about events at the Berkeley campus.

With Kaufman at the concert was her boyfriend, a nineteen-year-old Berkeley English major with shaggy brown hair parted in the middle like a British rock musician.

Jann Wenner excitedly shook Gleason's hand and put into motion a friendship that would revolutionize American music journalism.

Wenner had plunged into the rising San Francisco counterculture after meeting Kaufman. At Berkeley, Wenner balanced academics with a part-time job as a stringer for NBC News. He became involved in campus activism after joining SLATE, a left-wing political group founded in 1958 that ran campus political candidates and helped start the Free Speech Movement. The police violence at the 1964 Sproul Hall demonstration sickened Wenner, shook his faith in American institutions, and redoubled his belief in activism. During the spring of 1965, with Kaufman at his side, Wenner experienced LSD for the first time, and the two ventured into the kaleidoscopic world of the San Francisco psychedelic rock scene.

And now, standing in the phantasmagoria of "Dr. Strange" that October night, Wenner, Kaufman, and Gleason experienced a seminal event in American cultural history. A counterculture took root on the bank of San Francisco Bay and would spread its influence across the globe. As Gleason drove back to Berkeley after the dance, his mind reeled with the weekend's events, from the VDC march to the pageantry of "Dr. Strange." As a teenager in Chappaqua, Black jazz cadences pushed the boundaries of his imagination. The new sounds of San Francisco rock push those boundaries further out.

A few weeks after "Dr. Strange," another dance concert featured the Jefferson Airplane, along with the John Handy Quintet. The "San Francisco Mime Troupe Appeal Party" raised money for the Troupe after city police arrested its leader, Ronnie Davis. Organizing the "Appeal Party" was a visionary promoter who would change the course of music history with the help of Ralph Gleason.

8

A Sonic High (1965–67)

Without Bill Graham and the hard work and business know-how he threw into the Fillmore when the scene was starting, there might never have been an SF Sound to talk about. Give him credit, and give Ralph Gleason credit, without whose enthusiastic columns in the SF Chronicle, the city would have no doubt shut down those psychedelic superstructures before you could say "building inspector."
                                        Paul Williams, *Crawdaddy!* 1967[1]

The Promoter

Wulf Wolodia Grajonca, better known as Bill Graham, came to America as part of One Thousand Children, an effort to rescue mainly Jewish youth from Nazi-occupied Europe during the Second World War. Raised in a Bronx foster home, Graham moved to San Francisco in the early 1960s and began working for the San Francisco Mime Troupe, a theatrical group that gave free performances in Bay Area parks. Founder R. G. Davis incorporated leftist politics and jazz elements into the plays, and Gleason supported the Troupe in his column. When San Francisco police arrested Davis for performing without a permit in the summer of 1965, Graham held the "Appeal Party," a fundraising concert in the troupe's rehearsal loft. The crowd that showed up far exceeded the loft's capacity. This presented a problem because Graham was planning a second benefit.

"We've *got* to find a bigger place!" Graham told Gleason, aware that his friend had extensive knowledge of San Francisco's ballrooms, clubs, and auditoriums. Gleason suggested a grand old theater, the Fillmore Auditorium.[2] Owned by African American promoter Charles Sullivan, the 1912 building sat in the predominantly Black Fillmore district. The neighborhood became known as the "Harlem of the West" in the 1950s when the Fillmore featured major jazz and R&B artists such as Louis Jordan, Dizzy Gillespie, the Coasters, and Ray Charles. Sullivan made the Fillmore available to civil rights groups, including the Congress of Racial Equality and the Student Nonviolent Coordinating Committee. Malcolm X gave a speech there in 1961.

Gleason covered many of these events in his column. And so, when Graham called looking for a large hall to hold his benefit show, Gleason urged him to consider the Fillmore. Affordable venues for psychedelic rock dance concerts were scarce outside

Longshoremen's Hall. Plus, the Fillmore had a track record as a site of benefit shows for leftist causes—a perfect fit. Graham met with Sullivan, arranged to rent the building, and held "S.F. Mime Troupe Appeal II" on December 10, 1965. Gleason described the remarkable night in his column:

> A most remarkable assemblage of humanity was leaping, jumping, dancing, frigging, fragging, and frugging on the dance floor to the music of the half-dozen rock bands—the Mystery Trend, the Great Society, the Jefferson Airplane, the VIPs, the Gentleman's Band, the Warlocks and others.[3]

The Warlocks were the first iteration of the Grateful Dead and brought a powerful jam-band presence to the rock scene. With Gleason's help, Mime Appeal II kicked off the era of the San Francisco ballroom concerts.

As the ballroom scene got off the ground, Bob Dylan returned to the Bay Area for several concerts in December 1965. He gave a notable press conference with Gleason's help during the visit. KQED hosted the event, the only fully televised press conference of Dylan's career.[4] On December 3, 1965, Dylan arrived at the KQED studios with his new backup group, the Hawks, formerly the support band for rockabilly singer Ronnie Hawkins. Gleason and the musicians sip tea as they wait to go on air. When the time comes, Gleason escorts Dylan into the studio and enigmatically announces, "Dylan is a poet; he'll answer everything from questions about atomic science to riddles and rhymes."[5] Dylan turns the event into a surrealistic give-and-take with reporters largely unaware of his significance. Some questions get intriguing answers. When asked about performing live, Dylan answered that he and the Hawks were not "really performing [songs], just letting them be there."[6] After the press conference ends, Gleason thanks Dylan and the audience applauds. Gleason escorts Dylan off the stage, and the two chat while Dylan smokes a cigarette.

The next day in the *Chronicle*, reporter Michael Grieg described Dylan as an "anemic-looking young man" with a "fey smile."[7] Grieg assembled Dylan's quotes in such a way as to make the singer appear spaced out and vacuous. But young viewers knew Dylan communicated through free association and loved mocking the establishment press. Today, the press conference footage is considered a vital document of the early rock era; Dylan's responses continue to fascinate fans and scholars.

Following the conference, Gleason saw Dylan and the Hawks play at the Masonic Auditorium. It was the first time he heard Dylan live after the singer went electric. In his review, Gleason focused on the Hawks' performance, one of the first times he wrote about the musical characteristics rather than the social aspects of a live rock performance. Gleason wrote with a level of passion and detail equal to his best jazz reviews:

> Robbie Robertson, the lead guitarist in the Hawks, is a highly talented guitarist who can solo with intensity and communication, rivaling the best jazzmen. Rick Danko, bassist (he plays electric bass), swings like a great jazzman … The pianist (Richard Manuel) and the organist (Garth Hudson)—also electronic—contribute

Figure 8.1 Bob Dylan and Ralph Gleason at the 1965 KQED press conference for Dylan, who was in the Bay Area for a series of concerts. Courtesy of the Estate of Ralph J. Gleason, photo by Eric Weill.

great fills and backgrounds and aid the montage of sound necessary to flesh out the performance ...

The music they play is organized, routined, and arranged at least as much as most jazz groups and requires rehearsals ... In the arrangements of "It Ain't Me Babe," the virtuosity of the group is displayed.

Their sounds all deal with a different arrangement of the elements of music than we have been accustomed to so far. It poses interesting possibilities for future development. As a vehicle for reaching a mass audience with poetry, it is unequaled, which is one of the reasons the [Beat] poets have clustered around in admiring and envious throngs, having had their run at jazz and been outdistanced. Rock 'n' roll may be the answer.[8]

The Hawks were relatively unknown then, with no guarantee of the extraordinary success to come. Gleason went out on a limb to lavish praise on an untested band, and in the process, he legitimized the Hawks and their sound, later dubbed "Americana."

The concert capped a great year in San Francisco music. Revolutionary artists such as Dylan, the Rolling Stones, and the Byrds brought diverse rock styles into the local music scene. Bay Area musicians absorbed the new sounds and formed bands of their own, rooted in the city's folk, blues, jazz, and literary traditions. Luria Castell and Bill Graham hosted dance concerts that brought self-recognition to the rising community. Gleason documented it all like an ethnomusicologist taking notes on a cultural revolution he helped launch. Gleason wrote the first narratives of the San Francisco rock scene in his role as a participant observer. His texts are still cited today, such as in Sarah Hill's superb *San Francisco and the Long 60s*.[9]

A Sonic High

By early 1966, all the ingredients were in place for a thriving rock scene. San Francisco had the fans, bands, promoters, and venue operators needed for a cultural revolution. And it had a nationally respected jazz critic supporting the music in print and behind the scenes.

Journalists play an integral role in local music scenes. As sociologist Sarah L. Thornton writes in her study of club cultures, "Every music scene has its own distinct set of media relations" that sustain the action.[10] Scenes depend on the media for publicity, internal communication, and dissemination of their values. A journalist gains access to information and even levers of power if deemed trustworthy. Establishing and maintaining trust is a delicate dance between a journalist and members of a music scene.

Gleason learned this as a White journalist covering the racially segregated American jazz scene. Because he showed respect for Black musicians and a genuine willingness to help them, performers such as Miles Davis, Dizzy Gillespie, Duke Ellington, and Sonny Rollins, to name a few, trusted and befriended him. In the case of the San Francisco rock scene, age, not race, distinguished him from the scene's participants. Another critical difference was that Gleason didn't use hallucinogens and he gave up marijuana after the birth of his children. He didn't even drink because of diabetes.

Yet Gleason appreciated the sensory pleasures of drug-induced happenings such as the Trips Festival, co-produced by Ken Kesey and writer Stewart Brand in January 1966. Gleason had a sneak preview of these happenings when Kesey and the Pranksters took him on a multimedia excursion in Furthur in 1964. After that, Kesey hosted LSD-fueled parties at his La Honda ranch, then took them to other locations and called them "Acid Tests." The three-day Trips Festival at Longshoremen's Hall was the most prominent Acid Test. Gleason announced the event in his column and noted its roots in the city's culture:

San Francisco's reputation as a center for avant-garde activity, artistic and otherwise, seems about to be enhanced.

There is something going on here touching upon creative activity and, possibly, a lineal descendant of the non-objective film days and the well-remembered programs of Vortex.

Kesey says that he is expressing himself through the "Acid Tests" these days and not through the more orthodox methods of fiction.[11]

Gleason had been interested in the city's avant-garde art for years, including Vortex, an experimental light-and-sound show by San Francisco's Morrison Planetarium in the 1950s. He saw Kesey's Acid Tests as a psychedelicized version of the Vortex shows. Gleason gave Kesey's happenings an aura of respectability by framing the Acid Tests as a legitimate heir of the city's avant-garde movement.

The Trips Festival drew approximately 6,000 people who experienced performance art and concerts, such as the debut of Big Brother & the Holding Company before Janis Joplin joined. An essential event in the development of the rock scene, the festival represented a reconceptualization of music events, according to Brand:

> One of the main things is the idea of no spectators. The idea that an audience shows up to a certain kind of event expecting to do something, not just to see something. Raves came on through that. People came to the Trips Festival in outfits, stoned, and prepared to dance.[12]

On the first night, festival organizers pushed the boundaries of performance art a little too far for some participants. Gleason called the night's performance, "Nothing. A bust, a bore, a fake, a fraud, a bum trip."[13] Others agreed; counterculture historian Charles Perry called the night "unparalleled chaos in a crowded hall pulsing with undirected energy."[14] But on the second night, the focus was on the rock bands. Gleason compared the evening to the fantasy novel *The Circus of Dr. Lao*:

> The variety, imagination, degree of exoticism, and just plain freaky far-outness of the thousands who thronged the Longshore Hall defies description ...
>
> On stage, a succession of good rock 'n' roll bands, the Grateful Dead, Big Brother and the Holding Company, produced the kind of Sonic high that big bands used to, only the rock bands do a quicker and for more people.[15]

The crowds who flocked to the Trips Festival confirmed the growing demand for immersive performances that combined rock music, light shows, and dancing. Fans sought shows like the Family Dog concerts in which members of the rising counterculture transgressed repressive social norms among like-minded souls. These one-night heterotopias inspired other producers, such as Bill Graham, who began holding dance concerts at the Fillmore Auditorium every weekend.

Gleason became a regular, and Graham gave him a table and kept a supply of milk and chocolate bars on hand to help control his diabetes. Gleason and Graham developed a mutually reciprocal relationship in which Gleason gave the Fillmore coverage, and Graham gave Gleason scintillating shows to write about. Hardly a column went by without Gleason announcing an upcoming Fillmore show. He devoted entire columns to the venue, such as "Dance Renaissance in the Fillmore," an analysis of the free-form style of dancing at rock concerts, a dance style commonly ridiculed by older journalists but fascinating to Gleason.[16] At the Fillmore, Gleason witnessed significant trends and moments in rock music. For instance, he heard Grace Slick perform "Somebody to Love" as vocalist for the Great Society before she performed it with the Jefferson Airplane. Gleason listened to the nascent sounds of jazz rock at the Fillmore, such as when Great Society played Miles Davis's "Milestone."[17] He heard the first sounds of American blues rock by the Paul Butterfield Blues Band:

> The electronically amplified sound comes on with a roar like a couple of jets, but it swings, and it swings hard. Butterfield plays the harmonica in an exciting, shouting style, and he sings with conviction and spirit.
>
> The solo guitarist Mike Bloomfield is really an extraordinary player. He produces long, exciting, soaring solos that leap out over the sound of the band and come alive, whirring, and snapping through the hall.[18]

Gleason wrote that the electric guitar, as "played by a virtuoso musician like Bloomfield, becomes a true jazz sound with all the excitement of the best jazz solos."[19] Like his 1965 review of the Hawks, Gleason went beyond his typical sociological analysis of a rock performance to give the Butterfield performance a jazz-like critique focused on technical virtuosity and ensemble chemistry.

Predictably, just as the Bay Area psychedelic rock scene got rolling, some citizens and authorities reacted negatively. As noted earlier, despite the Bay Area's wide-open cultural values, local government was conservative. To control the ballroom dances, officials used outdated laws that prohibited under-18 youth from attending dance concerts, a carryover from the days when bartenders served alcohol at these events. Police applied the law to rock concerts even though they were alcohol-free. This crackdown ruined a night out for the Gleason family in April 1966 while they attended a concert by the Butterfield Blues Band and the Jefferson Airplane at the UC Berkeley Harmon Gym. As Ralph and Jean watched the show, their three children came and went. When the show ended at 11 p.m., Toby approached his parents and said campus police had apprehended Bridget, Stacy, and their friends. Gleason rushed to where they were, and security told him that unaccompanied minors were required to leave at 11 p.m. Gleason was outraged. He wrote in his column, "We wonder why the youth is losing its respect for authority."[20]

The crackdown on minors at rock concerts continued. A week later, on April 22, 1966, San Francisco police raided the Fillmore Auditorium and arrested fourteen juveniles and Graham. Police charged Graham with breaking the city's ordinance prohibiting teens under 18 from attending public dances. Gleason witnessed the arrests, and one of the police officers rebuffed him for asking questions. He recounted the incident in his column and wrote, "It's a crime in our society to be under 18 and having fun."[21] Graham appealed the charge and leveled one of his own, that police disliked White youth going into a predominantly Black neighborhood. He announced that the dances would continue until the appeal was resolved, and he continued producing extraordinary concerts. At one, Gleason witnessed the Butterfield Band work out a new instrumental that was "hypnotic as it built to climax after climax."[22] Yet untitled, the modal instrumental exemplified a growing alliance between blues, rock, raga, and jazz. The band later named the piece "East-West."

A Puppet Show

As the San Francisco psychedelic rock scene thrived in 1966, the city continued to host influential rock bands at large venues crowded with teen fans. Although rock music now attracted a young-adult audience, bands like the Rolling Stones and the Beatles continued to fill stadiums with screaming adolescent admirers. Gleason covered shows by both groups in 1966.

The Stones came into their own as live performers during this time with the dynamic stage moves of Mick Jagger. On July 26, Bay Area rock fans appeared in droves to hear the group at the Cow Palace. Gleason watches Jagger and the band tear into "Stupid Girl" from the recently released *Aftermath*. Dressed in a yellow shirt with a scarlet-lined black jacket and white bell bottoms, Jagger side-shuffle dances across the stage and bangs a tambourine to the beat of Charlie Watts on drums. "Look at that stupid girl out there," Jagger taunts as he points into the crowd with a bent wrist. The band finishes their last song, and Jagger profusely thanks the fans before he throws his tambourine into the crowd. Gleason enjoyed the show and wrote that Jagger "looked like some exotic tribal figure, the long blond hair cascading almost down to his shoulders."[23]

Despite Jagger's wild stage antics, the Rolling Stones were months away from their first scandals over drugs and risqué lyrics. For the Beatles, though, 1966 was a year of controversy as the band members began to express their views on religion, racial injustice, and war. In June, Capitol Records released *Yesterday and Today* with the infamous "butcher cover" that depicted the band seated in bloody butcher's smocks draped in dismembered doll parts. The group intended to challenge pop star photography conventions and protest the Vietnam War's brutality. The backlash was swift. Even former *DownBeat* editor Gene Lees disparaged the band for using the photo. Bowing to pressure, Capitol re-released the LP with a more conventional cover.

Gleason devoted a column to the controversy and concluded:

> Far from being offensive, the "butcher boys" cover strikes me as a subtle protest against the war, as well as an example of "black humor." Isn't there something paradoxical about the shrill reaction of disc jockeys and program directors to this cover at a time when the heads are being blown off real children and their bodies seared by American napalm in Vietnam?"[24]

Gleason called *Yesterday and Today* a minor, transitional album. His underwhelming reaction was understandable compared to the three rock masterworks he concurrently reviewed, *Aftermath*, *Having a Rave-Up with the Yardbirds*, and *My Generation*, all of which he praised.[25] When *Revolver* dropped in August, Gleason called it the "most outstanding pop album in years, possibly the best of all time." He wrote that the Beatles' "recorded art grows, it doesn't stay still."[26]

As *Revolver* sparked rave reviews, the Beatles sparked another controversy. The September 1966 *Datebook* magazine contained the infamous Maureen Cleave interview with Lennon in which he said, "We're more popular than Jesus now; I don't know which will go first—rock 'n' roll or Christianity."[27] Almost immediately, clergy in Southern states protested the statement, including a "ban the Beatles' records" campaign by a radio station in Birmingham, Alabama.

Gleason wrote:

> The fuss about Lennon's remark was a symptom of a sick society, really ... Only [radio] stations which didn't matter banned them. And as for burning discs, last week it was crosses, this week Beatles records.
>
> His antiwar remarks haven't been quite as sensational, though no less valid and no less important sociologically.[28]

As the controversy continued, Gleason saw the Beatles perform at San Francisco's Candlestick Park baseball stadium in the summer of 1966. He announced the upcoming concert in his column and joked that the band would be walking across water to play the show. Gleason predicted that when the band walked on stage, "the heavens will open and the sky part and earth tremble."[29]

Gleason invited his two daughters and their friends to the concert with him. As usual, he paid for the extra tickets, according to Bridget:

> I want to emphasize Dad's commitment to always paying his way. He would accept records and books for possible reviews but never slanted his reviews based on whether or not he'd bought the book or album or had been given it. And always—the multiple times we took our friends to concerts—he bought tickets for all of us beyond the one or two comped seats standard for a reviewer. And he always paid for his box at Monterey.[30]

At the time, Stacy was with her best friend at their family ranch in Wyoming. The friend's mother planned to drive them to the concert, but the car broke down. Ralph arranged for Stacy and her friend to take a Greyhound bus to San Francisco. A Gleason family friend picked them up at the bus station and delivered them to Candlestick Park, where they joined Ralph and Bridget.[31] Reunited, the group settled in to watch the show.

Huddled in the cool air, they watch an armored car deliver the Beatles to the stage, a platform in the center of the field surrounded by a chain-link enclosure. As a chorus of screams echoes across the stadium, a few fans break away and rush the stage only to be swooped up by security. Gleason and his entourage root for the kids. Lennon launches into "Rock 'n' Roll Music," and the band is off and running. "She's a Woman," "Nowhere Man," and "Paperback Writer" follow. McCartney closes the set with "Long Tall Sally" and replants American rock 'n' roll back in its native soil.

Figure 8.2 Ralph Gleason with the Beatles backstage at their concert in Candlestick Park, San Francisco, 1966. © Jim Marshall Photography LLC.

Figure 8.3 John Lennon and Ralph Gleason backstage at the Beatles concert in Candlestick Park, San Francisco, 1966. © Jim Marshall Photography LLC.

Yet Gleason detected ennui beneath the rush of songs. The screaming fans rendered the Beatles' songs—now heralded as art—inaudible. Fans whose manic behavior required a security barrier that encaged the Beatles as they performed. In his column two days later, Gleason wrote:

Is it worth it? As a spectacle, it is not without sociological interest, of course. As a performance, it is, like John Lennon says, a puppet show. It can hardly continue to be attractive to four such rational, intelligent, and talented human beings.[32]

The "puppet show" had already lost its attraction. The Beatles never toured again. Gleason at least enjoyed visiting the band backstage, captured by eminent rock photographer Jim Marshall.

The New Rock Criticism

Just weeks before the Beatles played Candlestick Park, they released *Revolver*, with its fascinating mix of pop music and experimentalism. Among other exceptional LPs released that year were *Aftermath* (Rolling Stones), *Pet Sounds* (Beach Boys), *Blonde on Blonde* (Bob Dylan), *Fifth Dimension* (Byrds), and *Parsley, Sage, Rosemary and Thyme* (Simon and Garfunkel). Music of this caliber inspired young journalists nationwide to take rock discourse to a higher level. Gleason read the new criticism with interest and influenced some of its writers.

New York City produced a group of pioneering rock writers such as the *Times'* Robert Shelton, who began covering rock music in late 1965 with a lengthy review of the garage rock band the Remains.[33] Music scholar Bernard Gendron cited Shelton's 1966 article "The Folk-Rock Rage" as a seminal text in the evolution of American rock criticism.[34] Shelton began as a folk music critic and brought attention to Dylan early in his career. Critical writings about folk music began in the early days of recording and continued in the digests *Broadside* and *Sing Out!* Paul Nelson co-edited the latter before he became a prominent rock critic.

Shelton covered the burgeoning rock scene in Greenwich Village, which produced bands that influenced the San Francisco scene, such as the Lovin' Spoonful. The Village provided a rich context for Shelton and other rock critics, including 22-year-old Richard Goldstein, who launched his "Pop Eye" column in the *Village Voice* in June 1966. Goldstein wrote with uncommon acuity:

> If *Rubber Soul* opened up areas of baroque progression and Oriental instrumentation to commercialization, *Revolver* does the same for electronic music. Much of the sound in this new LP is atonal, and a good deal of the vocal is dissonant. Instead of drowning poor voices in echo-chamber acoustics, *Revolver* presents the mechanics of pop music openly as an integral part of musical composition. Instead of sugar and sex, what we get from the control knobs here is a bent and pulverized sound. John Cage move over—the Beatles are now reaching a super-receptive audience with electronic soul.[35]

Goldstein represented a new breed of music journalist—the *rock critic*. He eschewed teen-mag journalism for critical writing based on analysis and close listening. His "Pop Eye" became one of the first rock columns. At that same time, college student

Paul Williams, 17, put together the first issue of *Crawdaddy!* in a Brooklyn basement. Williams shared Gleason's belief in rock music as a revolutionary force. A Swarthmore College student with an easy smile and a Beatles haircut, Williams launched *Crawdaddy!* on January 30, 1966. Like Gleason and company's *Jazz Information, Crawdaddy!* was a four-page mimeographed and stapled blast of fan enthusiasm tempered by searching intellects. Williams' first editorial captured the same kind of high-minded, independent spirit that infused the 1940s hot collector magazines:

> You are looking at the first issue of a magazine of rock 'n' roll criticism. *Crawdaddy!* will feature neither pin-ups nor news briefs; the specialty of this magazine is intelligent writing about pop music. *Billboard, Cashbox,* etc., serve very well as trade news magazines; but their idea of a review is "a hard-driving rhythm number that should spiral rapidly up the charts." ... The teen magazines are devoted to rock 'n' roll, but their idea of discussion is a string of superlatives below a folded-out photograph. *Crawdaddy!* believes that someone in the United States might be interested in what others have to say about the music they like.[36]

Crawdaddy! covered the San Francisco rock scene in the fall of 1966, just as the city's counterculture began to attract mass media attention. The October 1966 issue featured the article "San Francisco Bay Rock" by Gene Sculatti, a city native.[37] Nineteen-year-old Sculatti avidly read Gleason's *Chronicle* columns:

> Gleason was primarily a hometown booster; he was the town crier. Everything was happening so quickly and organically; nothing was planned. There were no venues, you had to go out and find them. A whole universe was being created and recreated weekly.[38]

Sculatti, Williams, and Goldstein were among the first rock journalists of their generation. They identified with the young musicians they wrote about and understood the anti-establishment tenor of rock music. After the Bay Area counterculture took root, young local writers like Sculatti put their talent to work. Others began their careers later but drew inspiration from Gleason's *Chronicle* columns. One was Joel Selvin, who became the *Chronicle*'s pop music critic, a *Rolling Stone* writer, and the author of twenty books. He began reading Gleason's columns at the age of 14, growing up in Berkeley:

> Ralph taught me everything as a kid reading him, and I looked under the hood.
>
> He was educating us; we knew nothing. He was very lectural in his tone. We all first read the bottom of his column—what concerts were taking place and when and where to get tickets. Who was playing in the clubs.
>
> The way he conveyed information was magical. He was able to pump things from the pulpit of the newspaper to the heart of the community.[39]

Another fan en route to a prominent writing career was Davin Seay, who, with Sculatti, later co-authored *San Francisco Nights: The Psychedelic Music Trip, 1965–1968.* Seay grew up in Monterey and read Gleason's column:

> Gleason's columns provided an essential link to the fledgling Bay Area music scene. In them, I first heard of the Dead, the Airplane, Big Brother, and Quicksilver—names that thrilled me to see in print. It all seemed quite strange and subversive, and while I can't say that Gleason's writing prompted me to go to the Avalon and the Fillmore for the first time, it provided a kind of legitimization to the experience when I arrived.[40]

Gleason also influenced another budding music writer, John Swenson, who would have a productive tenure at *Crawdaddy!* He later co-edited the first *Rolling Stone Record Guide* and edited *The Rolling Stone Jazz and Blues Album Guide*, assisted by Jean Gleason. Asked about Ralph's influence, Swenson said:

> I eagerly read all the jazz writers I could find, but I found too many pompous and severe in their judgments. There was not much joy in their writing, and I vowed never to write like that myself. Then I discovered Ralph J. Gleason in *Downbeat*, the *San Francisco Chronicle*, and *Rolling Stone*. Gleason was the first writer I encountered who fully understood and appreciated jazz but was also enthusiastic about the experimental sounds of rock and roll, especially the stuff made in San Francisco in the late 1960s. Gleason understood this music as well or better than anyone else writing about it.[41]

Gleason inspired one Bay Area reader to co-found a legendary rock fanzine. High school friends Greg Shaw and David Harris launched a mimeographed and stapled fanzine called *Mojo-Navigator Rock & Roll News* in August 1966. Like Sculatti, Shaw looked to Gleason as a model and wrote that the *Chronicle* columnist was "an inspiration to everyone I know who became a rock critic in the 1960s."[42] Shaw credited Gleason and *Hit Parader*'s Jim Delehant with inspiring him to co-found *Mojo-Navigator*. During the fall of 1966, *Mojo-Navigator* became a voice of the Bay Area counterculture when it featured some of the first lengthy interviews with emergent bands such as the Grateful Dead.

Gleason wrote that *Mojo-Navigator* was "run by stone rock fans who pack it with funnies and goodies and information unobtainable elsewhere." He said, "Interviews with local rock personalities and musicians and comments make this the liveliest and most essential thing around."[43] In the same column, Gleason vouched for Delehant's *Hit Parader* and all the music magazines published by Charlton Publishing, "the best coverage of pop music in this country."[44]

Also on Gleason's radar was a new music column in the UC Berkeley *Daily Californian*. Although the column "Something's Happening" appeared under the pseudonym "Mr. Jones," Gleason knew who the columnist was—Jann Wenner, the aspiring music writer he met at "Dr. Strange." Soon, the two would meet again.

The Acolyte

On May 9, 1966, Gleason returned to the Harmon Gym at UC Berkeley, where a few weeks earlier, he retrieved his children from overzealous campus police. Gleason is there to cover a show called "Peace Rock" with the Grateful Dead, Charlatans, and Great Society. Wenner is also there to review the show. He spots Gleason and bounds up the bleachers to re-introduce himself. "I know exactly who you are," Gleason replies. "I've been reading your column," an affirmation to the aspiring rock writer.[45] The two hang out for the rest of the concert. Bemusedly, they watch Bill Graham "running around yelling" to stagehands.[46] They stick their heads in the band's loudspeakers "right into the middle of the Dead's music" and chat with drummer Bill Kreutzmann.[47] Following the performance, each review the concert for their respective publications. In the *Daily Californian*, Wenner calls the Dead's rendition of "Midnight Hour" the high point of their performance.[48] Gleason also praises the song and writes, "Jerry Garcia, their lead guitarist, is an interesting soloist with a wild surge of inventiveness." Gleason liked how the Dead got a "groovy ensemble sound from the electric organ, lead and rhythm guitars, bass, and drums."[49] Though at an early stage of development and nearly a year away from releasing their first album, the band impressed Gleason and Wenner.

Following the concert, Gleason established a friendship with Wenner that grew into a lifelong collaboration. Gleason tutored Wenner in jazz, blues, and rock, using the San Francisco music scene as their classroom. Despite the generational divide, Wenner valued Gleason's views on music and politics. Ralph and Jean welcomed the young music fan into their home:

> I became a steady visitor, dropping by in the afternoons, looking to just sit around and talk. His living room had floor-to-ceiling shelves stuffed with books and records, as did the foyer, the dining room, and the bedrooms. Ralph liked that I was an enthusiastic student and acolyte, eagerly soaking up everything he had to offer. He was a sage. I nearly always stayed for dinner.[50]

Wenner recalls that he and Gleason "fell into this rare and reassuring place where you know an adult ... who thinks the same way you do and likes the same things, especially the music and the passionate nature of being young."[51] Like Gleason at Columbia University, Wenner increasingly put music above studies. After completing his junior year in the spring of 1966, Wenner dropped out of UC Berkeley and jumped into the global rock scene. A special issue of *Time* magazine caught his attention, "London: The Swinging City":

> London is switched on. Ancient elegance and new opulence are all tangled up in a dazzling blur of op and pop. The city is alive with birds (girls) and Beatles, buzzing with minicars and telly stars, pulsing with half a dozen separate veins of excitement. The guards now change at Buckingham Palace to a Lennon and McCartney tune, and Prince Charles is firmly in the longhair set ... In a once sedate

world of faded splendor, everything new, uninhibited, and kinky is blooming at the top of London life.[52]

Intrigued by the *Time* issue, Wenner traveled to London, taking a letter of recommendation from Gleason to Max Jones, the editor of *Melody Maker* whom Gleason befriended in London during the Second World War. Like Gleason, Jones used his deep experience as a jazz writer to influence the new generation of music journalists such as Chris Welch, a pioneering rock critic who wrote for *Melody Maker*.[53] Jones didn't have a full-time position to offer Wenner, but he gave him freelance assignments while the budding writer explored swinging London. Meanwhile, Wenner went through the travails of a long-distance relationship with Denise Kaufman. They became engaged in a flurry of transatlantic letters but then broke up.

Crestfallen, Wenner returned to the United States and moved into Overly Farms, a New York estate owned by the family of an old friend. Wenner and Kaufman stayed in touch, and she updated Gleason on her former fiancé and expressed concern about his emotional state. Gleason helped Wenner by finding him a job at a new Bay Area publication he helped launch. He sent Wenner a letter offering him the position:

> The reason I write is that *Ramparts* is taking over the *Sun Reporter*, which is the weekly Negro newspaper here, and turning it into a weekly thing roughly in the *Village Voice*, *New Republic* bag. We will cover local stories the metros don't cover, full coverage of the movement, literary, social, etc. etc. etc. I am going to be on the board of directors of this project. I would like to propose that you might be available for a part or full-time job as a reporter when we get going in October. You would fit into the whole thing very well. We're going to need coverage of flicks, art, books, plays, etc., etc., etc. Wide open.[54]

Wenner accepted the offer, returned to San Francisco, and went to work on the inaugural issue of *Sunday Ramparts*, published in October 1966. This position was Wenner's "first real job as a working journalist," thanks to Gleason.[55]

At *Sunday Ramparts*, Wenner developed a witty, wry, and insightful style. For example, he described the Iron Butterfly as a band with an "incredibly fast and tasteless lead guitarist."[56] Wenner wrote that Paul Revere and the Raiders were "probably the best teen-oriented rock group" and "some of their hard-rocking tunes are pretty moving."[57] Such favorable comments were uncharacteristic of the new rock writers who typically eschewed bands with teen followings.

Soon after Gleason gained a new friend in Wenner, he lost an old one when Lenny Bruce overdosed on morphine in August 1966. Two days later, Gleason published "The Sickness That Killed Lenny" and declared it was more than opiates that killed his dear friend:

> Lenny Bruce had an incurable disease. He saw through the pretense and hypocrisy, and paradoxes of our society, and all he insisted on was that we meet it straight on and not cop out or lie about it … And because he insisted on telling the truth as he saw it, the machine killed him. Like it killed Bud Powell and Billie Holiday.[58]

Jazz pianist Bud Powell had recently died after a life of mental illness, addiction, and scrapes with police. Like Bruce and Holiday, Powell perished from a system that slammed substance abusers into the legal system and complicated their odds of recovery. Being a close family friend, Bruce's death hit Gleason hard. Gleason had praised and defended Bruce in print and on the witness stand, seeing him as an exemplar of artistic integrity. And placed him among the most influential jazz, rock, and literary rebels of the time.

Another poignant example of Gleason's ability to empathize with someone suffering came at the end of 1966. It was Christmas Eve, and twelve-year-old Toby heard a knock on the front door. Opening it, he saw a frightening sight. A young friend of the family, ravaged by methamphetamine addiction, asks to see Ralph. Matted hair, sleep deprived, malnourished, and shaking in the cold. "Can I come in?" whimpered the beleaguered figure. Toby paused but let him in the hall where Ralph, Jean, Bridget, and Stacy joined them. Ralph went over and sat down next to the tragic figure, who numbly pleaded:

> I realize I'm strung out, and I almost OD'd. I have nowhere to go. You're the only people I know who ain't on dope, and I have to stop doing drugs and get out of town. But I'm scared and paranoid they're gonna get me. I don't wanna go to jail. I can't even move. I just hurt. If you can't help me, I don't know what I'm gonna do.[59]

When Gleason told him he could stay with them, the man broke down as he was taken to Gleason's office and set up on a cot. In the morning, the Gleasons welcomed him with a Christmas dinner and impromptu gifts that included a box of Poinciana-red Kleenex. The next day, Ralph gave him money so he could leave the Bay Area and start over. He never put a needle in his veins again. The individual was J. Poet, who became a successful music writer at the *Chronicle* and in music magazines such as *American Songwriter*.

The year 1966 was transformative for Gleason and the San Francisco rock scene. Within the Haight-Ashbury and Fillmore districts, a growing community of young people created an alternative lifestyle inspired by psychedelic visions. The San Francisco rock scene emerged from this counterculture with its bands, fans, venues, promoters, and media. With Gleason's help, the highly improbable came to pass. A city remote from the music industry and governed by conservative officials became the American Liverpool.

Hippies Run Wild—Jailed

Considering what was to come, the first two weeks of 1967 began uneventfully for Gleason. He helped to organize "Jazz '67," a series of performances, movies, and art exhibits hosted by UC Berkeley. The first concert showcased one of his favorite performers, Big Mama Thornton. In his first columns of the year, Gleason focused on jazz, including a jab at the US State Department for not using more jazz musicians in their overseas cultural programs.

But on January 13, Gleason announced a milestone cultural event:

> Tomorrow beginning at 1 p.m. on the Polo Field in Golden Gate Park, there will be a "Gathering of the Tribes" for a Human Be-In. It marks the first conscious get-together of all the elements in Brave New World.[60]

The Human Be-In set the stage for San Francisco's Summer of Love by bringing together the groups that made up the Bay Area counterculture. The event manifested principles of the movement, such as communalism, freedom of expression, and spiritual enlightenment. The Be-In also revealed a division in the community, as noted by Gleason in his announcement:

> Berkeley politicos who have been notorious for their squareness will join the Hashberry [Haight-Ashbury] hippies uninterested in politics to make an affirmation for life.[61]

Gleason had noted this division between activist "politicos" and apolitical "hippies" since he covered the "Dr. Strange" concert. Now, he sided with the hippie community that birthed the San Francisco rock scene. Gleason enthusiastically listed the scheduled bands and ended with, "If you want to know what is happening, you will not miss this. And if you want a glimpse of the future as it will be (poetically if not practically), dig it."[62]

That vision of a poetic future stretched out across the polo field of Golden Gate Park on January 14, 1967. Twenty-thousand people turned out on the pleasantly warm day, drawn by word of mouth and newspaper notices like Gleason's. Merrymaking freaks mingle with college students and curious onlookers. Beneath a maypole, a lithe, leotard-clad dancer undulates to the music. Gleason arrives shortly after 1 p.m. and sits on the embankment overlooking the field. Near him, a young person wearing a top hat and white scarf marvels at the crowd, "Look at them! Look at them! There's thousands of them!" Sitting next to Gleason is his friend James Hollingworth, manager of Quicksilver Messenger Service. Hollingworth says, "There has never been anything like it since the Persians." Gleason envisioned another historical setting. As richly costumed hippies fly brightly colored banners unfurling against the clear blue sky, the scene reminds him of the plains of Camelot, the mythical court of King Arthur and Lady Guinevere.

Gleason watches as Beat poets recite poetry. Allen Ginsberg and Gary Snyder chant, and some in the crowd join in. Others mill about, distracted. Signs and handbills express counterculture slogans like "Love is happening." LSD advocate Timothy Leary encourages the group to "Turn on, tune in, drop out." Jerry Rubin speaks out against the war. The Grateful Dead perform "Morning Dew" with Jerry Garcia playing the delicate filigree introduction, his bushy hair parted in the center and down to his shoulders. When the band launches into the jaunty "Viola Lee Blues," the crowd jumps to their feet and turns the grassy field into a pastoral ballroom. As the Dead end their three-song set, a golden fog of incense rises from the stage, and a parachutist lands in an adjacent field to a cheering crowd. Other San Francisco bands play, including Big Brother & the Holding Company, Jefferson Airplane, Quicksilver Messenger Service, and the Charlatans. When the setting sun marks the end of the Be-In, the crowd faces west and watches the sunset. Gleason walks back to his car to the sounds of music and bells. He thinks about John Lennon's "Tomorrow Never Knows" line: "Turn off your mind, relax, and float downstream."

But the stream becomes turbulent as revelers head back to Haight-Ashbury. Police arrested one group of Be-In participants because they were "high on LSD" and obstructed traffic as they walked home.[63] The next day, "Hippies Run Wild—Jailed" shouts the front page of the *Chronicle*.[64] An accompanying article derided the Be-In as a "bizarre union of love and activism" by "far out Berkeley political activists and the further out love hippies of the San Francisco Haight-Ashbury District."[65] Over the following days, the *Chronicle* assigns reporters to write additional articles about the aftermath of the Be-In that focus on the arrests.

In this anti-hippie climate, Gleason writes his column about the Be-In, "The Tribes Gather for a Yea Saying." He notes that the police response reminded him of the clampdown by authorities after Graham opened the Fillmore. This was not the first time Gleason had seen a clash between a youth subculture and the powers that be. He saw it during the swing era and again during the rock 'n' roll years. But Gleason knew how to combat moral panic. Fight misinformation with facts and bear witness to the positive. Then weave it all into a compelling narrative:

> The tribes gathered early in the day. Some came in their 20th-century teepees, old school buses, caravans, and VW buses lined the embankment overlooking the field. Tambourines, drums, flutes, and chiming bells appeared, and the air was filled with the buzz of voices and music.
>
> People sat on the grass and played harmonicas, tambourines, guitars, sitars, mandolins, flutes, and pennywhistles ... Two nuns watched demurely from the embankment ...
>
> Saturday's gathering was an affirmation, not a protest. A statement of life, not of death, and a promise of good, not of evil ... This is truly something new ... a new dimension to peace ...
>
> And so it ended, the first day of the great gatherings, no fights. No drunks. No troubles. Two police officers on horseback and 20,000 people. The perfect sunshine, the beautiful birds in the air, a parachutist descending as a Grateful Dead ended a song.[66]

But Gleason's bucolic image of the Be-In belied a violent act that occurred offstage. Organizers hired the Hells Angels to guard the electrical equipment that powered the event. When a festival-goer accidentally walked into the area, the bikers beat him badly. Meanwhile, back in the park, messages of peace and love prevailed for the rest of the day. Although aware of the incident, Gleason left it out of his column because he didn't want to play into the city's rising anti-counterculture sentiment. After Gleason's column ran, he received a letter from his friend Mark Spoelstra, a singer-songwriter and conscientious objector who was also aware of the Angels incident. Said Spoelstra, "You wrote about the beautiful part of the Be-In, but what about the Hell's Angels stomping that guy?" Spoelstra's words stayed with Gleason and haunted him two years later in the aftermath of Altamont.[67]

From his 1965 column, "Wild Weekend Around the Bay," to his 1967 column, "The Tribes Gather for a Yea Saying," Gleason constructed a fulsome account of the San Francisco rock scene during its formative period. Writing at two levels, he spoke to scene insiders but also to general readers inclined to see the ballroom dances and drug experimentation as threatening their sense of order. His ability to reach both worlds gave Gleason a communicative edge over writers catering to one world or the other.

Although rock music history was made that day on the grassy fields of Golden Gate Park in January 1967, coverage was mainly by local press. The most thorough and empathetic coverage came from *Newsweek* magazine by way of a San Francisco correspondent.[68] Rock journalism was in flux, coming out of a decade of teen magazine coverage. There were tiny signs of hope, however. *Crawdaddy!* advanced to saddle-stitched binding and replaced its photocopied typed pages with typeset pages. *Hit Parader* covered the Greenwich Village rock scene. But other than these exceptions, mass-circulation music magazines rarely provided thoughtful writing about rock music and its relationship to the emergent counterculture. A lack of solid criticism, despite the growing body of great albums such as *Blonde on Blonde*, *Aftermath*, and *Fifth Dimension*.

After Gleason got Wenner his job at *Sunday Ramparts* in the fall of 1966, the two lamented this lack of quality rock journalism. Author Robert Sam Anson wrote:

> What was needed, Gleason and Wenner reasoned, was a publication combining the professionalism of the straight press with the insights of the undergrounds, a magazine with weight and substance, a voice, in short, that would be listened to. But how?[69]

Gleason and Wenner discussed several publishing ventures at the time, including a rock encyclopedia and an anthology of rock writings. Neither idea gained traction. However, the notion of a new music magazine captured their imagination. Wenner even considered going in with rock promoter Chet Helms on a magazine Helms planned to publish called *Straight Arrow*. The promoter ran Family Dog Productions and held concerts at a former dance hall, the Avalon Ballroom, where Wenner was a regular. But Wenner eventually lost interest in *Straight Arrow*.[70]

Meanwhile, the schism widened between hippies and activists in the Bay Area counterculture. Underpinning this divide were disputes about social change, community economics, and the role of music in shaping society. Gleason weighed in on these debates which would put him in conflict with old allies.

The Politics of Cultural Revolutions

The Bay Area counterculture held opposing views concerning its relationship to mainstream society. The Haight-Ashbury community, home of the psychedelic rock scene, aimed for an alternative culture in which music drove social change. On the other hand, the Berkeley activist community, and its San Francisco followers, called for changing society through radical political means. As noted, Gleason saw this division early on.[71]

In the spring of 1967, the schism widened. The hippie community largely eschewed leftist radicalism, although it supported many of its causes, such as ending the Vietnam War and creating Black empowerment. At the same time, the radical movement began to critique the apolitical nature of the Haight community and its capitalistic ventures, including ballroom dance concerts. Among the most vociferous critics of the hippie lifestyle was Gleason's editor at *Ramparts*, Warren Hinckle. An imposing figure who wore an eyepatch and nattily dressed his corpulent frame in a bespoke suit with a bowtie and pocket square, Hinckle reshaped *Ramparts* into a leading political voice of the rising generation. As part of this effort, Hinckle hired Gleason, gave him cover stories, and had him edit the magazine's arts section. Gleason and Hinckle developed an effective working relationship based on trust.

And so, when Gleason saw the March 1967 issue of *Ramparts,* he couldn't believe his eyes. Without telling him, Hinckle took a story assigned to Gleason and wrote it himself.[72] To make matters worse, "The Social History of the Hippies" was the antithesis of the story Gleason planned to write. Hinckle depicted the counterculture as a dictatorial movement rooted in a "distinctly fascist trend, embodied in Kerouac" and based on a "totalitarian insistence on action and nihilism."[73] Hinckle wrote:

> This strain runs deeper and less silent through the hippie scene today. It is into this fascist bag that you can put Kesey and his friends, the Hell's Angels, and, in a more subtle way, Doctor Timothy Leary ...[74]

> The biggest Robber Baron is dance promoter Bill Graham, a Jewish boy from New York who made it big in San Francisco by cornering the hippie bread and circuses concession. His weekend combination rock and roll dances and light shows at the cavernous, creaky old Fillmore Auditorium on the Main Street of San Francisco's Negro ghetto are jammed every night.[75]

After this screed, Hinckle was more charitable toward Gleason, his contributing editor:

> Instrumental and spreading the word was the *Chronicle*'s highly regarded jazz critic, Ralph J Gleason. Gleason is read religiously by hippies. Besides explaining to his square readers what is happening, he is also the unofficial arbiter of good taste in the Haight-Ashbury community. Gleason was quick to tell Ken Kesey, in print, when he was out of line, and did the same for Dr. Leary.[76] Gleason's writings tuned in other members of the *Chronicle* staff, and the extensive, often

headline publicity the newspaper gave to the hippie scene (Kesey's return from a self-imposed Mexican exile was treated with the seriousness of a reasonably large earthquake) helped escalate the Haight-Ashbury population explosion.[77]

Hinckle concluded:

> The New Left has been flirting with the hippies lately, even to the extent of singing "Yellow Submarine" at a Berkeley protest rally, but it looks from here like a largely unrequited love ...
>
> The crisis of the happy hippie ethic is precisely this: it is all right to turn on, but it is not enough to drop out ...
>
> The danger in the hippie movement is more than overcrowded streets and possible hunger riots this summer. If more and more youngsters begin to share the hippie political posture of unrelenting quietism, the future of activist, serious politics is bound to be affected. The hippies have shown that it can be pleasant to drop out of the arduous task of attempting to steer a difficult, unrewarding society. But when that is done, you leave the driving to the Hells Angels.[78]

Hinckle's harsh assessment might seem surprising for someone in the San Francisco counterculture. Yet other writers had begun to critique the West Coast hippie movement, including journalist Joan Didion and New York rock critic Richard Goldstein. Although Gleason generally supported the hippie culture in his writings, he sometimes criticized it, as Hinckle noted.

Aristocratic English author and Oakland resident Jessica Mitford worked at *Ramparts*. One of the famous Mitford sisters known for their controversial political views, the communist heiress wrote about Gleason's reaction to the hijacking of his *Ramparts* assignment:

> He wrote a furious letter of resignation and demanded that this letter should be printed in the mag. He got no acknowledgement, nobody contacted him at all, it was never printed ... He'd never set foot in that place again. He was, in a word, simply *furious* with the lot of them.[79]

As Gleason terminated his relationship with *Ramparts*, he worked on an opening address for the "Rock 'n' Roll Conference" at Mills College in Oakland. Other speakers included academics and music industry members, including Bill Graham, Chuck Berry, Phil Spector, Marty Balin, and Jorma Kaukonen. The academic conference, likely the first on rock, represented the music's rising status.

On Friday night, March 17, 1967, Gleason kicked off the three-day event with his talk, "Like a Rolling Stone," based on an article he was writing for *American Scholar*, a literary journal. Standing at a lectern, he passionately argued that rock music shaped contemporary society more forcefully than political movements, including the New Left. Gleason laid out his theory of rock music as the chief communication conduit within the postwar youth culture. This speech was likely the first of its kind—an academic address that declared rock music's aesthetic and social significance with abundant evidence from Gleason's archives and personal experience.

Gleason also moderated two discussions at the conference. On Sunday, he led a panel with musicians and music industry members. That night, Gleason moderated a panel before an audience of students. He took questions from the young audience, including his daughter Stacy and Denise Kaufman, now a member of the all-woman rock group Ace of Cups. Gleason asked the audience, "Why is rock music important?" Stacy answered that rock mattered to her generation because they were "so wrapped up in this music that everything else relates to it."[80] The discussion moved to how rock culture divided young fans from their families. Kaufman declared, "My family is the band."[81] After the panel ended, the Jefferson Airplane performed, accompanied by a light show. Rock and rhetoric came together.

An important meeting occurred behind the scenes at the Rock 'n' Roll Conference. San Francisco photojournalist Baron Wolman was there photographing the conference for Mills College. Gleason knew the young photographer and introduced him to Jann Wenner. The three discussed the notion of founding a music magazine. The magazine idea gained more momentum after the conference ended. In June 1967, *Sunday Ramparts* ceased publication, leaving Wenner unemployed. He faced two options: launch the music magazine he'd been brainstorming with Gleason or take a civil service job that would have stuck him in limbo, the same indeterminate state Gleason endured as a young aspiring writer. Wenner drove to Ashby Avenue and told Gleason he was ready to launch their magazine. Gleason needed no convincing and later wrote, "We started to conspire that afternoon."[82] The two continued to meet regularly in Gleason's living room, where John Coltrane had pondered his next creative jump, and the Free Speech Movement found someone who spoke their language. Surrounded by walls of records that dated back to the birth of jazz, R&B, and rock 'n' roll, Gleason and Wenner envisioned a new direction for music journalism.

Monterey Pop

As Gleason and Wenner collaborated, an unassuming legal notice went out in Los Angeles newspapers:

> Certificate of Business Fictitious Name
>
> The undersigned certify they are conducting business under the fictitious firm name of Monterey International Pop Festival/67.[83]

The "fictitious firm" included John Phillips of the Mamas & the Papas, record producer Lou Adler, and publicist Derek Taylor. The legal notice announced a project they had worked on for months that now had a board of directors and an official name: the Monterey International Pop Festival.

Adler said the festival idea grew out of a conversation about "the general perception of rock 'n' roll, and that, while jazz was considered an art form, rock 'n' roll was continually viewed as a fad, a trend—and yet both were American-born musical genres."[84] The organizers decided to follow the altruistic spirit of the counterculture and donate profits to charity. Alder and his partners secured the Monterey County Fairgrounds where the jazz festival took place and scheduled the event for June during the anticipated "Summer of Love" when thousands of young people nationwide were expected to descend on San Francisco.

The Monterey Pop team needed someone to help line up San Francisco bands, and they reached out to Wenner, who was becoming known in Los Angeles rock circles. Wenner brought in Gleason and Bill Graham. The festival organizers arranged for a planning session at Gleason's house. When the day came, Adler, Taylor, and Rolling Stones manager Andrew Loog Oldham met in Gleason's living room to discuss the festival. The Stones' drummer Charlie Watts tagged along. Stacy remembers "he and Dad constantly pulling out old records for Charlie to listen to."[85]

Reportedly, the San Francisco bands initially balked at playing at the festival. The city's counterculture held a dim view of Los Angeles, home of the organizers. Recall Luria Castell's comment that Los Angeles was "too uptight" to nurture a rock scene. But Graham and Gleason persuaded the bands to perform, and Gleason alone convinced Big Brother & the Holding Company. In time, all the city's major rock bands agreed to perform, thanks to Wenner, Gleason, and Graham. "The first annual Monterey International Pop Festival is well along in its planning, and most of the programming is pretty well set," Gleason said in a May 1967 column.[86]

Gleason had unknowingly put the wheels in motion for the festival. The previous year, he persuaded Jimmy Lyons to book two rock bands for that year's Monterey Jazz Festival, the Jefferson Airplane, and the Paul Butterfield Blues Band. The event drew a young crowd that included rock promoter Alan Pariser. Inspired, Pariser approached Phillips and Adler about putting on a rock festival at the Monterey County Fairgrounds, and the idea blossomed into Monterey Pop.[87]

As the June 16 opening day grew closer, leading rock writers converged on Monterey. They included Robert Christgau for *Esquire*, Richard Goldstein for the *Village Voice*, Sandy Pearlman for *Crawdaddy!* and Ellen Sander for *Hit Parader*, who described the "gaggle" of rock writers on the jet ride from New York to California:

> Sandy Pearlman was quiet and obscure; Richard Meltzer had a top hat with a Sergeant Pepper emblem. We alighted from the stratosphere and made our way toward the fairgrounds to hunt down some press passes. Even as we neared the gates, we could feel something happening without knowing which entrance to go in. Cars, motorcycles, and campers lined the road for miles, and a pilgrimage of beautiful people was making its way toward the grounds.[88]

Ralph Gleason and his family also headed to Monterey, a drive they made annually since the jazz festival's inception in 1958. As a co-founder of Monterey Jazz, Gleason had nine years of extraordinary memories.

On opening night, gyres of humid Pacific wind hit the cold upswelling waters of the Monterey Bay canyon and condensed into a landscape-softening fog. Equally muted is Gleason's reaction to the first performers. He finds the Association canned, sees Johnny Rivers as a holdover from an earlier time, and thinks Lou Rawls is out of place at a rock festival with his polished nightclub act. But the sonic fog lifts when Eric Burdon and the Animals launch into "Paint it Black." Gleason delights in the opening riff by the band's violinist John Wheeler, made more dramatic by the psychedelic light show. By the time Simon and Garfunkel close the evening with "Punky's Dilemma," Gleason's faith in the festival is restored.[89]

At the Saturday afternoon show, Gleason relishes performances by the Paul Butterfield Blues Band, Steve Miller Blues Band, the Electric Flag, Quicksilver Messenger Service, and Big Brother & Holding Company. On the other hand, he loathes Canned Heat's performance.[90] By Saturday night, the audience swells to more than 8,000 people. Gleason watches in awe as festival staff toss thousands of orchids into the audience and onto the stage. Moby Grape opens the show, and although Gleason enjoys guitarist Skip Spence, he's unimpressed with the band's overall sound. Next up is South African trumpeter Hugh Masekela, whose performance Gleason finds tiresome and interminable. His spirits rise when the Byrds play a winning version of "Renaissance Fair." Gleason listens intently as vocalist David Crosby shares his opinions with the audience about the Kennedy assassination, the wonders of LSD, and the magic that is Monterey Pop: "I hope the artists know what they have here, the power of it to do good. It's an international force."[91] After decades of hearing vacuous show biz patter from performers, Gleason likes that rock musicians have something to say.

On Sunday afternoon, sitarist Ravi Shankar performs an Indian raga and tosses flowers to the audience, who give him a standing ovation. During the evening show, Gleason enjoys the set by the Blues Project and Janis Joplin's jaw-dropping "Ball and Chain," used in the film *Monterey Pop*. But Gleason is less impressed with the next act, the Who. When the hard rock quartet ends their set with Pete Townsend demolishing his guitar while smoke bombs go off, Gleason deems it a debauched and cynical ending that lacks musical value.

Gleason's mood lifts as the smoke rises and the Grateful Dead begins to play. Garcia's solos thrill the seasoned jazz critic who years ago reviewed the first records of Django Reinhardt, one of Garcia's influences. Gleason also appreciates the Dead's swinging rhythms and tight ensemble work.[92] But when the Jimi Hendrix Experience performs, Gleason reacts just as negatively as he did to the Who's auto-destructive performance. While most of the audience is electrified by Hendrix's sacrificial incineration of his guitar, Gleason yawns. The destruction of musical instruments was something Gleason despised and viewed as gimmicky. But as the festival ends with the Mamas & the Papas harmonizing on "Dancing in the Street," Gleason proclaims the festival a success.

Monday morning, Gleason wanders the fairgrounds while a cleanup crew picks up trash, and blurry-eyed revelers crawl out of sleeping bags. A lone singer plugs in an electric guitar and sings about serenity and camaraderie, reminding Gleason of David

Crosby's message to the audience. The anonymous guitarist provides a final grace note to the weekend.

The same day, the *Chronicle* published the first of Gleason's three columns about the festival. Not surprisingly, Gleason delivered both praise and criticism. He applauded how the festival—held before Woodstock—proved "you can have 35,000 long-haired, buckskin and beaded hippies in one place without a hassle."[93] He quoted local officials and citizens about the peaceful nature of the festival and its cultural value, which countered the negative press that inevitably followed counterculture events. Gleason expressed his displeasure about performances he disliked, especially the guitar-smashing climaxes by Hendrix and the Who. But he called the festival a triumph for the new generation.

A week after the festival, Gleason returned to his coverage of the San Francisco scene, which he lauded in "The Triumph of the New S.F. Music."[94]

> It has been evident for some time that a new generation of musicians playing (and, in the process defining) the electric, single-body guitar is emerging. In England, the leading exponents have been Jeff Beck, formerly with the Yardbirds, and Eric Clapton. But neither of these has done anything on record or in Beck's appearances here with the Yardbirds that is anywhere as impressive as the guitar playing of Jerry Garcia of the Grateful Dead, Jorma Kaukonen of the Airplane, or Steve Miller. And Mike Bloomfield is generally acknowledged to be ahead even of these players [both Miller and Bloomfield lived in San Francisco at the time].
>
> What has been going on, my instincts tell me, is the creation of a new musical language that includes not only the country and Western and blues influences but also is deeply touched by jazz.[95]

Gleason presents a powerful argument for the musical value of the San Francisco bands. By the time he runs out of column space, you get the feeling he is just warming up.

Also warming up was Wenner and Gleason's vision of an innovative music magazine that would speak for the new generation. The festival's success proved that rock music inspired a growing global music scene. But that scene lacked a publication with the heft to spread its values. Wenner and Gleason knew the time had come to stop talking and put their plan into action.

9

The *Rolling Stone* Generation (1967–69)

> *What Ralph wrote [in "Like a Rolling Stone"] was everything I believed about rock and roll, how serious it was, its deeper meanings, and how it had become an act of freedom and liberation. His essay was the philosophical underpinning of Rolling Stone, our thesis, and ultimately our name.*[1]
>
> Jann Wenner, in his 2022 memoir, *Like a Rolling Stone*

"I Have Never Been Subsidized by the C.I.A."

Gleason sits at his typewriter and begins his final draft of "Like a Rolling Stone," slated to be published in the autumn 1967 issue of *American Scholar*. He had worked on the article since he presented a preliminary draft at the "Rock 'n' Roll Conference" that past spring. Gleason starts with a sardonically light-hearted declaration: "I am not now, and I have never been subsidized by the CIA."[2] An ironic disclosure because the Central Intelligence Agency had surveilled Gleason because of his connection to Bay Area radical groups. *American Scholar* would leave the line out—readers might not get the joke.

With his books by Nietzsche, Plato, and other philosophers at hand, Gleason begins:

> Forms and rhythms in music are never changed without producing changes in the most important political forms and ways.

Plato said that.[3]

Guided by this thesis, "Like a Rolling Stone" becomes a nine-page argument on how music changes society. More specifically, the paper showed how rock music transformed a generation. In addition to *The Republic* by Plato, Gleason cited *The Birth of Tragedy Out of the Spirit of Music* by German philosopher Friedrich Nietzsche. The latter presents Nietzsche's belief that life is a struggle between the Dionysian (disordered) and the Apollonian (ordered). Gleason suggested the counterculture was a Dionysian movement.

"Like a Rolling Stone" begins with an analysis of how postwar technology influenced the baby boom generation:

Figure 9.1 Gleason in 1967. Photo by Barry Olivier. Courtesy of the Berkeley Folk Music Festival Archive, Charles Deering McCormick Library of Special Collections, Northwestern University Libraries.

Automation, affluence, the totality of instant communication, the technology of the phonograph record, the transistor radio, had revolutionized life for youth in this society … Popular music, the jukebox, and the radio were becoming the means of communication.[4]

Gleason encapsulates the history of rock music, beginning with its roots in rock 'n' roll. As he had in an earlier column, he uses three major artists to represent what he saw as three different directions in rock music:

The early Beatles were at the same a declaration in favor of love and of life, an exuberant paean to the sheer joy of living, and a validation of the importance of American Negro music.

Dylan, by his political, issue-oriented broadsides first and then by his Rimbaudish nightmare visions of the real state of the nation, his bittersweet love songs, and his pure imagery, did what the jazz and poetry people of the 50s had wanted to do – he took poetry out of the classroom and out of the hands of the professors, and it put it right out there in the streets for everyone.

The Rolling Stones' songs … were anti-establishment songs in a non-political sort of way … they hit out in rage, almost in blind anger and certainly with overtones of destructiveness, against the adult world.[5]

Gleason argued that these White musicians began their careers by imitating Black music but later broke free of imitation in songs like the Beatles' "Strawberry Fields." Gleason saw this as a positive move away from the phoniness and the lack of imagination of Caucasian musicians copying Black influences.[6] And just as he saw White rock musicians finding their ethnic identities, Gleason saw some contemporary Black musicians losing theirs:

> The Negro performers, from James Brown to Aaron Neville to the Supremes and the Four Tops, are on an Ed Sullivan trip, striving as hard as they can to get on that stage and become part of the American success story while the white rock performers are motivated to escape from that stereotype. Whereas in years past the Negro performer offered style in performance and content in song ... today he is almost totally [focused on] style with very little content.[7]

Music scholar Bernard Gendron took issue with the above statement by Gleason and wrote that it denied "cultural accreditation to contemporary black music."[8] Yet Gleason had heralded Black R&B and rock 'n' roll performers for over a decade. And some Black activists held Gleason's view. Professor of African American studies Reiland Rabaka writes:

> Many of the more critical members of the civil rights movement believed that the Motown sound was not the soundtrack to the civil rights movement but the soundtrack to selling out, black pop music that more or less encouraged African Americans to abandon the core principles and practices of the civil rights movement.[9]

Gleason never shied away from criticizing Black musicians he thought were selling out for commercial reasons. As early as the 1930s, he criticized Louis Armstrong and Fats Waller for compromising their music during the swing era, a view held by many hot collectors. But Gleason praised Armstrong and Waller when their artistry equaled their commercialism and did the same for Motown artists. He was particularly effusive with praise for Martha Reeves of Martha and the Vandellas. In his review of a concert by Motown artists, Gleason praised Reeve's "truly extraordinary" performance and said she was the "best singer that I have heard in years."[10] He also lauded other artists on the bill, including the Four Tops and Marvin Gaye. In 1967, Gleason identified a shift in soul music's center of gravity. In a lengthy column called "The Progression of the Soul Singers," Gleason wrote, "The Detroit era is moving on out as show business, and the sound of Memphis has become a heavy factor in today's popular music."[11] And so, the view of Motown Gleason expressed in "Like a Rolling Stone" was part of his broader and more nuanced concern that the Detroit sound risked losing its power as a voice for the Black community.

In addition to race, another theme in "Like a Rolling Stone" is the relationship between rock music and radical politics. Gleason noted the aggressive tone of the Rolling Stones' music and said the band's attitude "appealed to that section of youth whose basic position was still in politics and economics."

When the Stones first came to the West Coast, a group of young radicals issued the following proclamation of welcome: "Greetings and welcome Rolling Stones, our comrades, in the desperate battle against the maniacs who hold power. LONG LIVE THE REVOLUTION!!!"[12]

Gleason contrasted the tone of this rhetoric with the mood of the Human Be-In attendees who went to the event "to see the other members of the tribe, not to hear speeches—the speeches were all a drag from Leary to Rubin."[13] After his falling out with *Ramparts* editor Warren Hinckle, Gleason had become more critical of leftist radicals:

> The Square Left wrestles with the problem … Even *Ramparts*, which is the white hope of the Square Left, if you follow me, misunderstands … Bob Dylan says, "There's no left-wing and no right-wing, only up-wing and down-wing," and also, "I'll tell you there are no politics."[14]

Another theme of Gleason's article is how he saw the hippie community as a Dionysian movement, as described by Nietzsche in *The Birth of Tragedy*:

> Orgiastic movements of society leave their traces in music. Dionysiac stirrings arise either through the influence of those narcotic potions of which all primitive races speak in their hymns [dig that!] or through the powerful approach of spring, which penetrates with joy the whole frame of nature …
>
> There are people who, either from lack of experience or out of sheer stupidity, turn away from such phenomena and [confident] of their sanity, label them either mockingly or pityingly "endemic diseases." These benighted souls have no idea how cadaverous and ghostly their sanity appears as the intense throng of Dionysiac revelers sweeps past them.[15]

"Like a Rolling Stone" delivered a compelling argument that rock songs were the mantras of a new Dionysian movement. When Gleason and Wenner discussed names for their magazine, Gleason brought up the article and asked, "How about *Rolling Stone*?" Wenner loved the idea.

Believe in the Magic That Can Set You Free

Armed with a name and philosophy for their magazine, Wenner and Gleason went to work. The top priorities were securing capital, staff, office space, and a printer. Their endeavor reminded Gleason of his old *Jazz Information* days when he and Eugene Williams arranged for a room in Milt Gabler's record shop. Wenner reached out to family and friends and raised $7,500. He put in $1,500, and Gleason put in $2,000.[16] Gleason suggested using the Garrett Press, which had published the now-defunct *Sunday Ramparts*. They could save money by using the leftover typeset and reams of *Sunday Ramparts* layout pages with their distinctive Oxford rule border—a thick line next to a thin one that became a hallmark of *Rolling Stone*. "Ask them for free office space, too," Gleason advised. Wenner negotiated an agreement to occupy the former *Sunday Ramparts* printing facilities in a San Francisco warehouse district at 746 Brannan St., which became the first *Rolling Stone* headquarters, complete with free office space.[17]

While Wenner and Gleason were in the early stages of launching *Rolling Stone*, San Francisco experienced an unprecedented transformation. During the summer of 1967—famously called the Summer of Love—roughly 100,000 young people descended on the city's Haight-Ashbury district, where groups like the Family Dog and the Diggers struggled to provide shelter, food, and medical assistance. With free-flowing cannabis, psychedelics, and free concerts, the Dionysian scene Gleason predicted suddenly scaled up. Along with the massive influx came social pathologies. Poverty, reckless parenting, sexual abuse, and hard drug use increased, as detailed in Joan Didion's book *Slouching Towards Bethlehem*.

Within this cultural ferment, Wenner went to work on the first issue of *Rolling Stone*. With Gleason's help, Wenner created Straight Arrow Publishers and hired staff using the $7,500 he raised, the equivalent of $68,000 today. Early staffers included Michael and Sue Lydon, whom Wenner and Gleason met at the Monterey Pop Festival, and photographer Baron Wolman whom Wenner met at the Mills College rock conference. Wenner also hired correspondents, including Jon Landau in Boston. Gleason suggested that Wenner contact *Melody Maker,* which resulted in hiring Nick Jones as their London correspondent, the son of Gleason's friend Max Jones.

The team put the first issue together in the coming weeks, and Wenner formalized Straight Arrow as *Rolling Stone*'s publishing arm. Wenner set up a board of directors with himself as president and Gleason as vice president and appointed himself editor and Gleason consulting editor. Gleason pitched story ideas, shared his contacts in the music industry, and solicited record label advertising. Contracts came in from record companies Buddha, ATCO, and Chess, along with Bay Area businesses such as the Print Mint poster shop, Fillmore Auditorium, and local radio stations. Even though Wenner aimed for a broader circulation, *Rolling Stone* would be integral to the San Francisco rock scene. Everyone fell into their roles, and 746 Brannan hummed with activity for weeks. Finally, the big day arrived, and *Rolling Stone* No. 1 rolled off the presses on October 18, 1967.

On the cover was a photo of John Lennon wearing a Brodie helmet as Musketeer Gripweed in Richard Lester's *How I Won the War*. Frontpage headlines like "Where's the Money from Monterey?" and "Airplane High, But No New LP Release" clarified that *Rolling Stone* would take a no-holds-barred approach to the counterculture. In his first "Letter from the Editor," Wenner wrote:

> We have begun a new publication reflecting what we see are the changes in rock and roll and the changes related to rock and roll. Because the trade papers have become so inaccurate and irrelevant, and because the fan magazines are an anachronism, fashioned in the mold of myth and nonsense, we hope that we have

something here for the artists and the industry, and every person who "believes in the magic that can set you free."[18]

In today's world of over 200 music magazines, it's hard to imagine the radicalness of early *Rolling Stone*. As Wenner promised, the tabloid broke the rules of music magazines. *Rolling Stone* eschewed the glossy color formats of those magazines for a no-nonsense yet stylishly proletarian look. The writing pushed the boundaries of free speech with writing that was as profane or casual as everyday speech within a hip community. Wenner's magazine was no fanzine; the writing, photography, and graphic design balanced experimentalism with professionalism. *Rolling Stone* had flare.

Gleason contributed a regular column called "Perspectives," named after his old *DownBeat* column. In the title, Gleason made clear that his viewpoint would be expressed, not absolutist proclamations. In his first column titled "Sound is Without Color," Gleason challenged White rock fans who loved blues by lower-melanated musicians like Mike Bloomfield but ignored blues by Black musicians like Muddy Waters.[19] Gleason explained how White rock musicians made fortunes covering blues songs by Black songwriters who went unacknowledged and often poorly paid. In his debut *Rolling Stone* column, Gleason established a new dialogue with a new audience. Unlike his multi-generational *Chronicle* readership, Gleason's *Rolling Stone* readers were predominantly young adults, the generation he empathically wrote about in the *Chronicle*.

Gleason's presence permeated the first issue of *Rolling Stone*. On the masthead was "Consulting Editor: Ralph J. Gleason," just below Wenner's name as editor.[20] Other signs of Gleason's influence were the elegant *Sunday Ramparts*-style pages and typeset, a column by Nick Jones on the London scene, and John Carpenter's interview with Donovan that Gleason acquired from Carpenter.[21] The cover story was also Gleason's idea, an investigative report by Michael Lydon on the finances of the Monterey Pop Festival.[22]

The *Rolling Stone* team barely had time to catch its breath before going to work on the next bi-weekly issue. Gleason was a calming presence when glitches arose, such as problems with distribution. Or when a letter arrived from the Rolling Stones' lawyer threatening to sue over the use of the famous band's name, a threat that was soon retracted. Gleason's name on the masthead helped Wenner in many ways, such as getting in the door at major record labels to solicit advertising, or connecting with important music industry figures such as Jerry Wexler.[23]

As Gleason helped launch *Rolling Stone*, he continued his jam-packed agenda. He began writing a biography of Lenny Bruce but abandoned the project for unknown reasons.[24] Gleason wrote an article for *Evergreen Review*, "The Power of Non-Politics or the Death of the Square." In it, Gleason said, "Radical politics in the United States has demonstrated its bankruptcy too openly now to have any real attraction for youth anymore."[25] In contrast, he called the hippie subculture the "single most powerful social movement in the country."[26]

During this time, Gleason penned liner notes for essential albums such as *Sorcerer* by Miles Davis; *Parsley, Sage, Rosemary and Thyme* by Simon and Garfunkel; *Polka*

Dots and Moonbeams by Bill Evans; *The History of Otis Redding* compilation; and the box set *Billie Holiday: The Golden Years*. In addition, he was a contributing editor for a new magazine titled *Jazz & Pop*. He wrote twenty columns monthly for the *Chronicle* and two for *Rolling Stone*.

Encyclopedia Britannica hired Gleason to write "The Flower Children" for the 1968 *Britannica Book of the Year*, which signified his status as a leading counterculture authority. In the article, Gleason refined and augmented the narrative he developed in his *Chronicle* columns and articles such as "Like a Rolling Stone." He bolstered his points with quotes from historians and sociologists and explained how the counterculture affected him and millions of others:

> If the hippies have done nothing else—and if they do nothing else—they have made the rest of us reexamine our lives, look again at what we are doing and why we are doing it. In the process, they have challenged all the paradoxes and hypocrisies—as Bill Resner of the Straight Theater put it, "The dichotomy between what we've been taught and what's going on." This alone is a valuable service to humanity.[27]

Yet the San Francisco counterculture struggled to sustain its identity. On October 6, just twelve days before *Rolling Stone* issue No. 1 hit the Haight-Ashbury head shops, a mock funeral called "Death of Hippie" was staged by the Diggers. A Haight-Ashbury street theater collective, the Diggers played a prominent role in the San Francisco counterculture. Like their seventeenth-century namesake, the English Diggers, this group of community activists sought to free society of capitalism. They despised how the mass media presented a caricature of the city's counterculture, and the group paraded a coffin down Haight Street to protest.[28]

Gleason didn't put much stock in "Death of Hippie" and called it a charade, a PR stunt that "had little to do with reality."[29] He reminded readers there was a "San Francisco Sound in rock music and a San Francisco scene, and there is no other city with anything like it going today."[30]

Rock is Jazz?

> Last year, there appeared in print a remarkable statement: "The rock bands are really jazz bands; the guitar soloists ... are really jazz players."[31]

With those words, Leonard Feather challenged Gleason's recent comments comparing rock groups like the Band, the Grateful Dead, and the Paul Butterfield Blues Band with jazz bands because of their improvisatory soloists. Feather warned that there was an "undertone of defensiveness in the claim that rock is really jazz, as though this were an attempt to upgrade a young, growing, often maligned form by identifying it with one that has been established for half a century. And has achieved a belated modicum of recognition as a genuine art."[32] Twenty-four years after Gleason called out Feather for his "line of jive," Gleason fell under attack by his colleague.[33]

Gleason did blur the line between jazz and rock at times. For instance, in an April 1967 *Chronicle* column on Jerry Garcia, Gleason said, "The music that Garcia's group, the Grateful Dead, plays is really jazz."[34] Feather supported Gleason's rock music coverage but worried the term "jazz" could lose its historic identity if it included rock music. His comments appeared in *DownBeat Music '68*, the magazine's special publication about the state of jazz, rock, and pop. As scholar Matt Brennan documented in his book *When Genres Collide*, Feather's tirade against Gleason indicated two concerns in jazz circles, that critics would forsake jazz for pop and that the conflation of jazz and rock "further destabilized the definitions of jazz" already undermined by avant-garde jazz.[35] Brennan appreciates the consistency of Gleason's "radical aesthetic vision," based on the dissolution of genre categories.[36] Musical omnivores like Gleason comprehend the hybridity that innovates popular music and disrupts genre categories.

Gleason's friend, the late Nat Hentoff, also commented on the relationship between jazz and rock. Like Gleason, Hentoff wrote about rock music from a jazz perspective, although not nearly to the degree Gleason did. Hentoff said that because of Gleason's "seal of approval," jazz writers and fans gave rock music a chance. "You're reading Gleason, and you are a jazz person, and he [Gleason] is going into this other form of music [rock], so you think, 'Umm, this must be worth listening to.'"[37] Hentoff said Gleason communicated like a jazz musician, and his writing style developed through his experiences and friendships with jazz musicians, with no pretensions and from the heart. Hentoff added:

> We became great friends and regularly talked on the phone, and I always knew it would be a rich conversation. We were both a bit of a gossip. I would gossip about what was going on with me at *DownBeat*, and he would gossip about what was going on at *Rolling Stone*. He was one of the two or three most important writers on jazz.[38]

Thus, Gleason had at least one ally in his quest to build a mutual audience for jazz and rock. But now, Gleason faced a bigger problem: the *San Francisco Chronicle* went on strike.

Outside Agitator

The year 1968 started with a jolt at the *Chronicle*. The paper temporarily closed when the Mailers Union went on strike against the *Chronicle* and the *Examiner* in January. Over the next several months, the *Chronicle* produced only short, galley-quality editions. The newspaper suspended Gleason's column until March. Not one to sit idle, Gleason used his extra time to write a guest column for the *Daily Californian* titled "Outside Agitator."[39] When the strike ended in March, Gleason noted that the "big lesson" was how the "new forms of entertainment, such as the rock dances, established their lines of communication" to fans without the mainstream press.[40]

When the strike ended and Gleason resumed his routine at the *Chronicle*, he had exciting news: "The most extensive programming of jazz on television by any network gets underway Wednesday when National Educational Television presents four one-hour programs on the Monterey Jazz Festival."[41] The series presented a spellbinding series of performances by artists such as Dizzy Gillespie, the Modern Jazz Quartet, violinist Jean-Luc Ponty, guitarist Gabor Szabo, and the Don Ellis Orchestra. Gleason modestly neglected to mention that he co-produced the nationally broadcast documentary.

As the Monterey Jazz Festival documentary enjoyed national renown, the San Francisco rock scene experienced turmoil. It started when several bands led by the Grateful Dead began to hold dance concerts at a 1920s dance hall renamed the Carousel Ballroom. Gleason called the dances "huge successes," with each like a "family party."[42] The Carousel was the "best hall in town for rock concerts," he wrote, citing its good acoustics and generous capacity. "I think we are in for a season of interesting developments in the ballrooms." He admitted that management needed to be more precise about upcoming concert dates but praised the shows.[43] Gleason noted the growing rivalry between the Carousel and the Fillmore but said the competition increased the number and diversity of performances.[44] He even found comfort at a Carousel concert following the assassination of Senator Robert F. Kennedy in June 1968. After watching Kennedy's funeral on television, Gleason attended a Jefferson Airplane performance that soothed his grief with its "beautiful, quiet, friendly, warm, and loving audience."[45]

But problems arose that summer. "Court Shuts Carousel Ballroom," exclaimed a *Chronicle* headline. A local court found the venue's management guilty of not paying rent, canceling its liability insurance, and letting audiences trash the place. To cap it all off, the Carousel management "caused a lewd and lascivious word to appear on the street front marquis ... so lewdly repugnant that it will not be inserted herein."[46] A word too lewd for Gleason's *Chronicle* column and therefore lost to posterity. Although concerts continued at the Carousel while the case went to court, the ballroom eventually closed. Grateful Dead manager Rock Scully announced that Bill Graham would take over the venue. In a dramatic move, Bill Graham closed the original Fillmore, moved into the Carousel, and renamed it Fillmore West to distinguish it from his recently opened Fillmore East in New York City.

Gleason wrote two columns about the Carousel episode, one in the *Chronicle* and one in *Rolling Stone*. Gleason criticized the local counterculture's inability to organize concerts and other ventures. He called the movement's careless handling of finances a "death wish."[47] He said the Carousel fiasco revealed a problem "deep within the hippie mystique." Most disconcerting to Gleason was how the situation paralleled "the whole of American society."[48] With these columns, he criticized San Francisco hippies for the first time, a turning point in his relationship with the community.

Gleason also experienced a turning point in his rapport with *Rolling Stone* readers. In early 1968 several readers took issue with Gleason over his review of Dylan's *John Wesley Harding*, the singer's first album since his 1966 motorbike accident. Gleason wrote, "We can all relax now. Bob Dylan isn't dead."[49] Some readers found this patronizing, and one wrote a letter directly to Wenner and told him that Gleason was "horrible and detrimental to your good name."[50] The writer said, "teenyboppers go 'ick'" at the mention of Gleason and that the *Harding* review had a "hipper-than-thou" attitude.[51] Other readers joined in. "That piece on Dylan by Gleason is the biggest piece of trash I have ever read," said one.[52] Another Dylan fan wrote that although Gleason showed "more tolerance and willingness to listen" than "most critics of his generation," he over-analyzed *John Wesley Harding*.[53] Dealing with such comments was the price Gleason paid to be part of 1960s rock discourse.

Gleason sparked even more controversy three months later. In "Stop this Shuck, Mike Bloomfield," Gleason surprisingly blasted the beloved blues guitarist he supported in the past:

> Mike Bloomfield will never be a spade no longer how long he lives and how good he plays. White jazz musicians over the years have had the drive to sound black … But, tragically enough, the better they were at sounding black, the less they were themselves and the more obvious they were an imitation.[54]

Complaints from *Rolling Stone* readers appeared on the letters-to-the-editor page for weeks. "I've done my best in trying to tolerate Ralph Gleason's conviction that contemporary music is either black or white and that each should be played by musicians of corresponding skin color," wrote a reader, who said the column "took me over the brink."[55] The most substantial response came from Electric Flag vocalist Nick Gravenites who published his rebuttal in a *Rolling Stone* article, "Stop This Shuck, Ralph Gleason." He exasperatedly asked, "When is Ralph going to get out of his Black-White bag?"[56] Gleason's column continued to generate flak from readers. As the negative letters continued, it became clear that Gleason had lost his aura with a segment of the *Rolling Stone* readers. Wenner said Gleason was "quite right" about Bloomfield's appropriation of Black blues music, but the column was "a little overheated."[57]

Over the coming months, the Bloomfield controversy died away. But after a year of working at *Rolling Stone*, Gleason had become frustrated with his situation at the magazine. On September 4, 1968, Gleason poured out his vexations in a letter to Wenner:

Dear Jann:

Let us stop this charade. I resign as vice president of Straight Arrow effective immediately because I am totally out of sympathy with 1) the way you handle the business affairs of the corporation and 2) the way you handle personal relations.

In addition, I resign immediately as consulting editor of *Rolling Stone* because I can no longer accept responsibility for an editorial and reportorial policy with which I am not in sympathy and over which I have no control. Please remove my name from the masthead.

Following our conversation 10 days ago when you began sending me—daily—proofs of stories in type for me to read (something it took the entire publishing history of *Rolling Stone* to accomplish), I began to think that I have been seriously exploited by you in this venture. I wish to state to you, and to the other stockholders, in writing, that I have received the sum of $35 from *Rolling Stone* for my advice, consultation, and articles since the paper began. That you can expect me to continue, is what I'm talking about. When, in addition, you offer to buy my stock, my feeling of exploitation is reinforced.

I regret having to take this action, but I feel that I must retain my own integrity. I urge you to reexamine, in every possible way, the assumptions on which you operate.

Yours,
Ralph J. Gleason[58]

Two days later, Wenner wrote to *Rolling Stone*'s bank, Pacific National, and stated that Gleason was "no longer an authorized signature on our accounts."[59] In the following *Rolling Stone* issue: "Straight Arrow Publishers, Inc. regretfully announces the departure of Mr. Ralph J. Gleason from its board of directors. Mr. Gleason has also resigned his position as contributing editor on the staff of *Rolling Stone*."[60] Starting with the October 12, 1968, issue, Gleason was no longer on the masthead, and "Perspectives" was gone from the magazine, as though he was never there.

But at the *Chronicle*, it remained business as usual for Gleason. Over the coming weeks, he covered Miles Davis at the Both/And, Seatrain at the New Orleans House, and the Basie Band at Basin Street West. He covered a show by Donovan with his "guitar, his soft voice and the lilting love songs, the lines of Yeats and the feeling of peace."[61] He saw the Jimi Hendrix Experience at Winterland and reassessed his earlier adverse reaction to the group. Hendrix, Gleason raved, unleashed a "crashing, swirling hurricane of sound." The guitarist "communicates by a total instantaneous flash rather than by any kind of linear process." Gleason loved how Hendrix played the "Star Spangled Banner" with the "insolence of youth, as a pure revolutionary act."[62] This column predated Hendrix's iconic national anthem performance at the 1969 Woodstock Music Festival.

Meanwhile, *Rolling Stone* continued without their co-founder. On the surface, all looked good. A Pete Townsend interview. A Mick Jagger interview. Big headlines: "Janis Leaves Big Brother," "New Beatles Double Album Due." Insightful articles by top-notch critics such as Jonathan Cott, Jerry Hopkins, and Jon Landau. Gone were ads for San Francisco poster shops; in their place were full-page ads for albums like the Grateful Dead's *Anthem of the Sun*.

But the break-up undoubtedly weighed heavy on Wenner and Gleason. And so, they met to hash out their differences. *Rolling Stone* magazine was Gleason's primary means of communicating with the youth counterculture he helped to create. In many ways, his work there had been a labor of love, although he saw his low pay as a sign of disrespect for his work. But the magazine meant far more to Gleason than income. It represented regeneration, a continual feed of rejuvenating youth-culture music, and a readership with whom he could share each discovery like he did decades before when he told his young *Columbia Spectator* readers about the thrill of a Johnny Hodges solo or an impromptu jam session at the Onyx Club. Gleason agreed to return to *Rolling Stone* because it connected him to the youth subculture.

But there was one condition: Wenner would hire a new managing editor, John Burks, who worked at *Newsweek*'s San Francisco bureau. Wenner met with Burks and gave him the job. Gleason's name returned to the masthead as one of four contributing editors.[63] His "Perspectives" column also returned. It was as if Gleason never left.

Cash, the Band, and Joplin

Upon his return, one of Gleason's ideas brought *Rolling Stone* to national prominence. It happened right after John Lennon and Yoko Ono released their experimental album *Unfinished Music No. 1: Two Virgins*. On the front of the album is a full-frontal nude photo of Lennon and Ono. On the back of the album is a photo of the couple naked with their backs to the camera. The images provoked outrage, and Apple Records gave retailers brown paper wrappers to hide the nudes. Gleason suggested that Wenner obtain the photos and print them in *Rolling Stone*. Lennon and Ono obliged, and the images appeared in the November 23, 1968, issue. Their backside shot appeared on the cover, and their full-frontal landed inside as a center spread. Wenner printed double the number of copies than usual, and the issue still sold out. It was banned in Boston and provoked a nationwide reaction. You couldn't buy such good publicity. Gleason's idea "put *Rolling Stone* on the map," said Wenner.[64]

Some of Gleason's most significant contributions to *Rolling Stone* were his long-form articles about essential artists and concerts. The first was his 1969 article about Johnny Cash's performance at San Quentin State Prison. Cash never forgot the rave review Gleason gave him in 1956 and had carried the clip in his pocket ever since.[65] Now, a decade later, Gleason covered Cash's San Quentin show for *Rolling Stone* and the *Chronicle*.

On the evening of February 24, 1969, Gleason drives from his warm bungalow in Berkeley to the cold countenance of San Quentin State Prison, California's only death row penitentiary. The twenty-five-mile trip is a surreal journey to the flip side of the American Dream. The moon hangs over San Pablo Bay, and the nighttime sky is covered with "deep purple clouds [like] two-day-old bruises."[66] Arriving at the prison gate, a guard looks suspiciously at a brown paper bag on Gleason's front seat. Gleason quickly assures him it's not a gun but a quart of milk brought along as part of his diabetes regime. The guard lets Gleason enter, and he parks and walks through security.

Gleason reaches a large hall with rows of seats filled with prisoners. While a television crew sets up, Cash and his entourage wait on the sidelines. Gleason spots the singer, dressed in his trademark black frock coat. To Gleason, Cash looks like a "haunted man, deep scoops under his burning eyes and jaw muscles working like he was chewing invisible gum."⁶⁷ But when Cash strides onto the stage, he comes alive as inmates cheer and shout. In his deep Arkansas voice, Cash sings "San Quentin," written for the occasion. The inmate beside Gleason turns to him and says, "Cash is real; these cons would spot a phony in a hot minute."⁶⁸ Driving home after the show, Gleason feels relieved to be on the outside.

In his *Chronicle* column, Gleason wrote how "you could feel the inmates breathing" when Cash sang. He understood what Cash meant when he said prisoners make the "best audiences in the world."⁶⁹ Gleason captured the gritty setting with details such as a fork "thrown in some mess hall demonstration, embedded in the stucco block fifteen feet above the floor."⁷⁰ The column's theme: staging a concert in prison is an implicit protest against institutional inhumanity. A theme underscored by Cash's lyric, "San Quentin may you rot and burn in hell!"⁷¹

Three months later, Gleason published another significant article in *Rolling Stone*, "The Band at Winterland," an immense former ice-skating rink used by Bill Graham for shows too large to fit the Fillmore. After a shaky first night, the Band is back in fighting form. With Gleason hanging onto every note, Robbie Robertson bobs, sways, and pops out his signature Telecaster riffs. To Gleason, the solos sprang from the amplifier and "cracked around the hall like a whip."⁷² With his "bushy beard, swinging shoulders, and Mephistophelian visage," Drummer Levon Helm sat hunched over the mike as he sang.⁷³ Gleason's favorite song of the night was the closer, Little Richard's "Slippin' and Sliddin'":

> It was the best thing they did all weekend. It was looser, and it was down home dance music, and the people leaped with it and spun around and kicked and shouted. My God, it was great!⁷⁴

The show confirmed Gleason's admiration for the Band, whom he had praised since their days as Dylan's backup band, the Hawks. Following the group's name change, Gleason reviewed their debut album, *Music from Big Pink*. He lauded the album's "undiminishing delights, the stark imagery of the songs and the beautiful, clean, economical playing so tightly interwoven that it emerged as more exciting the leaner it became." He said *Big Pink* teemed with "poetry, imagery, metaphor and sound all molding together into a remarkable music-making association." Sensing the special bond between Dylan and his former backup band, Gleason wrote how *Big Pink* complimented *John Wesley Harding* and *Nashville Skyline*. When Dylan and the Band recorded a batch of songs released on the bootleg album *Great White Wonder*, Gleason said the best part was the "so-called 'Basement' tape" and concluded, "Despite a slightly fuzzy quality, the album "is superb."⁷⁵

"Superb" wasn't the word Gleason used to characterize Janis Joplin's new band. The singer left Big Brother & the Holding Company amidst rising stardom following *Monterey Pop* and *Cheap Thrills*. Joplin formed a new group, the Kozmic Blues Band, which debuted in San Francisco at Winterland in March 1969. Gleason attended with high expectations; after all, he had lauded Joplin's prowess since she joined Big Brother in 1966. A few days later, he wrote:

> Her new band is a drag. They can play OK, but they are a pale version of the Memphis-Detroit bands from the rhythm & blues shows, and Janis, though in good voice, seems bent on becoming Aretha Franklin …
>
> The best thing that could be done would be for her to scrap the band and go right back to being a member of Big Brother & the Holding Company (if they'll have her). There, she was something unique and special, and the whole of it was magnificent when it was right and never dull, and especially never pretentious or in bad taste.
>
> The publicity she has had may keep her up there as Janis Super Star if that is what she really wants. But there will have to be more than this to support it. It may go over in Indiana, after all, the Iron Butterfly and Canned Heat are big there too. But in San Francisco, and I suspect in New York as well, there are too many good things going on.[76]

Gleason's review devastated Joplin, according to the late Sam Andrew, guitarist for Big Brother and the Kozmic Blues Band:

> Janis read it in Stockholm the night that Bobby Neuwirth and I got drunk and walked all over town with the mayor. We came back to the hotel, and there Janis was in tears, distraught by this sentence: "She should go back to Big Brother and the Holding Company (if they will have her)." Janis was inconsolable … That there might have been some truth in Gleason's words didn't make them any easier to take. We still read Ralph J. Gleason when we could.[77]

Sometimes, we forget the impact of critiques on artists. Gleason's negative reviews were unbiased, even toward musicians he liked. Some musicians, including Frank Sinatra, improved their performances by following Gleason's critiques. Although Gleason praised Sinatra's work in the 1950s, he was critical of his later performances. This can be seen in Gleason's review of Sinatra's well-known televised performance at Madison Square Garden:

> It is simply weird now to see him all glossed up like a wax dummy, with that rug on his head looking silly, and the on-stage movement which used to be panther-tense, now a self-conscious hoodlum bustle.
>
> His possible appearance is the occasion for bodyguards and hush-hush phone calls and big security plans and a blanket of secrecy … For Frank Sinatra, whose voice made him the friend of millions of Americans, to carry on like a Caribbean dictator holding back history with bodyguards and secret police is simply obscene … I think he went somewhere that makes him alien now to me in a way he never was before.[78]

Sinatra seems to have taken the review in stride and later wrote, "Ralph often led me to better performances, and I am eternally grateful to him for that. He remains a rare and gifted friend."[79] An uncharacteristically complimentary and wholehearted remark from someone known for his antagonistic relationship with the press. When Sinatra didn't like his coverage, he often sent the journalist an angry telegram and sometimes threatened legal action.[80]

In addition to reassessing artists such as Sinatra, Joplin, and Bloomfield, Gleason reevaluated the San Francisco hippie community. An ambitious plan for a San Francisco rock festival brought him into conflict with the community he had supported for years.

Wild West

March 12, 1969. Gleason sits in the Jefferson Airplane's 1904 neoclassical mansion at 2400 Fulton Street in Haight-Ashbury. Joining him are Bill Graham, Jann Wenner, disc jockey Tom Donahue, and the managers of the Jefferson Airplane and the Grateful Dead. The occasion is the first meeting of the San Francisco Music Council. Their mission: organize the Wild West Festival, San Francisco's first major rock fest.[81]

The illustrious group was called together by Gleason's old friend and colleague Barry Olivier, director of the Berkeley Folk Music Festival. Olivier and the other council members envision a more ambitious version of the Be-In, to be held in Golden Gate Park and showcasing all the city's rock bands, including the Jefferson Airplane and Grateful Dead. Olivier wisely formed a group of Council members who collectively had the talent needed to stage a festival: promoters, band managers, and journalists. All had experience with previous festivals. But the planned event provoked an unexpected backlash from the counterculture community. Unknowingly, the Council made itself a target for a Haight-Ashbury community simmering with grievances.

Everything looked promising at the start. The Council met regularly to move their ambitious plan forward. Gleason organized the group's first press conference and called the festival a "celebration of San Francisco" in his *Chronicle* column.[82] But leaders in the Haight-Ashbury community saw the event as an exploitation, not a celebration. The underground newspaper *Berkeley Tribe* trashed the Music Council in an article that said the festival was "the latest attempt at rip-off by the media-oriented promoters, notably Bill Graham and friends." The piece included a list of demands by the community that included the donation of profits to the Black Panthers and the Haight-Ashbury Free Clinic. The *Tribe* article said that if the demands weren't met, Haight-Ashbury residents and other Bay Area hippie groups would go on strike and protest the event.[83]

The strike threat angered Gleason and the Council. A press statement likely written by Gleason stated that the festival would go forward even though "the Haight-Ashbury community (whom we have always counted upon as being sympathetic) have started a campaign of attacks which have jeopardized this entire project."[84] To make matters worse, the San Francisco mayor's office balked at approving the festival in light of potential demonstrations.

As the *Berkeley Tribe* article indicated, Gleason's old friend Bill Graham had already sparred with the counterculture community. Light show operators recently went on strike against Graham, demanding higher wages. Although the strike ended, Graham lost his clout in the counterculture. And now that community protested the Wild West Festival. Gleason bristled at those he called the "crazies of the rock scene" and wrote an anguished column about the attacks on Graham and the festival: "Paranoia is the sickness of contemporary American life and more dangerous than speed. Everybody believes the worst. Nobody trusts anyone."[85] He had made a similar comment about the Carousel Ballroom fiasco, blaming it on mistrust within the San Francisco counterculture.

In both cases, Gleason blamed the tensions on the infusion of radical politics into the music scene. Gleason wrote that radicals aimed to appropriate the rock scene for their purposes, "the last convulsion of the old politics."[86] To Gleason, the New Left succumbed to the same narrowmindedness that made the Old Left obsolete. In Gleason's mind, politics served culture, not vice versa. Rock would change society, and political forms would adopt. Gleason's columns sparked a backlash from the festival's opponents. Marjorie Heins wrote in the San Francisco underground newspaper *Dock of the Bay*, "Gleason's situation is a microcosm of the whole rock music mess. The bands talk about what the radicals do and the capitalists exploit."[87] Heins called Gleason's column a "hysterical defense of two current banes of local radicals," Bill Graham and the Wild West Festival. Heins said Gleason, like many liberals, had been "backed into a conservative position by revolutionaries."[88]

Faced with this unmovable opposition, the Music Council canceled the Wild West Festival. Just one week from opening day, months of planning, negotiations, and contracts came to naught. Gleason fired off passionate columns about the cancellation. In his *Rolling Stone* column, he said, "These are the paranoid years."[89] A frustrated New Left had gone mad, he observed. It would be rock, not radicalism, that would change society. Gleason called the radicals "musical parasites" who hosted on rock music.[90] He recounted a "fruitless discussion with one politico" who wanted to go to Vietnam and shoot American soldiers.[91] Seething, he noted, "This is the kind of irresponsible, reckless bullshit that will result in unimaginable repression if not in actual murders in the streets."[92] Less than a year later, the Kent State protest exploded into deadly violence.

Gleason expanded his critique and blamed both sides. It wasn't just the "infantile disorders among the hysterical elements of the so-called hip community."[93] The festival failed because the "naïve organizers of the Wild West (including yours truly) had not expected to be attacked and were shaken."[94] Gleason focused his fury on the San Francisco Mime Troupe, a group he had defended in his column for years. The Troupe leaders were "boll weevils looking for an audience and a stage."[95] Leaders triggered a "latent paranoia among the radical political organizations who have hated the rock bands" because they channeled "young people's creative energies into music" instead of political radicalism.[96]

The conflict between the Wild West organizers and the Haight-Ashbury community reflected the impact of radicalism on the counterculture. Gleason feared where this would lead and prepared an extended attack against leftist extremism.

10

We've Had All That (1969–74)

The political radicals have the right enemies; they have courage, and some of them, they even have a program for the improvement of society which makes a kind of sense.

But they all have the old approach. You can't make an omelet without breaking the eggs. True, man, true. But you better figure out how to make a revolution without killing people, or it won't work. We've had all that. We really have.

Nothing I have read by the SDS, and the rest is as relevant as Allen Ginsberg's poems. None of it says as much to me as Bob Dylan, and none inspires like the simple thing of the Beatles singing "Hey Jude" on TV.[1]

Ralph J. Gleason, "Is There a Death Wish in the U.S.?"

When Gleason wrote, "We've had all that," he referred to the political revolutions during his lifetime, most notably in Ireland and Cuba, that left thousands of people dead. He was undoubtedly aware of the sectarian strife in Northern Ireland about to erupt into the Troubles, a thirty-year conflict. And so, from 1969 to 1974, Gleason intensified his case that rock music, not militancy, would bring about the counterculture's vision of a better society.

Is There a Death Wish in the US?

"American Revolution 1969," *Rolling Stone*, April 1969. The cover photo says it all. A young bewildered-looking cop in riot gear crouches over a profusely bleeding protester he's pinned to the ground with his baton. The message is clear: activism means going to war.

Inside the *Rolling Stone* issue is a special insert with essays on the violent state of political protest in 1969. In his introduction, Wenner wrote, "Like it or not, we have reached a point in the social, cultural, intellectual, and artistic history of the United States where we are all going to be affected by politics. We can no longer ignore it."[2] Some of the articles in the insert called for a radical political response, even if it meant fighting violence with violence.

But Gleason titled his contribution "Is There a Death Wish in the U.S.?" and proclaimed, "Politics has failed."[3] He said the most effective "revolutionary acts" were musical performances like Jimi Hendrix's reinterpretation of the "Star Spangled Banner," an "act of protest whose power and convincingness were inseparable from its identity as a fiercely nonconformist act of individual expression."[4] A mouthful, but true. Gleason said the Beatles weren't simply more popular than Jesus; they were "more potent than the SDS [Students for a Democratic Society, a radical group]."[5] Gleason said to change society through music, and "out of it will come the programs. Out of it will come the plans. When the time is right."[6] Change the mode of the music, and you change the way of society, a cause-and-effect theory as old as Plato. Gleason increasingly dismissed politics in his *Rolling Stone* columns and called for a cultural revolution fueled by rock music.

According to Robert Draper, author of *Rolling Stone: The Uncensored History*, these writings annoyed the magazine's young editorial staff, already dismissive of Gleason because of his age.[7] The twenty-something team found the graying journalist's theories of a rock revolution discomforting, coming from a middle-aged person who romanticized swing jazz, their parents' music. Yet Gleason's concern over growing violence was grounded in fact. Nadya Zimmerman writes:

> The counterculture in the Haight-Ashbury district from late-1965 to mid-1967 dissolved and spread out. What had seemed to be a self-contained entity of refusal became more of an infectious, multifaceted ethos of rebellious pluralism.
>
> ... the counterculture made itself vulnerable to media co-option, to unraveling into an ethos that could incubate and tolerate ... violence.[8]

Gleason had already sensed this violent undercurrent in rock music, most notably the early music of the Rolling Stones. Recall that in 1967 he wrote that the band "hit out in rage, almost in blind anger and certainly with overtones of destructiveness ... this attitude appealed to that section of the youth whose basic position was still in politics."[9] Violence also lay beneath the counterculture's dalliance with the Hells Angels, which had troubled Gleason since the 1965 Vietnam Day march from Berkeley to Oakland when the Angels blocked and beat protesters. His fears intensified two years later when the Angels assaulted a reveler under the blue skies of the Human Be-In.

And so, when promoters announced the Hells Angels would provide security for a free concert featuring the Rolling Stones at the Altamont Speedway, Gleason was justifiably concerned. Although *Rolling Stone* and the *Chronicle* sent writers to cover the show, Gleason stayed home. On December 6, 1969, the Altamont Speedway Free Festival drew approximately 300,000 people to hear the Stones, Santana, Jefferson Airplane, the Flying Burrito Brothers, and Crosby, Stills, Nash & Young. Some hoped for a "Woodstock West" after the highly successful Woodstock Music and Art Fair held the previous summer in Bethel, New York. Instead, Altamont deteriorated into a day of violence caused by the aggressive tactics of Hells Angels. The hostility culminated in a gang member fatally stabbing concertgoer Meredith Hunter after Hunter drew a revolver.

Gleason wrote two *Chronicle* articles about Altamont. In the first, he quoted an attendee's astute observation, "There was no love, no joy. It wasn't just the Angels. It was everybody. In twenty-four hours, we created all the problems of society in one place: congestion, violence, dehumanization."[10] In his second column, "Who's Responsible for the Murder?" Gleason answered: the rock promoters who "put the Angels with a truckload of free beer in charge of security." Then more questions, "Is this the new community? Is this what Woodstock promised? Gathered together as a tribe, what happened? Brutality, murder, despoliation."[11]

Following the tragedy, Gleason urged Wenner to cover Altamont "like it was World War II."[12] The result was "Let It Bleed," a collaborative article by staff writers including Lester Bangs and Greil Marcus, published January 20, 1970. These writers called Altamont a festival of death bungled by the Rolling Stones' management team who organized the concert. Another article, "The Love Generation Hype in the News," blamed local media except for Gleason's *Chronicle* articles.[13]

Weeks later, Gleason couldn't get Altamont off his mind. For him and others, the concert triggered a crisis of faith—a deep and painful questioning of the counterculture movement. "What started as a dream on Haight Street in 1965," he wrote, "may very well have ended in Meredith Hunter's blood in front of the bandstand at Altamont." The concert was a "sociological cusp, a tribal moment of truth."[14] Altamont also altered Gleason's view of the band who played on as mayhem ensued. In an interview with a local underground newspaper, Gleason said, "I'm the enemy of the Rolling Stones. If these people are going to sing about violence, then they've got to handle and understand and expect violence."[15] When the Stones released *Let it Bleed*, Gleason wrote that listening was difficult "without visions of swirling Hells Angels and flying bottles and Denise [Kaufman] of Ace of Cups in the hospital with a fractured skull."[16] This assault affected Gleason personally because an empty beer bottle thrown from the crowd struck his young pregnant friend.

Predictably, some on the left disagreed with Gleason's response to Altamont and his condemnation of militant radicalism. Leftist writer Sol Stern fired back in an article in *Scanlan's Monthly* called "Altamont: Pearl Harbor to the Woodstock Nation." Like *Ramparts*' Warren Hinckle, Stern leveled a blistering critique against the counterculture and Gleason's support.[17] Stern wrote that Gleason, Wenner, and Bill Graham represented the "elite of the rock and roll industry," a perception created during the Wild West debacle. Stern called Gleason's "Death Wish" column "nonsense."[18]

Instead of responding, Gleason sent Stern's article to activist Jerry Rubin for his thoughts. Rubin replied to Gleason with a five-page typed letter:

> Yes, he does use you as a scapegoat, though it's really that he's using you as a handle to criticize the whole rock scene. I didn't like it, the criticism, I mean, because I felt it to be largely unfair toward both you and the people who made the music.[19]

But Rubin believed the Stern article was "to some extent justified, in that, I myself have often felt that you tend to be too uncritical of those you really dig and sometimes fail to catch when they go off the track."[20]

Neither Rubin nor Stern changed Gleason's views about Altamont. Gleason published a lengthy article about the tragic festival in the August 1970 issue of *Esquire* and meticulously reconstructed the chain of events that culminated in the Angels' violence. Gleason blamed the festival organizers, the media (including the *San Francisco Chronicle*), and Mick Jagger for creating the toxic environment. Stopping short of blaming the overall counterculture, Gleason wrote that no one "but the lunatic fringe of the underground press has suggested that Meredith Hunter's murder and the other accidents were anything but results of irrational, spontaneous violence." The perception of the Hells Angels as the "guardians of the children at the Great Human Be-In" was "part of the San Francisco rock mythology which ended abruptly at Altamont."[21] A mythology that Gleason helped create, now debunked in the awful aftermath of the concert.

A Young Irishman Haunted by Dreams

Although Altamont disrupted Gleason's belief that rock music was *always* an unequivocally positive force, he never lost faith that rock, in the right hands, *could* be a positive force. Refreshing Gleason's conviction was the new music of Dylan, the Band, and a singer-songwriter who blended Celtic traditions with American soul music.

One afternoon in early 1970, Ralph and Jean host special guests—Irish vocalist Van Morrison and his wife, Janet. Morrison is there to be interviewed by Gleason for a *Chronicle* profile. The couple recently settled into a house in Marin County across the Golden Gate Bridge from San Francisco, and Morrison had just released his masterwork *Moondance*. In songs like "Glad Tidings," the vocalist drew on Irish influences that few critics other than Gleason would have recognized. For example, Morrison's guttural "yarrrrragh" characterized the Celtic folk style Gleason heard in his father's recordings of Irish tenor John McCormack. Morrison's lyrics on *Moondance* drew from a heritage he shared with Gleason, Celtic paganism kept alive in folk songs and poetry.

The Morrisons talk about the musicians who delighted them over the years. They admired blues players like Albert King and Howlin' Wolf, former Coltrane drummer Elvin Jones, and R&B powerhouses like Ike and Tina Turner. The couple had never encountered anyone as knowledgeable about these artists as Gleason. As a result, the reticent Morrison opened up about his background and early musical influences. Gleason was impressed by how far the twenty-six-year-old had come so quickly.

Gleason's column, "A Young Irishman Haunted by Dreams," came out in March 1970. The lengthy piece included a profile and a review of *Moondance*:

> Unlike many of his contemporaries, Morrison is jazz-influenced; you can hear it in the edge he has to his voice. You can listen to it also in the way he phrases, as well as in the relationship between the melodic line and the rhythm of the number ... He wails. He wails as the jazz musicians speak of crying, as the gypsies, the Gaels, and the old folks in every culture talk of it.[22]

Gleason found *Moondance* to be one of those albums that grew richer with each listen, something he'd experienced with only a handful of rock records—those by the Band, the Beatles, Bob Dylan, and a few other artists. Although Morrison spoke the language of the blues, he sounded like a "young Irishman haunted by dreams, a poet, one of the 'children of the rainbow, living in the morning of the world.'"[23] Morrison's former wife, Janet Morrison Minto, called Gleason's *Chronicle* profile "another defining moment in Van's career and another important turning point in gauging the trajectory of his fame."[24]

A year later, in 1971, Gleason saw Morrison play at the New Orleans House, a Berkeley club popular with visiting musicians such as Eric Clapton. The nightspot was part of what Gleason called a "minor league circuit" of Bay Area clubs where emerging artists proved themselves and established artists enjoyed the intimate setting. Covering the show for *Rolling Stone*, Gleason walks into the packed 150-seat club and finds a vantage point. He spots Morrison, who finishes his glass of wine at the bar and steps on stage. As the set starts, Gleason loves the pacing, which begins softly with a few background instruments and intensifies until Morrison's full band wails. After the final song, the shy Morrison mumbles, "Thank you." But the audience clamors for more. Morrison obliges. After he finishes, the crowd, now on its feet, basks in the afterglow. A young man recognizes Gleason, walks up to him, and makes a request, "Please tell the man how great he is." Gleason says, "I will," knowing that even great artists welcome reaffirmation.[25]

After the show, Gleason steps out of the smoky club into the foggy night. As he walks to his car, he hears young fans singing songs from Morrison's performance, carrying the spirit of the show home. Knowing that Morrison will read it, Gleason honors the young man's wish when he writes his *Rolling Stone* review, "Van Morrison, you gave one of the greatest performances those people will ever witness, and you staked a claim to musical greatness in all our hearts that night."[26]

The Jefferson Airplane and the San Francisco Sound

> She wore black, and her pale skin almost glowed in the light that sifted through the ivy around the windows. Her blue-green eyes were direct as bullets ... she served tea in a substantial earthen-ware cup and sat on an exotic Indian sofa with a canopy over it.[27]

Gleason sits with Grace Slick in her San Francisco apartment, decorated with tapestries, posters, and Bay Area artifacts. Next to Slick is a stuffed seal, a leftover prop from a Hollywood Bowl show by the Jefferson Airplane. Gleason is there to interview Slick for his upcoming book, *The Jefferson Airplane and the San Francisco Sound*. As Gleason and Slick sip tea, they talk of many things: jazz saxophonist Archie Shepp, James Joyce's *Ulysses*, Lenny Bruce, and the San Francisco rock scene. Like Gleason, Slick believes rock music can shape society more effectively than politics. Gleason asks, "Do you see all this music as a crest of a whole revolution?"

Slick answers:

Probably. Part of it. I think the music's probably at the top. It hasn't been in the past as closely integrated with a revolutionary movement ... Music goes over the radio ... a pleasant way of getting your [political] ideas across, rather than a speech which is dull unless you're a fantastic orator ... plus, even if they are reasonable, nobody cares![28]

For his book, Gleason conducted lengthy interviews with the band's members, along with Jerry Garcia and Bill Graham. These dialogues provide a detailed firsthand account of how the San Francisco rock scene took off. Marty Balin discusses the band's interest in experimental music composer Edgar Varese. Jorma Kaukonen talks about his visit to the Philippines, where he taped the music of Indonesian orchestras called gamelans. Paul Kantner describes how the band wrote songs in the studio. Bassist Jack Casady talks about the role of improvisation in the band's music, and drummer Spencer Dryden recounts his roots in the Los Angeles jazz scene.

Slick said Gleason's portrayal of her and her bandmates was accurate, and she enjoyed reading the book. Gleason and Slick had met earlier, and she recalls seeing him at Jefferson Airplane shows leaning against a wall taking notes. "Gleason was gracious and pleasant, easy to have around."[29] A regular reader of Gleason's columns, Slick considered *Rolling Stone* a "joyous thing, a publication that wasn't stupid" like teen magazines.[30] *Rolling Stone* "had well-read writers," Slick noted, "which is what young readers wanted, so it was exciting to have *Rolling Stone* come on the scene."[31] Slick believes Gleason liked the Jefferson Airplane because the melodies of their songs "could have been from the 1940s when he was young."[32]

Like Slick, Kaukonen also read Gleason's columns and remembers him at the band's shows. Gleason had a "tweedy college professor persona," the guitarist recalled. Kaukonen appreciates how Gleason recognized the "new rock 'n' roll emerging in San Francisco as a valid art form."[33] Kaukonen added, "When Gleason covered a show, he wasn't there for the hang. He didn't socialize, and he didn't care what people wore ... it was all about the music."[34] Although Slick said reviews didn't sway the band, Kaukonen acknowledged that "we liked to see our name in print, and it legitimized us."[35]

The first chapter of *San Francisco Sound* was called "The Bands ... That's Where It's At," and it provided one of the first comprehensive histories of an American local rock scene. Gleason detailed how the San Francisco rock community flourished because of its network of self-reliant promoters who started as fans. He explained how this new scene was rooted in the city's bohemian past. The chapter drew heavily from Gleason's *Chronicle* columns.

Book reviewers generally gave *The Jefferson Airplane and the San Francisco Sound* positive reviews. Writing for the *Baltimore Sun*, rock critic Mike Jahn called Gleason's book a "precise, accurate and objective account" written by a person who has "seen many musical trends come and go and knows well how to account for them."[36] Reviews came in over the summer and continued through the end of 1970. John Grissim of *Rolling Stone* called the book "forceful and fascinating, and one of the better books on the music yet published."[37] The book was adopted by a San Francisco Institute of Art music course.

But two reviewers sharply criticized Gleason's book. The first was *Chronicle* reviewer Richard A. Ogar, a writer for the underground newspaper the *Berkeley Barb* and friend of beat poet Michael McClure. Ogar wrote as a counterculture insider who saw the middle-aged Gleason as an "outsider trying only too desperately to get in."[38] Ogar said Gleason "falls short of insight and perspective, relying instead on facile adulation and a bag of appreciative slang."[39] Ogar continued his tirade:

> Running back over the years, Gleason has selected a few golden moments and a batch of yellowed columns from the *Chronicle*, padding the mix like a freshman essay … The more considered comments are rarely more than rehashes of the old, and one begins to wonder if this is a history or an unrequested memoir …
>
> But the most distressing aspect of the interviews is Gleason's pure gush attitude towards his subjects.[40]

San Francisco native R. Serge Denisoff also criticized Gleason's lavish praise for his subjects. In a review that ran in the *Journal of Popular Culture*, Denisoff criticized Gleason's hagiographical approach:

> Ralph J Gleason of the *San Francisco Chronicle*, more by geographical accident than original interest, has become the historian of the San Francisco Sound. Like most religious converts, Gleason is very laudatory of his subject and the musicians who have made San Francisco the "American Liverpool." … The participant observer status of the author unfortunately provides a reader with little more than a short history of the evolution of the San Francisco Sound, held together by columns on various events … Gleason conveys much of the so-called charismatic approach to popular culture, that is, the glorification, if not deification, of cultural heroes.[41]

Denisoff said, "few new insights are gained" because the book relied so heavily on previously printed columns.[42] In his late twenties, Denisoff cared for rock music and wanted to see an accurate, fulsome account of the San Francisco scene from a fresh perspective. Denisoff and Ogar's comments foreshadowed those of some contemporary pop music scholars. For instance, rock scholar Ulf Lindberg said Gleason idealized psychedelic music.[43] Gennari wrote that Gleason was "a romantic with a utopian vision of a social and spiritual revolution sparked by musical prophets."[44]

Gleason's belief in these prophets dates back to his jazz conversion as a Chappaqua teen. He had a romantic's emphasis on subjectivity, as shown by his chosen journalistic medium, the column, in which Gleason could convey an ecstatic musical experience with uncommon immediacy and expressivity in a 500–1,000 word burst. Columns demand subjectivity, not scholarly objectivity. As noted in *Deadlines Artists: America's Greatest Newspaper Columns*, "The improvisational nature of the newspaper column is what sets it apart, the near-miracle that stories composed on punishing daily deadlines can resonate with beauty and power decades later."[45]

Ogar's and Denisoff's criticisms also smack of ageism. As we've seen, Gleason's age was an issue for some of his young readers and colleagues at *Rolling Stone* magazine. But as music scholar Andy Bennett points out in his book *Music, Style, and Aging*, older fans can "supply critical judgment" of a music scene and be "informal educators" about a scene's roots, "conveyors of both aesthetic and practical knowledge."[46] Like providing information about the "practical skills involved in successfully running dance music events," skills Gleason learned on the 1930s Columbia dance committees he chaired.[47] But as Bennett notes, conflicts can arise among different generational groups in a music scene, sometimes caused by "the inscription of age-related biases in particular sub-genres of music."[48] An oft-repeated credo of the 1960s counterculture was, "Don't trust anybody over 30."

Incidentally, Gleason knew Ogar planned to pan his book in the *Chronicle*'s book review column, so he turned his Sunday "Rhythm" column over to Ogar to publish his critique.[49] Gleason told a friend, "I ran the asshole's review in my own space to take the curse off it and look like a good guy."[50] Ogar's aggressive tone guaranteed that Gleason would ignore his comments.

Following the publication of *The San Francisco Sound*, Gleason wrote several columns about recent developments in jazz and rock. These writings show Gleason moving beyond the San Francisco rock scene. His review of the 1969 Big Sur Folk Festival with headliners John Sebastian, Joni Mitchell, and Crosby, Stills and Nash (CSN) shows this. Gleason praised CSN's harmonizing and called Stephen Stills one of pop music's best lyricists. He called Crosby's "Long Time Gone," a cautionary statement to the counterculture that progressive social progress crawls at a snail's pace. Gleason said the song's message added to the "themes of the new generation."[51]

Counterculture politics underlay Gleason's next column about the recent Woodstock Festival:

> One of the most important things that happened there, it seems to me, was missed completely [by the press]. Abbie Hoffman, who, with Jerry Rubin, started the Yippies, was rousted from the stage by the musicians as he attempted to take over the microphone when the Who was performing. Hoffman wanted to protest the festival. Last fall Jerry Rubin's speech at the Berkeley Community Theatre was booed and then ignored by the audience …
>
> All this is important, I suspect, because the strength of contemporary music is greater than the power of any music at any time in history, apparently, and everyone wants to hitchhike on it to power. But the music represents a much different approach than the traditional confrontation politics, though music people may share some common beliefs with politicos.[52]

A week later, Gleason reviewed *In a Silent Way*, Miles Davis's first fusion album. Also known as jazz rock, fusion is a blending of jazz with rock, funk, and R&B. Fusion notably emphasizes electronic instrumentation, including electric bass, electric guitar, and electric piano. Gleason found Davis's album revolutionary in its use of electric

Figure 10.1 Ralph Gleason with Paul Simon (seated) and Art Garfunkel (standing) at Big Sur Folk Festival, 1969. © Jim Marshall Photography LLC.

sounds interwoven with the bandleader's solos. He said, "Davis's playing extends from misty rumblings to bright, dancing runs and sharp jabs (he's a boxer, too) of high notes, but sets the mood at all times. At times he sounds like a blues singer."[53] Gleason praised the album and correctly predicted it would spark a revolution in jazz. He compared Davis to other modernist disruptors, James Joyce and Pablo Picasso.[54] Davis also figured prominently in an article Gleason just published that would garner a prestigious award.

Black Art

The article "Jazz: Black Art/American Art" appeared in the fall 1969 issue of *Lithopinion*. The quarterly celebration of the graphic arts was published by Amalgamated Lithographers of America, a labor union. In "Black Art," Gleason expanded his career-long argument that African Americans invented jazz and made its most significant developments:

Jazz is an art … the creation of black musicians and music completely original to the United States of America. Its first creators were black, and its most important, innovative players, the delineators of all its styles, and the greatest of its solo performers, right down to last night's session on the concert hall or the nightclub stage, have all been black men.

It is even possible to speculate that all the white jazz musicians could be eliminated from the history of the music without altering its development in any significant way.[55]

This last statement is highly problematic. White musicians such as Benny Goodman, Dave Brubeck, and Bill Evans revolutionized jazz during Gleason's lifetime. To decenter White privilege in the development of jazz, Gleason sometimes undervalued White contributions, a carryover from his hot collector days. He made a similar case in a chapter he wrote on jazz education for the book *The Creative College Student: An Unmet Challenge*:

The only music which is accepted as art and is indigenously American is jazz. The better a jazz artist is, the more he sounds like a negro (if he is not already one), and the very best musicians, but with one or two exceptions, are negroes. Negroes made this music. They created it, developed the basic styles, and are still its leading figures. All whites could be erased from the history of jazz, and the level and quality of jazz would be just where it is today.[56]

Gleason argued similarly about White blues musicians. Significantly, Gleason wrote "Jazz: Black Art/American Art" during the peak of the Black Arts Movement, a coalition of poets, writers, and musicians. Gleason admired its founder Amiri Baraka and his book, *Blues People*, a pioneering study of African American music and Black identity. Jazz historian John Gennari notes the similarity of Gleason's and Baraka's racialized views of jazz and how Baraka came under attack for "jazz exclusivism" by White fans and critics.[57] The fact is that not *all* jazz originators and innovators were Black, and Black experience isn't a prerequisite for being able to play jazz any more than White experience is necessary to perform "My Favorite Things," memorialized in Coltrane's fourteen-minute interpretation.

"Jazz: Black Art/American Art" reflects Gleason's excellent command of jazz history and his mental storehouse of colorful anecdotes, including those he heard firsthand from pioneering musicians. Gleason's abundant knowledge allowed him to do what he most loved—take his reader on a journey through the history of jazz. Gleason framed his tale as the story of a nation finding itself:

In an America coming of age at the turn of the [twentieth] century, seeking its identity as a world power, European music was the standard for culture; it was "classical" and "good." Anything American, therefore, must be somehow less valuable, especially anything which came from the black citizens who, so recently as to be within the memory of a majority of the adult population, had been slaves and officially only three-fifths human at that …

> White Americans found the world implied and represented by [jazz] to be exciting and fascinating, and valuable. They found it to be more honest, more poignant, and more dimensional than their own world ...
>
> So increasingly, the strange process of crossing the color line in reverse began, with whites imitating black speech, dress, style and music.[58]

Gleason won the ASCAP Deems Taylor Award for "Jazz: Black Art/American Art" in 1970. The prestigious prize is given to outstanding articles, liner notes, and books about music.

While Gleason worked on "Black Art," he published another analysis of popular music. "The Greater Sound" was published in the summer 1969 issue of *The Drama Review: TDR*, an art journal the MIT press printed. In it, Gleason expanded and refined the thesis of "Like a Rolling Stone" that it would be rock musicians, not radical militants, who would bring about the counterculture's vision of a better society:

> Today, all over the United States, American young people are being spoken to by revolutionists in words they understand, in the style that makes those words acceptable, and through an invisible medium that old professional politicos have not yet picked up on.
>
> This medium is the phonograph record.[59]
>
> If you want to reach young people in this country (and revolutions are made by the young; the old make counter-revolution), then write a song, don't buy an ad, or issue a statement.[60]

Gleason took on the "radical theoreticians" of the Frankfurt School who dismissed popular culture:

> The radical movement in the United States has always seen music as an arm of the revolution ... But radical theoreticians mis-assessed the phenomena of pop music. [To them] pop music meant mass culture and mass production and was, de facto, anti-art and anti-culture and manipulated by perverted money-makers.[61]

Gleason responded that subversive music corrodes capitalism from the inside out:

> American Enterprise will, in a kind of autolysis [obliteration of cells via their own enzymes], allow its own destruction to be preached via a product that is profitable.[62]

Meaning best-selling records by Dylan, the Band, and others, vinyl discs that upset the status quo, not just through their lyrics, but through their sound:

In a culture of noise – not just the jets roaring overhead and the trucks thundering on the streets, but the cyclic noise of the crashing of institutions and assumptions and conventions, the whole crescendo of a collapsing civilization – the only peace seems to be in the middle of an even greater sound in which a special kind of sonic high is produced and a new kind of one-to-one communication occurs.[63]

"Jazz: Black Art/American Art" and "The Greater Sound" show that Gleason excelled at long-form writing when he augmented his earlier ideas with new insights. When he published these articles in 1969, jazz and rock musicians explored new sonic territories. In Columbia's Studio B in New York City, Miles Davis prepared the way for jazz fusion with *Bitches Brew*. Across the continent, in Wally Heider's ultramodern studio in San Francisco, the members of the Jefferson Airplane recorded their fifth album, *Volunteers*. At the same time, *The Jefferson Airplane and the San Francisco Sound* hit the paperback spinner racks in bookstores across the country. But Gleason had far more to say about the band he helped make famous.

Go Ride the Music

While writing *The Jefferson Airplane and the San Francisco* Sound, Gleason filmed the Airplane and other San Francisco bands for a KQED television documentary called *West Pole*. He and Robert Zagone first discussed producing a rock film while working on the Duke Ellington documentaries for KQED.[64] After the Human Be-In, when television networks sent crews to San Francisco to film rock concerts, Gleason thought these films failed to capture the scene's holistic energy.[65] And so, in early 1968, Gleason convinced KQED to let him and Zagone film *West Pole* featuring performances by San Francisco bands and commentary on the scene.

The art of televised rock music was in its infancy. Teen programs like *American Bandstand* typically featured artists lip-syncing their hits. Two musical variety series, *Shindig*, and *Hullabaloo*, showed more promise, but the performances occurred in television studios, not natural settings like clubs. Gleason and Zagone were in unexplored territory. Zagone was interested in the underground films of Andy Warhol and appreciated how the pop artist-director used cinema verité in films featuring the Velvet Underground. Warhol incorporated aspects of psychedelia in these movies, such as projected light shows and multiple exposures. Zagone understood the limitations of adapting these techniques to a television program, but rather than being discouraged, the challenge spurred his creativity.

Gleason and Zagone made *West Pole* through KQED's National Center for Experiments in Television (NCET). The film reflects this spirit of innovation, fitting for the boundary-breaking bands: the Jefferson Airplane, Quicksilver Messenger Service, Grateful Dead, Steve Miller Band, Ace of Cups, and Sons of Champlin. Between performance scenes, Gleason narrated. Now with longish hair and a handlebar mustache Gleason looked at home in this setting and used his knowledge of music history to provide context. For example, he compared the San Francisco rock scene with the 1930s Kansas City jazz scene and told viewers about Bay Area dance halls during the swing era. Local rock ballrooms boomed, he said, because "dancing never stopped" in San Francisco.[66]

West Pole opens with a soulfully exquisite a cappella performance by the Ace of Cups, an under-recognized San Francisco band and among the first all-women rock bands. Gleason's friend Denise Kaufman sang and played guitar and harmonica in the group. Gleason mentored Kaufman and her fellow band members and gave them a place of honor in *West Pole*. In an unpublished remembrance shared with the author, Kaufman wrote:

> Ralph didn't expect a young musician to be Miles Davis. And if the sound was rough, he had the vision to know that with attention and care, it would grow and refine. So, he found a way to let me know my music touched him and to let it come ...
>
> Ralph's house was like your oldest and most comfortable slippers. Just felt good to be there. Books and records and stuff piled around to trip into for as long as you wanted. I could and did hang out there indefinitely ...
>
> When Simon and Garfunkel were coming on their first visit to the Bay Area ... we all ended up at Ralph's listening to Lenny Bruce tapes, which Paul loved. And then Ralph gave Paul and me tickets to the Ray Charles concert that night, so we hitched to San Francisco to see Ray. And caught a Grateful Dead set too, but Paul didn't like them much.[67]

Life then took a dark turn for Kaufman when her parents, concerned about her immersion in the counterculture, had her committed to a mental institution:

> When I got committed to the nut ward, Ralph couldn't believe it. He called me every day for three months, and we'd hang out on the phone for sometimes an hour a day. He hated hospitals worse than anything, but on Christmas, he came and got me so I could spend the day with the family. We all made presents for each other. It was great—lots of love in that family.
>
> In order to get out of the ward, I had to have a job. So, Ralph talked Max Weiss into hiring me to work at Fantasy. I worked upstairs doing promo for [Brazilian guitarist] Bola Sete and writing letters for Max and answering the phone. And John Fogerty worked downstairs packing records. That's when Creedence Clearwater Revival was still the Golliwogs, and they wore matching polka dot shirts, and I had to send their publicity photos, and I'd wince every time.
>
> During that time, the Ace of Cups began, and from the front, Ralph was our most solid fan. He took it on to supervise the band's musical growth, just as he had my own. When people called him up to ask about bands for jobs, he'd tell them to call us.[68]

Kaufman's remembrance drives home how, for Gleason, *West Pole* was far more than a historical account. The film manifested his warm relationships with Bay Area rock musicians like Kaufman.

West Pole premiered on August 16, 1968, and broadcast in KQED's viewing area. In his *Rolling Stone* review, art critic Thomas Albright praised the film's creators for capitalizing on videotape anomalies such as snow, scanlines, and unnatural color. Zagone's techniques foreshadowed the experiments of the early MTV era.

Gleason started to work on two more San Francisco rock documentaries in early 1970. He and his KQED crew met with the Jefferson Airplane, who agreed to be in the documentaries and suggested filming on location at Bay Area concerts. The project was green-lighted.[69] The documentaries would serve as two episodes of *NET Fanfare*, a new National Educational Television series about the performing arts that covered music from classical to rock. This series presaged similar programs like *Soundstage* and *Tiny Desk Concerts* produced later by NET's successor Public Broadcasting Service—another example of Gleason's far-reaching influence.

The *NET Fanfare* episodes were titled *Go Ride the Music* and *A Night at the Family Dog*. They included performances by the Jefferson Airplane, Grateful Dead, Quicksilver Messenger Service, and Santana. The Jefferson Airplane played a vital role in both films and Gleason "was instrumental in negotiating with the Airplane and their manager Bill Thompson during the pre-production stage," said Zagone.[70] The crew and the band met several times at the Jefferson Airplane mansion and devised a filming schedule.[71]

The crew filmed *Night at the Family Dog* at a new venue called the Family Dog on the Great Highway. The concert hall sat beside an amusement park so close to the Pacific Ocean that audiences could hear breakers hitting the seawall. Promoter Chet Helms opened the ballroom in 1969 after the city revoked his license for the Avalon because neighbors complained about the loud music. The building predated the swing era and must have reminded Gleason of long-ago nights at Long Island Sound casinos where he danced to the Jimmie Lunceford orchestra.

The KQED mobile video unit taped performances on two nights. The crew kept the camera lights low to accurately capture the ballroom's subdued lighting, and they filmed cinema verité style to preserve the naturalness of each scene.[72] Captured on tape were remarkable moments like the powerhouse percussion on Santana's "Soul Sacrifice" and Grace Slick's unearthly recitation of "Eskimo Blue Day." Additionally, Ron "Pigpen" McKernan's gritty performance of "Hard to Handle" with the Grateful Dead. The film showcased this underrated blues singer's ability to set a driving groove and carry the audience along.

The team filmed the next session at Pacific High Studios near Fillmore West. The cameras start rolling as roadies set up the Jefferson Airplane's equipment. Once onstage, Grace Slick, dressed in a blue kimono, stands icily. Suddenly, Slick unleashes a bone-chilling howl. The band dives into "Volunteers," and Kaukonen lights up the rhythm motif with vivid guitar fills. In "Plastic Fantastic Lover," Balin wails the lyrics looser and faster than on the album. Kaukonen leads the band as a camera operator focuses on him, a commanding figure with his lean but sturdy frame and shoulder-length brown hair. As Gleason once told Zagone, "Scope out the driving forces that move the band."[73]

The final session captures a show by the Airplane and Quicksilver Messenger Service at Winterland. Quicksilver augment their extended jams with new, more pop-oriented songs. Gleason and the crew also film backstage as vocalist Dino Valenti runs through a tune with bassist David Freiberg. The team later films Quicksilver at the Sonoma State University Peace Festival, where, after a few glitches, the cameras roll and capture an excellent set.

Go Ride the Music and *A Night at the Family Dog* premiered on educational stations nationwide in November and December 1970. Gleason wrote an article about the two films for the *Chronicle*. He also wrote a separate piece that ran in several newspapers nationwide. "San Francisco rock music is one of the most important strains in contemporary rock 'n' roll," he wrote, "combining poetry and protest and pure music in almost equal proportions."[74] Gleason stressed the rapport between performers and their audience and said the "belief in the power of music is central to the whole San Francisco music life. This is its first appearance on TV."[75]

In his *Chronicle* article, Gleason declared, "The music which made the mid-sixties a turning point in American social history is alive and well."[76] He noted that the programs would be broadcast nationally and said proudly, "San Francisco's contribution to contemporary music has finally had an adequate representation on film."[77]

Several television critics reviewed *Go Ride the Music* and *A Night at the Family Dog*. One reviewer praised the video effects and the behind-the-scenes look at the bands.[78] The *Miami News* critic called the films a "fine representation of the San Francisco groups and their sound."[79] Ironically, one of the few negative reviews was by the *Chronicle*'s John L. Wasserman, who called *Go Ride the Music* a "very uneven piece of work."[80] Wasserman sarcastically said that although the camera work was "effectively restless," it was "terrifically cliche as well."[81] Gleason never forgave him. Once again, one of Gleason's younger *Chronicle* colleagues slammed an accomplishment he took pride in.

Adding insult to injury, Wasserman published the review in "Lively Arts," the *Chronicle* column founded by Gleason and written by him since 1953.[82] But now Wasserman penned the column as well as "On the Town." As for "Rhythm," the descendant of "Rhythm Section," it no longer existed. You see, in the summer of 1970, before Wasserman panned *Go Ride the Music*, Gleason resigned from his full-time position at the *Chronicle*.

The Dream Simply isn't Over

Gleason's departure came after an unexpected chain of events. First, Fantasy founders Max and Sol Weiss sold the label to Saul Zaentz in 1967. In his mid-forties, Zaentz entered the music industry by managing Jazz at the Philharmonic concerts for promoter Norman Granz. Like Gleason, the middle-aged Zaentz listened with an open mind to young Bay Area artists like the Golliwogs, whom he renamed Creedence Clearwater Revival. In 1968, Zaentz released the group's self-titled debut album. Gleason wrote the liner notes:

Creedence Clearwater Revival is an excellent example of the Third Generation of San Francisco bands which gives every indication (as this album demonstrates forcibly) of keeping the strength of the San Francisco Sound undiminished.[83]

Gleason's liner notes focused more on the city's rock scene than on Creedence, which the band and others resented.[84] He certified the then-unknown band as part of an evolving Bay Area rock scene, even though the Creedence sound departed from the psychedelia of the early bands. The album and its single "Suzy Q" soon dominated the charts, which made Fantasy rich. The company had enjoyed a reputation as an esteemed jazz label but with limited financial success. That changed following Creedence's hit records. The band's success funded a wave of expansion at Fantasy, including a new $1.5 million facility in Berkeley. Along with the new building came an ambitious agenda that required hiring staff attuned to the revolutionary changes in popular music.

And who was more attuned than Ralph J. Gleason? He was already part of the Fantasy family, having written liner notes for 20 years. His name on the board of officers would bring distinction to the label. And so, in 1970, Zaentz asked Gleason to come on board as a vice president who would oversee individual projects rather than manage a department. Because of his experience at KQED, tasks would include producing movies for Zaentz's new film division. But the responsibility Gleason found most exciting was to scout and nurture new musical talent. Gleason accepted Zaentz's offer and resigned from the *Chronicle* in the summer of 1970. The transition must have been profoundly emotional. Gleason found his voice as a writer at the newspaper, and it was there that he became an eminent music journalist. But Gleason kept one foot in the door at the *Chronicle*. He arranged to keep his Sunday column in the paper's *This World* section, renamed "Ralph J. Gleason."

Gleason's routine at *Rolling Stone* remained unchanged. In "Perspectives," he addressed the malaise that descended over the counterculture following the Manson family murders, Altamont, the Beatles' break-up, and the Kent State massacre where National Guardsmen gunned down student protesters. He continued criticizing America for its social ills while providing sharp music critiques. One of these took aim at Dylan's latest album, *Self Portrait*. Roundly criticized by other reviewers, the album prompted Greil Marcus to ask in *Rolling Stone*, "What is this shit?"[85] In his review, Gleason said Dylan appeared to have forsaken society's underdogs, and *Self Portrait* lacked the fiery indignation of Dylan's previous albums.[86] In another column, Gleason took on three other counterculture heavyweights: "I do not want Richard Nixon running my world. But I don't want Tim Leary, Eldridge Cleaver, or Jerry Rubin to run it either."[87] And he continued to speak out against the militant left. "The calls for armed struggle, whether they be from Ann Arbor or Algiers, are calls to suicide."[88]

Yet the titles of Gleason's *Rolling Stone* columns at that time convey a sense of hope: "An End to Us and Them" (1971), "We Made It, We Survived" (1971), and "The Music is Still Where It's At" (1971). He never lost faith in rock music's power to improve the world. His October 1971 column, "The Dream Simply Isn't Over," encapsulated that belief:

I hear the authentic voices now every time I turn on the radio ...

At this minute in time, we are living in a garden of delights, in an atmosphere so filled with sounds of beauty and words of poetry that is truly incredible. From the Band to The Who, from Van to Carole [King] to the Dead and the James Gang. Hour by hour, new ones appear ...

The state of the soul of the community is always calculable by the songs of the realm, and right now, the songs of the realm are exceedingly good. They please the ear, and they please the mind. They are retained in the memory and ring in your head long after the radio or the record player is off. They come at you out of unexpected corners of your thoughts, are sparked again by shadows and shafts of sunlight, and the very process of living through a day brings a dozen of them into your mind.[89]

As Gleason settled into his new work routine, Saul Zaentz assigned him a major project. It teamed him up with his old friend Robert Zagone on a full-length motion picture.

Payday

A brilliant, nasty little chrome-plated razor blade of a movie ... a "road picture" that is not, for once, a sentimental odyssey, but rather a clear-eyed study of people whose lives are linked to the road, how they behave and what becomes of them. Its clarity is what makes it so extraordinary. It is a work of such dead-honest realism that it is hard to know how, except as a kind of literal truth, to take it.[90]
    Movie critic Peter Schjeldahl, writing in the March 11, 1973, issue of the *New York Times* about *Payday*, produced by Fantasy Films.

Gleason's first significant project for Fantasy was co-producing *Payday*, the company's first movie. The film tells the story of Maury Dann, a famous but downward-spiraling country singer who tours the South in a Cadillac like Hank Williams did in the 1950s. The movie reflected country music's 1970s spike in popularity, while holding onto its traditional rural audience.[91] Young listeners discovered the music through country rock albums like the Byrds' *Sweetheart of the Rodeo* and a new wave of outlaw artists like Willie Nelson and Waylon Jennings. By 1972, *Rolling Stone* critics such as Chet Flippo wrote prescient reviews of country musicians such as Tom T. Hall, whose homespun style belied the literariness of his songs.

The genesis of *Payday* began when Saul Zaentz announced he wanted to branch into feature films and charged Gleason with getting the new film division off the ground. Gleason brought in his KQED colleagues Robert Zagone and Irving Saraf, editor for *Anatomy of a Hit*, Gleason's Vince Guaraldi documentary. He put out the word that Fantasy sought screenplays and contacted Berkeley writer Don Carpenter who immediately mailed Gleason a script. After he read it, Gleason met with Carpenter and told him, "It's a bitch. What do we do now?" Carpenter told Gleason he wanted control over how his screenplay was adapted and that he had a partner who could produce the movie, Hollywood producer Martin Fink.[92] Gleason set up a meeting for Carpenter and Fink to pitch the film to Zaentz. When Carpenter entered the meeting, Gleason handed him a retainer, no questions asked; Zaentz loved the screenplay. Carpenter and Fink were on board as producers, with Gleason and Zaentz as executive producers.[93]

With his dark shoulder-length hair and bushy mustache, Carpenter was among a new breed of screenwriters who could pass for rock musicians. Like Gleason's friend Nelson Algren, Carpenter wrote sympathetically about dead-enders such as *Payday*'s protagonist, who struggled against social conventions and his worst instincts. Carpenter based Maury Dann on the hellraising actor Rip Torn, who agreed to play the role. Carpenter brought Torn into *Payday*'s creative process, and the two hung out at Bay Area country music bars soaking up the ambiance. Author and songwriter Shel Silverstein tagged along and regaled them with stories about country musicians.[94] Carpenter developed the storyline about Maury Dann's disastrous trip from Selma to Nashville to promote his new record album *Payday*. Dann grew up poor and struggled with stardom, excessive drinking, and womanizing. His troubles culminate in a knife fight and a deadly police chase.

Robert Zagone:

> Ralph was intrigued about what made musicians "tick," what made them play or sing as well as they did, what were the creative juices that went into the makeup of the artistry, and the ambient influences in their lives. The movie delves deeply into these issues, and Ralph appreciated Don Carpenter's writing skills and artistry. Ralph loved films so much that he wanted to write screenplays eventually. Producing *Payday* was a launching pad for these interests.[95]

Filming began in Selma, Alabama, and Gleason and Zagone visited the set. *Payday*'s producer Marty Fink escorted them around the site while Gleason verified that the work proceeded on schedule and within budget. Gleason and Zagone watched the crew film a card-playing scene inside a local hotel with Rip Torn and other actors. During filming, "cooperation was hammered out the hard way during some wild arguments" between Gleason, Carpenter, and Torn.[96] Carpenter said the "pressures were incredible. Everybody was fighting, but they were fighting for the picture, not their egos."[97]

On a more transcendent note, Gleason made a side trip to Selma's Edmund Pettis Bridge. On March 7, 1965, a group of civil rights activists crossed the bridge on a 54-mile march from Selma to the state capital of Montgomery. State troopers and citizen militias brutally attacked the unarmed marchers on the day that became known as Bloody Sunday. The protesters refused to give up and crossed the bridge unscathed on a third try. Twenty-five thousand protesters finally marched into Montgomery under the protection of President Lyndon B. Johnson's National Guard. Gleason was awestruck to visit the site of such a critical point in civil rights history.[98] Another emotional side trip was to a local Black church where Gleason attended a service and was captivated by the choir. He sat in the back, the only White person in the rural church. The parishioners accepted Gleason because he so profoundly enjoyed the music.[99]

Payday opened in New York City on February 22, 1973. The movie premiered in San Francisco on March 23, and the *Chronicle*'s movie critic gave it a rave review.[100] Other critics commended it, including, as noted, Peter Schjeldahl of the *New York Times*. Charles Champlin of the *Los Angeles Times* called *Payday* "one of those good, tough, economic, modest, thoroughly professional films which knows preciously where it's heading and which gets there with power and grace."[101] Lawrence Devine of the *Detroit Free Press* commended its raw authenticity and demythologizing view of rural America and country music.[102]

However, despite glowing reviews, the film failed to sell tickets as expected. Gleason blamed poor distribution. In a *Chronicle* column called "A Filmmaker's Woes," Gleason said it was difficult to distribute independent movies like *Payday* because big film companies control the distribution system that smaller companies rely on. Gleason said Fantasy sent *Payday* to "a very small sea of independent distributors" to circumvent this. "It is possible to do this and to make money at it," Gleason wrote, but the stress was "ulcer-making."[103] Because of the uneven distribution, *Payday* remained off the radar for many filmgoers.

Zagone said:

> We all regretted that *Payday* at the time never got the recognition it deserved. Don Carpenter and the line producer, Martin Fink, were great craftsmen, and they did an excellent job on a meager budget. Indeed, the best acting job that Rip Torn ever produced. In the current reviews of the Academy Award-winning film *Crazy Heart* with Jeff Bridges, knowledgeable critics all refer to its prototype *Payday*.[104]

Zagone called Gleason "an ardent movie-goer" and noted that Gleason's favorite film was *Casablanca*, the classic film noir starring Humphrey Bogart and Ingrid Bergman. Gleason even wore a trench coat similar to Bogie's and wrote a column about the film. Howard Koch, one of the screenwriters of *Casablanca*, read the column and asked Gleason to write an "Introductory Note" for a book version of the screenplay called *Casablanca: Script and Legend*.[105] Gleason used the opportunity to reflect on a bygone era:

> We could afford sentiment then, even in the darkest days of Hitler's victories. Is there sentiment now in revolutionary circles, one wonders?
>
> But *Casablanca* was back then, before all the words and all the promises became distorted, drained of their truth by broken promises and failed ambitions.
>
> Casablanca was how we thought we were, all right, a pure explication of the mood in which we entered World War II and a greater distance than Mars even from the way we eventually came out of it, seduced by power, corrupted by affluence.

It was good to go back again in time to those days when, despite all our faults, we still believed in our own basic virtue. If today we are lost and by the wind grieved, it helps some to see us at a time when we were not, when the hope of truth and good and positive affirmation was not so far away as the grim reality of today makes them seem.[106]

"Lost and by the wind grieved." In quoting this line from Thomas Wolfe's *Look Homeward Angel*, Gleason mourned the loss of the America of his youth.[107]

11

Ralph, This is Your City (1974–75)

Despite growing health problems, Gleason produced some of the sharpest writing of his career during his final years. Nothing stood in his way of giving his last testament on the enduring value of jazz as America's greatest musical legacy. Not even a new wave of frustrations at *Rolling Stone*.

The Mutilated Remains of My Dylan Article

In early 1974, Gleason felt dissatisfied with *Rolling Stone*'s direction. Some of his grievances were personal, such as the magazine's policy to not pay royalties on Straight Arrow Press reprints of articles by Gleason and other writers. Other complaints targeted *Rolling Stone*'s changing direction and Wenner's management style. Gleason lashed out in the press, sometimes with shocking candor. In an article in the *Columbia Journalism Review*, he said *Rolling Stone* "catered to the worst of yellow journalism," referencing *Rolling Stone*'s coverage of the 1973 payola scandal.[1] The statement understandably angered Wenner.[2] The following month, Gleason wrote in *Parade* magazine that Wenner "can charm the birds out of the trees when he wants to, but he can also be ruthless." He sarcastically called Wenner "the perfect publisher. He wants everything. He always has. He wants reprint rights to your material and syndication rights to it anywhere in the world. In my mind, *Rolling Stone* has cruelly exploited a whole lot of young writers who were so eager to appear in the paper they were perfectly willing to allow themselves to be stepped on."[3]

A week after the *Parade* article, despite the growing tension between them, Gleason and Wenner went to see Bob Dylan and the Band at the Oakland Coliseum, a stop on their "Before the Flood Tour." Gleason was there to cover the show in "Perspectives." The evolution of Gleason's article provides a case study of a contentious give-and-take between a leading rock writer and their editor.

After the concert, the two requested to meet with the musicians backstage. Security allowed Gleason backstage but not Wenner, which created further tension.[4] After the show, Gleason went to work on his column. A few days later, he sent his first draft to Wenner to look over. Wenner marked up the manuscript and returned it to Gleason for revision with a handwritten note about additional changes. The changes were sweeping. He instructed Gleason to cut 2,500 words and eliminate "repetitions, cliches, unpursued hyperbole, and non-essential content."⁵ Wenner asked for additional information about Dylan's album *Planet Waves,* where Dylan stood in relation to his contemporaries, and the meaning of the Dylan tour for rock music.⁶ That wasn't all. Wenner also asked for an analysis of whether the tour was another example of how Dylan was alienating his old fans while winning new ones. He also wanted Gleason to explore "themes of maturity, family, growing up" as "evident on both the LP and the tour." Anticipating Gleason's reaction, Wenner ended with, "I'll talk to you as soon as you take a valium."⁷

Gleason took the changes in stride and wrote Wenner, "You are a good editor. I buy everything that you changed."⁸ The two followed up with a friendly phone conversation about the changes. Gleason revised his column that day and sent the revised draft to Wenner for publication, along with a warm note.

> Dear Janno:
> Here 'tis/I hope you like it. As you will see, I followed your suggestions. After I had gotten over my initial over-reaction, they were clearly very useful points and I thank you for them …
> Luv.
>   rjg⁹

With that, Gleason assumed the editing process was over. But further edits were made, and Gleason went through the roof when he began to read the published column. He stopped reading and fired off a four-page heat-seeking missile:

> I have been unable to force myself to examine the mutilated remains of my Dylan article in detail even yet, but there are two points about it which I wish to bring up instantly and in the strongest terms possible.
>
> … The point I want to raise is the addition, and two places of words I did not write, would not have written, and in one case, feel fundamentally change the meaning of what I said by inserting something I would not have said.¹⁰

The first added word that upset Gleason was "one." Whereas Gleason wrote that Dylan had a "Minnesota iron-ore twang," the editor changed the phrase to "one Minnesota iron-ore twang." Gleason said "one word throws off the whole cadence of the paragraph." But the "mutilation" that really angered him was the revision of, "He [Dylan] survived the torture of the road, the accident, and all the shit that has gone down since." The revised text read, "He survived the torture of the road, the motorcycle Madonna accident, and all the big money business shit." Gleason was aghast, "motorcycle Madonna"? He never would have written anything so trite! Gleason raged on and called the revisions "insufferable and intolerable."¹¹

Gleason's sensitivity to these changes shows his longstanding resistance to the editorial revisions that are standard in journalism up to the last minute and not always announced to the writer in advance. In his response to Wenner, Gleason pointed out a broader issue:

This is not just old Ralph being paranoid or overly sensitive. It goes to the heart of *Rolling Stone*'s editorial philosophy. It is an example of editorial irresponsibility which, if you carry on with it, is going to result in serious objections by other writers as well as myself. You cannot establish *Rolling Stone* as a responsible magazine with claims to literary excellence if you act like this. People are not stupid, you know. And writers are not just commodities to be shaped and edited to suit your whim of the moment.[12]

Gleason cc'd his letter to editors John Walsh, Paul Scanlon, and Jon Landau. He added an interesting postscript about another one-word change, "was" to "were." He wrote: "Grammar takes second place sometimes to colloquial usage even in the august pages of the literary quarterlies and the *Times of London*. And, after all, this was an opinion column called 'Perspectives.'"[13]

The first half of 1974 had been a rough stretch for Gleason. From attacking Wenner in print to the dust-up over the Dylan column, the two old friends had repeatedly hurt one another with the precision of family members who know where the emotional pressure points are. These angry outbursts masked the pain. Yet correspondence between Gleason and Wenner shows that by the summer of 1974, they returned to their old banter. Gleason was back to pitching story ideas, such as exposing how New York drug laws were "entrapping methadone users." Wenner thanked Gleason in a note signed, "Love, Jann."[14] In another memo to "Janno," Gleason shared a reference to *Rolling Stone* in *Spy Story*, a novel by Len Deighton.[15] This correspondence conveys an easy familiarity. Through it all, they maintained a productive writer–editor relationship. Gleason had an uncommonly complex bond with Wenner, not as one-dimensional as sometimes reported. And their association continued to produce extraordinary results.

Farewell to the Duke

May is late to receive a Christmas card, even from someone as notoriously unpunctual as Duke Ellington. Gleason saw it as a bad sign, and he was right. Three days later, on May 24, 1974, Ellington died of pneumonia at 75. The news devastated Gleason. Ellington had been part of his life since he discovered the bandleader on late-night radio remotes in the early 1930s. Gleason proclaimed Ellington "God" in his college newspaper, with Johnny Hodges a close second. As a jazz writer in the post-swing 1950s, Gleason reminded readers of Ellington's continuing relevance. In the 1960s, Gleason documented Ellington's brilliance in two television documentaries.

And now Gleason eulogized his friend and called Ellington the "greatest composer this nation has produced."[16] Before these words reached *Chronicle* readers, Gleason indirectly memorialized Ellington through the columns of fellow critics. John Rockwell began his *New York Times* remembrance of Ellington with three paragraphs of Gleason quotes, including, "Ellington has created his own musical world which has transcended every attempt to impose category upon it."[17] Other writers followed suit, a testament to the importance they placed on Gleason's insight into the legendary bandleader.

Ellington's funeral was at the Episcopal Cathedral of St. John the Divine in New York City, where the second of his Sacred Concerts took place in 1968. Gleason watched the funeral on television but refused to be disheartened for someone who lived with such relish and productivity despite society's racial barriers.

Gleason had been working on a lengthy *Rolling Stone* article about Ellington for the past two years. Now was the time to finish it. In "Farewell to the Duke," Gleason wrote, "America's greatest composer, in the opinion of so many musicians, never got the acceptance his art deserved from American intellectuals."[18] He couched Ellington's story as the struggle of a 1920s Black genius turned away by the classical establishment, who then turned to popular music. Gleason detailed Ellington's process for composing songs such as "Black and Tan Fantasy," written in a taxicab during one of Ellington's "quick bursts of activity." Gleason recalled how Ellington showed up for a *Jazz Casual* television appearance five minutes before taping and told Gleason to forgo his usual introduction. "Now I'll sit at the piano and start to play," Ellington sweetly instructed Gleason, "you walk on and ask me what the tune is, and we'll go from there."[19] Gleason and his team captured a half-hour of Ellington and Billy Strayhorn playing piano duets while Ellington regaled the audience with stories. Near the end of the article, Gleason quoted French poet Blaise Cendrars who saw the Ellington orchestra during their 1939 European tour and exclaimed, "Such music is not only a new art form but a new reason for living."[20] For a generation of critics like Gleason, it was also a reason for writing.

Rolling Stone published "Farewell to the Duke" in July 1974.[21] After Gleason saw it, he wrote to Wenner, "The layout and the whole spread was very impressive, and I wanted to tell you and everyone that." Two weeks later, after he received his check for the article, he wrote again, "I thought we had agreed on $1,500 [about $9,000 today] for that piece. Am I wrong?"[22] Yes, things were back to normal between Gleason and Wenner.

As Gleason and other critics eulogized Ellington in print, musicians memorialized the pianist in music. One morning before breakfast Gleason answered the phone, and a voice said, "Miles wants to talk to you." And then the soft raspy voice of Miles Davis said, "I want you to hear something." Mesmerizing sounds came out of the phone's earpiece. Davis mused in his husky whisper, "I don't know what it is. I sat down at the piano, and this melody just came out. It's a thing I wrote for Duke." An iridescent dissonance with a hint of electronic shading. Prayerful, poetic. "It just came out," the trumpeter exclaimed, "I can't even find the music I wrote. I just sat down, and it came out. It came through me, and it just came out that way. Isn't that wild?"[23] The intimacy and spontaneity of that moment overcame Gleason. A jazz giant needed someone to share his excitement, and that someone was Gleason.

The freshly minted composition was "He Loved Him Madly," a track on Davis's album *Get Up with It*. Gleason reviewed the LP and said, "This music is very difficult to describe. We really don't have the vocabulary, in the sense of commonly understood terms, to talk about it … It is highly electronic and highly rhythmic with little melodies running all through it …" Soon after that, Gleason saw Davis perform, an "overwhelming, a mind-boggling hurricane of sound which included innumerable shadings, subtle variations and an infinity of interplay between him and the members of his band ... the music had the kind of arresting urgency and deep emotional high voltage of the very best modern music."[24] Not that Gleason had lost his love of swing music, a passion revitalized on a cross-continental return to his musical roots.

My Name is Nelson Riddle

In the summer of 1974, Gleason traveled to New York City for surgery to correct his longstanding Dupuytren's contracture, the condition that curled his fingers into a bent shape. Despite the seriousness of the trip, Gleason made time to visit people and places of his youth. Terrified of surgery, he had postponed the procedure but found a way to ease his stress. He would have the operation in New York City where his old friend Irwin Kaiser, now a prominent obstetrician, could be present.[25] Kaiser, as earlier noted, was Gleason's editor at the *Columbia Spectator* in the 1930s. The two remained close, as did their families. During a mid-1950s visit to Stockholm, Kaiser and his family spent time with Dave Brubeck, thanks to Gleason arranging it. At Columbia, Kaiser participated in the antiwar cause and, as editor, continued the *Spectator*'s important role in the 1930s student activist movement.[26] For Gleason, having his old friend present gave him the confidence to deal with his crippling condition.

Gleason and Jean boarded the Amtrak train from Oakland to New York in late July. Assigned to the last sleeper car on the train, Gleason said they "whipsawed across the U.S. like a couple of bags of laundry in the back of a pickup truck."[27] After transferring to Chicago, the trip went smoother and included an incredible chance meeting. One morning as Ralph and Jean sit in the dining car awaiting breakfast, a porter seats a passenger at their table. The stranger introduces himself: "My name is Nelson Riddle." Suspicious, Gleason replies, "Really?" "Really," Riddle counters, "The last time I looked." Gleason introduces himself, and Riddle answers, "You gave me a bad review in 1962." "You're right," admits Gleason, and braces for a fight.[28] What comes to mind is Dixieland cornet player Mugsy Spanier chasing Leonard Feather down a street in Greenwich Village after Feather gave him a bad review in *DownBeat*. Gleason tries to recall something positive he had written about Riddle, but before he can, the legendary pop conductor breaks into a smile—no harsh feelings. Gleason relaxes, and the three enjoy a pleasant breakfast as the world rolls past their window.

Finally, the train pulls into New York's Pennsylvania Station. To his horror, Gleason sees that the original McKim, Mead, and White edifice had been partially demolished, its civic grandeur gone. The entry tracks rerouted away from the building. As Yale architectural historian Vincent Scully observed, "One entered the city like a god; one scuttles in now like a rat."[29] This was one more example of the loss of place that unsettled postwar writers like Henry Miller. Gleason, too, was repelled by the train ride through the urban sprawl connecting Philadelphia to New York City.[30]

Gleason's surgery went fine. After he recovered, he spent a few days "nostalgically roaming the haunts of my youth."[31] He visited the West End Bar & Grill in Manhattan, where he hung out during his Columbia University days. There, he and Jean enjoyed a combo composed of ex-Ellington band members, including drummer Sam Woodward, who delighted Gleason. "Thin, almost gaunt, he would squeeze his eyes shut and dig in and play."[32] Swing singer Helen Humes joined the group and "rapped out a double chorus of medium tempo blues with the band filling in behind her, the horns alternating in the responses and Sam Woodward growling and muttering behind her."[33] By then, the club had swelled with college students who came for the cheap beer and the band; it gratified Gleason to see the younger generation enjoying swing jazz.

He and Jean visited another spot that stirred wistful memories, the Saratoga Race Course, where Gleason bet on races with his father in the 1930s. A mist from an early morning rain caused the gold turrets of the Queen Ann-style buildings to shimmer in the sunlight. To his pleasant surprise, Gleason sees a distant figure from the swing era. It's Cab Calloway, sharply dressed and strolling the grounds:

> That was the only bit of the old days that seemed to me to be the same. Everything else had gone to hell one way or another. Probably, I am suffering from the "you can't go home again" syndrome or plain old age.
>
> In any case, the gap between my memories and the set reality of that rainy day was entirely too wide.[34]

Such wistfulness is common, writes Svetlana Boym in "Nostalgia and Its Discontents,"

> Nostalgia is a sentiment of loss and displacement, but also a romance with one's own fantasy. Nostalgic love can only survive in a long-distance relationship. A double exposure ... of two images ... of past and present ... The moment we try to force it into a single image, it breaks the frame or burns the surface.[35]

For most of us, the places of our youth rarely stay as we remember them. For Gleason, the clash of past and present evoked bittersweet feelings. Yet, the trip to New York sparked a sense of nostalgia that permeated Gleason's writings for the remainder of his life. Recollecting his past brought meaning and well-being to Gleason as he grew older.

Their New York visit over, the Gleasons return home on a different route, this time on the Canadian Pacific Railway from Montreal to Vancouver and then south to California. To while away the time, Gleason smoked Cuban cigars and listened to piped-in music played by unidentified Canadian musicians who sounded "like the appalling jazz you hear on TV drama shows."[36]

Once home, Gleason returned to work at Fantasy. He brought in a new publicity director, Gretchen Horton, after she lost her job as Wenner's secretary. Gleason hired an assistant for Horton, Terri Hinte. The young staffer marveled at how deeply Gleason understood rock music, "which was supposed to be young people's music."[37]

> Gleason understood rock because he dealt with music based on what it was, rather than on preordained judgments. He did not put things in boxes. Despite my young age, I felt seen and respected by him as a person with something to contribute. He was directly responsible for my very first job in the record industry—where I have continued to work ever since, going on 50 years.[38]

Another young staffer who worked with Gleason at Fantasy Records was Merl Saunders Jr., then barely in his teens. His father was keyboardist Merl Saunders who collaborated with Jerry Garcia and recorded for Fantasy. In the mid-1970s, Merl Jr. worked in Fantasy's art department, bringing promotional art to Gleason for approval. "Intimidating for a 13-year-old," Saunders acknowledged, but Gleason was "always a gentleman's gentleman" and "always kind to me."[39]

During his four years at Fantasy, Gleason established solid working relationships. Along with his responsibilities as a vice president, he continued to write liner notes for the company and Prestige after Fantasy bought the legendary jazz label in 1971. He penned liner notes for recordings by John Coltrane, the Modern Jazz Quartet, and Miles Davis. Asked how his father liked working at Fantasy, Toby Gleason says:

> He dug it because it allowed him to work every day with a passel of close friends from his Lenny Bruce period, his television production period and because of his longtime association with the original owners of Fantasy, the Weiss brothers, Sol, Max and Milton. Max was kind of my "crazy Dutch uncle." Sol taught me recording technique and how to tell a hit record from the VU meter, a device that measures the signal levels during a sound recording.
>
> It allowed Dad a much saner schedule, a single place to work and nights at home with his family a lot more often. It also bought him a new car, a larger home and a modest vacation home in Stinson Beach. So, he got a lot of what he thought he both needed and wanted out of it.
>
> On the other hand, it took him away from daily involvement with his life's blood, music. Unfortunately, while his [Fantasy] friends enjoyed having him around and he enjoyed it, too, they really didn't have any clear idea of what they wanted him to do for them. So, he was kind of a minister without portfolio, and as such, adrift. I think this hurt him, spiritually and physically.[40]

Gleason's diabetes also took a toll. Yet he maintained a demanding schedule; in addition to his full-time job at Fantasy, Gleason continued to publish insightful columns for *Rolling Stone* and the *Chronicle*.

Those Brave Translunary Things

Writing only one *Chronicle* column a week liberated Gleason to pursue topics that truly interested him. Collectively, his *Chronicle* columns from 1970 to 1975 are an invaluable scrapbook of snippets from the history of post-counterculture rock. Not a fan of glam rock or proto-punk artists such as Iggy Pop, Gleason remained focused on musicians who synthesized the traditions of swing jazz, blues, folk, and country—the first sounds of Americana music.

You can see this in Gleason's 1975 profile of the Allman Brothers. The pioneering Southern rock band recently lost two key members, slide guitarist Duane Allman and bassist Berry Oakley. Gleason had called Duane Allman's "Goin' Down Slow" "an exquisitely beautiful blues, unusual in the continuity of its storyline, the brilliance of its images, and the variety of its changes. It haunted me."[41] In his profile of the band, Gleason said the Allman Brothers' appeal "rests in a combination of elements" found in jazz:

> To begin with, The Allman Brothers Band swings in the same sense that Count Basie swings. The rhythm is tight, propulsive, and exciting. It is also rock steady and impeccable.
>
> Rather than indulge in heavy clusters of sound and a bag of electronic tricks, the guitarists in the Allman Brothers band play linear solos. The two guitarists exchange solos in the same fashion a pair of tenor saxophone players might do so ...
>
> The Allman Brothers group represents the best side of the pop music scene in recent years, a side in which all elements of America's musical heritage are utilized, all influences absorbed, reworked, and played back to us in a new and individual style which, while it owes a debt to the past, is in no sense purely derivative.[42]

Gleason saw this same synthesis in an emergent Bay Area rocker:

> I am a stone Boz Scaggs fan and consider him one of the best singers and songwriters in pop music today, as well as an exciting example of a particular type of American singer ... I think Boz and Greg Allman, for instance, are indicative of something new in American culture. They both have, in slightly different ways but with the same urgent, creative intensity, managed to meld together elements of almost all American musical styles and categories into something original ...
>
> Some years ago, I wondered in these pages if the white man could sing the blues. The answer to that question is given every time either of these singers steps before a microphone. It is an emphatic "yes!" in their cases. They really have the wail.[43]

Gleason also wrote perceptive articles about 1970s rock musicians for *Rolling Stone*. When Bob Dylan went through significant changes in the mid-1970s, Gleason defended the singer-songwriter's music when some critics found the new songs tame compared to Dylan's 1960s work. Gleason had witnessed similar backlashes in jazz when Duke Ellington and Miles Davis changed the direction of their music.

Consequently, Gleason is open-minded when he sees Dylan and the Band at the Oakland Coliseum on February 11, 1974. Gleason sits with some young friends, expectantly waiting for the show to start. Then one of them exclaims, "God damn! It's him!" Dylan stands on a Persian rug in a pool of light within the dark cavernous space. He appears sleep-deprived but confident. Beside him is Robbie Robertson with a bright red Stratocaster that matches his shirt color. Behind them are Garth Hudson, Richard Manuel, Rick Danko, and Levon Helm. Robertson launches into the rollicking chords of "Most Likely You Go Your Way." The group falls in with a swampy but jaunty backbeat. Dylan spits out the lyrics in an edgy style halfway between singing and talking. Gleason wrote:

> The Band has never played better in person or on record. They were hard-driving, rocking, swinging accompaniments for Dylan and gave majestic performances on their own. Robbie Robertson played guitar obligatos or fills when Dylan was singing that compared in emotional intensity and artistic simplicity to Louis Armstrong behind Bessie Smith. Within the total sound of the band, a pulsing, cracking, shaking sound, there was an infinity of variety and internal musical activity ...
>
> Dylan's voice is stronger now. Very sure and very flexible. Surrounded by the overwhelming energy of the Band with Robbie's guitar whipping and cracking behind it, Dylan sometimes used his voice itself as an electric guitar, screaming and soaring and changing the sound of the words by that trick of appearing to smile by the way he pronounces words ...
>
> Nelson Algren once said about Ernest Hemingway something which also fits Dylan's achievement: "No American writer since Walt Whitman has assumed such risks in forming a style. They were the kind of chances by which, should they fail, the taker fails alone; yet should they succeed, succeed for everyone."[44]

When Columbia released Dylan's *Blood on the Tracks* in January 1975, Gleason listened to the album six times before he wrote his *Chronicle* review. He saw the album as a turning point in Dylan's artistry and proof of his creative vitality. Gleason delighted in the "humor which is frequently bubbling below the surface ... sardonic, ironic, joyful." He marveled at Dylan's nuanced delivery, in how Dylan "bends a note or the way he pronounces a word or drags it out over several syllables."[45] Gleason said *Blood on the Tracks* equaled Dylan's previous albums and was his best work since *Blonde on Blonde*.[46]

In March 1975, Gleason wrote a lengthy *Rolling Stone* article, "The Blood of a Poet," about Dylan's new music. In it, Gleason made the same argument he had since 1965, that Dylan was first and foremost a poet. He wrote how Dylan "made us dream everything, as Sainte-Beuve said poetry must do." Quoting poet Michael Drayton, Gleason said Dylan had in him "those brave translunary [ethereal] things that the first poets had."[47] In citing a nineteenth-century French literary critic and an Elizabethan poet, Gleason placed Dylan in a literary tradition that stretched back hundreds of years.

Nelson Algren teased Gleason for such comparisons and sent him a letter with one of his customary cartoons, this one depicting Algren conked out on the floor holding an article by Gleason that compared Dylan to Spanish painter Francisco Goya and William Shakespeare.[48] In 2008, the Pulitzer Prize Board awarded Dylan a Special Citation for his his profound impact on popular music and American culture, marked by lyrical compositions of extraordinary poetic power."[49] In 2016, Dylan was awarded the Nobel Prize in Literature.

We Gotta Get Rid of Nixon

To the degree Gleason lauded Dylan in the 1970s, he denigrated President Richard M. Nixon. And so, along with many fellow Americans, Gleason rejoiced on August 9, 1974, when Nixon resigned from office. Gleason had been among Nixon's sharpest public critics, something the White House took note of.

The counterculture had reviled Nixon since his first inauguration in January 1969. Gleason called him a "faceless, neat, mindless administrator with no sensitivity to pure humanity and no feeling for the individual."[50] Gleason recoiled when Nixon addressed the American people in May 1972 and announced the escalation of the Vietnam War.[51] He wrote a scathing *Rolling Stone* column about Nixon's escalation of the war the following month. The column title said it all, "We've Gotta Get Rid of Nixon." Gleason said Nixon's speech "frightened me out of my wits … We have to get this man out of office before he kills us all."[52] Gleason had planned to write a column about Nixon's deportation order against John and Yoko Lennon but set that aside to comment on the escalation speech. In the fall of 1972, when Nixon tromped Democratic candidate George McGovern, Gleason ramped up his anti-Nixon rhetoric. He compared the president's bombing of Hanoi with Hitler's invasion of Poland in its "sheer use of armed might to force a small country to bend to a superpower's will."[53] A harbinger of what would come fifty years later when Russia invaded Ukraine.

In the spring of 1973, Gleason and the country reeled from a different kind of Nixon bombshell. An investigation into a bungled burglary at the Watergate Complex produced evidence that linked the crime to Nixon's Committee to Reelect the President (CRP). As a result, the US Senate established a select committee to investigate. Televised hearings from May to August 1973 brought the investigation before the American public. The hearings revealed that White House Counsel John Dean prepared an "enemies list" of about 220 political opponents to be investigated by the Internal Revenue Service. The list included journalists such as jazz critic George Frazier. It also appeared that Nixon taped conversations between 1971 and 1973 with administration officials and staff who knew about the break-in, and the tapes proved the president's involvement. When the administration blocked attempts to subpoena the tapes, the public grew suspicious, prompting Nixon to famously declare, "I am not a crook."

Gleason and the nation sat glued to the televised hearings. Gleason gleefully wrote to his friend Fern Frazier (no relation to George), "God, how great it is to be, at this moment in history, an American with a color TV."[54] Gleason listened to the hearings each morning as soon as he got up. One day as he dressed, Gleason heard the testimony of James McCord, a CIA operative who helped with the burglaries and testified against Nixon. Gleason told Frazier, "McCord names them all, the roster of Anglo-Saxon Protestant White American thieves, liars, and deceivers."[55] Gleason was so absorbed that he continued listening to McCord's testimony while he ate breakfast and brushed his teeth. "Those obsequious young WASPS," he wrote, "keep telling their stories, spelling out their sellout … Watergate is the best course in civics this country has ever produced."[56] Gleason hoped the mass media reportage would unite the older and younger generations in a shared disgust of Nixon's subterfuge and, as a result, reduce public cynicism about the American political system. He asked Frazier, "Is it possible that the rascals can be caught? Can it be true that the arrogant, the corrupt, the forces of Darkness can be combatted successfully?"[57] After losing faith in political solutions in the 1960s, the Watergate hearings gave Gleason hope that politics could right wrongs.

Gleason continued his *Rolling Stone* critique of Nixon as the Watergate hearings continued into the winter of 1973. One column featured a pen-and-ink caricature of a Nixon as Pinocchio, dressed in rags, bent over, his nose spanning the page. He credited Bob Dylan's music with helping to make a more open society where corrupt politicians like Nixon could face impeachment.[58] A few weeks after Gleason's column hit the newsstands, another Nixon revelation came to light. White House Counsel John Dean had sent a second enemies list to the Internal Revenue Service. During the hearings, Commissioner of Internal Revenue Johnnie Mac Walters testified:

> On September 11, 1972, I met with John W. Dean, III, pursuant to his request, in his office at the Old Executive building. At that meeting he gave me a list of names and requested that IRS undertake examinations or investigations of the people named on the list.[59]

On the list of 576 citizens, "Ralph J. Gleason" was number 225.[60] The *San Francisco Examiner* published Gleason's name and other Bay Area residents on the list.[61] Being on the list elated Gleason. Terri Hinte remembers Gleason's "delight and pride at being included."[62]

Why was Gleason on the list? Likely because of his past affiliations with Bay Area radical groups the federal government surveilled. Gleason's four-year run of *Rolling Stone* columns skewering Nixon didn't help. To Gleason, it didn't matter why. He was delighted to be included, though he found the list absurd and refused to take it seriously. When a local television reporter asked him what he did to anger high officials in the White House, he answered, "I had no idea the officials in the White House were high."[63] Gleason said being on the Nixon Enemies List was the "highest honor a man's country could bestow upon him, and the only one an honorable man would accept."[64] As a joke, Gleason had a notepad made with "Enemies List" printed at the top of each sheet with a quasi-presidential seal below. He emblazoned his signature across the seal and gave the pages to friends.[65]

Being on a federal government watchlist didn't stop Gleason from going after Nixon in *Rolling Stone*. At that point in the Watergate investigation in early 1974, Nixon had admitted no wrongdoing. He still had public support and a chance to survive the hearing and retaliate against his critics. But Gleason proceeded unfazed. As the hearings continued, he intensified his commentary. He lambasted media outlets that failed to call out Nixon's lies and warned that Nixon wanted to divert the country's attention away from Watergate. He compared Nixon's deception to the "Goebbels technique of the Big Lie."[66] Adolf Hitler created the "Big Lie" strategy based on the theory that the public would believe a vast untruth because they assumed no leader would have the nerve to tell such a whopper. Hitler and Joseph Goebbels used the technique to convince the German people that Germany was the victim of a global Jewish plan to exterminate Germans. In recent years, the term has been used to describe the false claim by President Donald Trump that the 2020 election was rigged against him.

By the spring of 1974, Congress could no longer ignore the mountain of evidence against Nixon. Transcripts of the Nixon White House Tapes suggested severe improprieties. The televised proceedings moved from an investigation to an impeachment hearing. As citizens watched, the committee presented evidence that an American president undermined the principles of the Constitution, democracy, and basic morality. In a column called "Paranoia Follies," Gleason wrote, "Reading the transcripts is like a nightmare come true. Nobody believes in anything anymore. There is no trust anywhere. Which means, of course, that everybody can believe in everything." He called the 1972 election a "license to steal our morality." Nixon "defrauded me of my birthright as a citizen, and I want it back."[67]

In the summer of 1974, a group of Republicans met with Nixon and told him impeachment was certain. To avoid further disgrace, Nixon resigned on August 8, 1974. He was succeeded by Vice President Gerald Ford, who promptly pardoned him. Gleason immediately titled a column, "Look Out! Ford's as Bad as Nixon." He said Ford represented a "change in persona, not a change in political stance. Citizens should howl in protest because it is our souls they are maiming."[68] Yet Gleason saw the Watergate hearings as proof that the American political system could root out corruption. He said politics were "essential," and if "we can make ourselves heard, there is the chance—a slim one, I agree—that we can have some effect." But he also reiterated his core belief that "art supplies truth and reality when society does not."[69]

In hindsight, as egregious as Watergate was, it pales compared to Donald Trump's 2020 attempt to overthrow the election of President Joe Biden, followed by the January 6, 2021, insurrection. As of this writing, much of the Republican Party has failed to do what their 1970s predecessors did: repudiate their errant president. But the field of music journalism has largely shied away from commenting. One exception is *Rolling Stone*, which maintains its tradition as a liberal watchdog, a tradition Gleason played a significant role in creating.

Celebrating the Duke

As Gleason worked on his assignments at Fantasy and met his deadlines at *Rolling Stone* and the *Chronicle*, he also worked on a third book. It would be an anthology like *Jam Session*, but with one big difference—all the writings would be by Gleason, his last will and testament to the jazz musicians who gave his life purpose over the past five decades. This was reflected in the book's title, *Celebrating the Duke: And Louis, Bessie, Billie, Bird, Carmen, Miles, Dizzy, and Other Heroes*.

It began with Gleason's proposal to Atlantic-Little, Brown (later called Little, Brown and Company). The publisher accepted it, and Gleason went to work under the guidance of William Abrahams, one of the country's top editors and a Bay Area resident known for his warmth and deep literary knowledge.[70] Gleason searched his archives and other sources for potential entries, reading clips from the *Chronicle*,

Rolling Stone, Stereo Review, and other publications. He dug through his enormous record library, looking for relevant liner notes. The search turned bittersweet when Gleason's friend George Kaplan died from cancer. Kaplan had accompanied Gleason to many of the shows in the articles Gleason rifled through.[71]

Gleason filled *Celebrating the Duke* with articles about his favorite jazz musicians, from Ellington to Charlie Parker. All were Black, reflecting Gleason's tastes and his belief that the most outstanding jazz innovators were African American. Among the selections were two articles that won the ASCAP Deems Taylor award for music writing: "Jazz: Black Art/American Art" (1969) and "God Bless Louis Armstrong" (1972). Also, Grammy-nominated liner notes for *Bitches Brew, Ellington Era 1926–1940 Volume II*, and *Duke Ellington: The Pianist*. Another notable piece was "Farewell to the Duke," his *Rolling Stone* remembrance. A mixed tone of praise and regret runs through many of the book's pieces, exemplified in his 1959 description of Lester Young, a "poet, sad-eyed and mystical, hurt that the world was not in actuality as beautiful as he dreamed it."[72]

The writings illustrate Gleason's ability to produce inspired prose. Of Coltrane, he wrote, "The long solos, the unorthodox cries and sheets of sound, the hard tone, the swift changes of mood from the lyric to the turbulent urgency of his modal interpretations."[73] Miles Davis represented the "longing of contemporary man, locked within the terrible loneliness that only a crowd can bring, for beauty and tenderness and lyric celebration of joy."[74] Gleason recognized the tension between alienation and belonging that characterized jazz. But in the end, it was about making an instrument speak, as Gleason states in the book's final chapter, "Coda: The Piano Player":

No one in my memory has ever had the ability to make the piano growl and rumble the way Duke could, with those low clusters of notes and that heavy rhythm. He could stomp, in the old-fashioned sense, and he could rock like the all-time swinging pianists. And, of course, he could be melodic and rhapsodic, sometimes playing melodic lines that truly seemed to sing almost as if they had words.[75]

Gleason wrote a lengthy introduction to *Celebrating the Duke* in which he chastised those who were close-eared and praised his musical "teachers":

I have to say ... there are people—for whom I feel very sorry—to whom no kind of music that is a straight-ahead emotional hit is attractive. I think they are frightened by it. Some of my very best friends, in those days when John Coltrane was carving out his new sounds (and James Baldwin was explaining the sociological and poetic background), insisted that the New Jazz [Free Jazz] was a music of hate ... they were reacting to a new world in which their values and security were threatened by something strange and foreign to them. It was to be repeated a few years later when adult rock music emerged ...[76]

This book is dedicated to those musicians present in its pages (and those who unfortunately are not) for all the great moments, the magnificent highs of listening, for all I have learned from them, my true teachers, and above all, for their clear instruction in how to live.[77]

After he completed his manuscript, Gleason submitted it to Abrahams. "Superb," the editor declared.[78] What Abrahams received was more than an anthology; it was Gleason's closing argument about jazz, backed by decades of wave-making texts.

Mystery Train

As Gleason finished his book in the spring of 1975, he wrote a pair of columns that sum up his core values. The first was a *Rolling Stone* column called "A True Media Hero" about investigative reporter I.F. "Izzy" Stone. Stone was a dapper dresser with tussled hair and rolled-up sleeves, ready to fight political corruption with facts. With his bow tie and a broad grin, Stone was a familiar figure to the American Left. He published *I. F. Stone's Weekly* from 1953 to 1971, a one-writer, four-page newsletter highly respected for its meticulously researched reporting. Gleason wrote:

> Izzy Stone is the journalist as incorruptible man, as honesty personified, and, as such, brings to life an American myth: that the honest journalist, in the muckraking tradition of Lincoln Steffens, is a saint who can save us all by his integrity and his dedication to truth.[79]

Steffens, one of the forgotten reformists of the Progressive Era, energized California's leftist politics in the 1920s with controversial stands such as his support for the Russian Revolution. The reportage of muckrakers like Steffens inspired Gleason to become a journalist as a teen in Chappaqua. That tradition lived on in Stone, whom Gleason benighted a "true media hero … the reporter as poet … a jolly little man with teary eyes, a hearing aid, a built-in shit detector as sensitive as a Geiger counter, and a love of humanity that transcends politics." Stone exemplified an "American myth: that the honest journalist is a saint who can save us all by his integrity and dedication to the truth."[80]

The American character underlay Gleason's review of *Mystery Train: Images of America in Rock 'n' Roll Music* by Greil Marcus. Growing up in Menlo Park, Marcus had read Gleason since he was a kid:

> I didn't really understand his jazz columns, or even really know what jazz was, but his descriptions of the nightclub milieu and the heroic things that went on there was alluring. The pieces on Lenny Bruce, Ray Charles, Bob Dylan, the Monterey Folk Festival, and package rock & roll shows at the Cow Palace were exciting, because there was nowhere else to read about anything of that sort. His column on the climactic act of the Berkeley Free Speech Movement, "Tragedy at the Greek Theatre," was titanic.[81]

However, Marcus lost interest after Gleason began covering the rising rock scene. By that time, Marcus was the music critic for the underground paper the *San Francisco Express-Times*:

It began to seem that he'd turned himself from a chronicler into a publicist and had three or four columns he'd recycle endlessly. And I was just starting to feel like I had something to say, and he was old and in the way. So, my first few *Express-Times* columns had digs at Ralph over something he'd recently written.[82]

But one day, the young journalist called Gleason for help. Marcus was working on an article about the Coasters and needed a great group photo. A call to Gleason confirmed he had one, and Marcus headed to Ashby Avenue. Gleason welcomed him, and Marcus left with far more than a photo:

> For the next three hours, I listened to him explain the music business. How record companies and artists themselves would present themselves as your friends so that you wouldn't be able to write anything negative about them. How corrupt it was from top to bottom. How hard it was to maintain a point of view in the face of hype and conventional opinion, and how hard it was to say in print what you thought—that everything conspired against your being able to tell what you really thought. I left thrilled and shaken.[83]

Marcus added, "From that point on, I was at his house, and later the place on Spruce, all the time. At first, I just listened. Then we'd go back and forth. He was a sage, a confidant, an inspiration, the most generous person imaginable."[84] These back-and-forths continued when Marcus began *Mystery Train* in 1972. When he finished the book, Marcus gave Gleason a pre-publication manuscript. *Mystery Train* impressed Gleason, as he expressed in his *Chronicle* review:

> This is not only a book about rock 'n' roll, although it is that, too. It is much more; it is a book about the American character and the American soul in this time period. As such, it is the best thing I've read in ages. I read it straight through, and it reminded me more than once of Melville's *The Confidence Man*. And of Parrington, too ...
>
> There is no more illuminating book on our condition today. The fact that Marcus has written this out of an interest in rock and roll is only proof again that what the established structure has seen as trivia is, in fact, genius.[85]

As he did in the Izzy Stone column, Gleason referenced a little-known historical figure. Historian Vernon Louis Parrington was a leftist intellectual who, in 1927, launched the field of American Studies, Marcus's major at UC Berkeley. Gleason also referenced Herman Melville's final novel, *The Confidence Man*, a tale of mistrust that Marcus referenced in his analysis of the Band's "The Weight," a "dramatization of a deeply American instinct for separation, distance, suspicion, the mistrust of community, as a foreign country with every citizen a stranger, 'Don't Tread on Me' as the national motto."[86]

Gleason and Marcus shared an interest in the role of popular music as part of the American identity. Asked about this, Marcus replied:

> As you know, when Ralph came of age musically in the early 1930s, it was in popular arts like jazz in which the first true American culture emerged. For prescient critics like Ralph, telling the story of the Americanization of popular music became paramount, which I believe is what predisposed Ralph to take up this theme in his 1960s–70s writings.[87]

As Gleason worked on his Izzy Stone and *Mystery Train* columns, he voiced new concerns about *Rolling Stone*'s direction. Another confrontation with Wenner loomed.

I Am the Number One on Your Side

The conditions for the clash began in the fall of 1973. "Just a reminder to bring up the stock deal at the December Board meeting," Gleason wrote Wenner in November 1973.[88] He wanted to sell his shares in Straight Arrow and began negotiating the terms with Wenner and his board of directors.[89] Wenner conducted the transaction through Alan Rinzler, who managed the Straight Arrow Press. According to Rinzler, the stock deal was initiated by Wenner in an effort to push Gleason out of *Rolling Stone*. Gleason believed the offer was unfairly low, but accepted it because he needed the money. Though correspondence between Gleason and Wenner conveys a businesslike negotiation, by all accounts the transaction left Gleason furious with his fellow *Rolling Stone* co-founder.[90] Gleason continued to harbor frustrations over his financial dealings with *Rolling Stone* and likely felt increased pressure from the magazine to resign.

Adding to Gleason's distress was his belief that *Rolling Stone* was losing its cutting edge in the early 1970s as it became a household name. The 1960s counterculture itself was now mainstream and the magazine was part of that shift. Another shift driving *Rolling Stone*'s new direction was the fact that pop music was becoming more dominant than rock music and rock music was becoming more pop-influenced. Changes at *Rolling Stone* came with this new direction. Redesigning the magazine's format, and in 1977 moving its headquarters from San Francisco to New York City. Rock stars now competed with pop singers, television celebrities, and movie stars to get on the cover of *Rolling Stone*. In contrast, its competitors such as *Creem* and *Crawdaddy!* maintained a focus on rock music which limited their mainstream influence. By finding a sweet spot between relevance and profitability, *Rolling Stone* managed to become a huge success. However, some of the original staff were unhappy with the magazine's broadened scope, including Gleason.

Gleason's frustration with *Rolling Stone*'s new course of action came to a head when the magazine ran a May 1975 cover story on singer-songwriter John Denver, whose smooth faux-country sound was the antithesis of everything Gleason believed in. "Unbelievable, the nadir of RS," Gleason wrote Wenner in response to the Denver cover.[91] The remainder of the letter further reveals the depth of Gleason's frustration:

I wonder sometimes if you really trust anybody.

Your instincts are great, but you get seduced by something else. I'm not sure exactly what; sometimes I think you are a perpetual groupie: first music, then writers, then politics. But it gets in the way of your mind and destroys your perspective …

If you would let me, I could show you how to change the image [of *Rolling Stone*] fruitfully over a period of time, how to alter the approach to the record business usefully, how to expand the audience and how to handle the things you have not been successfully handling. For Christ's sake, hire me as a consultant or something. But do something!

And if you don't know by now that I neither want to ruin you nor steal the paper from you, you will never learn anything; use the sources you have which you can trust, and by God and Jesus I am the number one on your side.

Think about this old friend … Write when you get work.[92]

After reading this letter, it's natural to assume that Gleason was about to resign. Instead, he takes a more subversive action—he threatens to stay. Despite his aggravation, Gleason maintained an effective working relationship with Wenner, as evidenced in later correspondence between them and Gleason's continuing contributions to the magazine. Wenner confirmed that they remained "allies."[93]

Gleason's letter foreshadowed the controversy Wenner sparked in a 2023 *New York Times* article about his book, *The Masters*, a collection of interviews he conducted across his career with rock musicians. In the article, Wenner said that no Black or female artists were included in the book because none had been "articulate" enough for the kind of in-depth interviews he included. Additionally, he admitted to allowing the musicians he interviewed to edit their comments prior to publication.

In Gleason's letter, written 49 years ago, he cautions his young friend to not let his love for celebrity musicians cloud his journalistic objectivity. Throughout his career, Gleason maintained a professional distance from famous musicians and even counseled his children to do so. Therefore, it frustrated him that Wenner could be seduced by star power. Must also be noted: across a 40-year career Gleason consistently spotlighted women and Black musicians. These writings include countless interviews which convey deep respect for his subjects, regardless of their sex or race.

Janno, Where's My Bottle of Champagne?

Notwithstanding Gleason's differences with Wenner, the two maintained a cooperative working relationship. This can be seen in their correspondence, which provides a fascinating glimpse into their mid-1970s rapport and the workings of *Rolling Stone* as it became a leading publication.

Gleason regularly pitched ideas for articles. For example, he negotiated an idea for a book review in this May 1974 memo to Wenner:

> Janno,
>
> Did you know the Lenny Bruce book, despite your letter, etc., had been given to Tommy Smothers to review? Also, luckily, he turned it down. I have it now and will do it if I can ... However, Mike says it should run 850–1000 words. I'll try that, but this is something of a major work and I don't know if it can be done that tightly ... Good or bad, I know the RS audience will want to know about it. I already know it is packed with dope stories, bound in syringes and shrink-wrapped in baggies, Luv. rjg[94]

Wenner immediately sent a message to his staff to carry out Gleason's request for a greater word count:

> Gentlemen: please sked [schedule] up to 2,000 words for this review per RJG's requests. Thanks, Jann."[95]

The book to be reviewed was *Ladies and Gentlemen Lenny Bruce*, the 1974 biography of the groundbreaking comic by Albert Goldman. Gleason hated it. "This author is not worthy of his subject," he wrote, because of the "pedestrian, often shoddy way in which he goes about his task."[96] Gleason called it "an exploitation book ... junkie pornography." When the movie *Lenny* came out later in 1974, Gleason asked Wenner if he could review it, and Wenner agreed.[97] But when Gleason saw his review in print, he discovered it had been cut to fit available space. This, despite Gleason suggesting ways to run it in its entirety. Gleason sent Wenner a memo, "I only bring this up so that you should understand the working of the chain of command."[98] This was Gleason's diplomatic way of saying he should have had more say than the staffer who cut his article.

Yet, Gleason often complimented his co-workers at *Rolling Stone*. For example, he praised the October 24, 1974, issue with its Beatles lunchbox cover: "I just had to tell you how good a job I think Tony [Lane] did on the current issue. It is a big step forward and looks like a new book [magazine]."[99] Gleason also pitched articles for other writers. "This seems to have the making of a fine story," he wrote Wenner about how New York Governor Nelson Rockefeller implemented new drug laws "entrapping methadone users."[100] Wenner liked the idea and published "Rockefeller's Legacy: The Vicious Drug Laws of New York" by Thomas Powers.[101] The article foreshadowed similar investigative stories, which became a hallmark of *Rolling Stone*.

The exchanges between Gleason and Wenner could be lighthearted. In one instance, Gleason asks in a memo: "Janno, where's my bottle of champagne on the Wm. [Roth] campaign you lost to me?" The bet was likely about who would win the 1974 Democratic primary for California governor, which William M. Roth lost to Jerry Brown. Wenner told his assistant, "Get a bottle of French to R.J.G."[102]

When pressure built up at *Rolling Stone*, Gleason called colleagues and friends to let off steam. Critic Jon Landau recalls such conversations:

> Because I lived in Massachusetts, I mainly got to know Ralph on the phone, and we developed a very friendly relationship. Because Jann and I had been close, Ralph

sometimes called to mildly vent about some disagreement they were having and to perhaps enlist my support. But mainly, it was to talk about music, which he simply loved. One night he called me just as I was going out to a Neil Young (I think) concert, and as soon as I said that, he said, "Have a ball." That was Ralph; as long as the subject was music, he was having a ball.[103]

Gleason's journalism influenced Landau:

While Ralph was a brilliant intellect, he did not write in an intellectual style. When you finished reading a piece by Ralph, you knew exactly what he meant and where he stood. I could sometimes write too carefully, and I learned a little about how to be more straightforward from Ralph. "Jon, it's just Paris. Not Paris, France." I remember that one![104]

Gleason also influenced *Rolling Stone* readers. One poignant example was a letter from an Oklahoma reader handwritten on pages torn from a four-hole spiral notebook. "Without question," he wrote to Gleason, "your columns in *Rolling Stone* introduced and stimulated my interest in more writers, poets, and musicians that have been important to me than any other single influence." The list of influences testifies to Gleason's eclectic

Figure 11.1 Ralph Gleason, c. 1975. Courtesy of Gleason family, photo by Phil Bray.

tastes: John Keats, Arthur Rimbaud, Berthold Brecht, Franz Kafka, Bob Dylan, and Miles Davis. The letter ends, "I hope you realize, with all the bullshit coming down on us from every direction, the value of what you are doing."[105] Such feedback points to Gleason's effectiveness as a cultural mediator who shaped readers' tastes.

Gleason also received letters at *Rolling Stone* from famous individuals, including one of his favorite novelists, *Catch-22* author Joseph Heller. The letter responded to Gleason's rave review of Heller's novel *Something Happened*. Gleason said the book had a "strange style, almost an American stainless-steel kind of prose which on reflection could be a metaphor for the American Dream." He praised the novel for capturing the alienation of the times and compared it to the work of Kafka and Dostoevsky.[106] Heller responded:

> I've read your review and have been stricken almost speechless, by your praise, by your ability to express yourself so clearly and say so much in so little space, and by your willingness to say honestly what you feel without hesitating in fear you might find yourself alone out on a limb.[107]

A journalist could expect no higher praise from a fellow writer.

Ralph, This is Your City

A few days after Gleason turned in his manuscript of *Celebrating the Duke*, he received a call from his old friend, jazz historian Ira Gitler. They made plans to have lunch the next day, but the meeting never happened.

That night, Gleason suffered a massive heart attack. An ambulance rushed him to Berkeley's Alta Bates Hospital, where his stunned family began a vigil. Jean Gleason told friends he could not receive calls, but cards could be sent to Fantasy Records. The situation was dire, but Jean was hopeful. She told a caller there was reason for hope because "Ralph's heart was behaving properly" after the attack.[108]

But at 2:30 a.m., Gleason died. He was fifty-eight.

The news spread immediately. Family and friends reeled from the information. *Rolling Stone* editor Paul Scanlon broke the news to Wenner, who burst into tears. When Jonathan Cott told rock journalist Al Aronowitz the shocking news, Aronowitz turned to his wife and railed, "I feel like I'm on the front lines, and my buddy next to me just got hit. You motherfucker!! You bastard! You got some nerve dying when I need you so bad!"[109] Gitler, who expected to see Gleason that day, wandered the hilly streets of San Francisco, shocked over the sudden death of his old friend. After walking several blocks in a daze, Gitler encountered a street band blowing the blues as if for Gleason. Crying, Gitler said, "Ralph, this is your city."[110]

Over the following days, Jean and her children received a steady stream of visitors. Because Gleason was an atheist, there was no funeral. Jann Wenner visited with Gretchen Horton; when they arrived at the Gleason's Spruce Street house, it was bursting with journalists, musicians, professors, and activists, all swapping stories about Gleason.

As newspapers and magazines around the country published remembrances, Bay Area journalists mourned the loss of one of their own. *Chronicle* reporter Carolyn Anspacher wrote:

> Scholarly and possessed of almost impeccable taste, Gleason was among the first to view rock music as a legitimate art form and accord it the dignity of searching criticism. His fine and elegant prose, sometimes fiery, sometimes cold as ice [was] the ultimate word on both modern music and modern mores.[111]

John Wasserman wrote, "Ralph and Jean Gleason were as devoted as any couple can be."[112] In the *San Francisco Examiner*, Philip Elwood said Gleason "was responsible for the national acceptance of San Francisco as the center of the rock scene."[113] Elwood mused that Gleason could "identify racehorses as easily as he could the personnel of Jelly Roll Morton's Red Hot Peppers." He added, "His was a natural one-upmanship—he always was anxious to be first, and he usually was."[114]

Large metropolitan dailies reported the news. A *New York Times* reporter wrote, "Mr. Gleason was an acerbic but highly perceptive critic of jazz and pop music."[115] The reporter quoted Gleason about why he wrote about jazz:

> I want to share my enjoyment with other people. And I dig me as a critic, vain and arrogant as it may sound. I don't care if I make it with musicians. I wouldn't care if Miles [Davis] and I didn't get along—it happens that we do, but that could change. The important thing is that I stay straight with myself.[116]

The *Times* article said Gleason "set a precedent by reviewing the opening night of folk groups, pop artists, and jazz groups and their concerts with the same attention and space normally given to classical music."[117] Newspapers around the country reported the story. With a typo that would have amused Gleason, the *Des Moines Register* succinctly announced: "Dead. Jass and pop music critic Ralph J. Gleason."[118]

In the San Francisco offices of *Rolling Stone*, Wenner scrambled to create a special section to memorialize Gleason, his friend, mentor, contributing editor, columnist—and occasional sparring partner. While preparing the issue, Wenner asked Gleason's son Toby to call Miles Davis for comment. Toby calls the trumpeter, and the phone keeps ringing. Finally, Davis answers in his raspy voice, the "voice of death," as Toby describes it. The notoriously private and blunt musician growls, "If I don't answer the fucking phone, I don't want to be fucking bothered!" Davis hangs up.[119]

Determined to get a comment, Toby turned to a mutual acquaintance of Davis and Gleason, Rose Libby.[120] In the 1950s, as a teenager, Libby accompanied her brother, a pianist, to Sunday jam sessions at the Blackhawk. There, she met Ralph and Jean, and they became lifelong friends. Rose, Jean, and Ralph had dinner with Davis several times, which made Rose an ideal go-between. Davis took Libby's call and provided two quotes. The first, "I read him. He understands me."[121] High praise from someone who publicly criticized critics. But the iconic trumpeter's second comment made it into the *Rolling Stone* tribute, five words expressing anger, longing, and pain. A plea to the gods of fate: "GIVE ME BACK my friend."[122]

Conclusion

One Picket Left

On September 21, 1975, two months after *Rolling Stone* published Miles Davis's aching words, Dizzy Gillespie stood on the Monterey Jazz Festival stage and performed his moving tribute to Gleason. Two Black titans of American music paid tribute to a White critic who recognized the revolutionary promise of their music.

During a crucial period in the development of American music, Ralph J. Gleason supported artists like Miles Davis, Bob Dylan, and the Jefferson Airplane who challenged musical and social norms. Gleason chose to align himself with these marginalized musicians and gladly accepted the estrangement that followed. He transformed his alienation into a call for collectivity and discovered that loneliness dissipates when one bonds with like-minded outsiders.

Gleason had experienced this at a Winterland concert on April 3, 1968. The show benefited striking workers at San Francisco's pioneering FM radio station, KMPX. DJ Tom Donahue had created the template for underground rock programming, but management began to meddle with Donahue's playlists, and he resigned. Staff went on strike and demanded the burly, bearded, and beloved DJ be reinstated and put in charge of programming. Winterland's operator Bill Graham held an all-star benefit to raise money for the strikers; most attended the concert.

Gleason watches a new wave of San Francisco bands take the stage, including Mother Earth, whose vocalist Tracy Nelson brings her gospel-tinged voice to a crescendo, accompanied by a trumpet and tenor sax that unleashes a torrent of sound. Gleason listens, riveted. After Mother Earth, more rising bands take the stage—Moby Grape, It's a Beautiful Day, and Electric Flag. Gleason basks in the scene, the fulfillment of that night at "Dr. Strange" when the San Francisco counterculture discovered itself. As the Winterland benefit winds down, Gleason wonders who's keeping the strike vigil going at the radio station. And so he hops in his car and drives to the waterfront offices of KMPX. He arrives at about midnight to find a sole picketer, Whitney Harris, a young salesman keeping a lonesome watch. Gleason, though tired from the long night, joins Harris. He stays until dawn rises over the luminant Bay and the evening fog melts away. Harris wrote that Gleason "alone left the festivities and shared the strike line with the one picket left."[1]

Perhaps this was Gleason's greatest gift, to accept the essential loneliness of the human condition yet bridge that chasm by simply being there for others who chose solitude. Those who, through their art or their politics, leaned far into the abyss to find their gifts. As did a Bronx child of Chappaqua who reached into the night, spun the wheel of chance, and surrendered to the liberating sounds of Black jazz.

Notes

Introduction

1. Dizzy Gillespie, "Tribute to Ralph Gleason," *Monterey Jazz Festival: 40 Legendary Years* (CD: Warner Bros, 1997).
2. John L. Wasserman, "Monterey and All that Jazz," *San Francisco Chronicle*, September 22, 1975, 35.
3. Jessica Armstrong, interview with Nat Hentoff, February 27, 2013.
4. Jessica Armstrong, interview with Gene Sculatti, April 3, 2010.
5. Ted Gioia, "Music Criticism Has Degenerated into Lifestyle Reporting," *Daily Beast*, March 18, 2014, webpage retrieved June 5, 2023: https://www.thedailybeast.com/music-criticism-has-degenerated-into-lifestyle-reporting.
6. Gioia, "Music Criticism Has Degenerated into Lifestyle Reporting."
7. R. Serge Denisoff, "Review Essays," *Journal of Popular Culture*, Vol. 3, 1969–70, 857.
8. Matt Brennan, *When Genres Collide: Down Beat, Rolling Stone, and the Struggle between Jazz and Rock* (New York: Bloomsbury Academic, 2018); John Gennari, *Blowin' Hot and Cool: Jazz and its Critics* (Chicago: University of Chicago Press, 2006); Steve Jones, ed., *Pop Music and the Press* (Philadelphia: Temple University Press, 2002); Ulf Lindberg et al., *Rock Criticism from the Beginning: Amusers, Bruisers, & Cool-Headed Cruisers* (New York: Peter Lang, 2011); Devon Powers, *Writing the Record: The Village Voice and the Birth of Rock Criticism* (Amherst: University of Massachusetts Press, 2013); and Bruce Boyd Raeburn, *New Orleans Style and the Writing of American Jazz History* (Ann Arbor: University of Michigan Press, 2009).
9. Robert Sam Anson, *Gone Crazy and Back Again: The Rise of the Rolling Stone Generation* (Garden City: Doubleday & Company, 1981); Robert Draper, *Rolling Stone Magazine: The Uncensored History* (New York: Doubleday, 1990); Joe Hagan, *Sticky Fingers: The Life and Times of Jann Wenner and Rolling Stone Magazine* (New York: Vintage Books, 2017); Jann Wenner, *Like a Rolling Stone: A Memoir* (Boston: Little, Brown, 2022). The novel *Rising Higher* contains a character based on Gleason, "Sam Carney": Robert Stuart Nathan, *Rising Higher* (New York: Dial Press, 1981).

Chapter 1

1. This was likely New York City radio station WEAF, which ran a 12 am program called "Earl Hines' Orchestra." "Radio Program," *New York Daily News*, February 15, 1932, 41.
2. Ralph J. Gleason to Seymour Krim, December 13, 1969, 1.
3. Larry Starr and Christopher Waterman, *American Popular Music: From Minstrelsy to MP3* (New York: Oxford University Press, 2010), 59.
4. Uncredited, "The First Jass Band," *Chicago Tribune*, October 19, 1916, 2.

5   George S. Kaufman, "Broadway and Elsewhere," *New York Tribune*, March 11, 1917, 29. "Jazzbo," a derogatory term for a Black person, also meant "hokum," or vulgar comedy.
6   Uncredited, "Drum Banished as Too Luring," *Los Angeles Times*, November 12, 1916, 10.
7   Uncredited, "Evangelist's Tirade," *Los Angeles Times*, November 12, 1916, 10.
8   Ralph A. Gleason, U.S., Social Security Applications and Claims Index, 1936–2007. 1910 United States Federal Census. William R. Gleason, 1900 United States Federal Census.
9   Mary A. Quinlisk, 1910 United States Federal Census. Mary Quinlisk, New York, U.S., Arriving Passenger and Crew Lists (including Castle Garden and Ellis Island), 1820–1957.
10 Stacy Gleason, email message to author, August 21, 2022.
11 Ralph J. Gleason to Seymour Krim, December 3, 1969, 1.
12 Ralph A. Gleason, New York, U.S., Arriving Passenger and Crew Lists (including Castle Garden and Ellis Island), September 17, 1928.
13 Ralph J. Gleason, "Memories of the Morning Telegraph and a Fond Farewell," *San Francisco Chronicle This World*, April 23, 1972, 29. Stacy Gleason interview by Don Armstrong, December 2, 2021.
14 Ralph J. Gleason, *Celebrating the Duke: And Louis, Bessie, Billie, Bird, Carmen, Miles, Dizzy and Other Heroes* (Boston: Da Capo Press, 1995), xix.
15 Ralph J. Gleason to Seymour Krim, December 13, 1969, 1.
16 Joan Shelley Rubin, Paul S. Boyer, and Scott E. Casper, *The Oxford Encyclopedia of American Cultural and Intellectual History* (New York: Oxford University Press, 2013), 439–40.
17 Hamlin Garland, "The Traditions of America and Today's Way of Living," *Kansas City Star*, January 3, 1924, 18.
18 Uncredited, "Police Raid Two Places," *Buffalo News*, August 29, 1930, 21.
19 James F. Cosgrave, ed., *The Sociology of Risk and Gambling Reader* (London: Routledge, 2006), 185.
20 Gleason, "Memories of the Morning Telegraph and a Fond Farewell," 29.
21 Ibid., 29.
22 Ralph J. Gleason to Seymour Krim, December 13, 1969, 3.
23 Ibid., 1.
24 Ralph J. Gleason, "Good Will, Bad Taste and Merry Christmas," *San Francisco Chronicle*, December 24, 1959, 27.
25 Dunstan later parlayed his knowledge into writing books about horseracing. Hatton was also a sports columnist and coined the term "Triple Crown" for the country's three main horse races.
26 Ralph J. Gleason, "But the Jazz Band Was Missing," *San Francisco Chronicle This World*, October 13, 1974, 26.
27 Ralph J. Gleason to Seymour Krim, December 13, 1969, 2.
28 Ibid.
29 Bruce E. Konkle, "A Preliminary Overview of the Early History of High School Journalism in the U.S." Presentation at the Scholastic Journalism Division Research Paper Sessions for the AEJMC summer conference, Washington, D.C., August 2013.
30 Ralph J. Gleason to Seymour Krim, December 13, 1969, 2.
31 Ibid.

32 Marjorie R. Fallows, *Irish Americans: Identity and Assimilation* (Englewood Cliffs: Prentice Hall, 1979), 120.
33 Lawrence McCaffrey, *Textures of Irish America* (Syracuse: Syracuse University Press, 1998), 39.
34 Gleason, *Celebrating the Duke*, xxi.
35 Neil Leonard, *Jazz: Myth and Religion* (Oxford: Oxford University Press, 1987), 61–2.
36 Ibid., 62.
37 Suzanne L. Cataldi, *Emotion, Depth and Flesh: A Study of Sensitive Space* (New York: State University of New York Press, 1993), 49.
38 Ibid., 49–50.
39 Ralph J. Gleason interview by Studs Terkel, transcript, *Studs Terkel Radio Archive*, July 31, 1971. Webpage retrieved March 10, 2023 (three parts): https://studsterkel.wfmt.com/programs/ralph-gleason-discusses-jazz-jazz-artists-and-jazz-festivals-part-1.
40 Gunther Schuller, "Jazz and Musical Exoticism," in Jonathan Bellman, ed., *The Exotic in Western Music* (Lebanon: Northeastern University Press, 1998), 282.
41 Lewis A. Erenberg, *Swingin' the Dream: Big Band Jazz and the Rebirth of American Culture* (Chicago: The University of Chicago Press, 1998), 6.
42 Gleason interview by Studs Terkel, July 31, 1971.
43 Ibid.
44 Ibid.
45 Simon Frith, *Performing Rites: On the Value of Popular Music* (Cambridge, MA: Harvard University Press, 1996), 272.
46 Ibid., 273.
47 Ibid., 274.
48 Gleason interview by Studs Terkel, July 31, 1971.
49 Ibid.
50 Ibid.
51 Ralph J. Gleason, "What Ever Happened to that Other Piano Player, Anyway?" *San Francisco Chronicle Datebook*, August 23, 1959, 16.
52 Ibid.
53 David G. Dodd and Diana Spalding, eds., *The Grateful Dead Reader* (Oxford: Oxford University Press, 2002), 90.
54 David W. Stowe, *Swing Changes: Big-Band Jazz in New Deal America* (Cambridge, MA: Harvard University Press, 1994), 33.
55 Erenberg, *Swingin' the Dream: Big Band Jazz and the Rebirth of American Culture*, xiii.
56 For a Catholic Irish American family in the 1930s, a parochial institution would likely be first choice. See Robert McCaughey, *Stand, Columbia: A History of Columbia University* (New York City: Columbia University Press, 2012), 274.
57 Ralph J. Gleason to Seymour Krim, December 13, 1969, 1.

Chapter 2

1 Uncredited, "Butler Charges Modern Youth Lacks 'Manners,'" *Columbia Spectator*, September 27, 1934, 1.
2 Ibid., 1.
3 Uncredited, "Challenge and Reply: An Editorial," *Columbia Spectator*, September 27, 1934, 1+.

4   Jann Wenner, "Ralph J. Gleason: In Perspective," *Rolling Stone*, July 17, 1975, 10.
5   Louis Menand, "Regrets Only," September 22, 2008, webpage retrieved September 7, 2022: https://www.newyorker.com/magazine/2008/09/29/regrets-only-louis-menand.
6   Lionel Trilling, *Mathew Arnold* (New York: Harcourt, 1954), 192, 271–2.
7   Ralph J. Gleason to Seymour Krim, December 13, 1969, 1.
8   Uncredited, "20 Students Will Leave for Kentucky," *Columbia Spectator*, March 18, 1932, 1. "81 of Faculty Sign Petition on 'Terrorism,'" *Columbia Spectator*, March 3, 1932, 1.
9   Robert Cohen, *When the Old Left Was Young: Student Radicals and America's First Mass Student Movement, 1929–1941* (New York: Oxford University Press, 1993), 43.
10 Ibid., 22.
11 Amos Elon, "A Shrine to Mussolini," *The New York Review of Books*, February 23, 2006, webpage retrieved June 2, 2022: https://www.nybooks.com/articles/2006/02/23/a-shrine-to-mussolini/. Mathew Wills, "Silence in the Face of Intellectual Conflagration," December 10, 2021, Daily JSTOR, webpage retrieved June 2, 2022: https://daily.jstor.org/silence-in-the-face-of-intellectual-conflagration/.
12 Cohen, *When the Old Left Was Young*, 23.
13 Gleason interview by Studs Terkel, July 31, 1971.
14 Gleason, *Celebrating the Duke*, 64.
15 Tuliza Fleming, "It's Showtime! The Birth of the Apollo Theater," in Richard Carlin and Kinshasha Holman Conwill, eds., *Ain't Nothing Like the Real Thing: How the Apollo Theater Shaped American Entertainment* (Washington: Smithsonian Books, 2010), 72.
16 Ralph J. Gleason, "Apollo Was the Home of Black America," *San Francisco Chronicle This World*, February 16, 1969, 35.
17 Ibid.
18 Ibid.
19 Ibid.
20 Gleason interview by Studs Terkel, July 31, 1971.
21 Rudolf Fisher, "The Caucasian Storms Harlem," Robert Walser, ed., *Keeping Time: Readings in Jazz History* (New York: Oxford University Press, 1999), 64.
22 Langston Hughes, *The Big Sea* (New York: Hill and Wang, 1993), 225.
23 Patrick Burke, *Come In and Hear the Music: Jazz and Race on 52nd Street* (Chicago: University of Chicago Press, 2008), 3.
24 Ralph J. Gleason, "A New York Street Has Echoes Here," *San Francisco Chronicle Datebook*, November 11, 1958, 19D.
25 Ibid.
26 Ralph J. Gleason, "A Tribute to Hammond," *S. F. Sunday Examiner & Chronicle*, May 28, 1972, 26.
27 Ibid.
28 Ibid.
29 Ibid.
30 Merwin appears to have been known around campus as an avid jazz fan at the time. An alumnus wrote in the *Spectator* that "When we were new at Columbia, we spent a lot of time there [Times Square], but then Bob Smith and Keery Merwin imbued us with a passion for jazz and all our spare time was spent on 52nd Street, not Broadway." *Columbia Daily Spectator*, November 19, 1937, 2.
31 Gleason interview by Studs Terkel, July 31, 1971.

32 Dave Brubeck and Iola Brubeck, "Digging Jazz in Gleason's 'Jam Session,'" *San Francisco Chronicle This World*, January 26, 1958, 23.
33 Gleason, *Celebrating the Duke*, 64–5.
34 Ibid., 63.
35 Uncredited, "Thorns of Cactus Become Phonograph Needles," *Popular Mechanics*, November, 1923, 685.
36 Gleason, *Celebrating the Duke*, 64.
37 Ralph Gleason, "The Old Commodore's Closing Ends a Jazz Era," *San Francisco Chronicle*, November 11, 1958, 31.
38 Ibid.
39 Hugues Panassié, *Hot Jazz: The Guide to Swing Music* (New York: M. Witmark & Sons, 1936), 22.
40 Ibid., 23.
41 Ibid., 23–4.
42 Ibid., 25.
43 Charles Edward Smith, "Collecting Hot," *Esquire*, February 1934, 96+.
44 Ralph de Toledano, "Swing Music to be Featured in New Jester," *Columbia Spectator*, March 3, 1937, 4.
45 Uncredited, "Philolexian Listens to 'Swing' Concert," *Columbia Spectator*, February 28, 1936, 1.
46 Uncredited, "Fadiman to Talk to Philo Tonight," *Columbia Spectator*, February 13, 1936, 1.
47 Uncredited, "Columbia Review Appears Today," *Columbia Spectator*, November 17, 1936, 1.
48 Lionel Trilling, "Trilling Notes 'Pleasant' Change in Reviewing Current *Jester*," *Columbia Spectator*, January 13, 1936, 2.
49 Williams strove to create a new imagist mode of American poetry that captured the rhythms and idioms of everyday people. He later influenced the Beat Generation writers who went to Columbia including Allen Ginsberg.
50 Uncredited, "Higlif Issue of Jester 'Will Descend on Campus Any Day Now,' Says Rice," *Columbia Spectator*, November 29, 1938, 1.
51 Eugene Williams, "Williams Redefines Position on Local 'Intellectual Sterility,'" *Columbia Spectator*, February 9, 1938, 1.
52 Thomas Merton, *The Seven Storey Mountain: An Autobiography of Faith* (Orlando: Harcourt Inc., 1999), 87.
53 Mary Cummings, "Traveling on Unbeaten Paths," *Columbia College Today*, May 2001, retrieved November 17, 2022: https://www.college.columbia.edu/cct_archive/may01/may01_feature_rice.html.
54 Ibid.
55 Ibid.
56 Merton, *The Seven Storey Mountain*, 170.
57 Uncredited, "Spectator Call New Aspirants," *Columbia Spectator*, September 27, 1934, 1.
58 Uncredited, "Chase Named Editor," *Columbia Spectator*, April 15, 1935, 1.
59 Uncredited, "A Statement," *Columbia Spectator*, March 28, 1935, 1.
60 Ralph J. Gleason, "Wolfe is Rated above Wilder as Lean Jack Discusses Books," *Columbia Spectator*, April 30, 1935, 1.
61 Joyce Johnson, *The Voice Is All: The Lonely Victory of Jack Kerouac* (London: Penguin

Publishing Group, 2013), 96.
62 Advertisement, *Columbia Spectator*, March 29, 1935, 4.
63 Uncredited, "Co-Chairmen Ask Increased Sales," *Columbia Daily Spectator*, March 26, 1935, 1.
64 Erenberg, *Swingin' the Dream*, 4.
65 Robert Paul Smith, "Off the Record," October 21, 1935, *Columbia Spectator*, 2.
66 Ralph J. Gleason, "Sidelines," *Columbia Spectator*, November 15, 1935, 3.
67 Uncredited, "Boards Listed for Soph Dance," *Columbia Spectator*, February 21, 1936, 1. "Red Tompkins Will Do Music at Easter Prom," *Columbia Spectator*, March 12, 1936, 1.
68 Uncredited, "Kling Selected House Nominee," *Columbia Spectator*, March 30, 1936, 1.
69 Ralph J. Gleason, "Off the Record," *Columbia Spectator*, October 1, 1936, 4.
70 Ibid.
71 Vander Lugt, Mason. "Phonograph Monthly Review, Now Online," in *ARSC Blog: Blog of the Association for Recorded Sound* Collections, webpage retrieved March 10, 2023: https://arsc-audio.org/blog/2016/10/27/phonograph_monthly_review/.
72 Gilbert Seldes, "American Noises: How to Make Them, and Why," *Vanity Fair*, June 1924, 59.
73 Uncredited, "Writers, Beaten in Ky," *Daily Worker*, February 17, 1932, 2.
74 John Hammond with Irving Townsend, *John Hammond on Record: An Autobiography* (New York: Summit Books, 1977), 148–9 and 187.
75 Henry Johnson (John Hammond), "Music: The Development of 'Swing,'" *New Masses*, March 3, 1936, 27–8.
76 Gleason, "Off the Record," *Columbia Spectator*, June 1, 1937, 4.
77 Ibid., April 20, 1937, 2.
78 Ibid., April 13, 1937, 2.
79 Ibid., May 4, 1937, 2; ibid., April 6, 1937, 2.
80 Ibid., May 4, 1937, 2.
81 Ibid., December 1, 1936, 2.
82 Ibid., February 21, 1938, 2.
83 Ibid., October 30, 1936, 2.
84 Ibid., April 20, 1937, 2.
85 Ibid., December 3, 1936, 2.
86 Ibid., December 15, 1936, 2; ibid., January 13, 1937, 2; ibid., December 2, 1936, 2; ibid., April 28, 1937, 2.
87 Ibid., April 28, 1937, 2; ibid., January 13, 1937, 2; ibid., March 23, 1937, 2.
88 Pierre Bourdieu, *Distinction: A Social Critique of the Judgment of Taste* (Cambridge, MA: Harvard University Press, 1998), 326.
89 Uncredited, "Conference Hits Civil Liberties for Fascists," *Columbia Spectator*, May 14, 1934, 1. Ralph J. Gleason to Seymour Krim, December 13, 1969, 1.
90 Advertisement, "Mass Anti-War Pageant and Dance," *Columbia Spectator*, January 13, 1937: 4.
91 Uncredited, "Youth Congress to Hold Dance Affair to Feature Goodman, Ellington in Swing Session," *Columbia Spectator*, March 31, 1938, 4.
92 Uncredited, "Peace Council Adopts Plans for Magazine," *Columbia Spectator*, March 3, 1937, 1. Uncredited, "Constitution for Magazine is Adopted," *Columbia Spectator*, March 4, 1937, 1.
93 Ralph J. Gleason, "Peace Group Adopts Call: Plans Strike," *Columbia Spectator*, March 19, 1937, 1.

94 Robert R. Buchele, ed., *University Against War*, April 1937.
95 Ralph J. Gleason, "Off the Record," *Columbia Spectator*, March 23, 1937, 2.
96 Ted Gioia, *The History of Jazz* (New York: Oxford University Press, 2011), 154–5.
97 Robert S. Gerdy, "1,500 Assemble in Gymnasium for Fourth Columbia Strike," *Columbia Spectator*, April 23, 1937, 1.
98 Uncredited, "Peace: The Inside Story," *Columbia Spectator*, April 27, 1937, 1.
99 Ibid., 2.
100 Ralph J. Gleason, "Off the Record," *Columbia Spectator*, April 30, 1937, 2.
101 Ibid., June 1, 1937, 2.
102 Ibid., 2.
103 Uncredited, "Dr. Butler Scores Fascism," *Columbia Spectator*, September 23, 1937, 1.
104 Uncredited, "Facing the Facts," *Columbia Spectator*, September 23, 1937, 2.
105 Ralph J. Gleason, "Off the Record," *Columbia Spectator*, October 15, 1937, 2.
106 Stacy Gleason, email message to author, April 9, 2023.
107 Ralph J. Gleason, "Off the Record," *Columbia Spectator*, February 7, 1938, 2.
108 Ibid.
109 Ibid., February 11, 1938, 2. Clinton was actually an innovative musician who experimented with jazz-classical hybrids that presaged Third Stream jazz.
110 Ibid., February 7, 1938, 2.
111 Ibid.
112 Ibid., March 30, 1938, 2.
113 Ralph J. Gleason to Seymour Krim, December 13, 1969, 1.
114 Stacy Gleason, interview by Don Armstrong, December 2, 2021.

Chapter 3

1 Max Jones, "Ferdinand Joseph Morton – A Biography," *Jazz Music: Bulletin of the Jazz Sociological Society*, Vol. 11, Nos. 6 and 7, February/March 1944, 86–101. Webpage retrieved November 23, 2022: http://www.doctorjazz.co.uk/page8.html.
2 Terry Trilling-Josephson and Barney Josephson, *Cafe Society: The Wrong Place for the Right People* (Chicago: University of Illinois Press, 2009), 3.
3 Ralph J. Gleason, *Celebrating the Duke, and Louis, Bessie, Billie, Bird, Carmen, Miles, Dizzy and Other Heroes* (Boston: Da Capo Press, 1995), 80.
4 Eddy Determeyer, *Rhythm is Our Business: Jimmie Lunceford and the Harlem Express* (Ann Arbor: University of Michigan Press, 2006), 109–10.
5 Gleason, *Celebrating the Duke*, 65 and 66–67.
6 Kelly Gleason, email message to Jessica Armstrong, December 29, 2021.
7 Bruce Boyd Raeburn, *New Orleans Style and the Writing of American Jazz History* (Ann Arbor: University of Michigan Press, 2012), 4.
8 Ibid.
9 Uncredited, "Jazz Information, Please," *Jazz Information*, September 1939, 1.
10 Eugene Williams, "Editorial: A History of *Jazz Information*," *Jazz Information*, November 1941, 94.
11 Uncredited, *Jazz Information*, September 19, 1939, 1.
12 Ibid., 1.
13 Ralph J. Gleason, "Hot Lips Page – A Jazz Great Who was Underrated," *San Francisco Chronicle*, November 15, 1964, 25.
14 Ibid., 25.

15 Frederic Ramsey, Jr. and Charles Edward Smith, eds., *Jazzmen* (New York: Harcourt, Brace, and Company, 1939), xi.
16 Raeburn, *New Orleans Style and the Writing of American Jazz History*, 111.
17 Ibid., 180.
18 Williams, "Editorial: A History of *Jazz Information*," 96.
19 Raeburn, *New Orleans Style and the Writing of American Jazz History*, 51.
20 Williams, "Editorial: A History of *Jazz Information*," 98.
21 Ibid., 34.
22 Ralph J. Gleason, "On the Air: An Interview with Ralph Berton," *Jazz Information*, August 9, 1940, 13.
23 Ibid.
24 New York State, Marriage Index, 1881–1967 for Ralph J. Gleason. Uncredited, "Ralph Gleason to be Married."
25 Jean Gleason, "The Trials and Gratifications of a Winning Jockey," *San Francisco Chronicle This World*, June 4, 1961, 28.
26 Raeburn, *New Orleans Style and the Writing of American Jazz History*, 155.
27 Williams, "Editorial: A History of *Jazz Information*," 98.
28 Ralph J. Gleason, "A Short Analysis of Hot Jazz Record Collecting," *Hobbies*, May 1941, 35–6.
29 Ibid., 36.
30 Williams, "Editorial: A History of *Jazz Information*," 98.
31 Ibid., 99.
32 Gennari, *Blowin' Hot and Cool*, 69.
33 Ralph J. Gleason, "'Something Keeps A-Worryin' Me," *Jazz Information*, Nov. 1941, 36.
34 Ralph J. Gleason, "Send Me Down," *Jazz Information*, Nov. 1941, 91. *Send Me Down* was the latest in many jazz fiction works since the 1910s. As David Rife notes, the term "jazz fiction" refers to "those stories and novels in which the music figures in the narrative," including works that are "obviously imbued with the spirit of the music." David Rife, *Jazz Fiction: A History and Comprehensive Reader's Guide* (Lanham: Scarecrow Press, 2008), 2.
35 Gleason, "Send Me Down," 91.
36 Ibid.
37 Williams, "Editorial: A History of *Jazz Information*," 100.
38 Ibid., 101.
39 Uncredited, "From the Production Centers," *Variety*, August 5, 1942, 42.
40 Uncredited, "CBS Makes it Legal," *Billboard*, July 32, 1946, 6.
41 Ralph J. Gleason to Seymour Krim, December 13, 1969, 2.
42 Raeburn, *New Orleans Style and the Writing of American Jazz History*, 105 and 119.
43 Uncredited, "R. J. Gleason Joins OWI," *New Castle Tribune*, January 22, 1943, 1.
44 Uncredited, "The Cool Square," *Time*, March 9, 1959, 22.
45 Ralph J. Gleason, "A Christmas Eve Long Ago in London," *San Francisco Chronicle*, December 24, 1965, 12.
46 Ibid.
47 Toby Gleason, email message to author, January 10, 2022.
48 Ralph J. Gleason to Jean Gleason, November 7, 1944.
49 Uncredited, "Judy Cortada Set for Blue Affiliate Promotion Slot," *Billboard*, November 4, 1944, 6.

50 Bernard Gendron, "Moldy Figs and Modernists: Jazz at War (1942–6)," in Krin Gabbard, ed., *Jazz Among the Discourses* (Durham: Duke University Press, 1995), 32.
51 Ralph J. Gleason, "London Blues," *Record Changer*, July 1944, 12.
52 Leonard Feather, *The Jazz Years: Earwitness to an Era* (New York: Da Capo, 1987), 79.
53 Paul Edouard Miller, ed., *Esquire's Jazz Book* (Chicago: Esquire, 1943), 49–54.
54 Raeburn, *New Orleans Style and the Writing of American Jazz History*, 163.
55 Ralph J. Gleason, "Featherbed Ball," *Record Changer*, September 1944, 48.
56 Ibid.
57 Ibid.
58 Ibid., 54.
59 Bernard Gendron, *Between Montmartre and the Mudd Club: Popular Music and the Avant-Garde* (Chicago: University of Chicago Press, 2002), 126.
60 Gleason, "Featherbed Ball," 55.
61 Ibid., 54.
62 Ralph J. Gleason, "Cless Played Heart Out to Deaf Town," *DownBeat*, January 1, 1945, 10.
63 Uncredited, "Music: Bunk Johnson Rides Again," *Time*, May 24, 1943. Webpage retrieved December 16, 2022: https://content.time.com/time/subscriber/article/0,33009,933016-1,00.html.
64 Gleason, "Featherbed Ball," 54.
65 Ibid., 55.
66 Rudi Blesh, "Crawl Out of Bed – Winter is Over," *Record Changer*, March 1945, 7+.
67 Ibid.
68 Ibid., 15.
69 Ralph J. Gleason, "That Book Again," *Record Changer*, May 1945, 26.
70 Ibid.
71 Ibid.
72 Ibid.
73 Gleason, *Celebrating the Duke*, 103.
74 Uncredited, "Jam Aplenty!" *New York Daily News*, October 8, 1944, M68. Burke, *Come in and Hear the Truth: Jazz and Race on 52nd Street*, 122.
75 Jean Gleason, "Bunk Storms 52nd Street," *Record Changer*, April 1945, 7.
76 Ralph J. Gleason, "Bunk's Horn Knocks Out Cats at Ryan's," *DownBeat*, April 1, 1945, 1.
77 Jean Gleason, "Bunk Storms 52nd Street," 7.
78 Gleason, "Bunk's Horn Knocks Out Cats at Ryan's," 4.
79 Christopher Hillman, *Bunk Johnson: His Life and Times* (New York: Universe Books, 1988), 75–9.
80 Ralph J. Gleason, "Bunk Johnson Bringing Band to NYC for Job," *DownBeat*, September 15, 1945, 1.
81 Ralph J. Gleason, *Jam Session* (London: The Jazz Book Club, 1961), 90.
82 Hillman, *Bunk Johnson: His Life and Times*, 90.
83 Ralph J. Gleason, *Jam Session*, 93.
84 Ralph J. Gleason, *Bunk Johnson and His New Orleans Band—Hot Jazz*, RCA Victor—HJ-7, April 1946.
85 Ibid.
86 Ibid.

87 Gleason told a friend about the trip but not why he went. Ralph J. Gleason to Seymour Krim, December 13, 1969, 2.
88 Blesh, "Crawl Out of Bed – Winter is Over," 15.

Chapter 4

1 Lawrence Ferlinghetti, "The Changing Light," *How to Paint Sunlight: Lyric Poems & Others* (New York City: New Directions, 2002), 8.
2 Kenneth Rexroth, *An Autobiographical Novel* (New York: New Directions Books, 1991), 366.
3 Ralph J. Gleason to Seymour Krim, December 13, 1969, 2.
4 Bridget Gleason, interview by Don Armstrong, May 20, 2021.
5 Ralph J. Gleason to Seymour Krim, December 13, 1969, 2.
6 Gleason, *Celebrating the Duke*, 107.
7 Ibid.
8 Ibid.
9 Raeburn, *New Orleans Style and the Writing of American Jazz History*, 215.
10 Gleason, *Jam Session*, 134.
11 Ralph J. Gleason, "Music in San Francisco is a Dead Duck," *DownBeat*, August 13, 1947, 11.
12 Ralph J. Gleason, "The Gospel Queen is Gone," *San Francisco Chronicle This World*, February 6, 1972, 29.
13 Ibid.
14 Ralph J. Gleason, "Swingin' the Golden Gate," *DownBeat*, October 22, 1947, 14.
15 Ralph J. Gleason, "Off the Record," *Columbia Spectator*, January 7, 1937, 2.
16 Ralph J. Gleason, "Hamp Remembers that Dance Bands are for Dancing," *DownBeat*, November 19, 1947, 6.
17 Ralph J. Gleason, "Sound Without Any Identity," *San Francisco Chronicle Datebook*, March 16, 1969, 31.
18 Ralph J. Gleason, "Ex-S.F. Schoolmarm New Coast Lutcher," *DownBeat*, December 3, 1947, 6.
19 Ralph J. Gleason, "Should 'Happen' to T-Bone, He's Ready," *DownBeat*, December 31, 1947, 9.
20 Eugene Williams, "Jazz Expert? No Such Thing! – Gene," *DownBeat*, July 16, 1947, 4–5.
21 Herb Caen, "It's News to Me," *San Francisco Chronicle*, August 8, 1949, 13; Raeburn, *New Orleans Style and the Writing of American Jazz History*, 295 ftn. 87.
22 Nesuhi Ertegun, "A Style and a Memory," *Record Changer*, April 1943, 1.
23 Ralph A. Gleason, Find a Grave Index, 1600s-Current: https://www.findagrave.com/memorial/55595239/ralph-a-gleason.
24 Ralph J. Gleason to Seymour Krim, December 13, 1969, 2.
25 Ibid.
26 Stacy Gleason, email message to author, February 2, 2022.
27 Gleason, "Swingin' the Golden Gate," *DownBeat*, December 29, 1948, 6.
28 Ibid., October 21, 1949, 12.
29 Ralph J. Gleason, "TD Told to Open Ears to Bop," *DownBeat*, September 23, 1949, 1.
30 Ralph J. Gleason, "Broke, Alone, Billie Goes Back to Work," *DownBeat*, July 15, 1949, 3.

31 Ralph J. Gleason, "Bunk's an Amazing Story," *DownBeat*, August 26, 1949, 6.
32 Ibid.
33 Ralph J. Gleason, "That Real Gone Gal is Here," *San Francisco Chronicle This World*, July 17, 1949, 11.
34 Ralph J. Gleason, "Rhythm is Contagious with Hampton," *San Francisco Chronicle This World*, July 9, 1950, 15.
35 Larry Starr and Christopher Waterman, *American Popular Music: From Minstrelsy to MP3* (New York: Oxford University Press, 2010), 155.
36 Matt Brennan, *When Genres Collide: Down Beat, Rolling Stone, and the Struggle between Jazz and Rock* (New York: Bloomsbury Academic, 2018), 81.
37 R. H. Hagan, "The Concert Season," *San Francisco Chronicle This World*, October 1, 1950, 19.
38 Marjorie McCabe, "Jelly Roll and Jazz Have Come from New Orleans to Records," *San Francisco Chronicle This World*, December 14, 1947, 23.
39 Carlton McKinney, "New Popular Records in Review," *San Francisco Chronicle This World*, June 16, 1946, 17.
40 Advertisement, "Sweet 'n' Hot," *San Francisco Chronicle*, February 10, 1951, 11.
41 Ralph J. Gleason, "Rhythm Section," *San Francisco Chronicle This World*, February 11, 1951, 17 and 27.
42 Ibid., 18.
43 Brennan, *When Genres Collide*, 60.
44 Ralph J. Gleason, "On and Off the Record," *San Francisco Chronicle This World*, July 1, 1951, 25.
45 Robert McCary, "Kezar Rings to Blues, Bop, and a Side Order of Bach," *San Francisco Chronicle*, November 6, 1949, 16.
46 Ted Gioia, *West Coast Jazz: Modern Jazz in California 1945–1960* (Berkeley: University of California Press, 1998), 65.
47 Ibid.
48 Ibid.
49 Ralph J. Gleason, "Brubeck Plays His Own Jazz Style," *San Francisco Chronicle This World*, June 15, 1952, 21.
50 The Owl, "After Night Falls," *San Francisco Chronicle*, December 12, 1953, 8.
51 Ralph J. Gleason, liner notes for *Distinctive Rhythm Instrumentals*, Dave Brubeck. Fantasy 4, 1952, 33 1/3 rpm.
52 Tom Piazza, *Setting the Tempo: Fifty Years of Great Jazz Liner Notes* (New York: Anchor Books, 1996), 1.
53 Ibid., 4.
54 Ralph J. Gleason, liner notes for *Cal Tjader Trio*, Cal Tjader Trio. Fantasy 3-9, 1953, 33 1/3 rpm.
55 George Voigt, "Lyons of KNBC," *San Francisco Chronicle This World*, September 18, 1949, 25.
56 Derrick Bang, *Vince Guaraldi at the Piano* (Jefferson: McFarland & Company, 2012), 21.
57 Jimmy Lyons and Ira Kamin, *Dizzy, Duke, the Count and Me: The Story of the Monterey Jazz Festival* (San Francisco: San Francisco Examiner Division of the Hearst Corporation: 1978), 22.
58 Ralph J. Gleason, liner notes for *Vince Guaraldi Trio*, Vince Guaraldi Trio. Fantasy 3-225, 1956, 33 1/3 rpm.
59 Ibid.

60   Ibid.
61   Bang, *Vince Guaraldi at the Piano*, 49.
62   Ralph J. Gleason, "Charlie Mingus: A Thinking Musician," *Down Beat: 60 Years of Jazz* (Milwaukee: Hal Leonard, 1995), 77–8.
63   Ibid.
64   Ralph J. Gleason, "Miles Davis All Stars – Wonderful Improvisation," *San Francisco Chronicle*, May 24, 1955, 17.
65   Ralph J. Gleason, "Modern Jazz Influenced Strongly by Miles Davis," *San Francisco Chronicle*, February 2, 1956, 19.
66   Ralph J. Gleason, "The Tenor Saxophone is at a Crossroads," *San Francisco Chronicle*, May 30, 1957, 13.
67   Ralph J. Gleason, "The Booming Market in Modern Jazz," *San Francisco Chronicle This World*, November 7, 1954, 22.
68   Ibid.
69   Ralph J. Gleason, "Spinning the Zodiac on Your Turntable," *San Francisco Chronicle This World*, February 17, 1952, 21.
70   Bridget Gleason interview by Don Armstrong, May 20, 2021.
71   Ibid.
72   Ralph J. Gleason, "Frisco's Market St. Near 100% Solo Feature, and Big," *Variety*, August 8, 1954, 3.
73   Bob Levin, *The Pirates and the Mouse: Disney's War Against the Underground* (College Park: Fantagraphics Books, 2003), 14.
74   Kevin Starr, *Coast of Dreams* (New York: Knopf Doubleday Publishing Group, 2011), 485.
75   David Talbot, *Season of the Witch: Enchantment, Terror, and Deliverance in the City of Love* (New York: Free Press, 2012), 77.
76   Jann Wenner, "Ralph J. Gleason in Perspective," *Rolling Stone*, July 17, 1975, 42–3.
77   Ralph J. Gleason, "It's Time to Acknowledge that Sinatra is Really Good," 18.
78   Ralph J. Gleason, "Man, Nobody Can Top that Frank Sinatra," *San Francisco Chronicle*, March 27, 1956, 21.
79   Ibid.
80   Ibid.
81   Ralph J. Gleason, "Jeri Clicks with a Restrained and Tasty Style," *San Francisco Chronicle This World*, January 8, 1956, 17.
82   Ibid.
83   Ralph J. Gleason, "Patti Page Can Sing Anything from Hymns to Hill-Billy," *San Francisco Chronicle This World*, January 6, 1952, 16.
84   Richard A. Peterson, *Creating Country Music: Fabricating Authenticity* (Chicago: University of Chicago Press, 1997), 163–4.
85   Ralph J. Gleason, "A Song Ain't Nothin' But a Story Just Wrote with Music to It," *San Francisco Chronicle This World*, June 1, 1952, 25.
86   Charles Emge, "Hillbilly Boom Can Spread Like Plague," *DownBeat*, May 6, 1949, 1.
87   Ralph J. Gleason, "A Man Named Texas from Arkansas," *San Francisco Chronicle This World*, March 24, 1951, 11.
88   Ralph J. Gleason, "Eddy's the Man Who Helped Bring the Country Song to the Big Town," *San Francisco Chronicle This World*, July 15, 1951, 21.
89   Ralph Gleason, "Sixteen Tons – Theme for the American Debtor?," *San Francisco Chronicle*, January 3, 1956, 19.

90 Peter La Chapelle, *Proud to be an Okie: Cultural Politics, Country Music, and Migration to Southern California* (Berkeley: University of California Press, 2007), 144–5.
91 Ralph J. Gleason, "The Record World Has a Language All its Own," *San Francisco Chronicle This World*, October 27, 1955, 21.
92 Ralph J. Gleason, "There's Room for Elvis as Well as for Music," *San Francisco Chronicle*, September 18, 1956, 21.
93 Ralph J. Gleason, "Recent Popular Recordings," *San Francisco Chronicle This World*, August 19, 1951, 19.
94 Jerry Wexler, "Rhythm and Blues in 1950," *Saturday Review*, June 24, 1950, 49.
95 Jerry Wexler and Ahmet Ertegun, "The Latest Trend: R & B Discs are Going Pop," *Cashbox*, July 3, 1954, 56.
96 Ibid.
97 Ralph J. Gleason, "Sharp Youngsters Dig Rhythm, Blues Records," *San Francisco Chronicle*, August 17, 1954, 15.
98 Ralph J. Gleason, "Rock 'n' Roll Because the Kids Had to Dance," *San Francisco Chronicle This World*, January 29, 1956, 14.
99 Ibid.
100 Ibid.
101 Ibid.
102 Ralph J. Gleason, "Record of the Week," *San Francisco Chronicle This World*, December 25, 1955, 17.
103 Ralph J. Gleason, "The New Albums," *San Francisco Chronicle This World*, April 8, 1956, 23.
104 Ibid.
105 Ralph J. Gleason, "The Vocal Volcanics of the Man in the Pink and Black Shirt," *San Francisco Chronicle This World*, May 27, 1956, 21.
106 Ralph J. Gleason, "Presley Leaves You in a Blue Suede Funk," *San Francisco Chronicle*, June 5, 1956, 19.
107 Ibid.
108 Ralph J. Gleason, "Perspectives," *DownBeat*, July 11, 1956, 35.
109 Ibid.
110 Ibid.
111 Elizabeth King, "Elvis Was the King of Treating Women Like Shit and Luring 14-Year-Olds into Bed," *Vice*, October 7, 2016, webpage retrieved July 1, 2022: https://www.vice.com/en/article/3k8z39/elvis-was-the-king-of-treating-women-like-shit-and-luring-14-year-olds-into-bed.
112 Ralph J. Gleason, "It Looks as If Elvis Has a Rival – From Arkansas," *San Francisco Chronicle This World*, December 16, 1956, 21.
113 Ralph J. Gleason, "While a Drummer Bats the Offbeat, a Guitar Twangs and Haley Shouts," *San Francisco Chronicle This World*, August 7, 1955, 21.
114 Ibid.
115 Another critic who appreciated rock 'n' roll at that time was John S. Wilson, the jazz critic for the *New York Times*. John S. Wilson, "Stylists in Jazz," *New York Times*, April 15, 1956, A131.
116 Ralph J. Gleason, "A Critic's Explanation of Rock 'n' Roll Music," *San Francisco Chronicle This World*, July 24, 1956, 17.
117 Ralph J. Gleason, "History Repeats Itself in Rock 'n' Roll Uproar," *San Francisco Chronicle This World*, August 2, 1956, 19.

Chapter 5

1. Ralph J. Gleason, "Moore Brews a Batch of Jazz at the Cellar," *San Francisco Chronicle*, June 21, 1956, 19.
2. Jack Kerouac, *Desolation Angels* (London: Penguin Books, 2019), 132.
3. Stephen R. Duncan, *The Rebel Café: Sex, Race, and Politics in Cold War America's Nightclub Underground* (Baltimore: Johns Hopkins University Press, 2018), 8–19.
4. Ralph J. Gleason, liner notes for *The Brew Moore Quartet And Quintet*, Brew Moore. Fantasy 3, 1956, 33 1/3 rpm.
5. Uncredited, "Can't Be Fooled," *San Francisco Chronicle*, November 11, 1865, 3.
6. Vlbert Parry, *Garretts & Pretenders: A History of Bohemianism in America* (New York: Cosimo, 2005), 238.
7. Dunbar H. Ogden, Douglas McDermott and Robert Károly Sarlós, *Theatre West: Image and Impact* (Amsterdam: Rodopi, 1990), 17–42.
8. Bonnie Kime Scott, editor, *Gender in Modernism: New Geographies, Complex Intersections* (Champaign: University of Illinois Press, 2007), 114.
9. Michael Davidson, *The San Francisco Renaissance: Poetics and Community at Mid-Century* (Cambridge: Cambridge University Press, 1991), 38.
10. Ralph J. Gleason, "On and Off the Record," *San Francisco Chronicle This World*, February 17, 1957, 31.
11. Ralph J. Gleason, "Lively Arts," *San Francisco Chronicle*, March 26, 1957, 21.
12. Kenneth Rexroth, "Thou Shalt Not Kill (In Memory of Dylan Thomas)," *Poetry Readings in the Cellar*, Kenneth Rexroth and Lawrence Ferlinghetti with the Cellar Jazz Quintet. Fantasy 7002, 1957, 33 1/3 rpm.
13. Lawrence Ferlinghetti, "Autobiography," *Poetry Readings in the Cellar*, Kenneth Rexroth and Lawrence Ferlinghetti with the Cellar Jazz Quintet. Fantasy 7002, 1957, 33 1/3 rpm.
14. Ibid.
15. Ralph J. Gleason, liner notes for *Poetry Readings in the Cellar*, Kenneth Rexroth and Lawrence Ferlinghetti with the Cellar Jazz Quintet. Fantasy 7002, 1957, 33 1/3 rpm.
16. Ralph J. Gleason, "San Francisco Jazz Scene," *Evergreen Review*, Vol. 1 No. 2, 1957, 62.
17. Ralph J. Gleason, "Perspectives," *DownBeat*, November 14, 1957, 20.
18. Thomas B. Sherman, "Reading and Writing," *St. Louis Post-Dispatch*, October 6, 1957, 4C.
19. Noah J. Gordon, "The *Atlantic* Reviews *On the Road* in 1957: 'Most Readable,'" *Atlantic* online, September 5, 2014. Retrieved May 29, 2024: https://www.theatlantic.com/entertainment/archive/2014/09/ladder-to-nirvana-on-the-road-september-1957/379704/.
20. Robert Kirsch, "The Book Report," *Los Angeles Times*, October 4, 1957. Retrieved May 29, 2024: https://www.latimes.com/style/la-bkw-kerouacreview2sep02-story.html.
21. Gilbert Millstein, "Books of the Times," *New York Times*, September 5, 1957, L27.
22. Kenneth Rexroth, "It's an Anywhere Road for Anybody, Anyhow," *San Francisco Chronicle This World*, September 1, 1957, 18.
23. Ralph J. Gleason, "Jazz was the Voice of Kerouac's Generation," *San Francisco Chronicle This World*, September 1, 1957, 23.
24. Ibid., 18.
25. Ibid.

26 Ralph J. Gleason, "Kerouac's 'Beat Generation,'" *Saturday Review*, January 11, 1958, 75.
27 Gleason, "On and Off the Record," *San Francisco Chronicle This World*, April 6, 1958, 27.
28 Ibid.
29 Gleason gave his account of discovering Lenny Bruce in "Lenny Bruce, The Real Lenny Bruce," in Toby Gleason, ed., *Music in the Air: The Selected Writings of Ralph J. Gleason* (New Haven: Yale University Press, 2016), 198–201.
30 Ralph J. Gleason, "Rebels with a Cause—Jazz, Lenny Bruce," *San Francisco Chronicle*, April 8, 1958, 27.
31 Ralph J. Gleason, "'The Subterraneans' is a Joke with the Punch Line Missing," *San Francisco Chronicle This World*, July 3, 1960, 15.
32 Ralph J. Gleason, "Boris the Beatnik Can't Dig that Convention," *San Francisco Chronicle This World*, July 19, 1960, 29.
33 Ibid.
34 Ibid.
35 Ralph J. Gleason, "Perspectives," *DownBeat*, May 12, 1960, 45. Although Gleason never met Dylan Thomas, the Welsh poet's work was popular with the Columbia hot collector circle Gleason belonged to.
36 Ibid.
37 Ralph J. Gleason, *Jam Session*, 11–12.
38 Ibid., 230.
39 Ibid., 15.
40 Ibid., 157.
41 Raymond Lowery, "A Jam Session with the Big Names of Jazz," *News and Observer*, June 1, 1958, III–5.
42 Philip Gaskell, "Jazz on Paper," *Observer Christmas Books*, November 23, 1958, 6.
43 Ralph J. Gleason, "Letter from the Editor," *Jazz: A Quarterly of American Music*, October 1958, 1.
44 Nat Hentoff interview by Jessica Armstrong, February 27, 2013.
45 Ibid.
46 Kent B. Diehl, ed., *Monterey Jazz Festival 1958: Official Program* (Monterey: Herald Publishers, 1958), 1.
47 Ralph J. Gleason. "Monterey Will Be a Jazz Fan's Paradise," *San Francisco Chronicle This World*, July 20, 1958, 31.
48 Ralph J. Gleason, "Jazz Fans Flocking to Monterey Festival," *San Francisco Chronicle*, October 2, 1958, 31.
49 Ralph J. Gleason, "The West Coast Gets its First Big Jazz Event," *San Francisco Chronicle This World*, September 28, 1958: 27.
50 Ralph J. Gleason, "Jazz Festival Ends with Jam Session," *San Francisco Chronicle*, October 7, 1958, 13.
51 Ralph J. Gleason, "The Sound of Death Was a Part of Billie's Charm," *San Francisco Chronicle This World*, July 26, 1959, 15.
52 Bridget Gleason, email message to author, May 20, 2021.
53 Terrence O'Flaherty, "Chaff," *San Francisco Chronicle*, September 3, 1959, 35.
54 James Truitt, "Letters to the Editor," *San Francisco Chronicle*, September 8, 1959, 32.
55 Ralph J. Gleason, "It's Too Easy with a Format," *San Francisco Chronicle*, March 6, 1963, 43. Strayhorn later made it up to Gleason; After Ellington returned to New York, he made an audio-taped interview with the arranger and sent it to Gleason, but

too late to make it into the program. Toby Gleason, interview with Don Armstrong, July 22, 2022.
56 Sonny Rollins interview by Jessica Armstrong, June 22, 2014.
57 Ralph J. Gleason, "It Was a Good Year for Jazz, it Was a Bad Year for Jazz," *San Francisco Chronicle Datebook*, January 6, 1963, 19.
58 "Rock 'n' Roll Show Turned into Bedlam," *San Francisco Chronicle*, February 23, 1957, 1–2.
59 Ibid., 1–2.
60 Ralph J. Gleason, "The Riot Syndrome is Set in Motion," *San Francisco Chronicle*, July 28th, 1960, 30.
61 Ralph J. Gleason, "The Civic Freeze on Rock 'n' Roll Shows," *San Francisco Chronicle*, August 23, 1960, 25.
62 Ralph J. Gleason, "Negro, Teen Cultures Have World Effect," *San Francisco Chronicle*, September 1, 1960, 31.
63 Ralph J. Gleason, "There's a Wide Gap between Parents and Chubby Checker," *San Francisco Chronicle This World*, April 16, 1961, 15.
64 Ibid.
65 Ralph J. Gleason, "Organization Man as a Singer – Pat Boone," *San Francisco Chronicle*, February 12, 1959, 35.
66 Ralph J. Gleason, "Why Weren't the Real Stars on TV's Grammy Show?" *San Francisco Chronicle Datebook*, December 15, 1963, 25.
67 Ralph J. Gleason, "The Rhythm Albums," *San Francisco Chronicle This World*, May 6, 1962, 30.
68 Ibid.
69 Ralph J. Gleason, "Ray Charles Album of True Folk Blues," *San Francisco Chronicle*, September 12, 1957, 25.
70 Ralph J. Gleason, "The Bay Area Jazz Scene Picks Up Tempo for a 1961 Finale," *San Francisco Chronicle Datebook*, December 24, 1961, 20.
71 Ralph J. Gleason, "Album of the Week," *San Francisco Chronicle This World*, January 19, 1958, 29.
72 Ralph J. Gleason, "Sam's Modern Blues Sound," *San Francisco Chronicle*, September 8, 1963, 35.
73 Toby Gleason, ed., *Conversations in Jazz: The Ralph J. Gleason Interviews* (New Haven: Yale University Press, 2016), 10–11.
74 Fourteen of these interviews were published in *Conversations in Jazz: The Ralph J. Gleason Interviews*.
75 Ibid., xiii.
76 Nat Hentoff interview by Jessica Armstrong, February 27, 2013.
77 Ira Gitler, "Les McCann," *DownBeat*, August 4, 1960: 32.
78 Ralph J. Gleason, "If You Want a Definition of Jazz, Go Hear Cannonball," *San Francisco Chronicle Datebook*, October 25, 1959, 20.
79 Ralph J. Gleason, "Rhythm Albums," *San Francisco Chronicle This World*, September 4, 1960, 23.
80 John Tynan, "Les McCann & 'The Truth,'" *DownBeat*, September 15, 1960, 20.
81 Ibid.
82 Ibid., 21.
83 Ralph J. Gleason, "Les McCann—Biggest Storm since Brubeck," *San Francisco Chronicle*, November 17, 1960, 33.

84 Ralph J. Gleason, "The Lyric Beauty of Miles' Music," *San Francisco Chronicle*, September 11, 1963, 45.
85 Ralph J. Gleason, "Bridging the Years with a Trio of Saxes," *San Francisco Chronicle This World*, August 23, 1959, 27.
86 Ralph J. Gleason, "The Radical Jazz of Ornette Coleman," *San Francisco Chronicle*, December 17, 1959, 39.
87 Ibid.
88 Ralph J. Gleason, "Some Unknown Kid Came Along and Upset the Jazz World," *San Francisco Chronicle This World*, June 19, 1960, 21.
89 Ibid.
90 Harold Macmillan, "The Wind of Change Speech," February 3, 1960, webpage retrieved March 10, 2023: https://web-archives.univ-pau.fr/english/TD2doc1.pdf.
91 Ralph J. Gleason, "Perspectives," *DownBeat*, April 27, 1961, 66.
92 Ibid.
93 Frank Kofsky, *John Coltrane and the Jazz Revolution of the 1960s* (New York: Pathfinder, 2001), 159-60.
94 Gene Lees, "Down Beat Days," *Gene Lees Jazzletter*, February 15, 1982, 5.
95 Ralph J. Gleason, "Down Beat through the Years—A Reflection of 25 Years of Jazz," *San Francisco This World*, August 16, 1959, 31.
96 Nat Hentoff, *Speaking Freely: A Memoir* (New York: Knopf, 1997), 45.
97 Dorothy Kilgallen, "O'Toole Stardom Expected to Zoom with 'Lawrence,'" *Fort Worth Star-Telegram*, August 9, 1962, Section Four 6.
98 Ralph J. Gleason, "An Epitaph for C. Wright Mills," *San Francisco Chronicle*, April 3, 1962, 33.
99 Ralph J. Gleason to Alexander Hoffman, September 2, 1963.
100 Ibid., June 26, 1963, 1.
101 Ralph J. Gleason, "The Painful Voice of Desperate Sanity in a World Hiding," *San Francisco Chronicle This World*, July 2, 1961, 20.
102 Ralph J. Gleason to Alexander Hoffman, June 1, 1963, 1.
103 Ralph J. Gleason, "The Poet of the Losers has Paid the Dues," *San Francisco Chronicle This World*, October 22, 1961, 33.
104 Nelson Algren to Jean Gleason, no date.
105 Ralph J. Gleason, liner notes to *The Best of Lenny Bruce*, Lenny Bruce. Fantasy 7012, 1962, 33 1/3 rpm.
106 Uncredited, "Cops Seize Lenny Bruce—'Dirty Talk,'" *San Francisco Chronicle*, October 5, 1961, 1.
107 Ralph J. Gleason, "An Unorthodox Pulpit for Lenny Bruce," *San Francisco Chronicle*, October 10, 1961, 35.
108 Ibid.
109 *Lenny Bruce Trial Transcripts* (Robert N. Beechinor, Official Court Reporter), 70.
110 Ibid., 77-8.
111 Ibid., 89.
112 Ibid., 119.
113 Ibid., 157.
114 Ibid., 160.
115 Michael Harris, "Lenny Bruce Acquitted in Smut Case," *San Francisco Chronicle*, March 9, 1962, 1.

116 Laura M. Holson, "Lenny Bruce is Still Talking Dirty and Influencing People," *New York Times* online, October 13, 2018, retrieved April 10, 2023: https://www.nytimes.com/2018/10/13/arts/lenny-bruce-comedy.html#:~:text=In%201963%2C%20he%20was%20barred,to%20four%20months%20in%20jail.

117 Stacy Gleason, email message to author, April 9, 2023.

118 Paul Lyons, *New Left, New Right* (Philadelphia: Temple University Press, 1996), 50.

119 Ralph J. Gleason, "Coltrane's Sax Blows Instant Art," *San Francisco Chronicle This World*, November 24, 1963, 30.

120 Barry Shank, *The Political Force of Musical Beauty* (Durham: Duke University Press, 2014), 3.

121 Ralph J. Gleason, "Dick Gregory's Personal War," *San Francisco Chronicle*, June 5, 1963, 43.

122 Ralph J. Gleason, "The Gap between Cultures," *San Francisco Chronicle*, November 15, 1962, 43.

123 Ralph J. Gleason to Alexander Hoffmann, June 1, 1963, 2.

124 Ibid., June 24, 1963.

125 Ibid., September 2, 1963, 1.

126 Ralph J. Gleason to Eric Hobsbawm, December 4, 1963, 2.

127 Ralph J. Gleason to Alexander Hoffman, November 25, 1963, 1-2.

128 Ralph J. Gleason to Eric Hobsbawm, December 4, 1963, 2.

129 Ralph J. Gleason, "A Violent Act Defines Us," *San Francisco Chronicle*, November 25, 1963, 37.

130 Ralph J. Gleason, "A Violent Act Defines Us," 37.

131 Ibid.

132 Ibid.

133 Ibid.

134 Mick Jagger and Keith Richards, "Sympathy for The Devil" lyrics, Mirage Music Int. Ltd. C/o Essex Music Int. L, Mirage Music Ltd.

Chapter 6

1 Ralph J. Gleason, "Lenny Missed a Good Show," *San Francisco Chronicle*, January 10, 1964, 39.

2 Uncredited, "The Beatles 'Infest' England," *Sumter, South Carolina Item*, January 1, 1964, 3.

3 Ben Gross, "What's On?" *New York Daily News*, January 4, 1964, 236.

4 Ralph J. Gleason, "The Beatles' Mersey Sound," *San Francisco Chronicle*, February 5, 1964, 43.

5 Ibid.

6 Ralph J. Gleason, "Fertility Goddess Explains the Beatles," *San Francisco Chronicle*, February 7, 1964, 37.

7 Ibid.

8 Ralph J. Gleason, "Monterey's Test of Fire," *San Francisco Chronicle*, May 22, 1963, 43.

9 Ibid.

10 Ibid.

11 Ibid.

12. Ibid.
13. Ralph J. Gleason to Alexander Hoffman, June 1, 1963, 2.
14. Ralph J. Gleason, "On the Town," *San Francisco Chronicle*, November 6, 1963, 47.
15. Ralph J. Gleason, "Magic by Joan Baez," *San Francisco Chronicle*, March 25, 1963, 47.
16. Ralph J. Gleason, "On the Town," *San Francisco Chronicle*, December 9, 1963, 61.
17. Bob Dylan, "The Times They Are A-Changin,'" Universal Music Publishing Group.
18. Ralph J. Gleason, "A Folk-Singing Social Critic," *San Francisco Chronicle*, February 24, 1964, 43.
19. Ralph J. Gleason, "The Man with the Message," *The San Francisco Chronicle*, February 21, 1964, 39.
20. Ralph J. Gleason, "Miles Davis—Full of Surprises," *San Francisco Chronicle*, April 10, 1964, 47.
21. Ibid.
22. Ibid.
23. Ibid.
24. Ibid.
25. Ralph J. Gleason, "Great Jazz Show at the Masonic," *San Francisco Chronicle*, September 16, 1964, 49.
26. Ralph J. Gleason, "Jazz Comeback in North Beach," *San Francisco Chronicle*, November 4, 1964, 43.
27. Ralph J. Gleason, "The True Fire of Creativity," *San Francisco Chronicle*, November 20, 1964, 43.
28. Ralph J. Gleason, "The Swingingest Band Ever," *San Francisco Chronicle This World*, September 13, 1964, 43.
29. Ralph J. Gleason, "An Exercise in Serendipity," *San Francisco Chronicle This World*, April 28, 1963, 33.
30. Ralph J. Gleason, liner notes to *Jazz Impressions of Black Orpheus*, Fantasy, mono LP 3337, 1962.
31. Derrick Bang, *Vince Guaraldi at the Piano* (Jefferson: McFarland, 2012), 131.
32. *Anatomy of a Hit*, television series, National Educational Television & Radio Center, March 11, 1964.
33. Ibid.
34. Ralph J. Gleason, "Genuine Triumph in Odetta's Songs," *San Francisco Chronicle*, October 19, 1959, 25.
35. Ralph J. Gleason, "It's Country Song Week on the Capricious Market," *San Francisco Chronicle This World*, August 9, 1959, 31.
36. Ibid.
37. Ibid.
38. Ralph J. Gleason, "Where Would the Folk Singers be without Huddie?" *San Francisco Chronicle This World*, July 17, 1960, 31.
39. Ibid.
40. Uncredited, "The Berkeley Folk Music Festival Project," webpage retrieved March 10, 2023: https://www.michaeljkramer.net/the-berkeley-folk-music-festival-project/#:~:text=Directed%20throughout%20its%20duration%20by,the%20West%20Coast%20folk%20revival.
41. Ibid.
42. Ralph J. Gleason, "The Dilemmas in Folk Music," *San Francisco Chronicle*, July 1, 1964, 51.

43 Ralph J. Gleason, "Some Highlights at the Folk Festival," *San Francisco Chronicle*, June 30, 1964, 37.
44 Ibid.
45 Gleason, "The Dilemmas in Folk Music," 51.
46 Ibid.
47 Stacy Gleason, email message to author, December 24, 2021.
48 Ibid.
49 Rebecca Adams, email message to Jessica Armstrong, December 26, 2021.
50 Toby Gleason interview by Don Armstrong, March 17, 2021.
51 Tim Riley, *Hard Rain: A Dylan Commentary* (New York: Da Capo Press, 1999), 85.
52 Ralph J. Gleason, "The Voice of the New Generation," *San Francisco Chronicle This World*, October 11, 1964, 35.
53 Ralph J. Gleason, "The Intransigent Dylan Speaks from the Top Rungs," *San Francisco Chronicle This World*, November 22, 1964, 42.
54 Ibid., 42.
55 Ralph J. Gleason, "To Find the Melody, One Must find the Language," *San Francisco Chronicle Datebook*, August 12, 1962, 19.
56 Ralph J. Gleason, "Paul Krassner and the Realist," *San Francisco Chronicle*, December 13, 1963, 49.
57 Ken Kesey to Ralph J. Gleason, June 11, 1964, 1.
58 Rising New Journalism writer Tom Wolfe chronicled the cross-continental road trip in his book *Electric Kool-Aid Acid Test* (New York: Picador, 2008).
59 Ibid., 68.
60 Ralph J. Gleason, "Sometimes a Great Notion is More Demanding than a Cuckoo's Nest," *San Francisco Sunday Chronicle*, July 26, 1964, 32.
61 Ralph J. Gleason, "On the Road with Ken Kesey," *San Francisco Chronicle*, July 29, 1964, 41.
62 Ibid.
63 Ibid.
64 Ralph J. Gleason, "Mercy Me! It's the 'Mercy Beat,'" *The San Francisco Chronicle Datebook*, November 1, 1964, 23.
65 Ibid.
66 Ibid.
67 Ralph J. Gleason, "The Night They Almost Had a Riot, but Didn't," *San Francisco Chronicle*, November 21, 1964, 28.
68 Ibid.
69 Ibid.
70 Ralph J. Gleason, "The Jamaica Ska and Blue Beat," *San Francisco Chronicle*, June 3, 1964, 45.
71 Ralph J. Gleason, "A Gospel Singer: A Secular Guitar," *San Francisco Chronicle*, January 30, 1964, 41.
72 Ralph J. Gleason, "Rock 'n' Roll—Berry the Show," *San Francisco Chronicle*, April 15, 1964, 43.
73 Robert Cohen and Reginald E. Zelnik, editors, *The Free Speech Movement: Reflections on Berkeley in the 1960s* (Berkeley: University of California Press), 2002.
74 Wenner, "Ralph J. Gleason in Perspective," 45.
75 Malcolm Smith, "Kerr Links Demonstrator, Reds," *San Francisco Chronicle*, October 8, 1964, 2.

76 Wenner, "Ralph J. Gleason in Perspective," 45.
77 Ibid.
78 Ibid., 44–5.
79 *Western Regional SNCC Conference, Press and Public Relations, Saturday Workshop*, November 13–15, 1964, 1.
80 Ibid.
81 Ibid.
82 Ibid.
83 Ibid.
84 Ralph J. Gleason, "An Aural Record of The U.C. Struggle," *San Francisco Chronicle Datebook*, November 23, 1964, 23.
85 Ralph J. Gleason, "Songs Born of the UC Rebellion," *San Francisco Chronicle*, November 23, 1964, 51.
86 Ibid.
87 *Thirteenth Report of the Senate Fact-Finding Subcommittee on Un-American Activities*, California Legislature, June 18, 1965, 96–7. The DuBois Clubs of America launched in San Francisco in 1964. Sponsored by the Communist Party USA, the group took its name from famed African American sociologist W.E.B. DuBois who co-founded the National Association for the Advancement of Colored People (NAACP) in 1909.
88 Mario Savio, *Free Speech Movement Chronology*, webpage retrieved March 10, 2023: https://bancroft.berkeley.edu/FSM/chron.html.
89 Joel L. Pimsleur to Ralph J. Gleason, December 3, 1964. From "Inside Sproul Hall," webpage, Free Speech Movement Archives, retrieved April 6, 2023: https://www.fsm-a.org/stacks/pimsleur_narr64.html.
90 *Free Speech Movement Chronology*: https://bancroft.berkeley.edu/FSM/chron.html.
91 Ibid.
92 Ralph J. Gleason, "The Tragedy at the Greek Theater," *San Francisco Chronicle*, December 9, 1964, 49.
93 Advertisement, "We Support the Free Speech Movement," *San Francisco Chronicle*, December 9, 1964, 6.

Chapter 7

1 Ralph J. Gleason, "LPs—Great Bechet Sides," *San Francisco Chronicle This World*, January 24, 1965, 38.
2 Ralph J. Gleason, "A Record Year of Beatlemania," *San Francisco Chronicle This World*, January 17, 1965, 47.
3 *Inside America*, television series, British Broadcasting Corporation, June 20, 1965.
4 Keith Power, "Gleason to appear in British TV Series," *San Francisco Chronicle*, February 22, 1965, 43.
5 *Inside America*, television series, British Broadcasting Corporation, June 20, 1965.
6 Ibid.
7 Ibid.
8 Ibid.
9 Ibid.
10 Ibid.

11. Ralph J. Gleason, "Dylan's Songs—Protest, Poetry, Love," *San Francisco Chronicle*, April 7, 1965, 41.
12. Ralph J. Gleason, "The Poetry of a Singing Spokesman," *San Francisco Chronicle This World*, April 18, 1965, 27.
13. Ralph J. Gleason, *The Jefferson Airplane and the San Francisco Sound* (New York: Ballantine Books, 1969), 325.
14. Nadya Zimmerman, *Counterculture Kaleidoscope: Musical and Cultural Perspectives on Late Sixties San Francisco* (Ann Arbor: University of Michigan Press, 2008), 22.
15. Gleason, *The Jefferson Airplane and the San Francisco Sound*, 325.
16. Gary Kamiya, *Cool Gray City of Love: 49 Views of San Francisco* (New York: Bloomsbury USA, 2014), 312.
17. Ralph J. Gleason, "On Horseplayers and Byrd-Watchers," *San Francisco Chronicle*, May 5, 1965, 49.
18. Ibid.
19. Steve Batterson and Stephen Smale, *The Mathematician Who Broke the Dimension Barrier* (Providence: American Mathematical Society, 2012), 98.
20. Ralph J. Gleason, "Two Moments in a Revolution," *San Francisco Chronicle*, May 24, 1965, 51.
21. Ralph J. Gleason, "Rolling Stones—and Pandemonium," *San Francisco Chronicle*, May 17, 1965, 43.
22. Ibid.
23. Ralph J. Gleason, "The Times They Are a' Changin'," *Ramparts*, April 1965, 47.
24. Ibid., 48.
25. Ralph J. Gleason, "Bob Dylan Does as He Pleases," *San Francisco Chronicle*, September 8, 1965, 45.
26. Ralph J. Gleason, "Rock and Roll for Folk-Singers," *San Francisco Chronicle*, August 2, 1965, 47.
27. Ralph J. Gleason, "Rock and Roll—Folk Music of the Teenagers," *San Francisco Chronicle This World*, August 8, 1965.
28. Ralph J. Gleason, "Dylan Places Poetry in the Hands of Youth," *San Francisco Chronicle This World*, September 19, 1965, 21.
29. Ibid.
30. Ibid.
31. Ibid.
32. Ralph J. Gleason, "On Listening to Rock 'n' Roll," *San Francisco Chronicle*, August 11, 1965, 39.
33. Ralph J. Gleason, "A Quiet Pause with the Beatles," *San Francisco Chronicle*, September 3, 1965, 37.
34. Ron Fimrite, "Beatles Play S.F. as a Riot Rages," *San Francisco Chronicle*, September 1, 1965, 1.
35. Ralph J. Gleason, "Beatles' Last Visit?" *San Francisco Chronicle*, September 1, 1965, 43.
36. Ibid.
37. Ibid.
38. Ralph J. Gleason, "Coltrane Looks at the Mad World with Love," *San Francisco Chronicle This World*, March 7, 1965, 35.
39. Ibid.

40 Ibid.
41 Ralph J. Gleason, "The Solace of John Coltrane," *San Francisco Chronicle*, September 17, 1965, 24.
42 Ralph J. Gleason, "Monterey's Fat is Close to the Fire," *San Francisco Chronicle Datebook*, October 3, 1965, 27.
43 Ralph J. Gleason, "Cops and Guns in an 'Armed Camp,'" *San Francisco Chronicle Datebook*, October 10, 1965, 23.
44 Ralph J. Gleason, "Monterey Festival: Trumpets Galore," *San Francisco Chronicle*, September 20, 1965, 31.
45 Ibid.
46 Ralph J. Gleason, "John Handy—Breaking Barriers," *San Francisco Chronicle*, June 23, 1965, 47.
47 John Handy interview with Jessica Armstrong, May 25, 2014.
48 Jimmy Lyons and Ira Kamin, *Dizzy, Duke, the Count and Me* (San Francisco: The San Francisco Examiner, 1978), 45.
49 Gabe Meline, "From the Club to the Cathedral: Revisiting Duke Ellington's Controversial 'Sacred Concert.'" Webpage retrieved March 16, 2022: https://www.kqed.org/arts/10957761/from-the-club-to-the-cathedral-revisiting-duke-ellingtons-controversial-sacred-concert#.
50 John Handy interview with Jessica Armstrong, May 25, 2014.
51 Ashley Kahn, notes, *Duke Ellington*, DVD, Eagle Eye Media, 2005.
52 Percy Shain, "Night Watch," *Boston Globe*, March 12, 1964, 35.
53 Ralph J. Gleason, "Manifesto," *Ramparts*, October 1965, 64–5.
54 Ralph J. Gleason, "Man with the Golden Charm," *Ramparts*, October 1965, 69–70.
55 Ibid.
56 Nelson Algren to Ralph J. Gleason, undated, 1.
57 Ibid.
58 Ibid.
59 Jonathan Cott, "A Hard Day's Knights," *Ramparts*, October 1965, 35–42.
60 Hunter Thompson, *Fear and Loathing in America: The Brutal Odyssey of an Outlaw Journalist* (New York: Simon and Schuster, 2011).
61 John L. Wasserman, "The Matrix: Social Blues via the Jefferson Airplane," *San Francisco Chronicle Datebook*, August 29, 1965, 5. A brief review of the performance was also published in the August 13, 1965, *Oakland Tribune* in Perry Phillips' *Night Sounds* column.
62 Band-founder Balin disliked the "the choirboy sound" of the Byrds and instead preferred the more primal music of the Lovin' Spoonful who "hit you with the music … that's what we do" (Gleason, *The Jefferson Airplane*, 85).
63 Ralph J. Gleason, "Jefferson Airplane – Sound and Style," *San Francisco Chronicle*, September 13, 1965, 49.
64 Ibid.
65 Robert Yehling, "The *High Times* Interview: Marty Balin." Website retrieved March 10, 2023: http://web.archive.org/web/20050222091301/http://www.geocities.com/balinmiracles/hightimesart.html.
66 Jeff Tamarkin, *Got a Revolution! The Turbulent Flight of Jefferson Airplane* (New York: Atria Books, 2005), 41.
67 Ibid.

68 Wenner, "Ralph J. Gleason in Perspective," 46.
69 Uncredited, "Touring Students Meet Fidel Castro," *San Francisco Examiner*, July 2, 1963, 1.
70 Uncredited, "Gleason Talk," *San Francisco Chronicle*, February 19, 1965, 46.
71 Alice Echols, *Scars of Sweet Paradise: The Life and Times of Janis Joplin* (New York: Henry Holt and Company, 1999), 104–5.
72 Gleason, "Jefferson Airplane – Sound and Style," 49.
73 Ralph J. Gleason, "'The Family Dog'—Liverpool in S.F.," *San Francisco Chronicle*, October 22, 1965, 57.
74 Ibid.
75 Ibid.
76 Ralph J. Gleason, "Bob Dylan—Quiet and Gentle," *San Francisco Chronicle*, October 11, 1965, 47.
77 Fred Allgood, "Focus on UC—A New Era?" *San Francisco Chronicle*, September 19, 1965: I–9.
78 Wolfe, *The Electric Kool-Aid Acid Test*, 222.
79 Denise Kaufman, typewritten recollections written after Gleason's death in 1975, 1–2.
80 Gleason, *The Jefferson Airplane and the San Francisco Sound*, 4.
81 Darby Slick, *Don't You Want Somebody to Love* (Berkeley: SLG Books, 1991), 56.
82 Wenner, "Ralph J. Gleason in Perspective," 46.
83 Ralph J. Gleason, "Folk Cult's Bid to Deal with Reality," *San Francisco Chronicle*, June 28, 1965, 45.
84 Denise Kaufman interview by Jessica Armstrong, April 28, 2010.
85 Ibid.

Chapter 8

1 Paul Williams, ed., *The Crawdaddy! Book: Writings (And Images) From the Magazine of Rock* (Milwaukee: Hal Leonard, 2002), 175–6.
2 Bill Graham and Robert Greenfield, *Bill Graham Presents: My Life Inside Rock and Out* (Boston: Da Capo Books, 2004), 128.
3 Ralph J. Gleason, "Lesson for S.F. in the Mime Benefit," *San Francisco Chronicle*, December 13, 1965, 47.
4 "Bob Dylan Gives Press Conference in San Francisco," webpage retrieved March 8, 2023: https://www.rollingstone.com/music/music-news/bob-dylan-gives-press-conference-in-san-francisco-246805/.
5 *Dylan Speaks*, DVD, Eagle Media, 2006.
6 Ibid.
7 Michael Grieg, "It's Lonely Where I Am," *San Francisco Chronicle*, December 4, 1965, 36.
8 Ralph J. Gleason, "How to Readjust to the Rock Bands," *San Francisco Chronicle Datebook*, December 12, 1965, 23.
9 Sarah Hill, *San Francisco and the Long 60s* (New York: Bloomsbury Academic, 2016), Kindle eBook location 1217.
10 Sarah Thornton, *Club Cultures: Music, Media, and Subcultural Capital* (Middleton: Wesleyan University Press, 1996), 16.

11 Ralph J. Gleason, "The Acid Test and Other Marvels," *San Francisco Chronicle*, January 7, 1966, 47.
12 Gabe Meline, "Q&A: Stewart Brand Revisits the Trips Festival, 50 Years Later," website retrieved January 31, 2023: https://www.kqed.org/arts/11263131/qa-stewart-brand-revisits-the-trips-festival-50-years-later.
13 Ralph J. Gleason, "One Wild Night—A Trips Festival," *San Francisco Chronicle*, January 24, 1966, 49.
14 Charles Perry, *The Haight-Ashbury: A History* (New York: Wenner Books, 2005), 45.
15 Gleason, "One Wild Night – A Trips Festival," 49.
16 Ralph J. Gleason, "Dance Renaissance in the Fillmore," *San Francisco Chronicle*, March 14, 1966, 49.
17 Ibid.
18 Ralph J. Gleason, "Paul Butterfield's Take-Charge Guys," *San Francisco Chronicle*, March 30, 1966, 45.
19 Ibid.
20 Ralph J. Gleason, "What's Going on in this Place?" *San Francisco Chronicle Datebook*, April 24, 1966, 23.
21 Ralph J. Gleason, "S.F. Cops Strange Raid on Dancehall," *San Francisco Chronicle*, April 25, 1966, 51.
22 Ralph J. Gleason, "A Great Survey of American Music," *San Francisco Chronicle*, April 20, 1966, 39.
23 Ralph J. Gleason, "Who was that White Witch Doctor?" *San Francisco Chronicle*, July 29, 1966, 49.
24 Ralph J. Gleason, "A Capitol Stew over Beatles," *San Francisco Chronicle*, June 13, 1966, 53.
25 Ralph J. Gleason, "Rock LPs—Some Remarkable Experiments," *San Francisco Chronicle This World*, July 10, 1966, 31.
26 Ralph J. Gleason, "The Beatles' Hot Revolver," *San Francisco Chronicle This World*, September 25, 1966, 35.
27 Maureen Cleave, "How Does a Beatle Live?" *London Evening Standard*, March 4, 1966, 10.
28 Ralph J. Gleason, "It's Beatles Day at Candlestick," *San Francisco Chronicle*, August 29, 1966, 49.
29 Ibid.
30 Bridget Gleason email to author, attachment, April 24, 2022.
31 Ibid.
32 Ralph J. Gleason, "A Puppet Show for the Beatles," *San Francisco Chronicle*, August 31, 1966, 43.
33 Robert Shelton, "The Remains (Long-Haired Dropouts) to be Seen," *New York Times*, December 11, 1965, L23.
34 Gendron, *Between Montmartre and the Mudd Club*, 190. Robert Shelton, "Folk-Rock Rage," *New York Times*, January 30, 1966, X21.
35 Richard Goldstein, "Pop Eye," *Village Voice*, August 25, 1966, *Village Voice* online, retrieved April 6, 2023: https://www.villagevoice.com/2020/03/27/pop-eye-on-revolver/.
36 Williams, *The Crawdaddy! Book*, 10.
37 Ibid., 66 and 84–7.
38 Gene Sculatti, interview by Jessica Armstrong, April 3, 2010.

39 Joel Selvin, interview by Jessica Armstrong, November 10, 2010.
40 Davin Seay, interview by Jessica Armstrong, April 5, 2010.
41 John Swenson, interview by Don Armstrong, April 23, 2020.
42 Suzy Shaw and Mick Farren, *Bomp! Saving the World One Record at a Time* (Pasadena: AMMO Books, 2007), 15.
43 Ralph J. Gleason, "Gleason's Guide to the Sources," *San Francisco Chronicle Datebook*, November 13, 1966, 29.
44 Ibid.
45 Joe Hagan, *Sticky Fingers: The Life and Times of Jann Wenner and Rolling Stone Magazine* (New York: Vintage Books, 2018), 59.
46 Jann Wenner, interview by Don Armstrong, May 5, 2021.
47 Ralph J. Gleason, "Perspectives," *Rolling Stone*, January 20, 1972, 26.
48 mr. jones (Jann Wenner), "something's happening," *Daily Californian*, May 12, 1966, 12.
49 Ralph J. Gleason, "A Great Weekend for Dancing," *San Francisco Chronicle*, May 9, 1966, 31.
50 Jann Wenner, *Like a Rolling Stone: A Memoir* (New York: Little, Brown and Company, 2022), 39.
51 Ibid., 36.
52 Uncredited, "Great Britain: You Can Rock Across it on the Grass," *Time*, April 15, 1966. Webpage, retrieved February 2, 2023: https://content.time.com/time/subscriber/article/0,33009,835349,00.html.
53 Lindberg et al, *Rock Criticism from the Beginning*, 89.
54 Wenner, *Like a Rolling Stone: A Memoir*, 46.
55 Jann Wenner, interview by Don Armstrong, May 5, 2021.
56 Jann Wenner, "Rock," *Sunday Ramparts*, February 12–26, 1967, 7.
57 Ibid.
58 Gleason, "The Sickness That Killed Lenny," 47.
59 Wenner, ed., "Ralph J. Gleason in Perspective," 46.
60 Ralph J. Gleason, "A Brave New Whirl in the Park," *San Francisco Chronicle*, January 13, 1967, 39.
61 Ibid.
62 Ibid.
63 Uncredited, "Hippies Run Wild—Jailed," *San Francisco Sunday Examiner & Chronicle*, January 15, 1967, 1.
64 Ibid.
65 Uncredited, "They Came ... Saw ... Stared," *San Francisco Sunday Examiner & Chronicle*, January 15, 1967, 3.
66 Ralph J. Gleason, "The Tribes Gather for a Yea-Saying," *San Francisco Chronicle*, January 16, 1967, 41.
67 Thomas Maremaa and Andrew Gordon, "Have You Seen Your Critic, Baby?: Ralph J. Gleason," *The Every Other Weekly*, January 13, 1970: 4.
68 Uncredited, "Dropouts with a Mission," *Newsweek*, February 6, 1967, 92–95.
69 Robert Sam Anson, *Gone Crazy and Back Again: The Rise of the Rolling Stone Generation* (Garden City, NY: Doubleday & Company, 1981), 61.
70 Draper, *Rolling Stone Magazine*, 57.
71 Ralph J. Gleason, "Wild Weekend Around the Bay," *San Francisco Chronicle*, October 18, 1965, 51.

72 Peter Richardson, *A Bomb in Every Issue: How the Short, Unruly Life of Ramparts Magazine Changed America* (New York: The New Press, 2009), 107–8.
73 Warren Hinckle, "The Social History of the Hippies," *Ramparts*, March 1967, 17.
74 Ibid., 17–18.
75 Ibid., 24.
76 The previous fall, Gleason critiqued a Kesey Acid Test. Ralph J. Gleason, "The Acid Test That Never Was," *San Francisco Chronicle*, November 2, 1966, 49. Gleason had also written a scathing critique of a talk by Dr. Timothy Leary.
77 Hinckle, "The Social History of the Hippies," 24.
78 Ibid., 26.
79 Richardson, *A Bomb in Every Issue*," 108.
80 Nancy Turpin, "Night the Lights Happened," *Oakland Tribune*, March 25, 1967, 7.
81 Ibid.
82 Ralph J. Gleason, "Perspectives: One Hundred Rolling Stones," *Rolling Stone*, January 20, 1972, 26.
83 Legal notice, *Los Angeles Evening Citizen News*, April 13, 1967, 15.
84 Harvey Kubernik and Kenneth Kubernik, *A Perfect Haze: The Illustrated History of the Monterey International Pop Festival* (Solana Beach: Santa Monica Press, 2011), 8.
85 Stacy Gleason email message to author, April 17, 2023.
86 Ralph J. Gleason, "The Monterey Pop Festival," *San Francisco Chronicle*, May 8, 1967, 45.
87 Timothy Orr, "A Noteworthy Connection: How Monterey Jazz Fest helped inspire Monterey Pop," *Blog Monterey*, website retrieved January 13, 2023: https://www.seemonterey.com/blog/post/connection-to-the-monterey-jazz-festival-and-the-monterey-pop-festival/.
88 Ellen Sander, *Trips: Rock Life in the Sixties* (New York: Scribner, 1973), 100.
89 Ralph J. Gleason, "A Warm and Groovy Affair," *San Francisco Chronicle*, June 19, 1967, 43.
90 Ibid.
91 Ralph J. Gleason, "The Beautiful Pop Festival," *San Francisco Chronicle*, June 21, 1967, 47.
92 Ibid.
93 Gleason, "A Warm and Groovy Affair," 43.
94 Ralph J. Gleason, "The Triumph of the New S.F. Music," *San Francisco Chronicle This World*, July 2, 1967, 32.
95 Ibid.

Chapter 9

1 Wenner, *Like a Rolling Stone: A Memoir*, 57.
2 Ralph J. Gleason, original manuscript, "Like a Rolling Stone."
3 Ralph J. Gleason, "Like a Rolling Stone," *American Scholar*, Vol. 36 No. 4, autumn 1967, 555.
4 Ibid., 555–6.
5 Ibid., 557–61.
6 Ibid., 559.

7   Ibid., 558.
8   Bernard Gendron, *Between Montmartre and the Mudd Club*, 220–1.
9   Reiland Rabaka, *Civil Rights Music: The Soundtracks of the Civil Rights Movement* (Lexington: Lexington Books, 2016), 149.
10 Ralph J. Gleason, "Martha Reeves' Different 'Ode,'" *San Francisco Chronicle*, December 4, 1967, 51.
11 Ralph J. Gleason, "The Progression of the Soul Singers," *San Francisco Chronicle This World*, November 26, 1967, 41.
12 Gleason, "Like a Rolling Stone," 561.
13 Ibid., 562.
14 Ibid., 562.
15 Ibid., 563. Gleason previously published this passage in a *Chronicle* column in which he argued that the city of San Francisco should do more to support the rock dancehall scene: Ralph J. Gleason, "Musical Refuges from Hostility," *San Francisco Chronicle Datebook*, June 18, 1967, 31.
16 Wenner, *Like a Rolling Stone: A Memoir*, 58.
17 Draper, *Rolling Stone Magazine*, 64–5.
18 Jann Wenner, "Letter," *Rolling Stone*, November 9, 1967, 2.
19 Ralph J. Gleason, "Sound Without Color," *Rolling Stone*, November 9, 1967, 11.
20 Masthead, *Rolling Stone*, November 9, 1967, 1 and 2.
21 Draper, *Rolling Stone Magazine*, 68.
22 Hagan, *Sticky Fingers*, 89.
23 Draper, *Rolling Stone Magazine*, 70–4.
24 William Hogan, "Porter's Wildness in Paperback—Other Notes," *San Francisco Chronicle This World*, September 3, 1967, 32.
25 Ralph J. Gleason, "The Power of Non-Politics or the Death of the Square," in Jesse Kornbluth, ed., *Notes from the New Underground* (New York: Viking Press, 1968), 215.
26 Ibid.
27 Ralph J. Gleason, "The Flower Children," *Encyclopedia Britannica*, website retrieved June 14, 2017 (From the 1968 Britannica Book of the Year): https://www.britannica.com/topic/The-Flower-Children-2101574.
28 Michael Grieg, "Death of the Hippies," *San Francisco Chronicle*, October 7, 1967, 2.
29 Ralph J. Gleason, "Death and Life of the Carousel," *San Francisco Chronicle Datebook*, July 7, 1968, 23.
30 Ibid.
31 Leonard Feather, "Pop=Rock=Jazz: A False Musical Equation Dissected," *Down Beat Music '68*, Maher Publications, 1968, 16.
32 Ibid.
33 Ralph J. Gleason, "Featherbed Ball," 48.
34 Ralph J. Gleason, "The Sound of a New Generation," *San Francisco Chronicle Datebook*, April 9, 1967, 25.
35 Brennan, *When Genres Collide*, 111.
36 Ibid., 114.
37 Nat Hentoff, interview by Jessica Armstrong, February 27, 2013.
38 Ibid.
39 Ralph J. Gleason, "Outside Agitator," *Daily Californian*, January 22, 1968, n.p.
40 Ralph J. Gleason, "Lessons Learned from the Strike," *San Francisco Chronicle Datebook*, March 28, 1968, 23.

41 Ralph J. Gleason, "Extensive Jazz on Television," *San Francisco Chronicle Datebook*, May 19, 1968, 27.
42 Ralph J. Gleason, "This is the Way it All Happened," *San Francisco Chronicle*, February 28, 1968, 53.
43 Ralph J. Gleason, "A Great Weekend at the Carousel," *San Francisco Chronicle*, March 18, 1968, 41.
44 Ralph J. Gleason, "Competition, Change at the Ballrooms," *San Francisco Chronicle*, April 15, 1968, 42.
45 Ralph J. Gleason, "A Day of Love, Hurt and Sorrow," *San Francisco Chronicle*, June 10, 1968, 49.
46 Uncredited, "Court Shuts Carousel Ballroom," *San Francisco Chronicle*, June 8, 1968, 3.
47 Gleason, "Death and Life of the Carousel," 23.
48 Ralph J. Gleason, "Deathwish of the Hippie Ethic," *Rolling Stone*, August 24, 1968, 10.
49 Ralph J. Gleason, "Country Music Station Plays Soft," *Rolling Stone*, February 10, 1968, 10.
50 Charles B. White to Jann Wenner, January 20, 1968.
51 Ibid.
52 D. W. Record, "Correspondence," *Rolling Stone*, January 22, 1968, 3.
53 Jane Drago to Jann Wenner, January 29, 1968.
54 Ralph J. Gleason, "Stop this Shuck, Mike Bloomfield," *Rolling Stone*, May 11, 1968, 10. The derogatory word "spade" was part of the jargon of rock music culture of that time.
55 "Correspondence, Love Letters & Advice," *Rolling Stone*, May 25, 1968, 3.
56 Nick Gravenites, "Stop This Shuck, Ralph Gleason," *Rolling Stone*, May 25, 1968, 17.
57 Jann Wenner, interview by Don Armstrong, May 5, 2021.
58 Ralph J. Gleason to Jann Wenner, September 4, 1968.
59 Jann Wenner to Pacific National Bank, September 6, 1968.
60 Uncredited, "Regrets," *Rolling Stone*, October 12, 1968, 6.
61 Ralph J. Gleason, "Donovan's Genius to Speak to His Peers," *San Francisco Chronicle*, September 30, 1968, 46.
62 Ralph J. Gleason, "Jimi Hendrix in Great Show," *San Francisco Chronicle*, October 14, 1968, 52.
63 Draper, *Rolling Stone Magazine: The Uncensored History*, 79-80.
64 Wenner, *Like a Rolling Stone: A Memoir*, 76.
65 Ralph J. Gleason, "It Looks as If Elvis Has a Rival – From Arkansas," 21.
66 Ralph J. Gleason, "Johnny Cash at San Quentin," *San Francisco Chronicle*, February 26, 1969, 50.
67 Ibid.
68 Ibid.
69 Ibid.
70 Ibid.
71 Ibid.
72 Ralph J. Gleason, "The Band at Winterland," *Rolling Stone*, May 17, 1969, 236.
73 Ibid.
74 Ibid.
75 Ralph J. Gleason, "Bootleg Album of Bob Dylan," *San Francisco Chronicle Datebook*, December 7, 1969, 25.

76 Ralph J. Gleason, "No Opening Night Encores for Janis," *San Francisco Chronicle*, May 24, 1969, 45.
77 Sam Andrew, Facebook post, February 17, 2015: https://www.facebook.com/profile/100063591346342/search/?q=ralph%20gleason%20.
78 James Kaplan, *Sinatra: The Chairman* (New York: Doubleday, 2015), 857.
79 Wenner, ed., "Ralph J. Gleason in Perspective," 44.
80 Kaplan, *Sinatra*, 98.
81 Barry Olivier, "Meeting Notes," March 12, 1969.
82 Ralph J. Gleason, "Dual Benefits for Wild West," *San Francisco Chronicle*, July 7, 1969, 42.
83 Forrest Saulsbury, "True Grit for Wild West," *Berkeley Tribe*, August 1, 1969, 4.
84 Uncredited, "Statement of the Wild West Festival," August 6, 1969.
85 Ralph J. Gleason, "A Pure S.F. Wild West Event," *San Francisco Chronicle*, August 11, 1969, 43.
86 Ibid.
87 Marjorie Heins, "Gleason," *Dock of the Bay*, August 12, 1969, 1–2.
88 Ibid.
89 Ralph J. Gleason, "Festival Paranoia," *Rolling Stone*, September 6, 1969, 24.
90 Ibid.
91 Ibid.
92 Ibid.
93 Ralph J. Gleason, "The Cancellation of the Wild West Show," *San Francisco Chronicle*, August 15, 1969, 49.
94 Ibid.
95 Ibid.
96 Ibid.

Chapter 10

1 Ralph J. Gleason. "Is There a Death Wish in the U.S.?" *Rolling Stone* insert, April 5, 1969, 18.
2 Jann Wenner, introduction to "The Sound of Marching, Charging Feet," *Rolling Stone* insert, April 5, 1969, 1.
3 Gleason, "Is There a Death Wish in the U.S.?" 18.
4 Ibid.
5 Ibid.
6 Ibid.
7 Draper, *Rolling Stone Magazine: The Uncensored History*, 127–9.
8 Nadya Zimmerman, *Counterculture Kaleidoscope: Musical and Cultural Perspectives on Late Sixties San Francisco* (Ann Arbor: University of Michigan Press, 2008), 157–8.
9 Gleason, "Like a Rolling Stone," 561.
10 Ralph J. Gleason, "There was a Tab, in Ego and Money," *San Francisco Chronicle*, December 8, 1969, 49.
11 Ralph J. Gleason, "Who's Responsible for the Murder?" *San Francisco Chronicle*, December 10, 1969, 46.
12 Draper, *Rolling Stone Magazine: The Uncensored History*, 114.
13 Uncredited, "The Love Generation Hype in the News," *Rolling Stone*, January 21, 1970, 38.

14 Ralph J. Gleason, "The Lesson of the Altamont disaster," *San Francisco Chronicle This World*, December 28, 1969, 28.
15 Thomas Maremaa and Andrew Gordon, "Have You Seen Your Critic, Baby? Ralph J. Gleason," *Every Other Weekly*, January 13, 1970, 1–5.
16 Ralph J. Gleason, "The Stones' Music: Let it Bleed," *San Francisco Chronicle This World*, December 14, 1969, 63.
17 Sol Stern, "Altamont: Pearl Harbor to the Woodstock Nation," *Scanlan's Monthly*, March 1970, 37–54.
18 Ibid, 54.
19 Jerry Rubin to Ralph J. Gleason, February 9, 1970, 1.
20 Ibid., 1.
21 Ralph J. Gleason, "Aquarius Wept," *Esquire*, Aug. 1970. Webpage retrieved January 13, 2022: https://www.esquire.com/news-politics/a6197/altamont-1969-aquarius-wept-0870/.
22 Ralph J. Gleason, "A Young Irishman Haunted by Dreams," *San Francisco Chronicle This World*, March 1, 1970, 33.
23 Ibid.
24 Janet Morrison Minto, interview by Don Armstrong, March 8, 2021.
25 Ralph J. Gleason, "Van Morrison Does It Right," *Rolling Stone*, June 24, 1971, 26.
26 Ibid.
27 Gleason, *The Jefferson Airplane and the San Francisco Sound*, 155.
28 Ibid., 159–60.
29 Grace Slick, interview by Don Armstrong, April 9, 2021.
30 Ibid.
31 Ibid.
32 Ibid.
33 Jorma Kaukonen, interview by Don Armstrong, March 11, 2015.
34 Ibid.
35 Ibid.
36 Mike Jahn, "Few Raves for Rock Books," *Baltimore Sun*, December 6, 1970, 88.
37 John Grissim, "Books," *Rolling Stone*, July 26, 1969, 30.
38 Ralph J. Gleason, "The Airplane under Heavy Flak," *San Francisco Chronicle This World*, July 6, 1969, 29.
39 Ibid.
40 Ibid.
41 R. Serge Denisoff, "Review Essays," *Journal of Popular Culture*, September 1, 1969, 857.
42 Denisoff, "Review Essays," 856.
43 Lindberg, *Rock Criticism from the Beginning*, 190, ftn. 37.
44 Gennari, *Blowin' Hot and Cool*, 296–7.
45 John Avlon, Jesse Angelo, and Errol Louis, *Deadline Artists: America's Greatest Newspaper Columns* (New York: Overlook Press, 2011), 16.
46 Andy Bennett, *Music, Style, and Aging: Growing Old Disgracefully* (Philadelphia: Temple University Press, 2013), 130–1.
47 Ibid., 133.
48 Ibid., 134.
49 Gleason, "The Airplane Under Heavy Flak," 29.
50 Ralph J. Gleason to Seymour Krim, September 23, 1969.

51 Ralph J. Gleason, "A Special Quality at Big Sur," *San Francisco Chronicle*, September 15, 1969, 46.
52 Ralph J. Gleason, "The Impact of Woodstock," *San Francisco Chronicle*, September 1, 1969, 41.
53 Ralph J. Gleason, "Miles Triumphs 'In a Silent Way,'" *San Francisco Chronicle This World*, September 7, 1969, 31.
54 Ralph J. Gleason, "How Davis Changed History," *San Francisco Chronicle Datebook*, September 14, 1969, 33.
55 Ralph J. Gleason, "Jazz: Black Art/American Art," in Gleason, *Celebrating the Duke*, 5.
56 Paul Heist, ed., *The Creative College Student: An Unmet Challenge* (San Francisco: Jossey-Bass, 1968), 86.
57 Gennari, *Blowin' Hot and Cool*, 283.
58 Ralph J. Gleason, "Jazz: Black Art/American Art," in Gleason, *Celebrating the Duke*, 11.
59 Ralph J. Gleason, "The Greater Sound," *Drama Review: TDR*, Summer, 1969, 160.
60 Gleason, "The Greater Sound," 162.
61 Ibid., 165.
62 Ibid.
63 Ibid., 166.
64 Ralph J. Gleason, "Look and Listen ... with Rowe," *Richmond Times-Dispatch*, December 6, 1970, L-5.
65 Ralph J. Gleason, "The S.F. Rock Scene Revisited," *San Francisco Chronicle This World*, December 6, 1970, 31.
66 *West Pole*, DVD, Eagle Rock Entertainment, 2008.
67 Kaufman, typewritten recollections, 1–2.
68 Ibid., 2.
69 Ralph J. Gleason, "The S.F. Rock Scene Revisited," *San Francisco Chronicle This World*, December 6, 1970, 31.
70 Robert Zagone, interview by Don Armstrong, March 30, 2021.
71 Ralph J. Gleason, "A Look at Frisco Rock," *Provo Daily Herald*, November 30, 1970, TV 11.
72 Ibid.
73 Robert Zagone, interview by Jessica Armstrong, April 6, 2010.
74 Gleason, "Look and Listen ... with Rowe," L-5.
75 Ibid.
76 Gleason, "The S.F. Rock Scene Revisited," 31.
77 Ibid., 31.
78 Uncredited, "KQED Sets 2-Part Musical Special," *Fremont Argus*, December 6, 1970, 15–Z.
79 Susan Brink, "Lennon's Album and the Band Concert," *Miami News*, December 15, 1970, 7–A.
80 John L. Wasserman, "Riding the Airplane Music," *San Francisco Chronicle Datebook*, December 13, 1970, 23.
81 Ibid.
82 Ralph J. Gleason, "Jazz Scene: Goodman's Mysterious Collapse," *San Francisco Chronicle*, April 28, 1953, 20.
83 Ralph J. Gleason, liner notes for *Creedence Clearwater Revival*, Creedence Clearwater Revival. Fantasy 8383, 1968, 33 1/3 rpm.

84 Creedence biographer John Lingan criticized Gleason's notes as "largely a pocket history of the city's ballroom scene. Amazingly, Creedence wasn't even mentioned until the final paragraph, and then as 'an excellent example of the third generation of San Francisco bands' who 'give every indication of keeping the faith of the San Francisco sound undiminished.'" Lingan notes that on the cover of the band's *Cosmos Factory* album is a photograph of the group with a sign in the background that reads "3d Generation." Lingan says, "Creedence was the biggest pop act to ever come from the Bay. They didn't need a jazz man's approval." John Lingan, *A Song for Everyone: The Story of Creedence Clearwater Revival* (New York: Hachette Books, 2022), 130 and 250.
85 Chet Flippo, "History of Rolling Stone, Part 1," *Popular Music and Society* 3:3, 1974, 180.
86 Ralph J. Gleason, "Perspectives: Is it Out of Control?," *Rolling Stone*, August 20, 1970, 9.
87 Ralph J. Gleason, "Perspectives: An End to 'Us and Them,'" *Rolling Stone*, March 4, 1971, 27.
88 Ralph J. Gleason, "Perspectives: The Problem of Nonviolence," *Rolling Stone*, April 15, 1971, 27.
89 Ralph J. Gleason, "Perspectives: The Dream Simply Isn't Over," *Rolling Stone*, October 28, 1971, 30.
90 Peter Schjeldahl, "Payday Doesn't Shortchange You," *New York Times*, March 11, 1973, D13.
91 Starr and Waterman, *American Popular Music*, 322.
92 Judy Stone, "Payday—The Script Defied that Hollywood Treatment," *San Francisco Examiner Datebook*, March 11, 1973, 15–16.
93 Stone, "Payday—The Script Defied that Hollywood Treatment," 15–16.
94 Ibid., 16.
95 Robert Zagone, email message to Jessica Armstrong, April 6, 2010.
96 Stone, "Payday—The Script Defied that Hollywood Treatment," 15.
97 Ibid., 15.
98 Robert Zagone, email message to author, April 7, 2021.
99 Odette Pollar, interview by Jessica Armstrong, December 19, 2021.
100 Paine Knickerbocker, "Payday is Fascinating," *San Francisco Chronicle*, March 23, 1973, 49.
101 Charles Champlin, "Twang of Truth in 'Payday,'" *Los Angeles Times*, March 16, 1973, IV.
102 Lawrence Devine, "On Tour with a Twangy Tyrant," *Detroit Free Press*, August 16, 1974, 17.
103 Ralph J. Gleason, "A Filmmaker's Woes," *San Francisco Chronicle This World*, March 25, 1973, 26.
104 Robert Zagone, email message to Jessica Armstrong, April 6, 2010.
105 Ibid.
106 Gleason, "Introductory Note," 12–14.
107 Thomas Wolfe, *Look Homeward, Angel* (New York: Scribner, 2006), 3.

Chapter 11

1. Peter A. Janssen, "*Rolling Stone*'s Quest for Respectability," *Columbia Journalism Review*, January/February 1974, 65.
2. Anson, *Gone Crazy and Back Again*, 302.
3. Connecticut Walker, "The Young Publishing Wizard of *Rolling Stone*," *Parade*, February 3, 1974, 6.
4. Draper, *Rolling Stone Magazine: The Uncensored History*, 236.
5. Jann Wenner to Ralph J. Gleason, undated, 1.
6. Ibid.
7. Ibid., 2.
8. Ralph J. Gleason to Jann Wenner, February 19, 1974.
9. Ibid.
10. Ibid., 1.
11. Ibid.
12. Ralph J. Gleason to Jann Wenner, March 15, 1974, 3.
13. Ibid., 4.
14. Ibid., Jann Wenner to Ralph J. Gleason, June 28, 1974.
15. Ralph J. Gleason to Jann Wenner, October 29, 1974.
16. Ralph J. Gleason, "Duke Ellington—An Original," *San Francisco Chronicle*, May 27, 1974, 41.
17. John S. Wilson, "Duke Passed by, and We're all the Richer," *St. Petersburg Times*, May 25, 1974, 53.
18. Gleason, *Celebrating the Duke*, 156.
19. Ibid., 166.
20. Ibid., 168.
21. Ralph J. Gleason, "Farewell to the Duke," *Rolling Stone*, July 4, 1974, 34.
22. Ralph J. Gleason to Jann Wenner, June 24, 1974.
23. Ralph J. Gleason, "The Melody Just Came Out," *San Francisco Chronicle This World*, February 16, 1975, 24.
24. Ibid.
25. Toby Gleason, interview by Don Armstrong, April 9, 2022.
26. Uncredited, "Strike Finance Group Will Open Fund Drive," *Columbia Daily Spectator*, April 3, 1936, 1.
27. Ralph J. Gleason, "Riding the Rails with Riddle," *San Francisco Chronicle This World*, September 22, 1974, 23.
28. Ibid.
29. Paul Goldberger, "Design Notebook," *New York Times*, March 24, 1977, C14.
30. Gleason, "Riding the Rails With Riddle," 23.
31. Ralph J. Gleason, "Jazz Sessions at the West End," *San Francisco Chronicle This World*, September 8, 1974, 30.
32. Ibid.
33. Ibid.
34. Ralph J. Gleason, "But the Jazz Band was Missing," *San Francisco Chronicle This World*, October 13, 1974, 26.
35. Svetlana Boym, "Nostalgia and its Discontents," *The Hedgehog Review*, webpage retrieved July 20, 2022: https://hedgehogreview.com/issues/the-uses-of-the-past/articles/nostalgia-and-its-discontents.

36 Ralph J. Gleason, "The Canadian Pop Music Revolt," *San Francisco Chronicle This World*, September 29, 1974, 28.
37 Terri Hinte, interview by Don Armstrong, April 23, 2020.
38 Ibid.
39 Merl Saunders Jr., interview by Don Armstrong, March 21, 2021.
40 Toby Gleason, interview by Don Armstrong, April 5, 2021.
41 Ralph J. Gleason, "The Endless Blues Mystery," *Rolling Stone*, January 3, 1974, 11.
42 Ralph J. Gleason, "Super Pop from the Deep South," *San Francisco Chronicle This World*, January 19, 1975, 28.
43 Ralph J. Gleason, "Boz's Shows are a Gas," *San Francisco Chronicle This World*, January 12, 1975, 27.
44 Ralph J. Gleason, "Like a Rolling Stone, Again," *Rolling Stone*, March 28, 1974, 14.
45 Ralph J. Gleason, "In Praise of a Mouth Harpist," *San Francisco Chronicle This World*, February 9, 1975, 24.
46 Ibid.
47 A. H. Bullen, editor, *Selections from the Poems of Michael Drayton* (UK: n.p., 1883), 143.
48 Nelson Algren to Ralph J. Gleason, undated.
49 "The 2008 Pulitzer Prize Winner in Special Citations and Awards," webpage retrieved February 17, 2023: https://www.pulitzer.org/winners/bob-dylan.
50 Ralph J. Gleason, "Johnny Cash Meets Dick Nixon," *Rolling Stone*, April 30, 1970, 47.
51 Richard M. Nixon, Address to the Nation on the Situation in Southeast Asia, May 8, 1972.
52 Ralph J. Gleason, "We Gotta Get Rid of Nixon," *Rolling Stone*, June 8, 1972, 34.
53 Ralph J. Gleason, "What Are We to Do about Nixon?" *Rolling Stone*, February 1, 1973, 20.
54 Gleason to Fern Frazier, May 17, 1973, 1.
55 Ibid.
56 Ibid.
57 Ibid., 2.
58 Gleason, "The Bob Dylan/Richard Nixon Synchronicity," 13.
59 Statement of Information: Hearings Before the Committee of the Judiciary, House of Representatives, Ninety-Third Congress Pursuant to H. Res. 803, Book VIII Internal Revenue Service (Washington: U.S. Government Printing Office, 1974), 238.
60 Ibid., 255.
61 Uncredited, "Nixon Gave Medal to Scientist on White House 'Enemies' List," *San Francisco Examiner*, December 21, 1973, 20.
62 Terri Hinte, interview by Don Armstrong, April 23, 2020.
63 Ibid.
64 Toby Gleason, interview by Don Armstrong, April 12, 2022.
65 Ibid.
66 Ralph J. Gleason, "Nixon Candor: Contradiction of Terms," *Rolling Stone*, March 14, 1974, 11.
67 Ralph J. Gleason, "The Paranoia Follies: More to Come," *Rolling Stone*, July 18, 1974, 11.
68 Ralph J. Gleason, "Look Out! Ford's as Bad as Nixon," *Rolling Stone*, October 24, 1974, 30.
69 Ralph J. Gleason, "Something to Believe In," *Rolling Stone*, November 7, 1974, 24.

70 William Hogan, "Celebrating the Duke and RJG," *San Francisco Chronicle*, June 6, 1975: 43.
71 Ralph J. Gleason to Seymour Krim, February 12, 1975.
72 Gleason, *Celebrating the Duke*, 84.
73 Ibid., 128.
74 Ibid., 137.
75 Ibid., 265.
76 Ibid., xxii.
77 Ibid., xxiv.
78 William Hogan, "Celebrating the Duke and RJG," *San Francisco Chronicle*, June 6, 1975, 43.
79 Ralph J. Gleason, "A True Media Hero," *Rolling Stone*, July 3, 1975: 24.
80 Ibid., 24.
81 Greil Marcus, interview by Don Armstrong, February 9, 2021.
82 Ibid.
83 Ibid.
84 Ibid.
85 Wenner, "Ralph Gleason in Perspective," 47.
86 Greil Marcus, *Mystery Train: Images of America in Rock 'n' Roll Music* (New York: Plume, 2015), 208.
87 Greil Marcus, interview by Don Armstrong, February 9, 2021.
88 Ralph J. Gleason to Jann Wenner, November 28, 1973.
89 Ibid., June 6, 1974.
90 Alan Rinzler, interview by Don Armstrong, August 30, 2021.
91 Hagan, *Sticky Fingers*, 294.
92 Draper, *Rolling Stone Magazine*, 237.
93 Jann Wenner, interview by Don Armstrong, May 5, 2021.
94 Ralph J. Gleason to Jann Wenner, May 3, 1974.
95 Ibid. Handwritten reply by Jann Wenner on the bottom of the page.
96 Ralph J. Gleason, "Going Down with Lenny," *Rolling Stone*, June 20, 1974, 76.
97 Ralph J. Gleason to Jann Wenner, October 14, 1974.
98 Ibid., January 6, 1975.
99 Ibid., October 7, 1974.
100 Ibid., June 28, 1974.
101 Thomas Powers, "Rockefeller's Legacy: The Vicious Drug Laws of New York," *Rolling Stone*, March 27, 1975, 24+.
102 Ralph J. Gleason to Jann Wenner, October 20, 1974.
103 Jon Landau, interview by Don Armstrong, March 26, 2021.
104 Ibid.
105 Rick Clinton to Ralph J. Gleason, August 8, 1974.
106 Ralph J. Gleason, "Heller's American Nightmare," *Rolling Stone*, November 21, 1974, 28.
107 Joseph Heller to Ralph J. Gleason, October 29, 1974.
108 Philip Elwood, "Yesterday, We Were All Losers," *San Francisco Examiner*, June 4, 1975, 38.
109 Wenner, "Ralph Gleason in Perspective," 41.
110 Gleason, *Celebrating the Duke*, x. Gitler wrote this after Gleason died.

111 Carolyn Anspacher, "Music Critic Gleason Dies," *San Francisco Chronicle*, June 4, 1975, 38.
112 Wasserman, "Looking Back at Ralph Gleason," 54.
113 Untitled, "Music Critic Ralph J. Gleason Dies at 58," *San Francisco Examiner*, June 3, 1975, 2.
114 Elwood, "Yesterday, We Were All Losers," 38.
115 Untitled, "Ralph J. Gleason, Jazz Critic, Dead," *New York Times*, June 4, 1975, 42.
116 Untitled, "Ralph J. Gleason, Jazz Critic, Dead," 42.
117 Ibid.
118 Untitled. "Dead," *Des Moines Register*, June 4, 1975, 4.
119 Toby Gleason, interview by Don Armstrong, May 18, 2021.
120 Rose later went by Rose Van Thayer—Braan Imai.
121 Toby Gleason, interview by Don Armstrong, May 18, 2021. Rose von Thater Braan-Im, interview by Don Armstrong, July 29, 2021.
122 Wenner, "Gleason in Perspective," 44.

Conclusion

1 Whitney Harris, letter to the editor, *San Francisco Chronicle*, June 10, 1975, 36. Also see Michael J. Kramer, "When Hippies Went on Strike at KMPX-FM," webpage retrieved April 11, 2023: https://www.michaeljkramer.net/when-hippies-went-on-strike-at-kmpx-fm/.

Index

52nd Street, "The Street," New York City 19–21, 54
2835 Ashby Avenue, San Francisco (domicile) 71–2

Absolute Beginners (MacInnes) 109–10, 120
Ace of Cups 171, 193, 202–5
"Acid Tests" 154–5
activism 1
   American Student Union 27
   CORE 111–12, 122
   Free Speech Movement 122–8, 134, 149
   Payday movie 208–9
   Peace Council 32–4
   SLATE political group 149
   see also antiwar activism; civil rights movements; race, racism, and racial justice
Adams, Rebecca 115–16
addiction 62, 73–4, 164–5
Adler, Lou 171
Albright, Thomas 204
Algren, Nelson 101–2, 142–3, 208, 219
Allman Brothers 217–18
A Love Supreme (Coltrane) 139
Altamont Speedway Festival 192–4, 206
"Altamont: Pearl Harbor to the Woodstock Nation" (Stern) 193
American Bandstand 202
American Mercury 20
"American Noises: How to Make Them, and Why" (Seldes) 28–9
"American Revolution 1969" (*Rolling Stone*) 191
American Revolutionary War for England 107–8
American Scholar 170–1, 175–8
   see also "Like a Rolling Stone"
American Student Union (ASU) 27

Anatomy of a Hit (National Educational Television) 113, 142, 207–8
Anderson, Signe Toly 144
Andrew, Sam 187–8
Annenberg, Moe 11, 24
Ann's 440 Club 86
Another Side of Bob Dylan (Dylan) 116
Anson, Robert Sam 168
Anspacher, Carolyn 231
anti-Semitism 18, 27, 32–4, 41, 151, 221–2
   see also Hitler, Adolf and Hitler Youth; Nazi Party
antiwar activism 32–3
   ban the bomb 109, 125
   Vietnam War protest 125, 134–6, 157, 190, 220–2
   see also Vietnam Day Committee
Apollo Theater, New York 17, 19–20, 32–3
Appeal Party, San Francisco Mime Troupe 149, 151–2
Archy and Mehitabel (Marquis) 35
Armstrong, Louis 49–50, 52, 54–6, 90, 111, 177
Army induction center, Oakland 146–7
Arnold, Eddy ("Tennessee Plowboy") 74
Aronowitz, Al 230
ASCAP Deems Taylor Award 201, 223
Astaire, Fred 27–9
ASU (American Student Union) 27
Atlantic Records 75, 121
Atlantic-Little, Brown (later Little, Brown and Company) 222–3
Avakian, George 87–8
avant-garde 84, 98, 154–5

Baez, Joan 109–10, 115–16, 124–8
Baldwin, James 101
Balin, Marty 144, 196, 204
"Ball and Chain" (Joplin) 173
"Ballads, Songs, and Snatches" (Niles) 28
Baltimore Sun 196

ban the bomb 109, 125
"The Band at Winterland" (Gleason) 187
Band, The 181, 186-9, 201-2, 218-19, 225-6
Bangs, Lester 193
Basie, Count 21, 32-3
Batista, Fulgencio 99-100
Bay of Pigs 99-100
BBC (British Broadcasting Corporation) 130-2
Beat Generation 83-5, 116, 129-32, 166-7
    see also individual Beat artists...
Beatles, The 107-9, 119-20, 138-9, 146-7
    Beatles '65 129
    breakup 206
    Candlestick Park stadium, 1966 158-60
    Hard Day's Night 143
    "Help" 147
    Revolver 157-8
    "Strawberry Fields" 176-7
    Yesterday and Today 157-8
"Beau Broadway" column (Winchell) 11
bebop jazz 43, 54, 58-9, 62, 70
    see also individual bebop musicians...
Bechet, Sydney 54-5
Belmont racetrack 10
Bennett, Andy 198
Berkeley Barb newspaper 197
Berkeley, San Francisco
    Community Theater, April 1965 132
    Folk Music Festival 115, 127, 148, 176, 189
    New Orleans House 195
    Sproul Hall protest and FSM 122-8, 134, 149
    see also UC Berkeley
Berkeley Tribe 189-90
Berry, Chuck 93-4, 121-2
Berton, Ralph 44-5
Big Brother & the Holding Company 155, 166-7, 172-3, 187-8
"Big Lie" strategy 221-2
Big Sur Folk Festival 198
The Birth of Tragedy Out of the Spirit of Music (Nietzsche) 175, 178
Bitches Brew (Davis) 202, 223
Bix Beiderbecke Memorial Album 30

Black Nationalism 96, 97
Blackhawk club, San Francisco 68-9
Blackshear, Harold 59-60
Blesh, Rudi 52, 53, 65
"Blood of a Poet" (Gleason) 219
Blood on the Tracks (Dylan) 219
"Blowin' in the Wind" (Dylan) 110
"Blue Beat" culture 121
"Blue Drag" (Hines) 13
Blue Network 50
blues music 76-7
    see also individual blues musicians...
Boar's Head Society 23-4
"Bodies Upon the Gears" speech (Savio) 125-6, 127
Bonfá, Luiz 113
bookmaking 10-11
The Bookman magazine 28
Boston Globe 65-6
Both/And club, San Francisco 140, 185
Bourdieu, Pierre 31
Boym, Svetlana 216
Brand, Stewart 154-5
Brennan, Matt 65, 182
The Brew Moore Quartet and Quintet 82
Bringing it All Back Home (Dylan) 132-3
Brinkley, David 105
Britannica Book of the Year, 1968 181
British Broadcasting Corporation (BBC) 130-2
British Invasion 120-1
    see also Beatles, The
Brown, Charles 60
Broyard, Anatole 88
Brubeck, Dave 48, 67-8, 69, 90
Bruce, Lenny 85-7, 102-3, 164-5, 228
Bunk Johnson and His New Orleans Band—Hot Jazz 55-6, 62
Burgoyne, John 107-8
Byrds, The
    Fillmore Auditorium concert, 1965 153-4
    Monterey International Pop Festival 173
    Peppermint Tree show 133
    Rolling Stones, Civic Auditorium show 1965 135-6
    Sweetheart of the Rodeo 207

Café Society club, New York City 39–40, 43, 59–60, 121
California Aggie 58
"Call It Stormy Monday (But Tuesday is Just as Bad)" (Walker) 60
Calloway, Cab 216
Capitol Records 72–3, 157
Carousel Ballroom, San Francisco 183, 189–90
Carpenter, Don 207–8
Casablanca: Script and Legend 209
Casady, Jack 196
Casey, William C. 18
Cash, Johnny 78, 186–9
Cashbox 75
"Cast Your Fate to the Wind" (Guaraldi) 113
Castell, Luria 144–6, 148
Castro, Fidel 144–5
CBS (Columbia Broadcasting System) 12, 49
Celebrating the Duke (Gleason) 222–4
Cellar Jazz Club 81, 83–4
Central Intelligence Agency (CIA) 175–8
Champlin, Charles 209
Change of the Century (Coleman) 98–9
Charlatans 147–8, 163, 166–7
Charles, Ray 94–5
A Charlie Brown Christmas (Guaraldi) 69
Charlton Publishing Corporation 120, 162
Checker, Chubby 93
Chicago Tribune 11, 65–6
Christian, Charlie 43
CIA (Central Intelligence Agency) 175–8
civil rights movements 103–4, 111–12
  see also race, racism, and racial justice
civil war 27, 105
"Cless Played Heart Out to Deaf Town" (Gleason) 52–3
Cless, Rod 52–3
Clinton, Larry 35
clubs
  Ann's 440 86
  Blackhawk 68–9
  Both/And 140, 185
  Cellar 81, 83–4
  cultures written by Sarah L. Thornton 154
  Gate of Horn 102–3

Hot Club de France 31, 40
Hurricane 51
Jimmy Ryan's 54, 121
Jupiter 57
New Orleans House 195
North Beach nightclubs 82–6
Onyx 39, 54
Peppermint Tree 133
Red Dog Saloon 145
Swing 59–60
Three Deuces 54
Cochran, Eddie 93–4
Cohen, Robert 18
Cold War 66, 99–100, 104
  see also ban the bomb
Cole, Nat King 59, 73
Coleman, Ornette 98–9
"Collector's Corner" (McCarthy) 49–50
Coltrane, John 48, 70, 217, 223
  Jazz Workshop 139–40
  A Love Supreme 139
  "My Favorite Things" 200
  Ole Coltrane 95
  political revolutionaries, Cuba 100
Columbia Broadcasting System (CBS) 12, 49
Columbia Journalism Review 211
Columbia Records 202, 219
Columbia Spectator, Columbia Daily Spectator 1, 17, 23–7, 32–6, 127–8
Columbia University 15–16, 18–19, 32–4
comics *see* standup comics
Committee to Reelect the President (CRP) 220
committees
  House Un-American Activities Committee 66, 75, 100, 125
  Student Nonviolent Coordinating Committee 124
  US Oversight 93–4
  Vietnam Day Committee 134–5, 146–7, 149
Commodore Record Shop 17, 22, 40, 41
  see also Gabler, Milt
Communism 66, 100, 145, 170
Communist Party, U.S.A. 29
"A Concert of Sacred Music" (Ellington) 140–2

Condon, Eddie 87–8
The Confidence Man (Melville) 225
"Conflict at Berkeley: An Inside Story" (Pimsleur) 127–8
Congress of Racial Equality (CORE) 111–12, 122
Contino, Dick 66–7
Cooke, Sam 95
cool jazz 70
Cott, Jonathan 143, 230
country music 73–5
  see also individual country musicians...
Cow Palace, San Francisco 121, 138–9, 146, 148, 157, 224
Crawdaddy! 151, 160–1, 162, 168
The Creative College Student: An Unmet Challenge 200
Creedence Clearwater Revival 205–6
"A Critic's Explanation of Rock 'n' Roll Music" (Gleason) 76–9
Crosby, Bing 30
Crosby, Bob 36
Crosby, David 173–4, 198
CRP (Committee to Reelect the President) 220
Cuba 99–100, 105, 144–5
cultural intermediaries 3
Cummings, Mary 24

Daily Californian 162–3
  "Outside Agitator" 182–6
"Dance Renaissance in the Fillmore" (Gleason) 155–6
Dann, Maury 207, 208
Darrell, Robert Donaldson 28
Dave Clark Five (DC5) 120
Davidson, Michael 83
Davis, Miles 70, 73, 97–9, 217, 223
  Bitches Brew 202, 223
  Celebrating the Duke 223
  death of Ralph J. Gleason 231
  Get Up with It 214–15
  Gleason's befriending across racial barriers 154
  In a Silent Way 198–9
  Jazz Workshop, April 1964 111
  "Milestone" 155–6
  political revolutionaries, Cuba 100

Davis, Ronnie 149
de Beauvoir, Simone 142–3
de Toledano, Ralph 23–4
  Era of Good Feeling 40
  Frontiers of Jazz 87–8
  graduation 37
  Jazz Information 41–3
  New Leader 44
  Peace Council 32–4
"Dead. Jass and pop music critic Ralph J. Gleason" (*Des Moines Register*) 231
Deadlines Artists: America's Greatest Newspaper Columns 197
Dean, John 221
"Death of Hippie" 181
Debussy, Claude 15
Deighton, Len 213
Delehant, Jim 120, 162
Delta Upsilon fraternity 27
Denisoff, R. Serge 3, 197, 198
Denver, John 226–7
Des Moines Register 231
Desmond, Paul 68
Desolation Angels (Kerouac) 81
Detroit Free Press 209
Devine, Lawrence 209
diabetes 71, 104–5, 154
Didion, Joan 179
Diggers, The, street theater collective 179, 181
"Discs and Data" radio program 62, 68–9
Distinctive Rhythm Instrumentals (Brubeck) 68
"Dixieland Jass Band One-Step" 6
Dixieland music 6, 45–6, 55–6, 60–1
  see also individual Dixieland musicians...
Dock of the Bay newspaper 190
documentaries
  A Concert of Sacred Music 140–2
  Anatomy of a Hit 113, 142, 207–8
  A Night at the Family Dog 204–5
  Go Ride the Music 204–5
  Inside America 130–2
  Love You Madly, Duke Ellington 142
  West Pole 202–5
Domino, Fats 93
Donahue, Tom 189–90
Dorsey, Tommy 17, 30

Dostoevsky, Fyodor 230
DownBeat magazine 29, 40, 42–3, 47–8, 52, 54–6, 100–1
  improvisation 68, 69–70
  Ira Gitler review, "phony funk" 96
  jazz poetry 84
  political revolutionaries, Cuba 100
  "Swingin' the Golden Gate" column 59–61
DownBeat Music '68 182
draft, Second World War 48–9
The Drama Review: TDR art journal 201
Draper, Robert 192
"Driftin' Blues" (Moore) 60
Driftin' Cowboys, Hank Williams 74
Dryden, Spencer 196
DuBois, W.E.B. 145
Duncan, Stephen 81–2
Dunstan, Nelson 11
Duran, Eddie 69
Dylan, Bob 109–11, 115–16, 136–9, 146–7, 201–2, 211–13
  Berkeley Community theater, April 1965 132
  Blood on the Tracks 219
  Bringing it All Back Home 132–3
  John Wesley Harding 183–4
  Oakland Coliseum, Feb 1974 218–19
  Planet Waves 211–12
  and Richard Nixon 221
  Self Portrait 206
  televised press conference, 1965 152, 153
  "The Times They Are A-Changin'" 110, 142

"East St. Louis Toodle-Oo" (Ellington) 13
Eckstine, Billie 67
Ellington, Duke 12, 19–20, 51, 111
  Apollo Theater 17, 19–20
  in Chappaqua 14
  coining of swing jazz 12
  "A Concert of Sacred Music" 140–2
  death of 213–15
  early days of jazz 13–14
  "East St. Louis Toodle-Oo" 13
  Gleason's befriending across racial barriers 154
  homage to 222–4

Jazz Casual 91
Love You Madly 142
"Off the Record" 30
Peace Council and Elmer Snowden 32
Elvis Presley: A Southern Life (Williamson) 78
Elwood, Philip 88–9, 231
Encyclopedia Britannica 181
"Ephemera" 142–3
"Epilogue: The Moon of the Arfy Darfy" (Algren) 101–2
Erenberg, Lewis A. 13–14, 15, 26
Ertegun, Ahmet 75, 76
Ertegun, Nesuhi 51, 61, 121
Esquire 23, 29, 51, 59
Esquire Jazz Book, 1944 51
Evans, Gil 70
Evergreen Review 84, 180
Evers, Medgar 103–4

Fair Play for Cuba 105
Family Dog production company 145, 147–9, 155, 168, 179, 204, 205
Fantasy Records 68–70, 83, 86, 205–7, 216–17
  Brew Moore Quartet and Quintet 82
  "Cast Your Fate to the Wind" 113
  death of Ralph J. Gleason 230
  Lenny Bruce 86
  Payday movie 207–10
  Poetry Reading in the Cellar 84
"Farewell to the Duke" (Gleason) 213–15, 223
fascism 18, 27, 32–5, 39–41, 146–7, 151, 169–70, 221–2
Feather, Leonard 48, 51, 87–8, 181, 182, 215
"Featherbed Ball" (Gleason) 51, 53
Federal Writers' Project (FWP) 83
Ferguson, Otis 87–8
Ferlinghetti, Lawrence 57, 83–4
festivals *see also Monterey festivals*
  Altamont Speedway Festival 192, 193, 194, 206
  Berkeley Folk Music Festival 115, 127, 148, 176, 189
  Big Sur Folk Festival 198
  "Festival of Grace" 134–6, 140–2
  Newport Jazz Festival 90, 136–7
  Sonoma State University Peace Festival 205

Trips Festival 154–5
Wild West Festival 189–90
Woodstock Festival 185, 192–3, 198
Fields, Shep 30
Fillmore Auditorium, San Francisco 95, 151–7
Fillmore Street, San Francisco 57–9
Fillmore West 183
"A Filmmaker's Woes" (Gleason) 209
Fink, Martin 207–8
First World War 15, 17
Fisher, Rudolf 20
Fitzgerald, Ella 105
"The Flower Children" (Gleason) 181
folk music
    Berkeley Folk Music Festival 115, 148, 176, 189
    Big Sur Folk Festival 198
    Gate of Horn folk Club 102–3
    Monterey Folk Music Festival 109
    Newport Folk Festival 136–7
    racism 114–15
    revivalist movement 75
    Robert Shelton, new rock criticism 160
    see also individual folk musicians ...
"The Folk-Rock Rage" (Shelton) 160
Ford, Gerald 222
Four Tops, The 177
Francisco and the Long 60s (Hill) 154
Frazier, George 47–8, 88–9, 220–1
free jazz 98–100
    see also free jazz musicians
Free Speech Movement (FSM) 122–8, 134, 149
Frith, Simon 14
Frontiers of Jazz 87–8
The Future Lies Ahead (Sahl) 85–6

Gabler, Milt 17, 22, 40, 41, 45
Gaillard, Bulee ("Slim") 59–60
Garcia, Jerry 132–3, 166–7, 182, 196
    see also Grateful Dead
Garfunkel, Art 115–16, 199
Gate of Horn folk Club 102–3
Gaye, Marvin 177
Gleason, Stacy Rayburn 69–70
Gehman, Richard 87–8
Gendron, Bernard 52, 160, 177

Gennari, John 20
Gerry and the Pacemakers 119
Get Up with It (Davis) 214–15
Getz, Stan 130–1
Gilbert, Gama 65–6
Gillespie, Dizzy 1, 4, 54, 58, 59
    Gleason's befriending across racial barriers 154
    Jazz Casual 91
"Gin Mill Blues" (Crosby) 36
Gingrich, Arnold 51
Ginsberg, Allen 84, 87, 137, 142, 147–8, 166
Gioia, Ted 2–3, 68
Gitler, Ira 86, 96, 230
"The Gleason Beat" (BBC's *Inside America*) 130–2
Gleason, Jean (formerly Rayburn) 40, 44–6, 57–8, 61–4, 215–16
    2835 Ashby Avenue, San Francisco 71–2
    birth (and death) of Timothy Gleason 61–2
    birth of Joyce Bridget 63–4
    birth of Stacy Rayburn 71
    birth of Toby Ralph 71
    death of Ralph J. Gleason 230–1
    "The Gleason Beat" by the BBC 130–1
    Louis Armstrong 54
    Rolling Stone guides 162
    Van Morrison 194–5
Gleason, Joyce Bridget 63–4, 71, 90–1, 103, 115–16, 156–7, 158, 165
Gleason, Mollie 6–9, 45
Gleason, Ralph Aloysius 6–11, 61–2
Gleason, Ralph Joseph *see also individual musicians, music genres, music scenes, music festivals ...*
    activism and political values 11–12, 32–4, 99–199, 101, 103–4, 122–8, 134, 177–8, 191–2, 193 *see also* activism
    aesthetics 31, 59, 120
    adolescence 9–16
    behind-the-scenes support for musicians 54–6, 140, 144, 148, 151, 172
    birth 6
    books, written by *see Celebrating the Duke: And Louis, Bessie, Billie,*

Bird, Carmen, Miles, Dizzy, and Other Heroes, Jam Session, and *The Jefferson Airplane and the San Francisco Sound*
and the British Invasion 107–9, 119–20
and Lenny Bruce 85–6, 102–3
childhood 7–9
children *see* Bridget Gleason, Stacy Gleason, Timothy Gleason, Toby Gleason
Columbia Spectator 25–7 *see also* "Off the Record"
Columbia University 17–37
death and remembrances 230–1
diabetes 71–2
DownBeat, "Swingin' the Golden Gate" 59–61 *see also DownBeat*
"The Dream Simply Isn't Over" (*Rolling Stone*) 206–7
Fantasy Records, liner notes 68
Fantasy Records, vice-president of 206, 216–7
"Farewell to the Duke" (*Rolling Stone*) 214
folk music, on 114–16 *see also* folk music
"Gleason Beat," *Inside America* BBC documentary 129–32
and Bill Graham 151–2, 155–6
"The Greater Sound" (*The Drama Review TDR*) 201–2
horserace betting 10–11
hot jazz record collecting 22–4, 45–7
Irish heritage, origins 7–9
Jazz: A Quarterly of American Music 88–9
"Jazz: Black Art/American Art" (*Lithopinion*) 199–201
Jazz Casual 91–2
jazz conversion 5, 12–14
Jazz Information 40–8
journalism, first interest in 11
and Kennedy Assassination 105–6
"Like a Rolling Stone" (*American Scholar*) 170, 175–8
literature on Gleason 3
marriage *see* Jean Gleason

Monterey Jazz Festival, founding 90–1
Monterey Pop Festival, role in 171–2
Mystery Train: Images of America in Rock 'n' Roll Music (Greil Marcus), review 224–6
North Beach Beat scene 81–5
Office of War Information (OWI) 49–50
parents *see* Mary A. Gleason, Ralph A. Gleason
Payday movie 207–9
on race and music 12–4, 19–20, 44–5, 59, 90, 93–4, 96–7, 101, 103–4, 112–14, 131, 140, 177, 184, 199–201, 218, 223
at *Ramparts* 142–3, 169, 170
Record Changer 51–3
"Rhythm Section" column 66–7, 72–9
rock criticism, influence on 160–2
San Francisco Bay Area, move to 57–8
San Francisco Chronicle, start 63–7
television documentaries *see Anatomy of a Hit, A Concert of Sacred Music, Go Ride the Music, Love You Madly, Monterey Jazz Festival, A Night at the Family Dog, West Pole*
"The Tragedy at the Greek Theater" (*San Francisco Chronicle*) 127
"A True Media Hero" (*Rolling Stone*) 224
Watergate and Richard Nixon 220–2
Wenner, Jann, early friendship with 148–9, 163–4, *see also Rolling Stone*
Gleason, Stacy Rayburn 35, 36–7, 71, 115–16, 156–7, 165, 171, 172
Gleason, Timothy R. 61–2
Gleason, Toby Ralph 71, 95–6, 115–16, 156–7, 217, 231
Go Ride the Music (*NET Fanfare*) 204, 205
"God Bless Louis Armstrong" (Gleason) 223
Goebbels, Joseph 221–2

Goffin, Robert 51
Gold Rush era 82–3
Golden Gate Park, San Franciso 166, 189
Goldman, Albert 228
Goldstein, Richard 160–1
"Gollywog's Cakewalk" 15
Goodman, Benny 26
Gottlieb, Louis 88–9
G.P. Putnam's Sons 87
Grace Cathedral, San Francisco 134–6, 140–2
Graham, Bill 151–7
    Altamont Speedway Festival 193
    "The Band at Winterland" 187
    Fillmore West 183
    Jefferson Airplane 196
    Monterey International Pop Festival 172
    "Peace Rock" 163
    Wild West Festival 189–90
Grand Terrace Café, Chicago 5, 6
Granz, Norman 63
Grappelli, Stéphane 31
Grateful Dead 132–3, 181–3, 189, 202–4
    "Peace Rock" 163
    Summer of Love 166
    West Pole documentary 202–5
Great Depression 10–12, 15–16, 18–19, 82–3
Great Famine, 1840s 7–8
The Great Ray Charles (Charles) 94
Great Society 147–8, 155–6, 163
Greek legend 113
Greek Theater, UC Berkeley 126–8
"Greeley General Store" 10–11
Green, Abel 102
Greenwich Village, New York City 60
Gregory, Dick 103–4
Grieg, Michael 152
Guaraldi, Vince 69, 130–1, 135
    "Cast Your Fate to the Wind" 113
    Grace Cathedral 134–5, 140–2
    see also Anatomy of a Hit
Gullahorn, Barbara 134
Gullickson, Gordon 51

Hagan, R. H. 65
Haight-Ashbury district, San Francisco 165, 169–70, 179–81, 189–90
Haley, Bill 78
Ham, Bill 147–8

Hammond, John 36–7
    Esquire Jazz Book, 1944 51
    Second World War draft 48
    writing under Henry Johnson 29
Hampton, Lionel 43, 59–60, 63–4
Hancock, Herbie 111
Handy III, John Richard 111–12
    see also John Handy Quintet
Hanoi, bombing 220
Hard Day's Night (The Beatles) 143
"A Hard Rain's a-Gonna Fall" (Dylan) 109
Harlem, New York
    Apollo Theater 17, 19–20, 32–3
    early days of jazz 13–14
"Harlem of the West" *see* San Francisco scene
Harmon Gym, UC Berkeley 156–7, 163
Harris, David 162
Harte, Bret 82–3
Harvey, Bob 144
    see also Jefferson Airplane
Hatton, Charles 11
Hawkins, Coleman 43
Hawks, The 152–3
    see also Band, The
"He Loved Him Madly" (Davis) 214–15
"Heartbreak Hotel" (Presley) 77
Heide, Wally 86
Heins, Marjorie 190
Heller, Joseph 117, 230
Hells Angels 147, 167–8, 192–4
Helms, Chet 168
"Help" (The Beatles) 147
Henderson, Fletcher 13, 22
Hendricks, John 90–1
Hendrix, Jimi 185
Hentoff, Nat 89–90, 95–6, 182
Highway 61 Revisited 137–8
Hill, Bertha ("Chippie") 121
Hill, Sarah 154
"hillbilly" music 72–5
Hillman, Christopher 55
Hinckle, Warren 142, 169–70, 178
Hines, Earl ("Fatha") 5, 12, 13–14, 58, 111
Hinte, Terri 216–17, 221
Hitler, Adolf and Hitler Youth 27, 39–40, 221–2
    see also Nazi Party
Hobbies magazine 45–7

Hodges, Johnny 213
Hogan, William 118
Hohner Harmonica Company 148
Holiday, Billie 39–40, 62, 90, 164–5
Hollingsworth, James 166
Holly, Buddy 93–4
"honky tonk" 73–4
Hoover, Herbert 10
Horace Greeley High School 9–10, 14–15
Horace Greeley Tribune 11, 25
horseplaying/horseracing 9–12, 45
Horton, Gretchen 216–17, 230
Hot Club de France 31, 40
hot collecting 21–2
    Columbia University 23–4
hot jazz 22–3, 29–31
    Bunk Johnson and His New Orleans Band—Hot Jazz 55–6, 62
    Jazz Information 1, 41–5
    jazz origins 45–7
    Record Changer 51
    see also individual hot jazz collectors and musicians…
Hot Jazz: The Guide to Swing Music (Panassié) 22–3
Hot Record Society Shop 40
Hotel Mark Twain, San Francisco 62
"Hound Dog" (Presley) 77
House Un-American Activities Committee (HUAC) 66, 75, 100, 125
Howl (Ginsberg) 87
HRS Society Rag 40, 44, 51
Hullabaloo variety series 202
Human Be-In 166–8
Humes, Helen 215–16
Hunter, Meredith 192–3
Huntley, Chet 105
Hurricane Club 51
hymns 72–5

"I Can't Stop Loving You" (Charles) 94
I. F. Stone's Weekly 224
"I Want to Hold Your Hand" (The Beatles) 108
improvisation 22–3, 67–70, 181
In a Silent Way (Davis) 198–9
Inside America (BBC) 130–2

Irish nationalism and independence 7–9
Irish Republican Army (IRA) 7–8
"Is There a Death Wish in the U.S.?" (Gleason) 191–4
"It Don't Mean a Thing (If It Ain't Got That Swing)" (Ellington & Miley) 12

Jagger, Mick 106, 135, 157, 194
    see also Rolling Stones
Jahn, Mike 196
"Jailhouse Rock" (Presley) 77
Jam Session anthology (Gleason) 87–8
"Jazz '67" exhibitions 165
"Jazz Age", launching of 6
Jazz Alley 19–21
"Jazz: An International Language" 90
Jazz: A Quarterly of American Music (Gleason) 88–9
Jazz at the Philharmonic (JATP) music series 63
"Jazz: Black Art/American Art" (Gleason) 199–202, 223
Jazz Casual 91–2, 131, 140–1
jazz criticism, early 28–9
Jazz Hot 40
Jazz Impressions of Black Orpheus (Guaraldi) 113
"Jazz in American Society" course 129–30
Jazz Information 1, 41–5, 47–8, 53, 88–9
Jazzmen 43
Jazz Music 49–51
Jazz: Myth and Religion (Leonard) 12
jazz poetry 83–4
jazz rock (jazz fusion) 156, 198–9
jazz war, 1940s 50–2
Jazz Workshop club 111, 139–40
Jefferson Airplane 143–4, 147–9, 155–6, 166–7, 189
    West Pole documentary 202–5
The Jefferson Airplane and the San Francisco Sound 195–8
Jester magazine 17, 23, 24
Jim Crow 44–5
    see also segregation
Jimmy Ryan's Club 54, 121
"Jive" (columnist) 65
Jobim, Antônio Carlos 113

John Handy Quintet 140, 142, 149
John Wesley Harding (Dylan) 183-4
Johnson, James P. 47, 54-5
Johnson, Lyndon B. 208-9
Johnson, Willie Gary ("Bunk") 53, 54, 55, 62
Jones, Max 49-50
Joplin, Janis 173, 186-9
Journal of Popular Culture 3, 197
journalism 11-12, 79
  networking 43
  see also individual periodicals, journalists, newspapers, and magazines...
"Juke Box" column of *This World* 65
Jupiter Club, San Francisco 57
"Just Can't See for Lookin'" (Cole) 59

Kafka, Franz 229-30
Kaiser, Irwin H. 34
Kandy-Kolored Tangerine-Flake Streamline Baby (Wolfe) 143
Kantner, Paul 144, 196
  see also Jefferson Airplane
Kaufman, Denise 148-9, 164, 171, 193, 203-4
  see also Ace of Cups
Kaufman, George S. 6
Kaukonen, Jorma 196, 204
Kennedy, John F. and Jackie 87, 99-100, 105-6, 173
Kennedy, Robert F. 183
Kent State protests 190, 206
Kerouac, Jack 26, 58, 81, 84, 116, 119, 169-70
Kerr, Clark 123, 127
Kesey, Ken 101, 103, 117-19, 127, 146-7, 154-5, 169-70
King, Bertie 121
King Cole Trio 59
King, Elizabeth 78
King, Saunders 59-60
Kirsch, Robert R. 84
Kofsky, Frank 100
Kolodin, Irving 87-8
Kozmic Blues Band 187-8
KQED television broadcasting
  Bob Dylan press conference, 1965 152, 153

"Cast Your Fate to the Wind" 113
"A Concert of Sacred Music", Duke Ellington 140-1
Jazz Casual 91-2
Love You Madly, Duke Ellington documentary 142
West Pole documentary 202-5

Ladies and Gentlemen Lenny Bruce (Goldman) 228
Landau, Jon 228
Larchmont Casino 40
"The Last Time" (Rolling Stones) 135
Lead Belly (Huddie Ledbetter) 88, 114-15
Lees, Gene 100, 157
Lennon, John 158, 159, 160, 179-80, 186, 220
  see also Beatles, The
Leonard, Neil 12
Les McCann Ltd. Plays the Shout (McCann) 96-7
Les McCann Ltd. Plays the Truth (McCann) 96
Let It Bleed (Rolling Stones) 193
"Let It Bleed" (Wenner) 193
Libby, Rose 231
"Like a Rolling Stone" (Gleason) 170-1, 175-6, 177-8, 181, 201
Liles, Robert 65
Lindberg, Ulf 197
liner notes 68-9, 180-1, 217, 222-3
  Brew Moore Quartet and Quintet 82
  Bunk Johnson and His New Orleans Band—Hot Jazz 55-6, 62
  Creedence Clearwater Revival 205-6
  Jazz Impressions of Black Orpheus 113
  Ole Coltrane 95
  Poetry Readings in the Cellar 84
Lisbon, Portugal 49
Little Richard (Richard Wayne Penniman) 93-4
"Lively Arts" (Gleason) 72, 205
Liverpool, UK *see* Mersey Sound
Lombardo, Guy 30
"London Blues" (Gleason) 48-50, 51
London, UK scene 121, 163-4
"Long Time Gone" (Crosby) 198
long-playing (LP) albums 68
Look Homeward Angel (Wolfe) 26, 209-10

"Look Out! Ford's as Bad as Nixon"
(Gleason) 222
Los Angeles Times 209
"The Love Generation Hype in the News"
193
A Love Supreme (Coltrane) 139
Love You Madly (Gleason) 142
Lunceford, Jimmie 19–22, 28, 40
Lutcher, Nellie Rose 63–4
Lyons, Jimmy 62, 68–9, 90, 140

McCabe, Marjorie 65
McCann, Les 96–7
McCarthy, A. J. 49–50, 90
McCluggage, Denise 63–7
McCord, James 220–1
McGovern, George 220
MacInnes, Colin 109–10, 120
McKean, Gilbert S. 87–8
McKernan, Ron ("Pigpen") 204
Macmillan, Harold 100
Mademoiselle magazine 47–8
Madison Square Garden, New York 188–9
Mailer, Norman 134–5
Mailers Union strike 182–3
Mamas & the Papas 171, 173
The Man with the Golden Arm (Algren)
101–2
"Manifesto" (Gleason) 142
Manson family murders 206
Marcus, Greil 193, 224–6
Mark Twain Hotel 62
Marquis, Don 35
Marrow, Esther 141, 142
Marsala, Joe 30–1
Marsden, Gerry 119
Marshall, Jim 159, 160, 199
Martha and the Vandellas 177
Marxism 29
Mayfield, Percy 106
Meet the Beatles (The Beatles) 108
Melody Maker 49–50, 51
Melville, Herman 225–6
Merry Pranksters, The 117–19, 146–7
see also Kesey, Ken
Mersey Sound 108, 129–49
see also Beatles, The
"Merton Circle" 24
Merton, Thomas 24–5, 37

Merwin, Kerry 21–2
Metronome 29, 50–1
Metropolitan Review radio show 44–5
Miami News 205
"Milestone" (Davis) 155–6
Miley, James ("Bubber") 12
Milhaud, Darius 68
Miller, Glenn 48
Miller, Johnny 59
Mills, C. Wright 101
Mime Troupe, San Francisco 149, 151–2, 190
Mingus, Charles 69–70
Minkowski, Eugene 12
Mitchell, Joni 198
Mitford, Jessica 170
Modern Jazz Quartet 217
*Modern Sounds in Country and Western
Music* (Charles) 94
Mojo-Navigator Rock & Roll News 162
"Monterey Concerto for Percussion"
(Roach & Symphony) 90
Monterey Folk Festival 109
Monterey Jazz Festival 90–1, 99, 140–1
Monterey Pop Festival 171–4
Moondance (Van Morrison) 194–5
Moor, Johnny 60
Moore, Milton ("Brew") 81, 82, 92
Moore, Oscar 59
Morden, Marili 45
Morrison Planetarium, San Francisco 155
Morton, Jelly Roll 39, 231
"Most Likely You Go Your Way" (Dylan)
218–19
"The Motorcycle Gangs: Losers and
Outsiders" (Thompson) 143
Motown music 177
see also individual Motown musicians...
muckrakers 224
music criticism today 2–3
Music from Big Pink (The Band) 187
music scenes
journalists' role in 154
New York City jazz scene, 1930s 19–21
San Francisco jazz scene, 1940s 67
San Francisco jazz scene, 1950s 65–70
San Francisco rhythm and blues scene,
1940s 60–1
San Francisco rock scene, 1960s 129,
154–7, 196, 202

Music, Style, and Aging (Bennett) 198
musical identity and alienation 14, 233–4
Mussolini, Benito 18, 146–7
"My Favorite Things" (Coltrane) 200
Mystery Train: Images of America in Rock 'n' Roll Music (Marcus) 224–6
"Mystery Train" (Presley) 76–7

Nash, Graham 198
Nation of Islam 96, 97
National Broadcasting Company (NBC) 12, 50, 105, 149
National Center for Experiments in Television (NCET) 202–3
National Educational Television 113, 142, 207–8
National Guard 190, 206, 208–9
Nazi Party 27, 32–4, 41, 221–2
Nelson, Paul 160
NET Fanfare 204, 205
New Deal (Roosevelt) 11–12
Newhall, Scott 72, 104
New Leader 44
The New Masses 29
New Orleans House, San Francisco 195
New Orleans-style jazz 1, 6, 30–1, 36, 48, 52, 55–6
    Commodore Record Shop 40
    Jazz Information 43
    jazz revival 36, 43–4
    Metropolitan Review radio show 44–5
"New Popular Records in Review" (Liles) 65
New York Morning Telegraph 10, 11
New York City
    Beat Generation 85
    Columbia Records and *Bitches Brew* 202
    Commodore Record Shop 17, 22, 41
    folk music 75
    Frank Sinatra, Madison Square Garden 188–9
    HRS Society Rag 40, 44, 51
    Jazz Alley 19–21
    Lenny Bruce 86–7
    Nelson Rockefeller 228
    new rock criticism 160–1
    Paramount Theater 93
    Playland Amusement Park, Rye 40
    politics of jazz history-telling (1938–46) 39–56
    Town Hall concert, 1946 55
    see also Harlem, New York; *individual musicians and venues...*
New York Times 10, 29, 65–6
    death of Duke Ellington 213
    death of Ralph J. Gleason 231
    Payday movie 209
Newhall, Scott 72, 104
Newport Festivals 90, 136–7
newspaper music columns, history 65–6
Nietzsche, Friedrich 175, 178
A Night at the Family Dog (*NET Fanfare*) 204, 205
Niles, Abbe 28
Nixon, Richard 220–2
North Beach nightclubs 82–6
"Nostalgia and Its Discontents" (Boym) 216
Notes from a Sea Diary: Hemingway All the Way (Algren) 142–3
Notes of a Native Son (Baldwin) 101
nuclear war 109, 125
    see also Cold War

Oakland Auditorium 119
Oakland Coliseum, 218–19
Oakland Mills College 68
Oakland Paramount Theater 76
Oakley, Berry 217–18
"Off the Record" column 1, 17–37
Office of War Information (OWI) 49, 125
Ogar, Richard A. 197, 198
Oldham, Andrew Loog 172
Ole Coltrane (Coltrane) 95
Oliver, King 49–50, 52
Olivier, Barry 115, 176, 189
"On the Air: An Interview with Ralph Burton" 44–5
On the Road (Kerouac) 26, 84, 116, 118–19
One Flew Over the Cuckoo's Nest (Kesey) 101, 117
One Thousand Children movement 151
Ono, Yoko 186, 220
Onyx Club, New York City 39, 54
Operation Rolling Thunder 134
Original Dixieland Jass Band 6, 45–6
Orpheus and Eurydice, legend of 113
Ory, Edward ("Kid") 55–6, 61

Oswald, Lee Harvey 105–6, 173
"Outside Agitator" (Gleason) 182–6
Oversight Committee 93–4
Oxley, Harold 40

Pacific High Studios 204
Page, Oran ("Hot Lips") 43
Page, Patti 73
Paley, William S. 49
Palomar Ballroom, Los Angeles 26
Panassié, Hugues 22–3, 24, 40
Parade magazine 211
Paramount Theater, New York 93
"Paranoia Follies" (Gleason) 222
Pariser, Alan 172
Parker, Charlie 48, 54, 69–70, 100, 223
Parrington, Vernon Louis 225–6
Paul Butterfield Blues Band 156–7, 172, 173, 181
Payday movie 207–10
payola scandal 93–4
Peace Council 32–4
"Peace Rock" 163
Pearl Harbor 48–9
Peloquin, Jerry 144
 see also Jefferson Airplane
Peppermint Tree Club, San Francisco 133
Perry, Charles 155
"Perspectives" (Gleason) 180, 206–7, 212–13
Phillips, John 171–2
Philolexian Society 23–4
Phonograph Monthly Review 28
"phony funk" 96
Piazza, Tom 68
Piazza Venezia, Rome 27
Pimsleur, Joel 126
Planet Waves (Dylan) 211–12
Plato 175
"Platter Chatter" (Reynolds) 65–6
Playland Amusement Park, Rye, New York 40
Poetry Readings in the Cellar (Fantasy Records) 84
poets/poetry 81–4, 116, 166–7
 Beat Generation 83–5, 116, 129–32, 166–7
 see also individual poets...
police brutality 127, 156–7
"Pony Time" (Checker) 93

pop music, 1950s 72–3
"Pop Eye" column (Goldstein) 160–1
"Popular Records" (Riley) 65–6
Powell, Bud 164–5
"The Power of Non-politics or the Death of the Square" (Gleason) 180
Powers, Thomas 228
"The Preacher" (Silver) 96
presidential elections 11–12
Presley, Elvis 76–7, 93–4
"Presley Leaves You in a Blue Suede Funk" (Gleason) 77
"Press and Public Relations" panel 123–4
Printer's Ink journal 49
Prohibition 17
propaganda 48–9, 136, 221–2
protest
 "American Revolution 1969" 191
 Berkeley, Sproul Hall protest 122–8, 134, 149
 Bob Dylan 109
 and country music 74
 Diggers street theater collective 181
 Kent State protests 190, 206
 Wild West Festival 189–90
 see also activism; Dylan, Bob

Quicksilver Messenger Service 147–8, 166–7, 202–5
Quinlisk, Mary see Gleason, Mollie
Quintette du Hot Club de France see Hot Club de France

Rabaka, Reiland 177
race, racism, and racial justice 6–7
 CORE 111–12, 122
 Dick Gregory 103–4
 Fats Domino concert 93
 folk music 114–15
 Free Speech Movement 125
 Gleason's being accepted by the Black community 154
 "Gollywog's Cakewalk" 15
 James Baldwin 101
 Jazz Information 44–5
 Monterey jazz festival 140
 Newport Jazz Festival 90
 soul jazz and Nation of Islam 96

racetrack betting *see* horseplaying/
    horseracing
Raeburn, Bruce 45
Ramparts magazine 142–3, 169–70, 178
    see also Sunday Ramparts
Ramsey Jr., Fredric 43, 49
Rayburn, Bill 40, 45
RCA Records 55–6, 62
"Rebel Café" culture 82
Record Changer magazine 50–6
    clash with columnist known as "Jive" 65
    "London Blues" 48–50, 51
"Records" (Gilbert) 65–6
Red Dog Saloon, Virginia City, Nevada 145
Reeves, Martha 177
Reinhardt, Django 31
"Religions, Inc." (Bruce) 86
The Republic (Plato) 175
Revolver (The Beatles) 157–8
Rexroth, Kenneth 57, 83, 85
Reynolds, Fred 65–6
"Rhythm and Blues in 1950" (Wexler) 75
rhythm and blues (R&B) music,
    1940s–50s 60, 75–6
    see also individual R&B musicians…
"Rhythm Section" column (Gleason)
    66–7, 76, 79, 88
Richards, Keith 135
    see also Rolling Stones
Richmond, Howie 75–6
Riddle, Nelson 215–17
Riley, John W. 65–6
Riley, Tim 116
Rinzler, Alan 226
Roach, Max 90
Roaring Brook Grammar school 7
Robertson, Robbie 218–19
"Rock Around the Clock" (Haley) 78
rock criticism 160–2, 168
rock 'n' roll 76–9, 93–4
"Rock 'n' Roll Conference", Mills College,
    Oakland 170, 175–8
    *see also individual rock 'n' roll
    musicians…*
"Rock 'n' Roll Show Turned Into Bedlam" 93
"Rock 'N' Roll Took Because the Kids Had
    to Dance" (Gleason) 76
Rockefeller, Nelson 228

"Rockefeller's Legacy: The Vicious Drug
    Laws of New York" (Powers) 228
"Rocking in Rhythm" (Toledano) 23–4
Rockwell, John 213
Rolling Stone magazine
    1967–9 era 175–90
    Altamont Speedway Festival 192
    "American Revolution 1969" 191
    "Blood of a Poet" 219
    Celebrating the Duke 222–3
    death of Duke Ellington 213–15
    death of Ralph J. Gleason 230–1
    founding 171, 178–80
    Jefferson Airplane 196
    John Denver 226–7
    Joseph Heller 230
    "Perspectives" 180, 206–7, 212–13
    "A True Media Hero" 224
    The Uncensored History by Draper 192
    West Pole documentary 204
    "We've Gotta Get Rid of Nixon" 220–2
Rolling Stones
    Altamont Speedway Festival 192–3, 194
    Civic Auditorium show, 1965 135–6
    Cow Palace, July 1966 157
    Fillmore Auditorium concert, 1965 153–4
    Let It Bleed 193
    Rolling Stones, Now! 135
    "Sympathy for the Devil" 106
Rollini, Adrian 35
Rollins, Sonny 70, 91–2, 154
Roosevelt, Franklin Delano 11–12
Rossman, Michael 122–4
roots rock (Americana) 217–19
Rubin, Jerry Clyde 134, 135, 146, 166–7, 193
Russell, William 55

Sagen, Jon 148
Sahl, Mort 85–6
St. Louis Post-Dispatch (Sherman) 84
"San Francisco Bay Rock" (Sculatti) 161
San Francisco Chronicle 1, 2, 52, 53, 63–6,
    68–9
    1970–75 era 217–18
    Beatles, San Francisco "riots" 138–9
    death of Ralph J. Gleason 230–1
    folk music 75
    Free Speech Movement 123

"The Gleason Beat" by the BBC 131–2
Gleason family as recurring characters 71
Grieg report on Bob Dylan 152
Lenny Bruce 86–7, 102–3
"Lively Arts" 72, 205
Mailers Union strike 182
music columns 65
On the Road reviews 85
Payday movie 209
"Rock 'n' Roll Show Turned Into Bedlam" 93
shutting down of Carousel Ballroom 183
Summer of Love 166
syndication of "Rhythm Section" 88
This World Sunday magazine 63–4, 65, 66, 126–7, 206
West Pole documentary 205
San Francisco Examiner 182, 221, 230–1
San Francisco Express-Times 224–5
San Francisco Renaissance and bohemianism 81–3 *see also jazz poetry*
San Francisco 53, 55–7
  1946–56 57–79
  Beat Generation 26, 58, 81, 83–5, 116, 118–19
  Candlestick Park stadium, 1966 158–60
  Carousel Ballroom 183, 189–90
  Congress for Racial Equality 111–12
  counterculture 166, 169, 181, 183, 189–90, 192
  Cow Palace 121, 138–9, 146, 148, 157, 224
  death of Ralph J. Gleason 230–1
  Dixieland music 6, 45–6, 55–6, 60–1
  Fillmore Auditorium 95, 151–7
  Fillmore district 165
  Gleason's acceptance by the Black community 154
  Golden Gate Park 166, 189
  Grace Cathedral 134–6, 140–2
  Haight-Ashbury district 165, 169–70, 179–81, 189–90
  Jazz Workshop, 111
  Jefferson Airplane 195–9
  John Handy Quintet at the Both/And Club 140
  Mime Troupe 149, 151–2, 190
  Monterey Festivals 1, 90–1, 99, 109, 140, 141, 171–4
  Morrison Planetarium 155
  Music Council 189–90
  Oakland Paramount Theater 76
  rebel lifestyle, Bret Harte 82–3
  Renaissance 81
  riots and The Beatles 138–9
  San Quentin State Prison, Johnny Cash 186–7
  Summer of Love 166–8, 179, 180–1
  "Swingin' the Golden Gate" column 59–61
  Tenderloin district 68–9, 77
  Vietnam Day Committee 134–5, 146–7, 149, 192
  West Pole documentary 202–5
  see also Berkeley; *individual musicians & venues...*
San Quentin State Prison 186–7
Saraf, Irving 207–8
Saratoga Springs racetrack 10
Saturday Review 75
Saunders Jr., Merl 217
Savio, Mario 122, 123, 125–6, 127
Scanlan's Monthly 193
Scanlon, Paul 230
Schiller's Café, Chicago 6
Schjeldahl, Peter 207, 209
Schuller, Gunther 13–14
Scott, Jane 120
Sculatti, Gene 161, 162
Scully, Rock 183
Seay, Davin 162
Sebastian, John 198
Second World War 41, 48–9, 151
segregation 44–5
Seldes, Gilbert 28–9
Self Portrait (Dylan) 206
Selvin, Joel 161
Send Me Down (Steig) 48
The Seven Lively Arts (Seldes) 28
Shape of Jazz to Come (Coleman) 98
Shaw, Greg 162
Shelton, Robert 160
Sheridan Square, Greenwich Village 39–40
Sherman, Thomas 84
Shindig variety series 202

Shining Trumpets: A History of Jazz (Blesh) 53
"A Short Analysis of Hot Jazz Record Collecting" (Gleason) 45–7
"The Sickness That Killed Lenny" (Gleason) 164–5
Silver, Horace 96
Silverstein, Shel 208
Simon, Paul 115–16, 199
Sinatra, Frank 72–3, 188–9
"Sixteen Tons" (Travis) 74
ska music 121
 see also individual ska musicians...
SLATE political group 149
Slick, Darby 148
Slick, Grace 147–8, 155–6, 195–9, 204
 see also Jefferson Airplane
Slouching Towards Bethlehem (Didion) 179
Smith, Charles Edward 23, 43, 45–6, 49, 51
Smith, Malcolm 123
Smith, Robert Paul 23, 25, 27
Smith, Stephen W. 40, 45–6
Snowden, Elmer 32
Snyder, Gary 166
Socialist Party of America 44
"Somebody to Love" (Jefferson Airplane) 155–6
Something Happened (Heller) 229–30
"Something Keeps A-Worryin' Me" (Gleason) 47–8
"Something's Happening" (Wenner) 162
Sometimes a Great Notion (Kesey) 117–18
"Songs Born of The UC Rebellion" (Gleason) 125
Sonny & Cher 119–20
Sonoma State University Peace Festival 205
soul jazz 96, 97
 see also individual soul jazz musicians
soul music 95
"Sound is Without Color" (Gleason) 180
Southern, Jeri 73
Spanier, Mugsy 215
"Spanish Lady" (John Handy Quintet) 140
Spider newspaper 143
Sproul Hall protest, Berkeley 122–8, 134, 149
Spy Story (Deighton) 213

standup comics 85–7, 102–3, 164–5, 227–8
State Department ban on travel 144–5
Steffens, Lincoln 224
Steig, Henry 48
Stereo Review magazine 222–3
Sterling, George 82
Stern, Sol 193, 194
Stewart, Ian 135–6
Stills, Stephen 198
Stone, I.F. ("Izzy") 224, 225–6
"Stop this Shuck, Mike Bloomfield" (Gleason) 184
Straight Arrow magazine 168
Straight Arrow Publishers 179, 184–5, 211, 226
Strange Tales (Marvel) 145
"Strawberry Fields" (The Beatles) 176–7
strikes 182–3
 see also protest
Student Nonviolent Coordinating Committee (SNCC) 124
Stuyvesant Casino (New York City) 55
substance abuse *see* addiction
"Sugar Foot Stomp" (Henderson) 13
Sullivan, Charles 64, 151–2
Summer of Love 166–8, 172–4, 179, 180–1
Sunday Ramparts 164, 168, 171, 178–9
"Suzy Q" (Creedence Clearwater Revival) 205–6
Sweetheart of the Rodeo (The Byrds) 207
Swenson, John 162
Swing Club, West Oakland 59–60
swing jazz 12, 13–14, 19, 48
 Era of Good Feeling 39
 Peace Council, activism 32–4
 San Francisco Chronicle 65
 see also hot collecting/hot jazz; swing youth subculture, individual swing musicians...
"Swingin' the Golden Gate" column (Gleason) 59–61
"Sympathy for the Devil" (Rolling Stones) 106

"Take This Hammer" (Baldwin) 101
Talbot, David 72
Taubman, Howard 65–6

Taylor, Derek 171–2
Tempo magazine 42–3
Tenderloin district, San Francisco 68–9, 77
"Tennessee Waltz" (Page) 73
Terkel, Studs 88–9
Tharpe, Rosetta 121
Third Stream jazz 68
This World Sunday magazine 63–4, 65, 66, 126–7, 206
Thompson, Hunter S. 143
Thornton, Big Mama 165
Thornton, Sarah L. 154
Three Blazers, Johnny Moore 60
Three Deuces Club 54
"The Times They Are A-Changin'" (Dylan) 110, 142
Timmons, Bobby 96
Tjader, Cal 68, 69, 73
Tommy Tucker Orchestra 30
"Tongs and Bones" column (Liles) 65
Torn, Rip 208
Townsend, Pete 173
traditional jazz 6
    see also New Orleans-style jazz
"The Tragedy at the Greek Theater" (Gleason) 126–8
travel bans 144–5
Travis, Merle 74
Treasury of Jazz (Condon and Gehman) 87–8
"The Tribes Gather for a Yea Saying" (Gleason) 168
"A Tribute to Dr. Strange" dance concert 145, 147–9
Trilling, Lionel 18
Trips Festival 154–5
"The Triumph of the New S.F. Music" (Gleason) 174
"A True Media Hero" (Gleason) 224
Truman, Harry S. 66
Twain, Mark 82
Tyler, T. Texas 74
Tynan, John 96

UC Berkeley
    Daily Californian 162–3, 182–6
    Harmon Gym, 156–7, 163
    "Jazz '67" exhibitions 165

SLATE political group 149
Vietnam Day Committee 134–5, 146–7, 149, 192
Ulanov, Barry 23–4, 48, 50–1, 87–8
Unfinished Music No. 1: Two Virgins (Lennon & Ono) 186
United Kingdom
    Irish nationalism and independence 7–8
    London, UK scene 121, 163–4
    Mersey Sound 108, 129–49
    see also individual UK musicians...
University Against War magazine 32
University of Heidelberg 27
US Office of War Information 49, 125
US Oversight Committee 93–4
US State Department ban on travel 144–5

Valens, Ritchie 93–4
Van Doren, Mark 18
Van Morrison and wife Janet 194–5
Vanity Fair magazine 28–9
Varese, Edgar 196
Velvet Underground 202
Venezuela 105
Vietnam Day Committee (VDC) 134–5, 146–7, 149, 192
Vietnam War protest 125, 134–6, 157, 190, 220–2
Village Voice 160–1
The Vince Guaraldi Trio 69
"A Violent Act Defines Us" (Gleason) 106
Vortex, light-and-sound show 155

A Walk on the Wild Side (Algren) 101–2
Walker, T-Bone 59–60
Waller, Fats 177
Walters, Johnnie Mac 221
Warhol, Andy 202
Warlocks, The 132–3
WASPS (White Anglo-Saxons) 220–1
Wasserman, John L. 143, 205, 231
Watergate scandal hearings 220–2
Watson, Doc 115
Watts, Charlie 135–6, 157, 172
    see also Rolling Stones
Watts race riots, Los Angeles 140
Webb, Chick 19–20, 31
"The Weight" (The Band) 225–6

Weiss, Max & Sol 86, 205–6
  see also Fantasy Records
Welles, Orson 55
Wenner, Jann 3, 149, 163–4, 168, 171, 211–13, 226–30
  death of Ralph J. Gleason 230–1
  "Let It Bleed" 193
  "Like a Rolling Stone" 170–1, 175–6, 177–8
  Monterey International Pop Festival 174
  New York Times interview, 2023 227
  Rolling Stone 175–6, 178–80, 184–6, 189
  writing under "Mr. Jones" 162
West Coast Jazz 70
West Pole documentary (KQED) 202–5
"We've Gotta Get Rid of Nixon" (Gleason) 220–2
Wexler, Jerry 75, 76, 180
When Genres Collide (Brennan) 182
White ignorance 104
White, Mike 111–12
White savior complex 101–3
White Southern teens and R&B music 75–6
White supremacy 104
  see also Hitler, Adolf and Hitler Youth; Nazi Party; race, racism, and racial justice
Who, The 173
"Wild Weekend Around the Bay" (Gleason) 168
Wild West Festival 189–90

Wilder, Thornton 25–6
Williams, Cootie 13
Williams, Eugene 24, 37, 40–8, 53, 54–5, 61–2
Williams, Hank 73–4
Williams, Paul 151, 161
Williams, Tony 98, 99, 111
Williams, William Carlos 23–4
Williamson, Joel 78
Winchell, Walter 11
"Winds of Change" column 81–106
"Wolfe is Rated above Wilder" (Gleason) 25–6
Wolfe, Thomas 25–6, 209–10
Wolfe, Tom 143
Wolman, Baron 171
Woodstock Festival 185, 192–3, 198
Woodward, Sam 215–16
Works Progress Administration (WPA) 83

Yesterday and Today (The Beatles) 157–8
youth subcultures *see also San Francisco counterculture*
  rhythm and blues, rock 'n' roll 75–6
  swing 13–15

Zaentz, Saul 86, 205–7
  see also Fantasy Records
Zagone, Robert 141, 142, 202–5, 207–10
Zimmerman, Nadja 192